Economic Analysis of Law in China

Economic Analysis of Law in China

Edited by

Thomas Eger

Professor of Law and Economics, University of Hamburg, Germany

Michael Faure

Professor of Comparative and International Environmental Law, University of Maastricht, The Netherlands

Zhang Naigen

Professor of Law, Fudan University Shanghai, China

Edward Elgar

Cheltenham, UK • Northampton, MA, USA

Published by
Edward Elgar Publishing Limited
Glensanda House
Montpellier Parade
Cheltenham
Glos GL50 1UA
UK

Edward Elgar Publishing, Inc.
William Pratt House
9 Dewey Court
Northampton
Massachusetts 01060
USA

A catalogue record for this book is available from the British Library

Library of Congress Cataloguing in Publication Data

Economic analysis of law in China / edited by Thomas Eger, Michael Faure, Zhang Naigen.
p. cm.
Includes bibliographical references and index.
1. Law—Economic aspects—China. I. Eger, Thomas, 1949– II. Faure, Michael (Michael G.) III. Naigen, Zhang, 1955–
KNQ440.E26 2007
343.51′07—dc22

2006102431

ISBN 978 1 84720 036 5

Printed and bound in Great Britain by MPG Books Ltd, Bodmin, Cornwall

Contents

Figures and tables

FIGURES

TABLES

Contributors

Du, **Julan**, Chinese University of Hong Kong, Hong Kong, China

Eger, **Thomas**, Institute of Law and Economics, University of Hamburg, Hamburg, Germany

Faure, **Michael**, METRO, Maastricht, The Netherlands

Garello, **Pierre**, Centre d'Analyse Economique, Université Paul Cézanne, Aix-Marseille 3, Aix-en-Provence, France

Jiang, **Qing-Yun**, Law Faculty, Tongji University, Shanghai, China

Jing, **Yijia**, School of International Relations and Public Affairs, Fudan University, Shanghai, China

Kamperman Sanders, **Anselm**, Maastricht University, The Netherlands and IEEM Intellectual Property Law School, Macau, China

Liu, **Yajun Lucy**, Goldman Sachs, Hong Kong, China

Ogus, **Anthony I**., University of Manchester, Manchester, United Kingdom and METRO, Maastricht, The Netherlands

Philipsen, **Niels J**., METRO, Maastricht, The Netherlands

Schüller, **Margot**, German Institute of Global and Area Studies (GIGA) – Institute of Asian Affairs, Hamburg, Germany

Van den Bergh, **Roger**, Rotterdam Institute for Law and Economics, Erasmus University Rotterdam, Rotterdam, The Netherlands

Wang, **Hui**, Catholic University of Leuven, Leuven, Belgium

Wei, **Jian**, Law and Economics Research Institute of Economic Research College, Shandong University, Jinan, China

Wong, **Sonia M.L**., Lingnan University, Hong Kong, China

Xue, **Shanguo**, Law and Economics Research Institute of Economic Research College, Shandong University, Jinan, China

Zhang, **Jianwei**, Law School, Fudan University, Shanghai, China

Zhang, **Naigen**, Center for International Law at Law School, Fudan University Shanghai, China

Abbreviations

AIDS	Acquired Immune Deficiency Syndrome
AR	Abnormal Return
ASAC	Assets Supervision and Administration Commission
BIT	Bilateral Investment Treaty
CCCPC	Central Committee of the Communist Party of China
CCER	China Center for Economic Research
CCP	China Communist Party
CD	Compact Disc
CEN	Comité Europèen en Normalisation
CENELEC	Comité Europèen en Normalisation Électrotechnique
CEO	Chief Executive Officer
CICPA	Public Professional Body of Chinese Institute for Certified Public Accountants
CLC	International Convention on Civil Liability for Oil Pollution Damage
CMC	China Maritime Code
CNY	Chinese Yuan
CPA	Certified Public Accountant
CSRC	China Securities Regulatory Commission
DG	Director General
EC	European Communities
ECJ	European Court of Justice
EU	European Union
FDI	Foreign Direct Investment
FTA	Free Trade Agreement
FTC	Federal Trade Commission
GDP	Gross Domestic Product
GIOV	Gross Industrial Output Value
HCRS	Household Contract Responsibility System
HIV	Human Immunodeficiency Virus
IAS	Institute for Advanced Studies
IFC	International Finance Corporation
IMF	International Monetary Fund
IPO	Initial Public Offering
IPR	Intellectual Property Rights

M&A	Mergers and Acquisition
MEPL	Marine Environmental Protection Law
MMORPG	Massive Multiplayer Online Role Playing Game
MOC	Ministry of Commerce
NTB	National Tax Bureau
OECD	Organisation for Economic Co-operation and Development
PT	Particular Transfer
RMB	Ren Min Bi (Chinese currency)
SAR	Special Administrative Region
SEO	Seasoned Equity Offering
SEZ	Special Economic Zone
SOE	State Owned Enterprises
SSNIP	Small but Significant and Non Transitory Increase in Price
ST	Special Treatment
TI	Transparency International
TRIPS	Trade-Related Aspects of Intellectual Property Rights
TVE	Town and Village Enterprises
UK	United Kingdom
UN	United Nation
US	United States
VAT	Value Added Tax
WIPO	World Intellectual Property Organization
WTO	World Trade Organization

Preface

1. GOALS OF THIS BOOK

This book focuses on the application of law and economics to Chinese law and to the development of the economic analysis of law in China. The reason seems relatively clear: the interesting domain of law and economics has been developed within the context of the American (common and regulatory) legal system in the 1960s and 1970s and has later also been applied by many scholars in Europe to the civil law. The interesting question obviously arises as to the extent to which this expanding domain of law and economics is also suited to application to developing economies like China. There is a growing interest in law and economics in China as well, more particularly in law schools with a strong multidisciplinary background, like Fudan University, Beijing University and Shandong University. Many young Chinese lawyers and economists are aware of the wide literature in this domain and apply it in their research. However, until now there has not been a closer cooperation between European law and economics scholars and Chinese scholars in order to analyse more precisely to what extent the law and economics models that have so far been within the context of developed countries can be used for a country like China as well.

This book attempts to answer precisely that question. We therefore hope that this book may be of interest both to scholars generally interested in the economic analysis of law and to Chinese lawyers, economists and social scientists interested in developing legal institutions with an eye on economic efficiency. Traditional (European and American) law and economics scholars may benefit from applying their traditional models to Chinese law by grasping the opportunity to test traditional models in new fields, given the rich material available in China. Within the particular Chinese context of the rapidly growing economy, law and economics may be a particularly suitable instrument for examining how a legal system can be developed to meet the needs of that particular rapid development.

2. METHODOLOGY

The methodology used in this book is of course the economic analysis of law. Traditional neoclassical, but also public choice models will be used to address the Chinese legal system. The book is the result of cooperation between Chinese and European law and economics scholars. However, the method chosen is not the conventional one where the European scholar is solely concerned with the analysis of his or her national (or European) legal system and the Chinese scholar deals only with Chinese law. On the contrary, the European law and economics scholars directly apply an integrated approach throughout these pages, whereby an effort is made to apply conventional models directly to Chinese law. Furthermore, the Chinese law and economics scholars use the law and economics models to address particular problems from Chinese law with an attempt to explain whether law and economics can be of any use in analysing the particular features of the Chinese legal system today. A particular challenge to which a lot of attention is paid in the book consists, of course, of the fact that many aspects of the Chinese legal system today do not correspond at all with what economists would advise as an efficient legal system. For instance, a few chapters pay a lot of attention to the fact that informal and personal relations play an important role within the Chinese (not only political but also economic) context. It is the well-known concept of 'guanxi' (literally 'relations') that explains a lot of the particular Chinese legal context. A lot of attention is obviously also paid to the fact that, differently than in the US or Europe, the state involvement in China is still spectacularly high. That has important implications, for instance, for the area of corporate law, but also for securities. To some extent, it is, methodologically, not difficult to come to the (too straightforward) conclusion that some of these traditional features of the Chinese legal system do not directly fit into the neoclassic paradigm on which the economic analysis of law is built. However, the contributors to this book do not stop with that simple conclusion but rather try to take the analysis further by analysing whether, even within this particular Chinese context (of guanxi and high state involvement), law and economics can still contribute to a better understanding of the legal system.

In that sense, the reader will also notice that many of the chapters in this volume are both of a positive and of a normative nature. Most contributors use law and economics in a positive way, to explain the particular shape of the Chinese legal system in particular areas. However, most contributors do not stop there, but also indicate how the Chinese legal system (or particular proposals, for example with respect to competition law) could be changed if the policy maker would wish to make the legal rules in those particular areas more in line with predictions concerning economic efficiency. Therefore, the contributions to this book are certainly not merely theoretical, but have practical and policy implications as well. The reader will notice specific analyses of, for example, the Chinese tax system, competition law, intellectual property or professional regulation in China. Every time Chinese law is confronted with predictions from the law and economics literature and some conclusions in that respect are formulated, that could be used at the policy level as well, of course, if one considers economic efficiency as a criterion for shaping legislation.

3. TOPICS

Of course, even though this book has the ambitious title 'Economic Analysis of Law in China', the volume does not at all attempt to provide a comprehensive economic analysis of Chinese law. This volume is a collection of essays rather than a Chinese version of Posner's well-known 'Economic Analysis of Law'. The various contributions rather focus on the validity and applicability of traditional law and economic models in the context of a country like China. Therefore, the topics chosen are not merely chosen because of their relevance from the Chinese legal perspective, but of course also from the perspective of law and economics theory. For instance, many traditional economic models may assume that an efficient enforcement of regulation can take place within the context of effective legal protection. It may thus be interesting to examine whether other and perhaps different legal rules are necessary if it appears that one cannot in all circumstances rely on an independent administrative agency, whereby civil servants merely work for the benefit of the public. Thus a particular analysis of the Chinese legal system is of interest since it can bring important insights into the consequences of opportunistic behaviour concerning the way in which legal rules should be shaped. The same is of course the case for the other examples mentioned, such as the importance of 'guanxi' within the context of the Chinese legal system, but also the high involvement of public authorities and, more particularly, the state.

Given this background, this volume has selected a number of topics within Chinese law which are centred on a variety of problem areas. A first group of chapters deals with basic features of the Chinese economic system. Unavoidably, primary attention has to be paid to the regulation of competences for law making and regulation within the Chinese context. Hence the economics of federalism has to be applied to Chinese law. Next, a fundamental issue is of course the way in which the tax system is used, whereby the question arises whether the taxation system in China corresponds to basic economic notions of efficient taxation. A very basic feature, as already mentioned, is the high reliance in China on informal relations and 'guanxi'. The question arises what the relevance of these social practices is for the development of an efficient legal system within the Chinese context.

A second set of contributions deals with specific aspects of the Chinese legal system from an economic perspective. These chapters take particular aspects of Chinese law and apply traditional law and economics insights to them. In that respect, attention is paid to competition policy and professional regulation, as well as to opportunistic behaviour and regulatory arrangements. In addition, law and economics of course also must be applied to the area of corporate law, financial securities and, more broadly, commercial law. Traditional economics of corporate law must thus be applied to monitoring problems in Chinese stock companies and the question also arises as to how capital markets are regulated in China, given the high-level protection awarded to so-called special treatment firms (with a high state involvement). Since China is also increasingly exposed to the virtual world, the question also arises as to how traditional economics of property rights can be applied to problems of virtual property rights as well.

The third part deals with China in the world economy. Indeed, to an important extent, regulations in China may affect China's position within the world economy. This is, for instance, the case for regulation concerning marine oil pollution, but more particularly for the important area of intellectual property law, given the specific problems that arise within the context of China in that respect.

4. FRAMEWORK AND PARTNERS

The book originated from cooperation between the three editors of this book, Professor Zhang Naigen, Professor of Law at Fudan University, Professor Thomas Eger, Economist at Hamburg University and Professor Michael Faure of the Maastricht European Institute for Transnational Legal Research (METRO). Professor Thomas Eger and Professor Michael Faure have a longstanding cooperation through their membership of the European Association of Law and Economics. Professor Eger and Professor Faure individually established contacts with Professor Zhang Naigen, one of the experts in law and economics in China. Within the context of the Erasmus Mundus Programme, 'European Master in Law and Economics' Professor Zhang Naigen spent several longer research periods at the University of Hamburg, where the project that served as the basis of this book could be prepared.

The chapters contained in this book are a selection of papers that were presented at a China–Europe conference on law and economics which was held in March 2006 at the Law School of Fudan University in Shanghai. An anonymous refereeing process was used to select the papers.

5. STRUCTURE OF THE PRESENTATION

It has already been stated above that the book is divided into three main parts. Part I deals with basic features of the Chinese economic system. It contains a contribution by Thomas Eger and Margot Schüller on 'A Comparison of Chinese and European–Style Federalism from a Law and Economics Perspective'. The second chapter in this part is by Pierre Garello and deals with 'The Road to Efficient Taxation in China'. The third chapter is by Jianwei Zhang and Yijia Jing dealing with 'Legal Pluralism in the Governance of Transitional China.'

Part II deals with specific aspects of the Chinese legal system from an economic perspective. Chapter 4, written by Roger Van den Bergh, deals with 'The Economics of Competition Policy and the Draft of the Chinese Competition Law'. Chapter 5, by Niels Philipsen addresses 'The Law and Economics of Professional Regulation. What Does the Theory Teach China?'. Anthony Ogus addresses 'Regulatory Arrangements and Incentives for Opportunistic Behaviour' in Chapter 6. Subsequently Chinese authors address specific aspects of the Chinese legal system. In Chapter 7, Julan Du, Lucy Liu Yajun and Sonia Wong deal with 'Special Treatment Firms and Administrative Governance of Capital Markets in China'. Qing-Yun Jiang in Chapter 8 deals with 'Monitoring Problems versus Fiduciary Duties in Chinese Stock Companies'. Jian Wei and Shanguo Xue address in Chapter 9 'The Stable Self-Enforcement and Distribution of Property Right: The Right to Virtual Property in MMORPG'.

Part III contains contributions addressing 'China in the World Economy'. Chapter 10, by Anselm Kamperman Sanders, deals with 'Intellectual Property Law and Policy and Economic Development with Special Reference to China'. Chapter 11, by Michael G. Faure and Wang Hui, provides an 'Economic Analysis of Compensation for Oil Pollution Damage in China'.

Part IV consisting solely of Chapter 12 contains a set of concluding remarks by the editors.

6. CONTRIBUTORS

The contributors to this book come, as was made clear, from various universities in Europe and in China. Michael Faure and Niels Philipsen are from Maastricht University. Wang Hui works at the Catholic University of Leuven. Anthony Ogus is affiliated to Maastricht University as well as Manchester University. Roger Van den Bergh works at the Rotterdam Institute for Law and Economics. Anselm Kamperman Sanders is affiliated to Maastricht University and with Macau as well. Pierre Garello works at the Université Paul Cézanne in Aix-en-Provence. Thomas Eger is from the Institute of Law and Economics at Hamburg University, whereas Margot Schüller works at the German Institute of Global and Area Studies (GIGA) – Institute of Asian Affairs in Hamburg. Jianwei Zhang and Yijia Jing are from Fudan University in Shanghai. Julan Du, Lucy Liu Yajun and Sonia Wong are from Hong Kong (Chinese University, Goldman Sachs and Lingnan University). Qing-Yun Jiang received a PhD from Hamburg University and currently works at the Law Faculty of Tongji University in Shanghai. Jian Wei and Shanguo Xue are affiliated to the Law and Economics Research Institute of Shandong University in Jinan.

A complete list of the contributors and their affiliation is provided after the table of contents.

7. ACKNOWLEDGEMENTS

As editors of this book, we are grateful to the many people who made this project possible. In this respect we refer both to the conference held in March 2006 at Fudan University in Shanghai and to the publication of the book. First of all, we would like to thank the Science Committee of the Law Faculty of Maastricht University and the German Research Foundation for financial support. In addition, we are grateful to Fudan University for providing financial support for the organization of the conference. We owe a special thanks to Katherine Walker and Sönke Häseler of Hamburg University who revised the English of some of the non-native English speakers. We are especially grateful to Henning Curti, Kid Schwarz, Alexander Schall, T. Somashekar and Peter Weise for providing useful comments on earlier versions of some of the contributions in this volume. We also owe thanks to the administrative centre of the Maastricht European Institute for Transnational Legal Research (METRO) and especially to Silvia Workum for editorial assistance in the preparation of the publication of this book. Finally, we are truly grateful for the – as usual – excellent and professional cooperation with the people working at Edward Elgar, our publisher, for all their assistance in the publication of this book.

The texts were finalized in September 2006, and for that reason developments after that date have not been treated.

Thomas Eger Hamburg/Maastricht/Shanghai, September 2006
Michael Faure
Zhang Naigen

PART I

Basic features of the Chinese economic system

1. A comparison of Chinese and European-style federalism from a law and economics perspective

Thomas Eger and Margot Schüller

1. INTRODUCTION

China's transition from a planned to a market economy has been very successful, although the reforms have been quite different from those proposed by most Western observers. Despite the fact that property rights were not well defined or formally secured, and that one party dominated the political system, China has become one of the fastest-growing economies in the world. What are the reasons for this success?

Following the tradition of Hayek, Tiebout and Brennan/Buchanan some scholars place emphasis on the political decentralization initiated by the Chinese central authorities and the competition between provinces and lower level political entities triggered by this decentralization.[1] In the EU, a specific federalist structure has been evolving, whereby the Member States transferred, step by step, more and more competences to supranational authorities. One important goal of European integration was to create a common market and thereby to improve the economic performance of the Member States.

Two questions arise. First, under what conditions will a federal structure contribute to economic growth? Secondly, what are the specific features of the federal structures in the EU and China, respectively, and what are their social costs and benefits?

In the next chapter, we will briefly present the concept of market-preserving federalism, which tries to find an answer to the first question. Thereafter, we will discuss to what extent the federal structures in the EU and in China are expected to have economically beneficial consequences, and whether China can learn something from the EU experience.

2. THE CONCEPT OF MARKET-PRESERVING FEDERALISM

'The fundamental political dilemma of an economic system is this: A government strong enough to protect property rights and enforce contracts is also strong enough to confiscate the wealth of its citizens.'[2] Consequently, the question arises as to 'what form of political system is required so that a viable, private market economy is a stable policy choice of that political system?'[3]

A market-preserving federal structure is a specific type of federalism, which consists of political institutions that credibly commit the state to honour economic and political rights and to abstain from confiscating the wealth of its citizens. Whereas any federal system is characterized by (1) a hierarchy of governments and (2) an institutionalised autonomy of each government, a market-preserving federal system has three additional characteristics:[4] (3) the lower-level governments have primary regulatory responsibility over the economy; (4) a common market is ensured, preventing the lower governments from using their regulatory autonomy to erect trade barriers against the goods and services from other political units; (5) the lower governments face a hard budget constraint, that is, they have neither the ability to print money nor the access to unlimited credit (in the case of fiscal problems, there is no bail-out of the lower by the higher government).

In the following, we will focus on point 4, the establishment and protection of a common market, because this element is a crucial issue in both the EU and China. If we look at the European Community, the Customs Union, which abolishes all internal tariffs and establishes common external tariffs, was already completed by 1968. But only since the mid-1980s have systematic efforts been made to achieve the final goal of a single market. Initiated by the Commission and supported by the judgments of the ECJ, many of the remaining non-tariff barriers to trade, as well as barriers to the free movement of services, persons and capital, have been removed step-by-step. Especially through the abolishment of non-discriminatory barriers to free movement, which result from differences in the national legislations of the Member States, it has become clear that increasing success in establishing a common European market by mutual recognition or by harmonization of national laws might undermine Member States' primary regulatory responsibility over the economy (point 3). Hence, it is of crucial importance for the future of the European Union to see how the important trade-off between promoting the common market and preserving Member States' responsibility for economic policy is solved and should be solved.

In China, on the other hand, political authority has been transferred from the central state to the provinces. Consequently, lower-level political authorities gained responsibility over the economy, which is in accordance with point 3. However, this increased responsibility of the lower-level political authorities also increased their incentive to erect barriers to trade in order to support their local economy (violation of point 4). As Montinola, Qian and Weingast put it:[5] '. . . China lacks an adequate mechanism for policing the internal common market'. What is the message? Establishing a market-preserving federal structure is a tightrope walk between the Scylla of segmenting the market into different (inefficient) local markets and the Charybdis of depriving the lower-level political entities of their ability to make independent policy decisions.

3. FEDERALISM, EUROPEAN STYLE

3.1 Integration by Primary and Secondary Community Law

The process of European integration is accompanied by a more or less permanent shift of responsibilities from the Member States to supranational 'European' authorities. In comparison with the European Union's more humble beginnings – a limited number of Member States (6), a low degree of market integration by establishing barely anything more than a Customs Union and a restricted set of common policies, such as Common Trade Policy, Common Agricultural Policy, Common Competition Policy and Common Transport Policy – today's European Union consists of 25 Member States, has abolished not only all internal tariffs, but in addition many discriminatory and non-discriminatory barriers to the free movement of goods, services and factors of production, and has extended the Community's (supranational) responsibility to areas such as environmental protection, consumer protection, health and safety, research and technological development and so on and so forth.

Although the public discussion on European integration usually focuses on money (which Member States are net-payers or net-receivers?) the EC is basically not a spending spree but a machinery to produce legal norms.[6] The European budget amounts to about 1 per cent of the GDP, an extremely low percentage compared to Member States' national budgets (about 30 per cent–50 per cent). However, the everyday life of people living in the EU is increasingly affected by European legal norms. Hereby, we have to distinguish between *primary law*, the articles of the relevant Treaties agreed upon by the Member States (from the EEC Treaty of 1957 to the Treaty of Nice, which came into force in 2003) that determine which policies, by which proceeding, the supranational authorities of the European Community are in charge of, and *secondary law*, regulations, directives and decisions, which the responsible supranational institutions are empowered to enact.

In a few words, the process by which the Community enacts legislation (secondary law) can be described as follows. The highest authority in the legislative process is not the European Parliament but the Council, which consists of the relevant ministers of the Member States. Originally, most of the legislative decisions had to be made unanimously, that is, every Member State had a veto right. But, owing to several changes in primary law, at present, most legislative Community acts have to be decided by qualified majority (about 70 per cent). However, usually only the European Commission has the right of legislative initiative. Whereas the Commission represents the supranational, federal element of European Integration, the Council represents, to some extent, the intergovernmental element, especially in case of unanimous decisions. Originally, the European Parliament had to play the smallest part in the legislative process, but, since then, the European Parliament's position has been systematically strengthened. Today, in most areas the so-called 'co-decision procedure' is applied, whereby it is always possible for Parliament to reject proposals by the Council. However, the Parliament still cannot force the Council to accept amendments.

There are three types of Community legislation. *Regulations* are binding upon all the Member States and are directly applicable within all such states (example: regulation on mergers). *Directives* are only binding as to the end to be achieved while leaving some choice as to form and method open to the Member States. *Decisions* are binding in their entirety only on those to whom they are addressed.

Whereas the Customs Union, the elimination of all internal tariffs and the harmonization of the external tariffs, was already completed in 1968, a year and a half earlier than expected, the Common Market, that is, the free movement of goods, services, labour and capital, was developing very slowly up to the mid-1980s. Many non-tariff barriers to free movement continued to exist, most of them resulting from differences in national laws (or law enforcement). There was no single European market, but a puzzle consisting of segmented national markets of the Member States. Since European primary law authorized the supranational Community institutions from the very beginning to abolish not only all tariffs and quantitative restrictions between Member States, but also all measures of equivalent effect and all impediments to the free movement of persons, services and capital, the Commission was required to look for appropriate strategies in order to achieve this aim. The traditional strategy of the European Commission was an ambitious programme of detailed regulatory harmonization.[7] A lot of money, time and effort was invested in harmonizing not only product standards, but also qualification and education requirements for many professions and more. But after almost 30 years of harmonization, it has become evident that this strategy has failed to address the issue of a Common Market: it is too expensive, too slow and not appropriate for heterogeneous Member States with different economic structures and different policy preferences of the population.

The Commission, under the guidance of president Jacques Delors, responded to this development with an ambitious plan for the single market.[8] In 1985, a White Paper, 'Completing the Internal Market', was published under the direction of the British Commissioner, Lord Cockfield, which identified three principal obstacles to the completion of the single market: *physical barriers to trade* (such as border controls), *technical barriers to trade* (such as divergent national product standards, other regulations, conflicting business laws) and *fiscal barriers to trade* (such as differing rates of VAT and excise duties). On the basis of this White Paper, the Single European Act was signed in 1986 by the Member States; this constitutes the first significant amendment of primary Community Law since the Treaty of Rome. It provided the necessary legal means to remove still-existing obstacles to the completion of the single market, and gave the Community a precise deadline for the completion of the single market – the end of 1992. One important element of the new regulatory strategy of the Commission was the 'new approach' towards technical harmonization and standardization, which to some extent replaced the traditional 'vertical' approach of detailed harmonization. The 'new approach' essentially consists of the following elements:

- As long as technical standards are not harmonized the principle of mutual recognition, as developed by the European Court of Justice in *Dassonville* (1974) and *Cassis de Dijon* (1979), holds (see below).
- Legislative harmonization (especially by directives) is limited to the adoption of essential safety and health standards. Thereby, time-consuming debates in the Council on technical details are avoided.
- Harmonization of detailed technical specifications which satisfy the adopted safety and health standards is entrusted to specialized standardization organizations such as CEN or CENELEC. If products comply with the harmonized standards they are presumed to conform to the essential health and safety requirements established by the directive.

With respect to the other basic freedoms, similar developments have taken place. For example, in order to foster free movement of services and the right of establishment, Community authorities originally tried to harmonize detailed qualification and educational standards for different sectors and professions. But progress with this 'vertical' approach of harmonization was slow and, for that reason, detailed sectoral harmonization has been replaced since the end of the 1980s, to some extent, by mutual recognition of qualifications. However, the Commission's proposal of a services directive, which intended to establish the 'principle of origin' not only for goods, but also for services, faced strong opposition and was replaced in February 2006 by a highly attenuated version.[9]

'Free movement of persons' originally meant that nationals of Member States who wanted to be economically active in other Member States were protected from discrimination on grounds of nationality. This narrow interpretation of 'free movement' has been broadened by secondary law and ECJ judgments in the sense that also non-economic movements of persons and of relatives from non-EU countries are protected, and that also non-discriminatory barriers to the free movement of persons are prohibited (subject to some derogations).

A latecomer to liberalization is free movement of capital, whereby government control of capital movements between Member States was completely abolished only in the second half of the 1980s. All in all, even though many barriers to the free movement of goods, services and production factors have been abolished during the last 50 years, there is still a large degree of segmentation into national markets, with respect to services resulting from differences in national regulation. This affects also the free movement of capital, which is impeded by still-existing national differences in the regulation of the banking and insurance sector.[10]

Although these measures contributed to a considerable extent to the establishment of a single European market this development would not have taken place without the large number of ground-breaking decisions by the European Court of Justice in favour of free movement, and in many cases against the interests of Member States wishing to regulate their economies according to their own preferences.

3.2 Fostering Integration through the European Court of Justice

Today's Community Law is to a large extent judge-made law. Hereby the preliminary ruling procedure, as laid down in Article 234 EC (ex-Article 177), the 'jewel in the Crown' of ECJ's jurisdiction,[11] played, and still continues to play, the most important role. This procedure aims at enabling national courts to ensure uniform interpretation and application of European Union law in all Member States. Under the preliminary ruling procedure any national court or tribunal may (and under certain conditions must) refer a question to the ECJ on the interpretation of a rule of Community law, if it considers it necessary to do so in order to resolve a dispute before it. Because of the preliminary rulings and the consequentialist, integration-friendly interpretation of Community law, the Court has developed concepts such as direct effect, supremacy and Member States' liability for violations of Community law. Thereby, 'individuals have been drawn into the process of making the common market a reality in their own States'.[12]

In the following, some important ECJ judgments are discussed which have helped to remove barriers to free movement and have contributed to establishing a common market. Since the mid-1970s, the Court has had to decide on a number of cases referring to Article 28 and 30 EC (ex-Articles 30 and 36). Article 28 EC prohibits quantitative import restrictions and also 'measures of equivalent effect'. Article 30 EC contains an exhaustive list of derogations from the prohibition of Article 28 EC. National measures that restrict the free movement of goods can be justified on grounds of public order, as well as other reasons serving important interests that are recognized by the Community as valuable, provided that the national measures are proportionate and do not constitute a means of arbitrary discrimination or a disguised restriction on trade between Member States.

In the *Dassonville* judgment from 1974, the Court defined the notion 'measures having equivalent effect to quantitative restrictions' very broadly: 'All trading rules enacted by Member States which are capable of hindering, directly or indirectly, actually or potentially, intra-Community trade are to be considered as measures having an effect equivalent to quantitative restrictions.'

Five years later, in the *Cassis de Dijon* judgment from 1979, the Court confirmed the broad interpretation of Article 28 EC and hence introduced the principle of mutual recognition, which means that goods lawfully produced and marketed in one Member State can, in principle, be sold in another Member State without any restriction. However, in the same judgment the Court invented, in addition to the express derogations of Article 30 EC, further derogations from the prohibition of Article 28 EC, an open list of so-called 'mandatory requirements', which can justify non-discriminatory measures of equivalent effect to quantitative restrictions:

> Obstacles to movement within the Community resulting from disparities between the national laws relating to the marketing of the products in question must be accepted in so far as those provisions may be recognized as being necessary in order to satisfy mandatory requirements relating in particular to the effectiveness of fiscal supervision, the protection of public health, the fairness of commercial transactions and the defence of the consumer.

In the following years, the ECJ has been applying the principle of mutual recognition to a number of related cases, such as cases on Belgian margarine (1982), German purity requirement for beer (1982), Italian noodles (1988), and so on. The open list of mandatory requirements has been extended, but the derogations are always subject to a strict proportionality test.

In order to avoid a too far-reaching application of the *Dassonville* principle, which would undermine Member States' regulatory autonomy, the Court in *Keck* (1993) decided to make a distinction between product requirements, where Article 28 EC should be applied, and selling arrangements, such as the German restrictions on opening hours, where Article 28 EC should not be applied. However, the lack of a clear-cut distinction in the *Keck* judgment between what is to be regarded as a product requirement, as opposed to a selling arrangement, has created a certain amount of legal uncertainty amongst lawyers.

But, apart from decisions on the free movement of goods, the Court was also concerned with the other basic freedoms. A groundbreaking judgment was *Gebhard* (1995), which was related to Article 43 EC on freedom of establishment. Here, the Court stated explicitly that the application of the principles developed in cases on the free movement of goods should be applied to all basic freedoms:

> It follows, however, from the Court's case law that national measures liable to hinder or make less attractive the exercise of fundamental freedoms guaranteed by the Treaty must fulfil four conditions: they must be applied in a non-discriminatory manner; they must be justified by imperative requirements in the general interest; they must be suitable for securing the attainment of the objective which they pursue; and they must not go beyond what is necessary in order to attain it.

These tendencies of these ECJ judgments have been of pivotal importance for European integration and for the establishment of a common market. According to the Treaty, the cornerstone of the four freedoms is the principle of non-discrimination on grounds of nationality, that is, equal treatment of domestic and foreign (economic) actors.[13] The great advantage of this principle is that it does not interfere with the national regulatory autonomy of the Member States. Every Member State is allowed to follow an economic policy according to national preferences, provided domestic and foreign actors are treated equally. The big problem with this narrow approach towards the principle of non-discrimination is that equal treatment of unequal actors itself may lead to discrimination resulting from additional burdens on imported goods, services and production factors. If, for example, there are different national safety standards for cars, a car producer who exports cars to several other Member States has to know all the different standards and has to produce a variety of cars in order to comply with the standards in each country of destination. Thereby, new barriers to entry of national markets are established.

In order to abolish as many invisible barriers to free movement as can be justified, the European Court of Justice is beginning to apply a broader market access test. This means that national measures preventing or hindering market access are, in general, considered to be unlawful, irrespective of whether they actually discriminate against imports and migrants (see the *Gebhard* judgment). The great advantage of this approach is that it supports free movement and speeds up the establishment of a common market. The problem, however, might be that it causes reverse discrimination to the detriment of national producers and undermines, to some extent at least, national regulatory autonomy. National authorities have to accept goods and activities in their territories, which are subject to other Member States' regulations. The consequence is that consumers, who are buying specific goods and services, and labour force and capital, which are deciding on a specific location, will opt at the same time for a specific regulatory regime. Since some countries face a gain and others a loss of consumers, labour force and capital regulatory competition may take place; that is, the losers will adapt their regulatory regimes to the preferences of the mobile consumers, labour force and capital. The highly disputed question is as to whether this regulatory competition would lead to a race-to-the-top or to a race-to-the-bottom. The answer to this question partly depends on the assumptions as regards efficiency of regulatory state activity. In cases where government regulation of economic activities constitutes an efficient response to market failures, regulatory competition may reintroduce the market failures by the backdoor and may lead to a race-to-the-bottom.[14] In cases where government regulation of economic activities is the result of inefficient rent seeking, regulatory competition may exert socially beneficial pressure on lawmakers and governments, and thereby may lead to a race-to-the-top.

The extent of regulatory competition among EU Member States is, first of all, restricted by some derogations, that is, *express derogations* as determined in Article 30 EC with respect to the free movement of goods, in Article 55 EC with respect to free movement of services, in Article 39 (3) and (4) EC with respect to employees, in Articles 45 and 46 EC with respect to right of establishment, and in Article 58 EC with respect to free movement of capital and, in the case of non-discriminatory barriers to free movement, the *mandatory requirements* as developed by the European Court of Justice. All derogations are narrowly defined and subject to a proportionality test. Secondly, although the centralized model to harmonize national regulations, which obviously abolished regulatory competition, was replaced by the decentralized model of the market access test and mutual recognition, some harmonization continues to exist which also restricts regulatory competition. Moreover, the integration-friendly case law of the European Court of Justice has contributed, to some extent, to increasing pressures for harmonizing national laws.

4. FEDERALISM, CHINESE STYLE

Chinese-style federalism is not based on explicit constitutional foundations or associated with Western types of democracy, thus contrasting sharply with Western federalisms. When applying the concept of market-preserving federalism, however, the focus of analysis turns to the relationship between different levels of government. According to Montinola, Qian and Weingast,[15] the nature of the relationship between the central and local entities changed in China, owing (1) to the political decentralization giving local governments stronger influence over a broad range of economic issues, (2) to the new market-oriented approach towards economic development by the political leadership, and (3) to the policy of integration into the global market. In the following sections, we first will concentrate on the question of how decentralization influenced the behaviour of local governments to support economic development. We will then look at the impact of decentralization on the establishment and protection of a unified or common market in China.

4.1 Decentralization of Economic Power

Bardhan and Mookherjee[16] point to different notions of decentralization at any given level of government; for example, (a) to the notion of authority over legislation or implementation of local regulations, composition of government spending, and delivery of public services, (b) that of finances, including setting and collecting taxes, borrowing from higher-level government or markets, and (c) that of democracy: whether local government representatives are elected locally or appointed by higher-level governments. In the case of China, decentralization concentrates mainly on the devolution of economic power (a) and (b), especially on the control over fiscal revenues and state-owned enterprises, as well as over financial institutions.

Decentralization with a focus on the central government transferring power to and sharing revenues with governments at local levels in China was not confined to the economic reform period of the 1980s. In his recent publication,[17] Jinglian Wu stressed that, already in 1957, the Central Committee of the Communist Party of China (CCCPC) decided to introduce decentralization as a key policy measure in the Great Leap Forward campaign, which represented an attempt to achieve rapid economic growth. The 1958 decentralization gave local governments a crucial role in economic planning, in the allocation of materials and equipment, in the review and approval of capital construction projects and in labour administration. In addition, local governments received more power in the administration of finance and tax collection, and most of the enterprises subordinated to ministries of the State Council were transferred to them. The resulting fierce competition of local governments over scarce resources and their concentration on large-scale infrastructure and heavy industry had an extremely negative impact on economic efficiency and agricultural production and led to a widespread famine. In 1960, the central government recentralized the administration of government finance, credit and enterprises. Another wave of decentralization started in 1970, this time motivated by the political leadership's assessment of a possible war and invasion of China. Decentralization was similar to the one of 1958, but contributed even more strongly to regionalism as each province and city was urged to establish an independent and integrated industrial structure of its own. As a reaction to serious economic problems associated with this policy, the central government recentralized economic power in the following years once again.

Decentralization in 1979 focused on changing fiscal relations between the central and provincial governments. In order to provide local governments with incentives to promote local business, fiscal contracts between the central and local governments were introduced. In a nutshell, there were basically six types of revenue-sharing contracts with provinces.[18] According to Jin, Qian and Weingast,[19] these contracts usually lasted for around five years. They defined the revenue basis for the central and local governments, with local revenues accounting for about two-thirds of total budgetary revenues. Based on a pre-determined sharing scheme, which widely varied among provinces, the local revenue was then divided between the central and local governments. During the course of the reform, many provinces were able to retain 100 per cent of the total local revenue.

Another strong incentive for local government to support economic development was the existence of extra-budgetary funds. As most of the fiscal revenue was administered by local governments, they were able to reduce the effective tax basis by transforming budgetary into extra-budgetary revenues, which the central government could not control.[20]

Fiscal contracting motivated local governments to promote economic development. In order to increase their fiscal revenue and create new employment in their localities, local government supported the emergence of domestic non-state enterprises and enterprises financed by foreign investment. With Town and Village Enterprises (TVEs) being the most important source of local revenues, Qian[21] stresses that local governments and these enterprises shared similar interests. Studies on the emergence of TVEs show the crucial role of local governments in the development of non-state enterprises. Despite ambiguous property rights of TVEs, their number increased rapidly in the 1980s and 1990s. In many cases, local officials got directly involved as shareholders of TVEs, helping to secure protection from local governments. Alternatively, these social arrangements provided necessary protection to underpin economic activities.[22]

Without the support of local governments, the fast growth of the private sector would be difficult to explain. A study by the International Finance Corporation (IFC) on the private sector development concluded that (domestic) private entrepreneurs had to function in an environment of significant legal and political uncertainties, with their property rights unprotected, and facing many restrictions. They were forced to establish close links with local bureaucracy to receive official support for their development: 'Because of China's marked decentralization and strong bureaucratic incentives to promote local development, however, the system was flexible enough and reasonably responsive to demands for legislative measures to allow the cumulative development of the domestic private sector.'[23] Up to the end of the 1990s, many large enterprises were reluctant to register as private enterprises. Gregory and Tenev[24] point to the fact that they disguised their true identities by maintaining the formal status of a collective or state-owned company. This status allowed some degree of local government involvement, in exchange for protection against ideological attacks, as well as easy access to land, bank loans and tax breaks.

To summarize, fiscal decentralization had a very positive impact on local economic development. However, it contributed to a sharp reduction of the central government's share in fiscal revenues. By 1993, this share, in total revenue, had fallen to 22 per cent. Another problem of fiscal contracting was that it worked in favour of large and powerful provinces, which were able to achieve an advantageous revenue-sharing arrangement in the bargaining process with the central government, thus contributing to regional disparity.[25] In 1994, a new system of revenue sharing between central and the local government was adopted as part of an overall tax reform, which aimed at enlarging the central government's share in budgetary revenue and its capacity to redistribute fiscal resources. The newly introduced tax-sharing system divided fiscal revenues between the central government and local governments, according to different types of taxes. Besides the local tax bureaus, national tax bureaus were set up at a local level, responsible for collecting national tax. VAT has become the major indirect tax to be shared between the central government and the local government at a fixed ratio of 60:40.[26]

Studying the effect of fiscal decentralization on local government behaviour, Jin, Qian and Weingast[27] stress the strong link between incentives and local development as well. Efforts of local governments to support economic development include policies to relax control over the emergence of non-state enterprises, by lowering entry barriers, eliminating fees and protecting these enterprises against ideological attacks. Using a panel data set of 29 provinces from 1970 to 1999 and including extra-budgetary revenue in their analysis as well, the authors came to the conclusion that fiscal decentralization gave provincial government an incentive to support economic development and reform, especially non-state enterprises. Even after the 'fiscal contracting system' was replaced by the tax sharing system in 1994, the authors find a strong correlation between incentives and economic development in the post-1994 period (2004, p. 4).

The fact that the central government's share in budgetary revenue increased to about 50 per cent by 1997 is regarded by Esarey[28] as an indication of successful centralization and as inconsistent with Weingast's market-preserving federalism. He argues that the 1994 tax reform represented a major reduction in the local governments' ability to influence local economic policy. According to the author, the power of local governments has decreased further since 2000, when the State Council prohibited the allocation of tax rebates to domestic and international businesses by local governments. Other authors, however, stress that local government's role in fiscal policy remained rather strong. Bohnet et al.[29] point to the unsuccessful attempt of the central government in the 1994 tax reform to introduce a second-round redistribution in order to redirect fiscal resources to less developed provinces. They argue that, even after the new tax reform was introduced, a large proportion of intergovernmental transfers comprised vertical grants, allocated as before in a non-transparent ad hoc fashion. The predominant part of intergovernmental transfers consisted of 'returned taxes', based on the provinces' 1993 tax base rewarding wealthy regions with increased transfers. This was a compromise vis-à-vis the rich provinces that were reluctant to accept the new tax system. That the central government had to rely on the emission of treasury bonds to finance its ambitious Western China Development Programme in 1999, instead of being able to redistribute fiscal resources among provinces, is another indicator that richer local governments were able to protect their interests.[30]

That the central government had difficulties in enforcing its new tax policy is demonstrated by the establishment of its own tax administration structure, which began to operate beside the existing local tax authorities in the post-1994 period. The central government's weak position in revenue-sharing prior to 1994 had been at least partly related to divided loyalties of tax administration officers working at the lowest level of government without much central government supervision. After the reform, the National Tax Bureau (NTB) became responsible for collecting value added tax (VAT) and other central and shared taxes. Their tax officers at the local level now must report to the provincial NTB, which evaluates their performance and determines their rewards.[31] To summarize, the 1994 tax reform hardened the fiscal budget constraints of local governments to some extent, but left enough incentives to increase local tax revenues.[32]

Economic reform since 1978, however, was not limited to fiscal decentralization, but was extended to a range of reform policies, including the liberalization of prices. Montinola, Qian and Weingast[33] point out that local governments played an important role in the transition from the dual price system of the initial reform period to the liberalization of prices across the board in later years. Reform of state-owned enterprises was also delegated to local governments as the de facto owner of most small and medium-sized state-owned enterprises (SOE). The transfer of responsibility for SOE management reform to local governments first occurred in 1958 and was followed by a second attempt in the late 1960s. In the course of these reforms, local governments were assigned the control over some 10 000 SOEs. By the mid-1990s, over 75 per cent of SOEs were subordinated to provincial and municipal governments. They were urged by the central government to be more accountable for the economic results of these enterprises and allowed to experiment with various reforms, including privatization. Only about 25 per cent of SOEs, which represented the largest companies and industrial groups, remained under the control of the central government and were transferred to the newly established State Assets Supervision and Administration Commission (SASAC) in May 2003 for further restructuring.[34]

With strong incentives to increase their revenues, local governments encouraged industrial enterprises under their control to increase investment and production, as well as profitability. The expansion of investment and industrial production contributed to China's fast economic growth, but owing to increased competition from the private sector, state-owned companies were faced with declining profits and mounting debts. To prevent state-owned enterprises from going bankrupt, local government put pressure on state-owned banks to bail companies out.[35] The fact that local governments (which Granick[36] called 'regional principals') were able to exercise strong influence on banks' credit allocation was due to their organizational weakness. Until 1984, a mono bank system existed, in which the central bank and its regional branches also acted as commercial banks. They were subordinated under a dual leadership of the central bank's headquarters in Beijing on the one hand, and the regional committee of the

Communist Party on the other.[37] At the local level, banks were under pressure from regional principals to allocate credits to state-owned companies and were often used as 'treasuries for local governments'.[38] The political power of regional principals led to a special relationship between bank managers and local party cadres, often resulting in collusive behaviour.[39] Even during the 1990s, when new banks were allowed to enter the banking sector, the predominant role of state-owned banks was preserved. By 1994, the state-owned banks' share of credit funds and deposits still amounted to about 70 per cent. They remained under strong pressure from regional principals to finance public investment projects and inefficient state-owned companies.[40]

The financial situation of small and medium-sized enterprises deteriorated further in the 1990s, owing to strong competition from TVEs. Zhou and Shen[41] showed that, in 1994, the majority of the loss-making state-owned enterprises were small ones. Faced with the mobility of capital on the one hand, and a hardening of their budget constraints on the other, the pressure to privatize state-owned enterprises became very strong for local governments.

Already some years before the CCCPC proclaimed the policy to 'Grasp the large and liberalize the small (Zhua da fang xiao)' at the 15th Party Congress in September 1997, county and district government started to sell off small and medium-sized enterprises.[42] Between 1994 and 2001, the number of state-owned enterprises in the industrial sector decreased by around 40 000.[43] According to statistics of SASAC, 80 per cent of small state-owned companies at the district level and 60 per cent at the township level were privatized by March 2003 (Schüller, 2003c). In sum, we can observe that local governments pushed for rapid privatization of 'their' state-owned enterprise after competition had increased and budget constraints hardened. With access to state-owned banks for bailing out loss-making enterprises becoming more difficult by the end of the 1990s, local governments were faced with a mounting fiscal burden and, thus, had an incentive to privatize and restructure state-owned enterprises.[44]

Despite various policies to reform state-owned enterprises, ownership transition still lags behind those in Eastern Europe.[45] In terms of its share in industrial output and its claim on resources, the state-owned sector remained comparably large. Because of the emergence of share-holding enterprises, a clear-cut differentiation between state-owned and private enterprises has become difficult. In 2004, state-owned enterprises and state-controlled companies together contributed 35.2 per cent to the Gross Industrial Output Value (GIOV) and 42.4 per cent to the value added of industry. Compared to 1985, the state-owned and state-controlled enterprises' share in GIOV went down by almost half. In contrast, the shares of foreign invested

Table 1.1 Ownership structure of industrial enterprises

	1985	2000	2004
Share in value-added of industry			
State-owned and state-controlled enterprises	–	54.3[2]	42.4[2]
Collective-owned enterprises	–	12.1	5.3
Foreign invested enterprises (FIE)	–	23.9	27.8
Individual/private enterprises	–	5.2	15.1
Share in gross industrial output value			
State-owned and state-controlled enterprises	64.9	47.3[2]	35.2[2]
Collective-owned enterprises	32.1	13.9	5.7
Foreign invested enterprises (FIE)	–	27.4	31.4
Individual/private enterprises	1.2[1]	6.1	16.5

Note: The shares in this table do not add up to 100%; [1] include foreign invested enterprises as well; [2] include state-holding enterprises; – not available.

Source: NBS (1990, p. 416), NBS (2005, p. 488).

enterprises (FIE) and private enterprises increased remarkably amounting to 31.4 per cent and 16.5 per cent (see Table 1.1).

Another indicator of the crucial role the state sector is still playing in the economy is the high share of state-owned units and shareholding units in total investment in fixed assets. In 2004, state-owned units absorbed 35.5 per cent of investment in fixed assets; share-holding units invested a share of 25.1 per cent.[46]

4.2 State-initiated Local Competition

At the beginning of economic reform, when markets were not established or not functioning well, the helping hand of the government to initiate competition was required. In the financial sector, for example, the right to issue shares on the stock market was allocated to individual provinces on the basis of a quota set by the State Planning Commission, the central bank and the China Securities Regulatory Commission (CSRC). The quota reflected the authorities' regional development goals, provincial differences in production structure and industrial development.[47] Ideally, regulatory authorities in matters of local security would choose those companies with a good performance in initial public offerings (IPO). Heilmann,[48] however, shows that competition among various localities over IPOs was often distorted by political patronage, lobbyism and corruption. The multi-step administrative admission process favoured collusion among the participating bureaucrats and companies. Although the allocation of quotas was an adequate mechanism under the condition of information asymmetry, it contributed to a deterioration in the quality of listed companies. Since August 2004, the CSRC has been working on a new IPO policy which is more market-oriented and aims at avoiding the underpricing of IPOs.[49]

The creation of Special Economic Zones (SEZs) at the beginning of the 1980s worked as another form of policy-supporting competition among localities. Guangdong and Fujian were allowed first to make SEZs accessible; other municipals were permitted to set up Economic and Technological Development Zones at the end of the 1980s, in order to develop faster than other regions. According to Goodman,[50] this policy resulted in 'a highly differentiated economic geography and pattern of regionalism that has suggested to some a replay of the "warlord era" of the 1920s, except that power is now based on economic rather than military might'. SEZs profited from a series of preferential policies introduced by the central government. These privileges enabled them to offer strong incentives to foreign companies in order to absorb foreign investment and technology.[51]

Being in competition with localities over corporate investments, local governments tried to direct resources to their own localities by offering tax exemptions and other forms of investment incentives. Inter-jurisdictional competition was especially strong with regard to foreign direct investment (FDI), because it not only generated local revenues through taxes and fees, but also was an important evaluation criterion for promoting government officials. They created a business-friendly environment by establishing local special zones or by allowing the free use of land by foreign companies.[52] During the course of competition with other localities over domestic investment and FDI, local government not only offered all sorts of tax breaks and tax exemption, but also designed special policies for attracting investment in high-tech sectors. The number of specific regions eligible for tax incentives, for example special economic zones, high-tech zones, economic development zones, bonded areas and so on increased rapidly. The various tax incentives increased the problem of China's economic fragmentation.[53]

This behaviour offers a good example of the way competition among jurisdictions was extended to factors of production, such as capital and labour.[54] In order to attract these factors to their jurisdiction, local governments had an interest in providing specific public goods, such as infrastructure and access to markets, as well as to secure rights for factor owners. In China, however, for various reasons, the mobility of labour remained limited; therefore, competition amongst jurisdictions, for the most part, concentrated on competition over capital.

4.3 Local Protectionism: The Dark Side of Chinese-style Federalism

In the last section, we showed that, despite poorly defined property rights and a weak legal system, China's economy grew very fast, thanks to adequate incentives for local governments to behave in a way compatible with market-preserving federalism. Decentralization, however, created conditions for local governments to set up trade barriers to protect their enterprises and markets against outside competitors.[55] Sonin[56] explains the existence of trade barriers across provinces by the relative weakness of the federal centre, and by rents extracted inside a specific region that provide incentives and resources to erect trade barriers.

In line with the three principal obstacles to a common market in the EU mentioned in section 2, we will look at the reasons for physical (cross-(local) border controls), technical and fiscal barriers to trade that contributed to the problem that China's market is not very well integrated.

Local protectionism in China is often related to the protection of one province against another province by erecting trade barriers across provinces.[57] However, protectionism is not restricted to the provincial level but can include lower administrative levels as well. Besides restrictions on the free movement of goods, the strength of the limitations on the mobility of labour remained even stronger. The distortion of the labour market relates to the strong urban–rural divide, cemented by the household registration system, which tied peasants to the countryside. Although this system has, to a certain extent, been relaxed, labour mobility remains limited, because of the rudimentary state of the national social security system.

There were a number of reports on local interference with inter-provincial trade since the mid-1980s. In these reports, local governments were criticized for retaining low-priced raw materials, in order to support companies within their jurisdiction, or for blocking the inflow of manufactured goods from other provinces, to better protect 'their' companies.[58] In November 1990, the State Council published a circular in reaction to the growing tensions amongst provinces over inter-provincial trade issues and ordered the elimination of all market barriers that restrict inter-provincial trade. Other examples of interference in trade between administrative units included the prohibition of beer 'imports' from Heilongjiang province via the neighbouring province of Jilin, discrimination of inflows from other provinces through high taxes by Jiangsu province, or restrictions on cotton sales to other provinces by Xinjiang province. This province also blocked the inflow of bicycles as well as television sets from other areas.

According to Huffmann,[59] local governments used their regulatory control of retail consumer and agricultural products to restrict inter-provincial transportation and distribution of products. Health and sanitation certificates with local conditions were applied as non-tariff barriers to nationally approved food products, and local laws required local wholesale purchases of alcohol and tobacco products.

Trade barriers were enforced by control stations along the main transport roads connecting provinces. These stations levied various kinds of fees and taxes on more competitive products from other regions. The central government reacted especially sensitively when local administrative units were challenging the central government's authority over tax issues.[60]

During the 1990s, the number of official media reports on local protectionism went down. The end of price control over consumer and capital goods, together with the improvement of the transport infrastructure, contributed positively to a stronger competition among provinces. In view of the accession to the WTO, however, local protectionism has become an important issue for discussion between the WTO member states and China.[61] The central government reacted to this discussion and published a State Council decree in April 2001, which prohibited protectionism by localities in any form. According to this decree, which consists of 28 articles, no unit or individual is allowed to interfere in the sale and purchase of products and services from other parts of the country.[62]

In the following years, this topic reappeared in official documents and policy papers, showing that the problems were not resolved. In September 2004, the Ministry of Commerce (MOC) set up an anti-monopoly office, with the focus on supporting a 'unified and open national market'. In a comment by MOC, local protectionism was criticized as being a threat to the establishment of a national market system.[63] In some industries, the problem of local protectionism was very difficult to solve. MOC, for example, issued a policy paper on automobile trade in March 2005 that urged local governments to stop interfering in the decision of local agencies. To support local automobile production, government agencies were urged to buy only locally produced vehicles.[64]

Bai et al.[65] point to the question of how local protectionism can be measured, as there are no tariffs or quotas on inter-regional trade, but rather administrative decrees. The authors have analysed the impact of local protectionism on regional specialization, assuming that protectionism has a significant impact on the degree of specialization. Based on a panel set of 32 two-digit industries in 29 Chinese regions over a period of 13 years between 1985 and 1997, their empirical findings have supported their hypotheses on the relationship between protectionism and regional specialization. They showed that local governments tend to protect those industries that generate high profit and tax yields, compared to industries characterized by a large share of state ownership. Their study revealed 'the overall time trend of China's regional specialization of industrial production has reversed an early drop in the mid-1980s, and registered a significant increase in the later years'.[66]

4.4 The Role of Law in Fostering the Common Market

The example in section 3 demonstrates the crucial role of the legal system in creating a Common Market in the EU. Although there has been a huge increase in the volume of laws and regulations in China, significant problems exist which are related to local protectionism, especially (a) in the making of laws and regulations and (b) in the enforcement of laws and regulations.

According to Dali Yang,[67] legal protectionism is primarily due to perverse incentives, attributable to the fact that local governments have appointive and financial power over judicial and law-enforcement departments. The situation is similar with regard to procuratorates funded by local governments. Because the judicial system lacked adequate funding, procuratorates and courts themselves had to get involved in commercial business up to 1998, when the central government prohibited their commercial activities. Analysing the lack of judicial independence, Jiang[68] concludes that local courts have little budget autonomy and little discretion in personnel management. The author refers also to an empirical study on 'Judicial Reform' based on interviews with 288 judges who admit that there is no judicial independence. According to the China Security Commission Report to the US Congress dated July 2002, over 90 per cent of the 180 000 judges in China were members of the CCP, making them subordinate to the nationwide structure.[69]

Jiang[70] shows that local protection has an impact not only on trials, but also on the enforcement of law. Local authorities, such as local courts, tax offices and banks tend to have a strong bias to protect local economic interests and therefore it is difficult to enforce court orders. A uniform implementation of law across China remains difficult, because 'local governments exercise a very high degree of power over local organs of state, including courts and procuratorates, because they fund their operation. Local courts are often unwilling to make a finding adverse to a local company, entity, or government agency for this reason. . . . Courts, in practice, lack effective coercive powers to enforce their judgements'.[71]

The loose enforcement of intellectual property rights (IPR) by local governments is an example of localism, resulting from the fragmentation of authorities. Contrary to national policies and attracted by the short-term benefits of not enforcing IPR, local leaders have a strong incentive to neglect enforcement. That the budget and career management of staff of local administrative entities responsible for IPR enforcement is dependent on the respective local government adds to the problem of enforcement by the local level.[72]

As a result of the systemic problems of the judicial system, the successful enforcement of World Trade Organization (WTO)-related rules and regulations was doubted by some observers. The China Security Commission Report to the US Congress from July 2002, for example, questioned whether the central government was able to oppose trade barriers across provinces and regarded this problem as a major obstacle to China's efforts to fulfil the WTO obligations.[73] However, the accession to the WTO offered a unique chance to introduce international rules, regulations and procedures that streamline the domestic judicial system. The basic principles of free trade, with non-discrimination and national treatment as the corner stones, and the central elements of transparency, certainty and predictability can play a crucial role in the domestic market. The WTO accession required that national laws, regulations and rules be applied in a uniform, impartial and reasonable manner across China. So far, much progress has been made by adapting national laws and regulation to international standards.

5. CONCLUSIONS

Although the European Union is certainly not a federal state, but represents a unique mixture of federal and confederal elements, and although China is not a federal state in the sense that this term is used by most Western scholars, the EU and China can be considered as two variants of 'federal structures', since both are characterized by a hierarchy of governments and by some degree of institutional autonomy of each government, whereby lower-level governments have primary regulatory responsibility over the economy.

What could China learn from Europe's experience? It has been shown that European integration has from the very beginning been driven by an inherent tension between the establishment of a common market, that is, the enforcement of the four basic freedoms, and the regulatory autonomy of the Member States. In order to foster the development of a Common Market, the European Commission and the European Court of Justice strive to centralize more regulatory activities at the EU level and to weaken the regulatory autonomy of the Member States. At least with respect to those regulatory activities that are confronted by heterogeneous preferences among Member States and that do not cause any spillovers or economies of scale, centralization is overstated and lowers social welfare.

In China, some 30 years ago, a development was initiated which aimed at strengthening the regulatory autonomy of provinces in order to improve the incentives of lower-level governments to support economic growth. However, this decentralization has induced lower-level governments to create barriers to entry to the regional markets in order to support their regional economies. Thus, in contrast to the development in the EU, China has been experiencing an overemphasis on decentralization, with the consequence that the Chinese economy is segregated into a multitude of regional markets.

From this point of view China would be well advised to determine the allocation of competences among the different government levels in an appropriate constitutional document, in a way that restricts regional protectionism by central government and through proper judicial control, whereas central government's activities should be restricted by a narrowly defined catalogue of competencies at a central level.

NOTES

1. Weingast (1995), Montinola, Qian and Weingast (1995), Weede (2000), Jin, Qian and Weingast (2004).
2. Weingast (1995, p. 1).
3. Weingast (1995, p. 2).
4. Weingast (1995, p. 4).
5. Montinola, Qian and Weingast (1995, p. 53).
6. Pelkmans (2001, p. 36).
7. Egan (2001, pp. 61ff).
8. Barnard (2004, pp. 11ff).
9. For the problems with mutual recognition in service markets see Pelkmans (2005, pp. 107ff).
10. For details see Wagener, Eger and Fritz (2006, chs 7 and 8).
11. Craig and De Búrca (2003, p. 432).
12. Barnard (2004, p. 17).
13. Barnard (2004, pp. 17ff).
14. Sinn (2003).
15. Montinola, Qian and Weingast (1995, pp. 2–3).
16. Bardhan and Mookherjee (2005).
17. Jinglian (2005, pp. 44–54).
18. Bahl (1999, pp. 149–73); Bohnet (2003, pp. 66–72); OECD (2002, p. 661).
19. Jin, Qian and Weingast (2004, pp. 6–11).
20. Bohnet et al. (2003, pp. 91–3); Wong (2000, pp. 5–7); Herrmann-Pillath (1991, p. 12).
21. Qian (2003).
22. Zhang (2005, pp. 1–3).
23. IFC (2000, p. 19).
24. Gregory and Tenev (2001, p. 14).
25. Schüller (2003a, pp. 103–4).
26. Cao, Qian and Weingast (1997, p. 15).
27. Jin, Qian and Weingast (2004).
28. Esarey (2002, pp. 11–15).
29. Bohnet et al. (2003, p. 126).
30. Schüller (2003a, p. 113).

31. Bohnet (2003, p. 117); Bahl (1999, pp. 47–69).
32. Cao, Qian and Weingast (1997, p. 16).
33. Montinola, Qian and Weingast (1995, p. 11).
34. Meyer et al. (2002, p. 252; SASAC homepage: http://www.sasac.gov.cn).
35. Imai (2003, p. 3).
36. Granick (1990, pp. 20–47).
37. Byrd (1983, p. 10).
38. Byrd (1983, p. 10).
39. Herrmann-Pillath (1991, p. 301).
40. Schüller (2003b, p. 195).
41. Zhou and Shen (1997).
42. Imai (2003, pp. 3–5).
43. Imai (2003, p. 12).
44. Cao, Qian and Weingast (1997, p. 4).
45. Yusuf et al. (2006, pp. 116–27).
46. NBS (1990) and NBS (2005).
47. Su and Fleisher (2000, pp. 243–4).
48. Heilmann (2001, pp. 8–10).
49. CSRC (2004, p. 8).
50. Goodman (1994, p. 1).
51. Wang and Hu (1999, p. 178).
52. Zhang (2005, pp. 5–6).
53. OECD (2002, pp. 633–4).
54. Montinola, Qian and Weingast (1995, p. 8).
55. Montinola, Qian and Weingast (1995, p. 14).
56. Sonin (2005, p. 4).
57. Sonin (2005, p. 2).
58. Watson, Findlay et al. (1989).
59. Huffmann (2003).
60. Schüller (1990, pp. 826–8).
61. Biddulph (2002).
62. Xinhua News Agency (30.4.01).
63. News Guangdong (17.9.2004).
64. China Daily (24.8.05).
65. Bai et al. (2003).
66. Bai et al. (2003).
67. Dali Yang (2005).
68. Jiang (2004, pp. 56–7).
69. Sonin (2005, p. 3).
70. Jiang (2004, p. 207).
71. Biddulph (2002, p. 205).
72. OECD (2005, p. 32).
73. Sonin (2005, p. 21).

REFERENCES

Bahl, R. (1999), *Fiscal Policy in China. Taxation and Intergovernmental Fiscal Relations*, Ann Arbor, Michigan: University of Michigan.

Bai, Ch.-E., Y. Du, Z. Tao and S.Y. Tong (2003), 'Local protectionism and regional specialization: evidence from China's industries', The University of Hong Kong (<http://www.bus.umich.edu/KresgeLibrary/Collections/Workingpapers/wdi/wp 565.pdf>).

Bardhan, P. and D. Mookherjee (2005), 'Decentralization, corruption and government accountability: an overview', in S. Rose-Ackermann (ed.), *The International Handbook on the Economics of Corruption*, Cheltenham, UK and Northampton, MA, USA: Edward Elgar, revised June 2005 (<http://www.bu.edu/econ/workingpapers/papers/Dilip%20Mookherjee/wp2005/decorr.pdf>).

Barnard, C. (2004), *The Substantive Law of the EU. The Four Freedoms*, Oxford: Oxford University Press.

Biddulph, S. (2002), 'Enhancing China's rule of law', in H. Holbig and A.Robert (eds), *China's Accession to the World Trade Organization, National and International Perspectives*, London: Routledge, pp. 193–226.

Bohnet, A. et al. (2003), *Theoretische Grundlagen und praktische Gestaltungsmöglichkeiten eines Finanzausgleichssystems für die VR China* (Theoretical Foundations and Policy Recommendations for a System of Fiscal Revenue Sharing in the PR China), Frankfurt a.M: Peter Lang.

Byrd, W. (1983), *China's Financial System: The Changing Role of Banks*, Boulder, Colorado: Westview Press.

Cao, Y., Y. Qian and B.R. Weingast (1997), 'From federalism, Chinese style, to privatization, Chinese style' (<http://www.econ.stanford.edu/faculty/workp/swp97049.pdf>).

China Daily, 'Local bias harms economy', in <http://www.chinadaily.com.cn>, 24.8.05.

CSRC (China Securities Regulatory Commission) (2004), 'Trial implementation of IPO pricing policy', <http://www.csrc.gov.cn>, 30.8.2004, posted on the website 11 November 2005.

Craig, P.P. and G. de Búrca (2003), *EU Law. Text, Cases, and Materials*, 3rd edn, Oxford: Oxford University Press.

Dougherty, S. and R. Herd (2005), *Fast-Falling Barriers and Growing Concentration: The Emergence of a Private Economy in China*, OECD Economics Department, ECO/WKP (2005), 58 (<http://www.olis.oecd.org/olis/2005doc.nsf/43bb6130e5e86e5fc12569fa005d004c/f25d982344f508c2c12570de003209eb/$FILE/JT00196117.PDF>).

Egan, M. (2001), *Constructing a European Market: Standards, Regulation, and Governance*, Oxford: Oxford University Press.

Esarey, A.W. (2002), 'Reconsidering Weingast market-preserving federalism in contemporary China', Columbia University, Political Science Department, New York, (<http://www.columbia.edu/~as48/Comparative%20Federalism_files/MPF%2002-02-04.pdf>).

Goodman, D.S.G. (1994), 'The politics of regionalism: economic development, conflict and negotiation', in D.S.G. Goodman and G. Segal (eds), *China Deconstructs, Politics, Trade and Regionalism*, London: Routledge, pp. 1–20.

Granick, D. (1990), *Chinese State Enterprises. A Regional Property Analysis*, Chicago and London: University of Chicago.

Gregory, N. and S. Tenev (2001), 'China's home-grown entrepreneurs,' *The China Business Review*, January–February, 14–21, 27.

Heilmann, S. (2001), 'Der Aktienmarkt der VR China (II): Schlüsselakteure und inoffizielle Spielregeln (*The Stock Market in the PR China (II): Key Actors and Unofficial Rules of the Game*)', *China Analysis No. 4*, Center for East Asian and Pacific Studies, Trier University (<http://www.china.ahk.de/gic/biznews/industries/finance/aktienmarkt2.pdf>).

Herrmann-Pillath, C. (1991), *Institutioneller Wandel, Macht und Inflation in China. Ordnungstheoretische Analysen zur Politischen Ökonomie eines Transformationsprozesses* (*Institutional Change, Power and Luflation in China. Institutional – Theoretic Analyses on the Political Economy of a Transition Process*), Baden-Baden: Nomos.
Huffman, T.P. (2003), 'Wal-Mart in China: challenges facing a foreign retailer's supply chain', *China Business Review*, Sept–Oct.
Imai, K. (ed.) (2003a), 'Dynamics of ownership transformation: privatization of small and medium scale enterprises', *Beyond Market Socialism. Privatization of State-owned and Collective Enterprises in China*, Tokyo, Japan: Institute of Developing Economies, pp. 9–26.
Imai, K. (ed.) (2003b), 'Privatization in China', *Beyond Market Socialism. Privatization of State-owned and Collective Enterprises in China*, Tokyo, Japan: Institute of Developing Economies, pp. 1–6.
International Finance Corporation (IFC) (2000), *China's Emerging Private Enterprises*, Washington, DC: IFC.
Jiang, Q.Y. (2004), *Court Delay and Law Enforcement in China. Civil Process and Economic Perspective*, Wiesbaden: Gabler.
Jin, H., Y. Qian and B.R. Weingast (2004), 'Regional decentralization and fiscal incentives: federalism, Chinese style', working paper, Hoover Institution and Department of Political Science, Stanford University.
Jinglian, W. (2005), *Understanding and Interpreting Chinese Economic Reform*, Mason: South-Western College Publishing.
Meyer, M.W. et al. (2002), 'Decentralized enterprise reform: notes on the transformation of state-owned enterprises', in A.S. Tsui and Ch.-M. Lau (eds), *The Management of Enterprises in the Peoples' Republic of China*, Bostan, Dordrecht, London: Kluwer, pp. 241–74.
Montinola, G., Y. Qian and B.R. Weingast (1995), 'Federalism, Chinese style: the political basis for success in China', *World Politics*, **48**(1), 50–81.
National Bureau of Statistics (1990), *China Statistical Yearbook 1990*, Beijing.
National Bureau of Statistics (2005), *China Statistical Yearbook 2005*, Beijing.
News Guangdong, 'Ministry Sets up Anti-monopoly Office' (<www.newsgd.com>, 17.9.2004).
OECD (2005), *Governance in China*, Paris.
Organisation for Economic Co-Operation and Development (OECD) (2002), *China in the World Economy. The Domestic Policy Challenges*, Paris.
Pelkmans, J. (2001), *European Integration. Methods and Economic Analysis*, 2nd edn, Harlow: Prentice-Hall.
Pelkmans, J. (2005), 'Mutual recognition in goods and services: an economic perspective', in F.K.P. Schioppa (ed.), *The Principle of Mutual Recognition in the European Integration Process*, Basingstoke: Palgrave, pp. 85–128.
Qian, Y. (2003), 'How reform worked in China', in D. Rodrik (ed.), *Search of Prosperity: Analytic Narratives on Economic Growth*, Princeton: Princeton University Press, pp. 297–333.
Schüller, M. (1990), 'Rundschreiben des Staatsrates zur Aufhebung der internen Marktzutrittsbeschränkungen ("The State Council's Circular on the Abolishment of Barriers to Entry to the Internal Market")', *in China aktuell*, November, 826–9.
Schüller, M. (2003a), 'China's western development program: a Chinese version of Germany's "Rebuilding the East"?', *Provincial China, Research News, Analysis*, **8**(2), 118–43.

Schüller, M. (2003b), 'Der institutionelle Wandel der Finanzintermediation in der VR China ("The Institutional Change of Financial Intermediation in the PR China")', in T. Eger (ed.), *Institutionen und wirtschaftliche Entwicklung* (*Institutions and Economic Development*), Schriften des Vereins für Socialpolitik, Berlin: Duncker & Humblot, pp. 183–218.
Schüller, M. (2003c), 'SASAC bestimmt Regeln über den Transfer von Vermögenswerten staatseigener Unternehmen' ("SASAC determines regulations on the transfer of state-owned enterprises' assets"), in China aktuell, December, 1452.
Sinn, H.-W. (2003), *The New Systems Competition*, Oxford: Blackwell.
Sonin, K. (2005), 'Provincial protectionism', New Economic School/CEFIR, CEPR and Institute of Advanced Study, May (<http://ctool.gdnet.org/conf_docs/Sonin_Paper_Parallel1_Session4.pdf>).
Su, D. and B.M. Fleisher (2000), 'Explaining IPO underpricing in China', in B. Chen, J.K. Dietrich and Y. Fang (eds), *Financial Market Reform in China*, Boulder: Westview Press, pp. 243–60.
Tsui, A.S. and Ch.-M. Lau (eds) (2002), *The Management of Enterprises in the People's Republic of China*, Boston, Dordrecht, London: Kluwer.
Wagener, H.-J., T. Eger and H. Fritz (2006), *Europäische Integration. Recht und Ökonomie, Geschichte und Politik* (European Integration. Law and Economics, History and Politics), Munich: Vahlen.
Wang, S. and A. Hu (1999), *The Political Economy of Uneven Development. The Case of China*, Armonk, New York/London: M.E. Sharpe.
Watson, A., C. Findlay et al. (1989), ' "Who won the wool war"?: a case study of rural product marketing in China', *The China Quarterly*, **118**, 213–41.
Weede, E. (2000), *Asien und der Westen: Politische und kulturelle Determinanten der wirtschaftlichen Entwicklung* (Asia and the West: Political and Cultural Determinants of Economic Development), Baden-Baden: Nomos.
Weingast, B. (1995), 'The economic role of political institutions: market-preserving federalism and economic development', *Journal of Law, Economics, and Organization*, **11**, 1–31.
Wong, C. (2000), *Central–local Relations Revisited: the 1994 Tax Sharing Reform and Public Expenditure Management in China*, World Bank Office, July.
Wu, J. (2005), *Understanding and Interpreting Chinese Economic Reform*, South-Western, Mason, Ohio: Thomson.
Xinhua News Agency, 'State council issues local protectionism ban', 30.4.01.
Yang, D. (2005), 'Can China overcome Balkanization?' (<www.pnl.gov/China/Balkaniz.htm>, 27.10.05).
Yusuf, S., K. Nabeshima and D. Perkins (2006), *Under New Ownership. Privatizing China's State-owned Enterprises*, New York: The World Bank.
Zhang, X. (2005), 'Asymmetric property rights in China's economic growth', paper presented at the session on 'Land Rights and Social Security in China', of the Annual American Economics Association Meetings, Boston, 6–8 January, 2006.
Zhou, F. and Y. Shen (1997), 'Letting go small SOEs is good for enhancing the quality of state assets', in *Realistic Choice: Preliminary Summary of the Practice of Reforming Small State-Owned Enterprises*, Shanghai: China Reform and Development Report.

2. The road to efficient taxation in China

Pierre Garello

1. INTRODUCTION[1]

The recent economic history of China is simply fascinating. During the past 25 years, China's GDP has grown at an average annual rate of 9 per cent, driving China to the top five world economies with a GDP per capita of 1410US$ in 2005. What accounts for such a rapid development? Institutional changes without a doubt. Indeed, during that period, The People's Republic of China has engaged in profound reforms on almost every front, from property laws (with a large programme of privatization) to competition law, and has opened itself to globalization. Tax laws are no exception to this rapid structural change. China has undertaken major tax reforms in 1978, 1983, 1994 and 2004.

In 2004, total tax revenue in China hit 2.57 trillion Yuan (US$313 billion), up 25.7 per cent on a yearly basis.[2] Still, the share of tax revenue in GDP has remained surprisingly low compared to OECD countries: in 1999, that share was 13 per cent for China, compared to 27.7 per cent for OECD countries and 30.2 per cent for EU countries.[3] This places China at a crossroad. How can growth be further fostered? And what use should be made of the proceeds from growth? Some analysts plead in favour of greater fiscal centralization and higher taxes, while others point in the opposite direction. The purpose of this study is to rely on law and economics to see which elements have to be considered when making these choices.

The design of a fiscal system obviously requires many things, among them the choice of what we could call 'a political vision' – that is, what kind of society we wish to live in – and it is not the purpose of this chapter to discuss alternative visions. Whatever vision one wishes to develop, however, it is essential to remain aware of the incentive dimensions attached to each alternative fiscal system if one does not want that vision to be mere illusion. The goal of this chapter is precisely to describe, relying on well established economic principles, the main incentives associated with various fiscal systems.

Not surprisingly, the literature on fiscal policy is voluminous, and a choice must be made here on how to synthesize, preferably in a useful way, such a tremendous amount of theoretical and empirical research. To guide us in this choice we could use what I would call a 'political' approach, acknowledging from the start that tax policies are designed with two goals in mind: first, to provide financial resources necessary for the production by the state of some specific goods and services, and, second, to serve as a tool for redistributing wealth from one subset of the population to another subset. Following this approach one would then attempt to synthesize the literature in a two-part presentation, starting with a discussion of the efficient financing of a state's production before turning to a study of the design of efficient redistributive policies. Such an approach will however quickly lead to the greatest confusion, and this for two reasons. First, wealth redistribution already occurs via the financing of public goods and services (as, for instance, when governments decide to finance those goods with a progressive income tax), and second, the very necessity to redistribute wealth greatly depends on the dynamics of the economy which itself is dependent upon the set of incentives entailed by the existing fiscal system.

Instead of considering state's production and redistribution as two separate topics, we propose the following, progressive, approach. In section 2 we will deal with what is, according to economic theory, the proper role of the state in financing goods and services (the demand side of public finance if one wishes). This provides a first approximation of how much money (leaving out purely redistributive goals) should be raised through taxation. The next three sections will be organized around the question of how to collect that money and, in particular, of how centralized the fiscal system should be. In section 3 we make the implicit assumption that the fiscal system is fully centralized. In such an environment we run the traditional cost–benefit analysis to compare various modes of financing: progressive v. flat income tax, excise taxes or general consumption taxes, and so on. In section 4 we look at the redistributive dimension of those fiscal policies as well as some specific tools for redistribution. Finally, in section 5 we drop the assumption of a centralized tax authority. This allows us to analyse the merits and shortcomings of fiscal decentralization. As will be seen, decentralization not only tends to improve the quality of the supply of public goods but it also allows for a better adjustment of supply to demand. In section 6, a general description of China's present fiscal system is offered and analysed with the tools previously introduced. This will lead us to the conclusion that, in order to maintain its impressive economic development, China must (i) resist fiscal centralization and instead delegate more fiscal power to lower levels of government, thus bringing more consistency (and competition) into the system, and (ii) favour 'passive' tax policies which do not use taxation with the hope of fine-tuning economic development or reaching a pre-specified allocation of wealth.

2. TAXING FOR WHAT REASONS?

Historically states have used their power to tax for many purposes and with various degrees of success.[4] The constitutional movement starting in the thirteen century stemmed precisely from the desire to limit such power.[5] As philosophers, lawyers, politicians, and indeed citizens were discussing those limits, economists developed their own approach to the question. Hence, the last book of Adam Smith's *magnum opus*, *The Wealth of Nations*, is entirely devoted to a discussion of the principles of 'good taxation'. During the following two centuries, as the ratio of tax revenues to GDP grew steadily, economists slowly reached a broad consensus on what, in theory, taxes should be used for.

It is nowadays largely recognized that most goods and services are better provided by a decentralized system based on private property and contract, that is to say, by the market. It is not the place here to restate the argument, but it is enough to recall that the price system (when prices are the outcome of free trade) provides efficient signals of relative scarcity and, through profit opportunities, invites everyone to look for better solutions to answer the needs of as many as possible. There was however a caveat to that general statement: the market is an efficient provider only of those goods and services which can be privately acquired, by which we mean that their owners can choose, if they wish, to foreclose access to others.[6] For the other goods, known among economists as 'public goods', the prediction is that no entrepreneur will be willing to engage in their production for fear of free-riding. Indeed, by the very nature of those goods, once the good is produced any one can benefit from it, whether or not he accepts to pay a price for that service. The temptation is therefore strong to let others pay for the good, and if every one follows that line of reasoning, no one will be willing to contribute and the entrepreneur foolish enough to engage in its production will soon realize he is losing money. Expecting such an outcome, no reasonable entrepreneur will undertake the production of a public good in the first place.

In order to have such a public good produced a way must be found around the free-riding problem. In small communities, reputation and retaliation may do the job.[7] Sometimes, it is also possible to tie the production of the public good to the production of a private good (hence, advertising companies might be happy to provide and maintain free bus shelters – a mild form of public goods – as long as they can post their advertising on the shelter's walls). But a clear alternative is of course to force everyone to contribute to the production of the good. This is what taxation does. But, if forcing everyone to contribute can guarantee that the public good will be produced, that solution also presents some obvious shortcomings that need to be quickly recalled, if only to invite us to use that tool with due care.

The first of those shortcomings is that it requires *everyone*, including those who care little for that good, to contribute. This naturally is not efficient in terms of allocation of resources. To remedy this efficiency, some economists, starting with Lindhal, have tried to design a system where each citizen will contribute according to the degree of satisfaction he or she derives from that good. Hence someone to whom the public good is very useful will contribute a lot and someone to whom the good is useless will contribute nothing. This however raises a new problem: will citizens honestly reveal their preferences? Will there be no free-riding via wrong reporting to the central authority? Somehow, we are almost back to where we started.

A second shortcoming of taxation follows logically from the first. If the quantity and quality of public goods to be produced have to be decided through an indirect mechanism (the central authority, or the vote of elected representatives), then, taking into account the fact that those who decide will contribute at best a tiny part to the financing, clearly the chances that the quantity and quality produced will approach the quantity and quality which would have been produced had the citizens' preferences been known are very low (for various reasons easy to imagine, ranging from corruption to mere ignorance).[8]

A last shortcoming associated with the provision of public goods by the state (regardless of its mode of financing) is that the state's employees are not necessarily experts in the production of those goods, so that, even assuming the quantity and quality to be produced are known, the production will not be done at the lower cost. Out-sourcing can, however, greatly help solve that problem. Hence, when a state auctions a contract for the production of a public good it can benefit from the technological and managerial knowledge possessed by private companies. In other words, in those circumstances where it is efficient to raise taxes to provide some public goods for the population, it is preferable to entrust the production to private enterprises (which will be in competition at the auctioning stage).

To sum up, economists have long acknowledged that it could be efficient to rely on taxation to finance the production of some specific goods, while, at the same time, pointing out the various imperfections of that solution. Now the good news, as far as efficiency is concerned, is that there are not so many 'public goods'. Clearly, schools, transportation services, swimming pools and the like are not public goods since it is perfectly possible to exclude those who do not wish to contribute to their financing. Even roads, bridges and canals do not have the characteristics of a public good. It is relatively easy to impose a toll and, if a well developed capital market exists, such large projects can be privately funded and profitable. Some have objected to the private production and financing of those goods on the ground that poor citizens will not be able to afford them once they are entirely privately managed. The traditional answer of the economist is that, if those goods are really basic, a money transfer or a voucher system (that is, a transfer 'in nature') can be established which, admittedly, will also require taxation, but at a much lower level, since the good is likely to be produced at lower cost and the state will pay only for the needy.

Before turning to the study of the most efficient ways of financing public goods, a final remark is in order to explain what appears first like a paradox. Indeed, if the above analysis is correct, that is, if a vast majority of goods and services are better produced by the market, what then can account for the rapid – some would rather say, exponential – growth in taxation which took place during the last two centuries in most developed countries? This paradox becomes thicker if we are mindful of the fact that, in those countries, wealth per capita has been booming over that period, so much so that the poorest citizens of the twenty-first century are incomparably wealthier than a poor citizen of the beginning of the twentieth century; and that steep increase in a state's spending is even more surprising when we take into account the fact that technological advances have partially transformed some public goods into private ones.[9] Part of the answer to that paradox is provided by Public Choice theory, a branch of economics that aims at understanding the mechanisms through which representatives are selected and decisions are taken by the bureaucrats as well as members of parliament. A presentation, even superficial, of those theories would however lead us too far away from our present topic.[10] Another solution to that paradox lies in what could be called an increasing aversion to wealth inequality. The question is then whether policies aiming at reducing wealth inequalities have achieved their goals and, most importantly, whether the quality of life of the poorest has been improved relatively to what it would have been absent those policies.[11] We come back to those topics in sections 3 and 4 below.

3. EFFICIENT TAXATION IN THE CONTEXT OF A UNIQUE FISCAL JURISDICTION

In this section and the following one we assume that there is *a single* fiscal jurisdiction which must find the most efficient way of levying a given amount of tax revenues and allocate those revenues. Before going further we must attempt to define what economists mean by an 'efficient' tax. As we will soon realize, such a definition can be found only for specific contexts and does not easily translate into policy recommendations. The effort nonetheless conveys important lessons for the design of a 'good' fiscal policy and is, in that sense, worthy.

The path to such a definition lies in the observation that any tax policy introduces a bias in the allocation of resources (in particular, in the allocation of labour time) and that, therefore, tax policies should be designed so as to minimize that bias. To illustrate that principle it might be useful to look more closely at the effects of a simple excise tax.

Let us assume that the S_0 and D_0 curves below represent the supply and demand for, let us say, cigarettes in the absence of tax. The quantity of cigarettes produced and sold will be Q_0 at price P_0. Assume now that an excise tax of t is levied per unit sold. If the companies were already producing at the level for which price just covers marginal cost, the effect of taxation is to move the supply curve upward by an amount just equal to t (the distance E_1A on the graph). The after-tax equilibrium is E_1, where a quantity Q_1 is sold at price P_1, the amount left to the companies per unit sold being $(P_1 - t)$.

As we can see, the effects of such a simple tax are extremely rich. Besides providing tax revenues for the government (the shaded rectangle with area $t \times Q_1$), it reduces production, and therefore the corresponding demand for labour and capital. Furthermore, since the new price is higher, it is possible

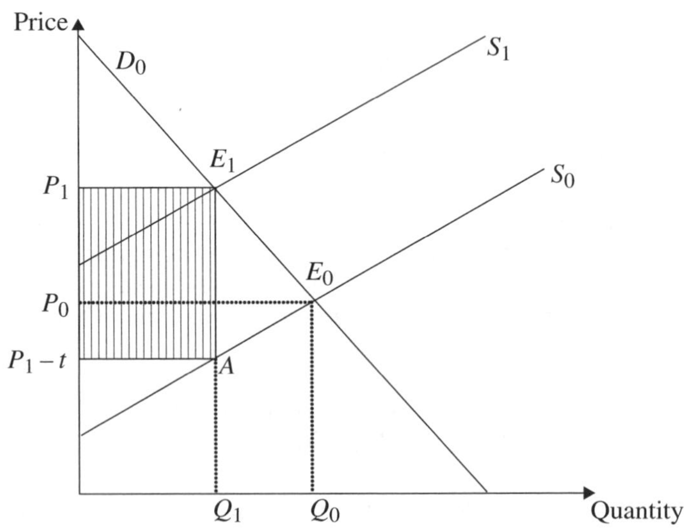

Figure 2.1 The effect of an excise tax

that consumers will decide to spend more on that good (and therefore reduce their consumption on other markets), this depending naturally on the degrees of elasticity of the various demand functions. To classify the various consequences attached to an excise tax, it is convenient to make the simplifying assumption that tax revenues represent benefits to society. Using the variations in consumers' surplus and companies' profit and comparing it to tax revenues gives then a first approximation of the net result. Coming back to the figure, we see that consumers' surplus has been reduced by an amount corresponding to the area $P_0E_0E_1P_1$, while producers have lost the equivalent of $P_0E_0A(P_1 - t)$. Since tax revenues correspond to the shaded rectangle $P_1E_1A(P_1 - t)$, clearly the welfare loss supported by consumers and producers of cigarettes *exceeds* the amount of tax receipts by an amount corresponding to the triangle E_1E_0A. The excise tax has generated a kind of deadweight loss, also called 'excess burden'.

We are now in a better position to understand what an efficient way of raising tax is, according to economic theory: the efficient tax policy is the one which minimizes the deadweight loss attached to taxation. In Adam Smith's words: 'Every tax ought to be so contrived as both to take out and keep out of the pocket of the people as little as possible, over and above what it brings into the public treasury of the state.'[12]

If we follow that criterion we quickly find out that the most efficient tax is also the simplest one: *a lump sum tax* paid by each citizen. The reasons for the 'superiority' of the lump sum tax are easy to grasp.[13] Because it applies to everyone regardless of their economic activities, there will be no money lost in rent seeking, no choice to be made between legal or illegal work, no distortion in relative prices and therefore in the allocation of scarce resources (in particular the arbitrage between labour and capital would remain unchanged). Also the administrative cost would be extremely low. But there is of course a dark side to the lump sum tax, namely, its political cost. Indeed the lump tax is largely perceived as unfair, violating in particular what is, to many, an undisputable principle of justice: the contributory capacity principle.

Without the lump sum tax we will therefore have to look for a second best. But, in the realm of taxation, even that appears a hard task.[14] Let me, however, briefly summarize some well known results which can guide us towards more efficient tax policies, keeping in mind that each of those theoretical results is derived under a very specific set of assumptions and usually does not hold in a more general context. In particular those results assume zero collecting cost.

1. A unique tax rate for all taxable consumption goods is usually not optimal. If this result may appear counter-intuitive it is because one

usually forgets that a very important good, leisure, is not taxable. The efficient consumption taxes should therefore put more burdens on goods which are complementary to leisure.

2. An approximation of this rule consists in taxing at a higher rate those goods with lower price elasticity. That rule is known as the inverse-elasticity rule, and is based on Ramsey's work. Practically it means that, if you do not tax all goods, then you should tax in priority those goods for which the demand is less elastic (which is why excise taxes bear usually on such things as energy products, or goods related to addiction such as tobacco or alcohol).
3. If you tax personal income, a lump sum tax will have less distortion than a flat rate tax (the latter is equivalent to a decrease in wage and has therefore a revenue effect and a substitution effect, while the former has only a revenue effect), which will itself be preferable to a progressive tax (which has a higher substitution effect). Indeed, it can be shown that, even if one cares about the poorest, it is not necessarily a good idea to impose high marginal tax rates on the rich. To quote Slemrod (1990, p. 165): 'Simple models of optimal income taxation do not generally point to sharply progressive tax structures, even if the objective function puts relatively large weight on the welfare of less well-off individuals.'
4. If you tax a company's income, better use a kind of lump sum tax and avoid exemptions and other tax incentives which introduce bias in resource allocation.
5. Better tax assets than income; this gives incentives to make the best use of those assets.
6. A tax on capital gain is largely unnecessary: better tax consumption or income.

Unfortunately, none of those results easily translates into policy recommendations[15] and the theoretical lack of 'economic efficiency' of a tax policy can sometimes be more than compensated by the fact that this policy can be run at low administrative cost. For, indeed, administrative costs and more specifically collecting costs are likely to be high since taxation rests on coercion and individuals tend to resist coercion.

As a consequence, it might be advisable to give a bonus to those taxes which are more transparent and/or can be collected at low costs. Hence, a powerful argument can be found in favour of a generalized (consumption-type) VAT, or a flat rate income tax. In any case, the advice would be to avoid using taxation as a tool for redistribution (as opposed to using the revenues from taxation to redistribute wealth) and to renounce using taxation as an incentive tool. There would be indeed an inconsistency in, on one hand, relying on the market for resource allocation, while on the other hand, trying to control resource allocation via fiscal incentives. The last solution, instead of leading the economy closer to the target, is most likely to lead to the adoption of sophisticated strategies by individuals and companies which will attempt to grasp any available 'fiscal gifts' and avoid fiscal burden.

It might be useful at this point to say a few words about externalities. Indeed, as we know, while some economists (following Arthur Pigou) have suggested that inefficiencies due to externalities could be remedied via taxation and subsidizing, others (following Coase) have shown that another remedy can be found in a refinement of existing rights and duties (property law and tort law). In both cases, the idea is to implement an incentive scheme with the objective of 'internalizing the externality'. There exists, however, a major difference between the Pigouvian and the Coasian approaches stemming from the fact that rights are tradable and can therefore 'circulate' as market participants change their views on the economic value of those rights, while the tax rate is based on the knowledge of a few and, by its very nature, is much less flexible. In a dynamic world of changing knowledge, economists tend naturally to favour the Coasian solution instead of the tax solution.

4. REDISTRIBUTION AND FISCAL POLICY IN A DYNAMIC PERSPECTIVE

As pointed out in the introduction, taxation can serve as a tool for redistribution in two ways: first, taxation redistributes wealth when, for instance, the wealthiest contribute a larger share to the financing of public goods and second, taxation is necessary to raise the money to be redistributed.

Before going further, let us recall that to work at the two levels simultaneously is generally not a good idea because it raises serious incentive problems. To see why, enough is to take the case of the so-called 'negative income tax'. Let R denote personal income, t the income tax rate, and S a threshold separating the population into two categories: those who pay income taxes and those who do not but benefit instead from money transfers. What any individual with revenue R pays or receives is hence given by the function $T(R) = (R - S)t$, those whose income is below S *receiving* from the state the amount $(S - R)t$. Clearly such a policy creates the wrong incentives since a poor person who starts working will receive less money from the state. The temptation is strong, therefore, to turn to the illegal market in order to keep the benefits of low-income workers. For that reason redistributing devices based on such mechanisms have come to be known as poverty traps.

There are two reasons why one may wish to redistribute. One is to reduce wealth inequalities, the other to make the poor richer. Clearly, the short-term effect of redistribution is to realize both. In the long run, however, things are much more complex. Economic development relies heavily on rule of law and private entrepreneurship motivated by profit. Therefore economic development, which makes everyone wealthier, including the poorest, might require an *increased* degree of wealth inequality; and, inversely, fighting against wealth inequality might slow down economic progress and keep many in poverty. If there is such a trade-off between the two – and there is strong evidence that such a trade-off exists[16] – it will have to be decided on political grounds.[17]

The literature on tax and growth is a rich one. In a recent study, Patrick Minford and Jiang Wang compare two rival models of the effects of public spending: the first one, labelled the 'activist' model, is based on the supposition that public spending (on *R* and *D* in that case) fosters growth. The second model, the 'incentivist' model, is built around the idea that public spending reduces growth by penalizing incentives through higher taxes. Using data from the 1970–2000 period they conclude: 'What we have found is that there appears to be no identifiable effect of *R* and *D* and other capital subsidies on growth but that there is an effect of taxation depressing growth. In this we join a growing literature that finds similar negative tax effects on growth.'[18]

The two figures below, taken from a study by Garello and Spassova (2006), confirm the previous findings: countries with high public spending

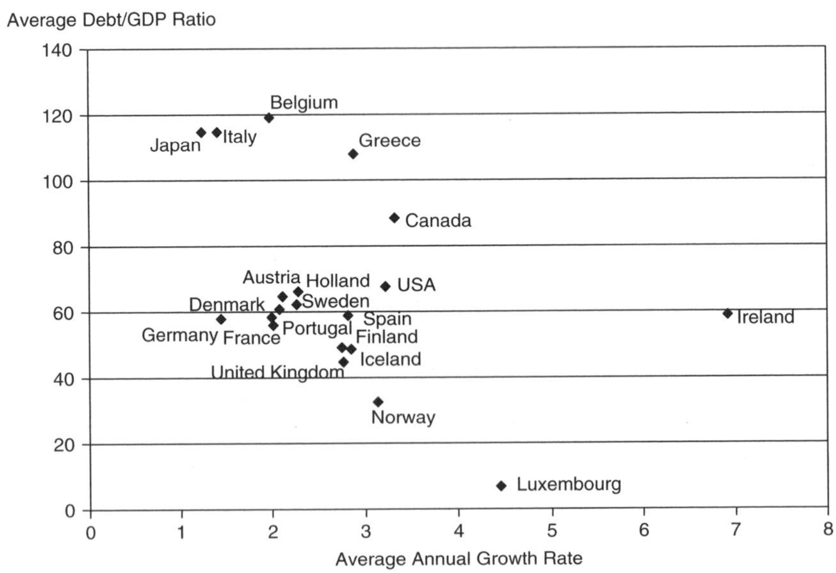

Figure 2.2(a) The debt–growth relationship (average level, 1992–2004)

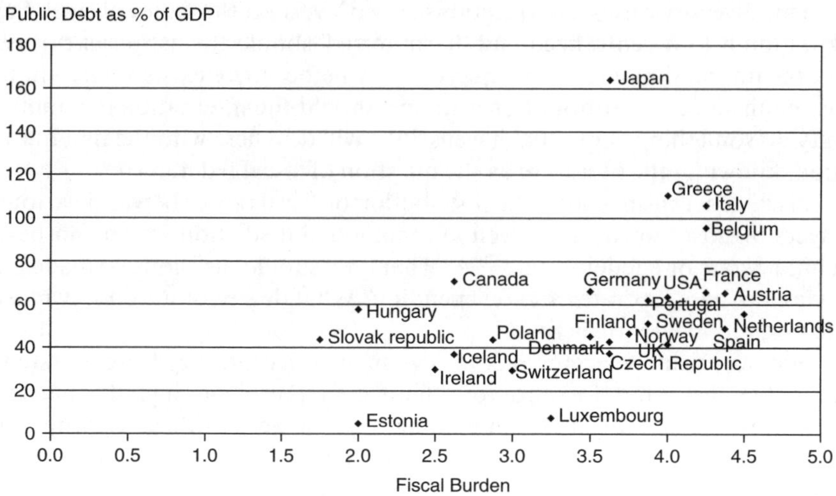

Figure 2.2(b) Public debt and fiscal burden (2005)

tend to have lower growth and high fiscal burden; inversely, low fiscal burden tends to be associated with higher growth and healthier public finance.

The tendencies shown in these figures corroborate another well-known effect to be kept in mind when designing a fiscal policy: the Laffer-curve effect. The economist Arthur Laffer has indeed reminded us that increasing tax rates does not necessarily result in higher tax revenues for the obvious reasons recalled above: higher tax rates generate tax avoidance, tax evasion and slower growth, thus reducing the tax base.

Summarizing the evidence, it is reasonable to conclude that, economic growth being probably the best way to fight poverty, an extensive use of taxes for purely redistributive purposes is not advisable.

5. THE NECESSITY OF DECENTRALIZED AND COMPETING FISCAL JURISDICTIONS

The three previous sections have shown how, because of the number of parameters to be taken into account, the science of taxation is bound to remain a very imperfect one. We must in particular emphasize the fact that, besides the use of efficient taxing techniques, some 'political' choices (or value judgments) have to be made concerning the level of redistribution to be implemented. It is therefore not surprising to observe a great variety of fiscal systems throughout developed economies.

This diversity raises new questions at two levels. At the national level, the question is how centralized and 'harmonized' should the fiscal system be? At the international level, the question is whether there exists such a thing as unfair tax competition. For instance, should the international community do something about 'tax havens'? We will deal here with the first question, known in the literature as the question of fiscal federalism.[19]

Fiscal federalism studies the distribution of fiscal power between various layers of government in a given autonomous jurisdiction which can be a unitary state or a federal state.[20] At what level should decisions be made on taxes, tax base, tax rates and on spending? What degree of autonomy must be given to local jurisdictions?

Not surprisingly, arguments in favour of a decentralized fiscal system resemble those put forward to defend a market economy; the market economy being indeed nothing other than a decentralized system for wealth creation and resource allocation. One of the most fundamental advantages of a decentralized system is to allow for a better use of local and tacit knowledge, a knowledge not easily transferred to a central decision maker.[21] Another related advantage is to free individual creativity: in a market economy virtually every market participant is invited to behave like an entrepreneur, looking for better ways to serve consumers, with heterogeneous preferences and varying purchasing powers, while making profit at the same time. The market economy thus opens the door to a competition process during which discovery takes place, and new knowledge is acquired and used to the benefit of a large number.

Similar benefits are to be expected from competition between various fiscal jurisdictions. Competition would allow different jurisdictions to offer different levels of 'public services' according to the needs and preferences of local populations. In a decentralized fiscal system, citizens (or experts, or politicians, or taxpayers' associations) would be able to compare the costs and qualities of the public goods and local services provided in various jurisdictions (for example, water supply, waste collection, school system, public transportation, physical security, and so on). The less efficient providers would therefore be much easier to spot and it would be possible to imitate the best practices. This is the principle of yardstick competition.

Beyond yardstick competition one can also expect citizens to exit from the jurisdiction which does not offer a satisfying ratio of tax burden to quality of services and move towards a preferred one.[22] Of course, the possibility to exit exists even in the absence of fiscal decentralization: one can always migrate to another country (or to the illegal market). But it is probably less expensive to move to a nearby region or district than to move to another country. Hence fiscal decentralization opens new choices for a wider range of the population. In a fundamental sense, because it gives more reality to the option of 'voting with one's feet', fiscal decentralization increases the quality of a democracy.

Combining yardstick competition with lower barriers to exit will put pressure on the administration, hence providing an interesting means of control, somewhat similar, although not as powerful, to the control a regular consumer can exert on producers.[23]

If many nations have been moving towards a more decentralized system,[24] some, such as England or Ireland, have maintained a highly centralized one. This suggests that fiscal decentralization might also have some disadvantages compared to centralization. The most often mentioned potential weaknesses of decentralization can be classified in two categories. The first one includes all the usual arguments in favour of large-scale production. Economies of scale are probably the first to come to our mind. It can be convincingly argued, for instance, that national defence is best organized at the national level; that having each region organizing its own defence against an external aggressor is not an optimal solution.

A second category of frequently invoked argument against decentralization has to do with the presence of spillover effects and strategic behaviours on the part of local authorities: strategic behaviours which could quickly turn into a 'race to the bottom'. The mechanism can be illustrated with the following example. Assume we have two autonomous and competing jurisdictions, *A* and *B*. If jurisdiction *A* decides to implement a programme involving a large redistribution of wealth and many public services, the fiscal burden for the wealthiest taxpayers of that jurisdiction is likely to be heavy. The neighbouring jurisdiction, *B*, can then make the choice of a low fiscal burden together with less wealth redistribution and public services. This strategy will be even more likely when the public services implemented by jurisdiction *A* are subject to spillover effects, as when citizens (taxpayers) of jurisdiction *B* have the possibility to go to the theatre, or to use the public swimming pools or the public gardens maintained by the taxpayers of jurisdiction *A*. Owing to the quality of redistribution programmes offered to the poorest citizens of jurisdiction *A*, it is also very likely that the poorest of jurisdiction *B* will migrate to jurisdiction *A*, while the wealthiest of jurisdiction *A* decide to avoid the high fiscal burden and move to jurisdiction *B*. If such behaviour is observed, the financial situation of jurisdiction *A* will obviously not be sustainable. Jurisdiction *A* will sooner or later have to lower the quality of its public services, or the amplitude of its redistribution programmes. A 'race to the bottom' will be initiated.

These arguments are to be taken seriously because they have served as the main obstacle to most decentralization processes and, more generally, to institutional competition. Regarding the presence of economies of scale and spillover effects, it must be noted that their presence does not necessarily call for centralization. One can indeed imagine that local jurisdictions will *voluntarily* choose cooperation if they can benefit from economies of scale (and then split between them the benefits resulting from higher productivity); and if they fear that the threat of free-riding behaviour will lead to an 'under-production' of public services, they might also enter into some kind of contractual arrangement.[25] Central tax authorities therefore have an important role to play, which is to allow and even facilitate such cooperation between local jurisdictions, and if need be to enforce agreements between them.

But there is also the question whether a race to the bottom is likely to take place in those countries where a more or less decentralized system is chosen. First, from a theoretical point of view, 'the bottom' will in fact be the lowest level of public services that might pass a voting decision in one of the jurisdictions, and this is likely to be far from zero and could even be increasing over time.[26] Also, from an empirical point of view, history shows that, if jurisdictions tend to cut programmes when other jurisdictions do so, they also tend to enlarge their programmes when others do. But, most importantly, it has been shown that the best way for a poorer region to narrow the economic gap with a richer region is by keeping (at least temporarily) their level of public services and welfare programmes low. This has been observed, for instance, in the economic development of the Southern states in the US.[27] Evidence is therefore simply that 'races to the bottom' do not occur.[28]

If the fear of a race to the bottom appears largely unfounded it does not follow that fiscal decentralization always brings the expected return. Indeed, looking at the level of fiscal decentralization and the way it relates to economic growth and fiscal burden, one can observe that some highly centralized countries are performing well as far as economic growth and public spending are concerned.[29] Should we conclude from this that in the realm of taxation competition is not effective? We do not think so. As suggested by Curzon-Price et al., a more plausible explanation to what could seem a paradox in the light of the fiscal federalism literature is that fiscal decentralization will bear its fruits only if it is well done, that is to say, if the local jurisdictions benefit from a true autonomy and are accountable for their choices. Looking more closely at the fiscal institutions of various 'decentralized' countries, this opinion receives support. Typically the local jurisdiction has discretion on how to spend the money, but no discretion on what type of tax can be levied. In brief, centralization might be better than half-way and therefore incoherent decentralization, but is likely to lose the battle against genuine decentralization.

Finally, let us emphasize that the evolution of institutions is a slow process and that it takes time for individuals to adjust to a new institutional logic. Knowing that most developed economies are emerging over centuries during which a highly centralized system was in place, more than a few years will be necessary for local jurisdictions to learn the best way of using their newly granted autonomy. And their chances of learning will be real only if there is *a clear commitment from central authorities* and if the latter do not bail out local jurisdictions which are in trouble, or do not leave to those jurisdictions the possibility to experiment with new fiscal policies.

6. ASSESSING CHINA'S ACTUAL FISCAL STRUCTURE

Since the opening up in 1978, China has engaged in major fiscal reforms. Hence, in 1984, profit delivery was replaced by tax payments, transforming enterprises in independent entities. In 1994, the barriers of local protectionism were largely abolished, dividing the central and local revenue into tax categories (before, revenues were divided by proportion). Those reforms were pushing in the right direction of greater accountability and fiscal coherence and Bao seems to be right when writing that 'The guidance of our tax system reform is to simplify the tax system, widen the tax base, lower the tax rate and tighten tax administration' (2004, p. 522). Hence, at least at first glance, China's tax reforms appear to have been promoting efficiency. Is that first judgment confirmed when we go into greater detail?

Comparing China's main fiscal indicators to those of a typical OECD country, the first striking fact is, as noted earlier, that the ratio of tax revenues (and more generally of state budget) to GDP, although steadily increasing, remains low (see Table 2.1, taken from BOFIT Review, 2005). In the rest of this section we first give more specifics on the nature of the actual fiscal system, leaving for a second sub-section our comments about the degree of decentralization prevailing in that system.

Table 2.1 Fiscal indicators (percentage of GDP)

	1997	1998	1999	2000	2001	2002	2003	2004*
Revenues	11.6	12.6	13.9	15.0	16.8	18.0	18.5	19.3
Expenditures	12.4	13.8	16.1	17.8	19.4	21.0	21.0	20.8
Balance	−0.8	−1.2	−2.1	−2.8	−2.6	−3.0	−2.5	−1.5
Government debt				22.8	23.6	25.1		

Note: * = preliminary results.

Sources: Budget: National Bureau of Statistics of China; debt: IMF.

6.1 Is China Using the Right Taxes?

As shown in Table 2.2 below (taken from Bao, 2005), China is relying essentially on VAT and income tax for rising funds, and of those two sources, income tax remains relatively low. These two types of taxes accounted in 2001 for 77 per cent of total tax revenues. The other revenues were provided by resource taxes, property taxes (including an important stamp tax on private legal transactions), agricultural taxes, specific taxes and custom duties.

Below we briefly present the main components of tax revenues before passing on to their critical appraisal.

6.2 Personal Income Tax

Direct taxes represent about 25 per cent of total tax revenue in 2001 (to be compared with an average of 35 per cent for OECD countries). Personal income tax includes a tax on wages and salaries, levied on a monthly basis, with a lump sum deductible amount of 800 Yuan and rates between 5 and 45 per cent (see Table 2.3 for the 2005 data). It is therefore a progressive tax, as is the tax on personal income from business activities (the latter with a progression from 5 to 35 per cent).

Passive income such as interest, capital gain and royalties is taxable at a standard rate of 20 per cent.

6.3 Corporate Income Tax

A limited company was liable for tax at the rate of 33 per cent in 2005. This tax is made up of a 30 per cent national tax and a 3 per cent local tax. In specific, legally defined areas company tax is 24 per cent or 15 per cent.[30] It must be noted also that this enterprise income tax is *progressive*: there exist lower rates (18 per cent and 10 per cent) for firms with lower incomes.

Table 2.2 Tax revenue

	Total tax revenue (Hundred million Yuan)	VAT + consumption tax (%)	Personal income tax (%)	Tax on foreign enterprises (%)	Tax on domestic enterprise (%)	% of total tax
1995	5974	64.2	2.2	0.9	12.5	79.8
2001	15 116	53.0	6.6	3.4	14.0	77.0

Source: Bao (2005), based on China Statistical Year Book.

Table 2.3 Taxes and income

Tax rate (%)	Income (CNY)
5	1–500
10	501–2000
15	2001–5000
20	5001–20 000
25	20 001–40 000
30	40 001–60 000
35	60 001–80 000
40	80 001–100 000
45	100 001 and above

6.4 Consumption Taxes

These are excise taxes on 'luxury' goods. Their rates range between 10 and 50 per cent. At present 11 types of products are subject to consumption tax: cigarettes, wine, cosmetics, skin and hair care products, expensive jewellery, gems and jade, gas and diesel oil, vehicle tyres, motorcycles, sedan automobiles, and fire crackers and fireworks.

6.5 Value Added Tax (VAT)

The VAT applies to sales of goods and is conceived as a turnover tax (it is a production-type VAT as opposed to a consumption-type VAT prevailing in most VAT countries) with very limited scope for sales of services (which are subject to the business tax). Its rate is 17 per cent (the normal rate) or 13 per cent (for basic subsistence goods and farming products). Exported goods are exempted from VAT.

6.6 Business Tax

This tax is again levied on turnover of taxable services and some transfer of assets; its level is low (8 per cent or less).

6.7 Assessing the Current Tax System

Like the vast majority of fiscal systems, the Chinese one is fairly complex so that efficiency could be enhanced through mere simplifications. A first, often suggested, simplification is the suppression of the business tax. The idea is to have all sales, on goods *and on services*, subjected to the same tax.

That tax could be, and this is a second efficiency-enhancing move, a consumption-type VAT since the actual production-type VAT penalizes the purchase of assets by a company, and more generally penalizes capital-intensive techniques.[31]

In light of the discussion of the previous sections, it would be probably a good idea to reduce the number of gradations of the progressive income tax, and to suppress the progression of the corporate income tax (which might slow down the growth of mid-size companies, the best engine of growth and employment). Again let us recall that it is wise to move away from policies designed to modify resource allocations. Tax incentives, as a rule, lead to unforeseen results and, in that field more than any other, if the immediate effect is satisfactory, the long-term effect turns out to be disappointing.

Another reform often suggested is the suppression of the many charges and fees imposed by local jurisdictions and their replacement by taxation. As will be explained in the next sub-section (and as was suggested by the discussion in section 2), this is not necessarily a good idea. As a matter of fact, the main lesson to be drawn from economic analysis is probably that, in the absence of a clear consensus on what the optimal taxation policy could be, local jurisdictions should have the freedom to experiment with new policies and to adjust them to local conditions.

6.8 Is the Central/Local Jurisdictions Split Well Designed?

To evaluate the degree of decentralization of the fiscal system in China is not an easy task, and comparing it to other countries is a perilous exercise owing to the size of this economy of over 1.3 billion inhabitants. Today, the structure of fiscal jurisdictions follows the structure of the government with, globally, three layers: the central jurisdiction, 31 provincial jurisdictions and thousands of sub-provincial jurisdictions (prefectures, cities, townships, towns and city districts).

Looking just at the distribution of tax revenues and public expenditures (see the figures below), we are tempted to conclude that this system is highly *decentralized*, the figure being comparable to that of a federal state such as the USA or Germany. Indeed, more than two-thirds of expenditures are made at the provincial or sub-provincial levels (and the trend toward a larger share for local expenditures is stable), and the ratio of central revenue to total tax revenues reached a low of 22 per cent in 1993, before rising to the 50 per cent level following the 1994 tax reform.[32]

But, as pointed out in previous sections, what matters most in terms of efficiency is the degree of autonomy of the various jurisdictions, or, to put it differently, the degree of fiscal coherency: to what extent are the various

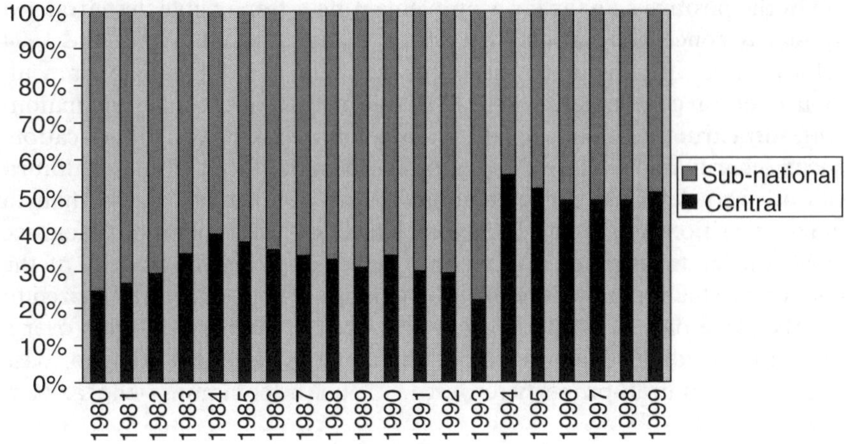

Source: OECD (2002), based on China Statistical Year Book, 2000.

Figure 2.3(a) Central/local share of government budget revenues

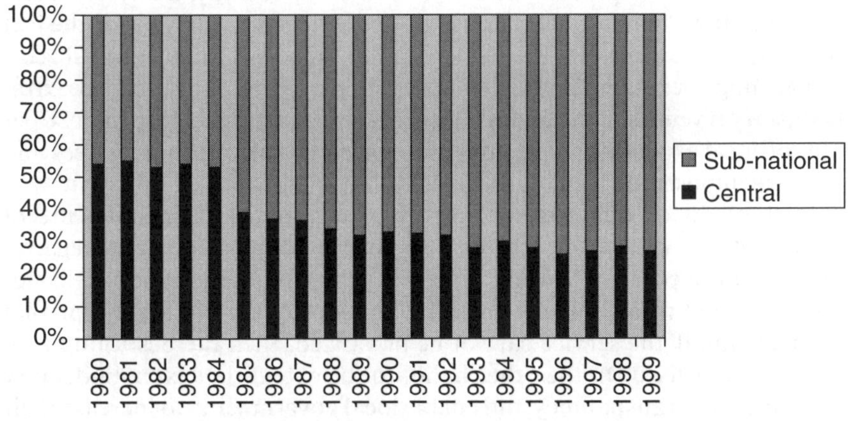

Source: OECD (2002), based on China Statistical Year Book, 2000.

Figure 2.3(b) Central/local share of government expenditures

layers of the fiscal system accountable for their choices? Are they free to choose their tax bases and tax rates as well as the nature and level of expenditures? If answers to those questions are positive, then the benefits from fiscal competition will soon show up. Otherwise, irresponsible behaviour is likely to surface. In the case of China, answers to these questions are ambiguous, which means that China is at a crossroads.

On the positive side (as far as implementing a responsible decentralized system is concerned), efforts have been made, especially since the 1994 reforms, to clearly divide the tasks between central and local government. Hence central government will be in charge of national defence and nationwide infrastructures, while local governments are taking care of education, social security and welfare. Also, it has been noticed that Chinese authorities at every level have gained more clearly defined tax rights than in many transition economies. Indeed each layer of government has exclusive rights on the taxation of a given base, hence avoiding the tragedy of the commons which rapidly develops when many authorities are authorized to tax the same base.[33] As Berkowitz and Li put it: 'When tax rights over a tax base are divided among more than one government, the tax base becomes a common-property resource . . . and the commons – the tax base – is "over-grazed." '[34]

On the negative side one can first point to the fact that this assignment of responsibility is still very theoretical and that, in practice, many responsibilities are still shared (see Table 2.4). It can also be pointed out that contracts passed between central and local governments binding the latter's budget are not scrupulously followed. More importantly, many observers will judge the Chinese system as a highly centralized one in view of the fact that, with few exceptions, the tax legislation process is totally centralized.

This might explain the tremendous role played by the so-called extra-budgetary revenues in the financing of local expenditures. More than 26 per cent of local expenditures are indeed financed by various charges, fees and surtaxes imposed by local authorities.

In the light of our previous survey of economic theory, that use of extra-budgetary expenditures can be seen as a positive or a negative feature. It is a positive feature to the extent that, if a public service is not a public good (that is, if it is possible to identify the consumers of that service), and if the service cannot be privatized, then the best thing is to resort to user fees. On the other hand, to the extent that extra-budgetary practices lack transparency and enable local governments to increase their budget beyond what was politically decided, they might just add to waste and corruption.

Putting everything together, it seems that China, which has already implemented a division of labour between the various layers of tax administration, still has to take the step of giving true autonomy to lower levels, that autonomy being granted not only to provincial jurisdictions but also to sub-provincial ones which, as shown in Figure 2.4, spend much more than they earn. If that (courageous) step is not taken, China will progressively fall into a new centralization process which, in the case of such a large economy, is likely to lead to a poor allocation of resources.

Table 2.4 Share of central and local governments in major expenditure items (% of total spending in each category)

Expenditure item	Central government	Local government
1. Expenditure for capital construction	43.9	56.1
2. Circulation fund for SOE	50.7	49.3
3. Innovation and new product funds	23.1	76.9
4. Geological prospecting expenditure	98.8	1.2
5. Expenditure for government administration	6.9	93.1
6. Operating expenses for industrial, commercial and communication department	38.2	61.8
7. Operating expenses for culture, education, science and health care	11.2	88.8
8. Expenditure for national defence	99.3	0.7
9. Expenditure for armed police troops		
10. Expenditure for social security and welfare	3.7	96.3
11. Agriculture aids	10.9	89.1
12. Price subsidies	51.1	48.9
13. Expenditure for urban maintenance and construction	0	100
14. Aid funds for less developed regions	0	100
15. Others	26.3	73.6
Total	28.9	71.1

Note: All data are for 1998.

Source: OECD (2002, p. 688).

7. THE CHALLENGE FACING CHINA

The fiscal situation of China remains a very unusual one in the sense that China is nowadays one of the largest world economies and, contrarily to other large economies, the share of public revenues and expenditures relative to GDP remains remarkably low. China can use that opportunity to bring more transparency progressively to the fiscal system and more accountability at all levels of governments, thus reaping all the benefits of a healthy fiscal competition.

But China can also take a diverging road, centralizing its system and relying on public expenditures in the hope of fostering growth and securing welfare. At a time when most developed countries are struggling with a welfare system established after the second World War, a system which turns out to be non-sustainable, it would be a pity if China were to adopt

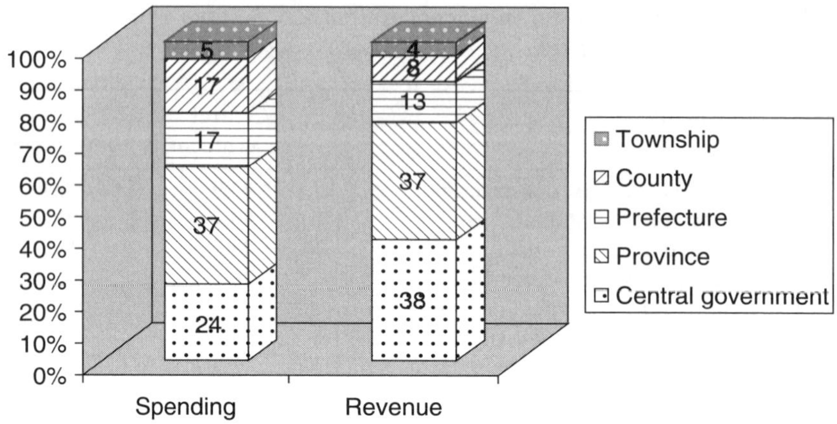

Source: Molnar (2005, p. 4).

Figure 2.4 Spending and revenue of government levels (2002)

the same scheme. China should therefore be careful not to stop the growth trend with the implementation of an intrusive tax system and economic control. To do so, it will be necessary to resist calls for increased taxation such as the one recently formulated by the OECD or the World Bank. One can read the following in the last OECD comprehensive survey on China:

> There is probably little disagreement over the need to increase the level of taxation in China. As indicated earlier, there has been a declining trend in the ratio of tax revenue to GDP over the past 20 years. Even compared to some developing countries, the ratio in recent years has remained low.
>
> China faces heavy pressure on expenditure in the near term to further develop its social security system, to provide support to unemployed and laid-off workers, and to continue to build infrastructure. It is clear that the current level of tax revenues is insufficient to finance all of these. In 1996, the World Bank estimated China's financing gaps and concluded that additional expenditure needed was equivalent to about 6 per cent of GDP. The major spending gaps are in the areas of health and education (2.3 per cent of GDP) and infrastructure (1 per cent of GDP). Social insurance, pensions and environmental protection are other areas where expenditure gaps now exist or are likely to occur.[35]

As recalled above, the economic history of the last two centuries shows that a high fiscal burden tends to be associated with lower growth. Another temptation to be resisted is to use taxation for equalizing economic development throughout the country. True, between 1978 and 2000, the Gini coefficient (a measure of income inequality) went from 0.16 to 0.458, and the gap between regions is widening. But, during that same period, disposable income per capita of urban residents was multiplied by 18.3, while disposable income for peasants was multiplied by 16.8.[36] What is more, to quote Bao (2004, p. 145), 'the situation of the whole society was relatively stable which showed that this gap was approved by the society'.

Facing a crossroads, China should give priority to the implementation of a coherent fiscal decentralization and not asphyxiate current economic growth with a heavier fiscal yoke.

NOTES

1. I wish to thank the participants in the Law and Economics conference in Shanghai as well as the participants in the CAE seminar in Aix-en-Provence for very helpful comments.
2. As of 2 March 2006, 1€ = 9.68 CNY = US$ 1.21.
3. Data from OECD (2002, p. 630). The figures for OECD and EU countries do not include social security contributions. If those contributions are included, we obtain 37.3% for OECD countries and 42% for EU countries.
4. See Webber and Wildavsky (1986) for a history of taxation.
5. Brennan and Buchanan (1980).
6. When such a 'private good' is managed collectively, we run inexorably into the so-called 'tragedy of the commons'. See Hardin (1968).
7. See Coase (1974).
8. Owing to lack of space, I ignore here the question of aggregating individual preferences. But it is well known, at least since the work of Arrow, that there is no satisfactory way for aggregating individual preferences into 'social preferences'.
9. Physical protection of persons and goods is a good illustration of that phenomenon. It is today possible to buy some protecting devices (using, for instance, alarms and the telephone) which will protect a given house or factory without protecting those located in the neighbourhood, so that free-riding on others' investment is no longer an option to protect one's property.
10. The explanatory power of Mancur Olson's logic of collective action is, in our view, particularly strong: a public project which benefits a small, easily identified, group of individuals and whose cost will be spread over a large set of taxpayers so that the individual cost will be 'negligible', has great chances of being adopted by the representatives, even though it does not have the characteristics of a public good (see Olson, 1965).
11. The literature on development highlights a trade-off between increasing the wealth of the poorest and reducing inequalities similar to the trade-off between risk and return on the capital market.
12. Smith (1981, p. 826). Recent studies (for example, Jones, 2004), show that, for OECD countries, the cost of raising one euro would be between 1.2 and 1.3 euros (without taking into account administrative costs). On this, see also Robson (2005).
13. For a demonstration of that well-known result, see for instance Slemrod (1990).
14. For a survey of optimal taxation, see Slemrod and the references provided there (1990).
15. As Slemrod says (p. 168): 'The leap from the blackboard to the real world is a large one when it comes to taxation'.
16. See, for instance, Rosenberg and Birdzell (1986).
17. One of the founding fathers of Law and Economics, Aaron Director, gave his name to a law predicting how decisions regarding redistribution policies will be made in a context of majority voting. On this, see Stigler (1970).
18. See Minford and Wang (2005, p. 19).

19. A discussion on international tax competition would lead us too far away from the main concern of this chapter.
20. For a comprehensive survey on fiscal federalism, see Oates (1999). Fiscal federalism should not be confused with the narrower topic of 'federal finance', the latter focusing exclusively on the study of the fiscal system of a federal state.
21. Classical references on the dynamics of the market include Hayek (1945), or Kirzner (1973).
22. Hirschman (1970), Tiebout (1956).
23. Bruno Frey has even suggested that the jurisdictions which are in competition for providing various goods and services could overlap territorially. This is the idea behind his concept of Functionally Overlapping Competing Jurisdiction. See Frey and Eichenberger (1996) for more details, including some historical illustration of the practical working of that system.
24. See, for instance, the fiscal reforms in France (1981), Spain or Italy. Federal states tend of course to have a fairly decentralized fiscal system, but the case of Germany, and the historical evolution of Federal taxation in the USA, show that even Federal states can be fairly centralized as far as taxation is concerned. For a comparative study of fiscal decentralization throughout European countries, see the special issue of the *Journal des Economistes et des Etudes Humaines* (2003).
25. It must also be noted that many of those public services are not public goods in the economic sense of the term. That is to say, that it is perfectly possible to exclude from their consumption those who do not contribute to their payment. We could for instance have different prices for the theatre, or the swimming pool, or access to public transportation, for residents and non-residents of the local jurisdiction.
26. To come back to the previous illustration, the wealthiest inhabitant of jurisdiction *A* can pressure their representatives to lower taxes, and the poorest of jurisdiction *B* can put pressure on theirs to increase the level of redistribution, both tendencies being likely to improve the quality/cost ratio of public services.
27. See Oates (1999) for references. Today, this debate is of particular importance in the EU where the two theses are opposed. One of them, pushed in part by the Commission and the OECD, favours fiscal centralization (or harmonization) coupled with wealth redistribution towards the poorest countries. The other thesis favours tax competition and lower redistribution and is often supported by new EU countries. It is interesting to note that the 'poor' countries are in favour of competition and the rich ones oppose it.
28. What may occur instead is that some groups will lose their privileges. But this is an entirely different question.
29. This is for instance the case of England and Ireland. For a complete survey of those studies, see Curzon-Price and Garello (2003).
30. See OECD 2002 (p. 633) for the detail of the specified regions benefiting from lower corporate income taxes.
31. The coastal regions' businesses tend to use labour-intensive production while the inner country regions use capital-intensive production (mining, for instance). The prevailing form of VAT therefore further penalizes the non-coastal regions.
32. In 2000, the share of central government revenues to total tax revenues (including social security taxes) was 30% in Germany and 46.3% in the USA. Leaving out social security taxes, the share of central government revenues in Germany becomes similar to that observed today in China, while that share in the US exceeds 50%.
33. See Berkowitz and Li (2000).
34. Berkowitz and Li (p. 370). The authors contrast the situation of China with that of Russia. In Russia, a survey of small firms revealed that each firm has been controlled on average by 5.42 different agencies from regional, local or sub-local levels.
35. OECD (2002, p. 637).
36. Data from Bao (2004).

BIBLIOGRAPHY

Bao, L. (2004), 'China: the characteristics and trend of the new tax system reform', *Intertax*, **32**(10), 519–23.

Bao, L. (2005), 'China: how should tax policies regulate personal income tax distribution?', *Intertax*, **33**(3), 143–54.

Berkowitz, D. and W. Li (2000), 'Tax rights in transition economies: a tragedy of the commons?', *Journal of Public Economics*, **76**(3), 369–97.

Bils, B. and T. Koivu (2005), 'Regional inequalities widening further in China', *BOFIT China Review, Yearbook 2005*, Bank of Finland, Institute of Economies in Transition.

Brennan, G. and J.M. Buchanan (1980), *The Power to Tax: Analytical Foundations of a Fiscal Constitution*, Cambridge: Cambridge University Press.

Brueckner, J.K. (2001), 'Strategic interaction among governments: an overview of empirical studies', *WP*, **88**, Institute of Government and Public Affairs, University of Illinois.

Coase, R.H. (1960), 'The problem of social cost', *Journal of Law and Economics*, **3** (October), 1–44.

Coase, R.H. (1974), 'The lighthouse in economics', *Journal of Law and Economics*, **17** (October), 357–76.

Coase, R.H. (1991), 'The institutional structure of production', *Journal des Economistes et des Etudes Humaines*, **2** (4 December), 431–9.

Curzon-Price, V. and J. Garello (2003), 'Index of fiscal decentralisation: methodology and findings', *Journal des Economistes et des Etudes Humaines*, **13**(4), 441–78.

Feld, L.P. and G. Kirchgässner (2003), 'The impact of corporate and personal income taxes on the location of firms and on employment: some panel evidence for the Swiss cantons', *Journal of Public Economics*, **87**, 129–55.

Frey, B.S. and R. Eichenberger (1996), 'FOCJ: competitive governments for Europe', *International Review of Law and Economics*, **16**, 315–27.

Garello, P. (2003), 'The dynamics of fiscal competition', *Journal des Economistes et des Etudes Humaines*, **13**(4), 421–40.

Garello, P. and V. Spassova (2006), 'Looking, without success, for a good reason not to worry about public debt', *IREF Working Paper* (available at <http://www.irefeurope.org>, *The Journal for the New Europe*) **3**(1), 5–38.

Gramlich, E.M. and H. Galper (1973), 'State and local fiscal behavior and federal grant behavior', *Brookings Papers on Economic Activity*, **1**, 15–58.

Hardin, G. (1968), 'The tragedy of the commons', *Science*, **162**, 1243–8.

Hayek, F.A. (1945), 'The use of knowledge in society', *American Economic Review*, **35** (4 September), 519–30.

Hines, J.R. Jr and R.H. Thaler (1995), 'Anomalies: the flypaper effect', *Journal of Economic Perspectives*, **9**(4), 217–26.

Hirschman, A.O. (1970), *Exit, Voice, and Loyalty*, Cambridge, MA: Harvard University Press.

Hors, I. (2005), 'China's governance in transition: adjusting relation across levels of government', *BOFIT Review*.

Inman, R.P. and D.L. Rubinfeld (2000), 'Federalism', in B. Bouckaert and G. De Geest, *Encyclopaedia of Law and Economics*, Cheltenham, UK and Northampton, MA, USA: Edward Elgar, pp. 661–91.

Jones, C. (2004), *Applied Welfare Economics*, Oxford: Oxford University Press.

Journal des Economistes et des Etudes Humaines (2003), **13**(4), Special issue on fiscal policies in Europe.
Kirzner, I. (1973), *Competition and Entrepreneurship*, New York: New York University Press.
Krug, B., Z. Zhu and H. Hendrischke (2004), 'China's emerging tax regime: devolution, fiscal federalism, or tax farming?', *ERIM Report Series*, ERS-2004-113-ORG.
Laffer, A.B. (2004), 'The Laffer curve: past, present, and future', *Backgrounder*, **1765**, 1 June, Heritage Foundation.
Minford, P. and J. Wang (2005), 'Public spending and growth', *IREF Working Paper* (available at <http://www.irefeurope.org>).
Molnar, M. (2005), 'The challenges facing public spending policy', *BOFIT Review*.
McKinnon, R.I. (1997), 'Market-preserving fiscal federalism in the American monetary union', in M. Blejer and T. Ter-Minassian (eds), *Macroeconomic Dimensions of Public Finance: Essays in Honor of Vito Tanzi*, London: Routledge, pp. 73–93.
Oates, W.E. (1999), 'An essay on fiscal federalism', *Journal of Economic Literature*, **37**, 1120–49.
OECD (1998), *Harmful Tax Competition: An Emerging Global Issue*, OECD.
OECD (2002), *China in the World Economy: The Domestic Policy Challenge*, OECD.
Olson, M. Jr (1965), *The Logic of Collective Action – Public Goods and the Theory of Groups*, Cambridge, Mass: Harvard University Press.
Rabushka, A. (1987), 'Taxation, economic growth, and liberty', *Cato Journal*, **7**(1), 121–48.
Robson, A. (2005), 'Taxation, individual incentives and economic growth', *IREF Studies* (<http://www.irefeurope.org/col_docs/doc_27_fr.pdf>).
Rosenberg, N. and L.E. Birdzell Jr (1986), *How the West Grew Rich: The Economic Transformations of the Industrial World*, New York: Basic Books, Inc. Publishers.
Scully, G.W. (1989), 'The size of the state, economic growth and the efficient utilization of national resources', *Public Choice*, **63**, 149–64.
Slemrod, J. (1990), 'Optimal taxation and optimal tax systems', *Journal of Economic Perspectives*, **4**(1), Winter, 157–78.
Smith, Adam (1776), *An Inquiry into the Nature and Causes of the Wealth of Nations*, reprinted in H. Campbell and A.S. Skinner (eds) (1981), Glasgow edition of the works and correspondence of Adam Smith Vol. 2 Indianapolis Liberty Fund.
Stigler, G. (1970), 'Director's law of public income redistribution', *Journal of Law and Economics*, **13**(April), 1–10.
Tiebout, C.M. (1956), 'A pure theory of public expenditures', *Journal of Political Economy*, **64**, 416–24.
Webber, C. and A. Wildavsky (1986), *A History of Taxation and Expenditure in the Western World*, New York: Simon and Schuster.
Wilson, J.D. (1999), 'Theories of tax competition', *National Tax Journal*, **52**(2), 269–304.

3. Legal pluralism in the governance of transitional China

Jianwei Zhang and Yijia Jing

1. INTRODUCTION

In recent years the transitions of Russia and China have attracted serious attention of scholars in law and economics. While law and economics provides more than one perspective in studying transition, it is interesting to apply legal pluralism to the evolution of the governance structure in the transition. By applying legal pluralism, we can identify many obstacles to the systematic provision of the rule of law in transitional countries, due to incomplete laws and inefficient courts, lack of political order and prevalent distrust of corrupt bureaucrats and law-enforcement agencies. These situations make laws appear as dummies and will finally challenge the fundamental role of the government in the provision of law and order. It is not rarely that, in some transitional countries, various alternative governance mechanisms, most of which are non-legal or illegal and are derived from informal institutions, become popular and compete with the government in providing, if not destroying, order. Economic transition and growth are more difficult in these countries. Such experiences, combined with the experience of relatively successful transitional countries, indicate that the maintenance of law and order under a situation of incomplete laws needs a relatively stable and solid political order. To improve the performance of governance, it is critically important to reach a healthy balance between multiple governance resources. The absence of a streamlined governance system may lead to the 'outsourcing' of governance authority to corrupt officials and the mafia.

China and Russia offer a good opportunity to analyse comparatively the interaction between transition, institutional reform and governance, and also the interactions between formal and informal institutions. Take China as an example: although the political and economic systems have changed significantly since the late 1970s, the social cooperative mechanisms have not been damaged as seriously as in Russia. In Russia, these mechanisms have been destroyed by vicious Guanxi Rule entrepreneurs, such as the mafia and corrupt officials. Regarding the mutual interaction between formal and informal institutions and its effect on the economy, China's stable political order has been able to maintain social capital, restrain opportunism, promote transaction efficiency, deepen the division of labour and induce productive investment. This has brought China an annual 9 per cent GDP growth rate for two and a half decades. In contrast, virtuous social capital has been dissipated by political disorder in some transitional countries, notably Russia, where predation and torts prevail. The whole society was trapped in a zero-sum or even negative-sum game. Such countries, to different extents, experienced economic decline. So our questions are the following. What fundamentally explains the different transitional results of China and Russia, which had seemingly similar transitional processes? How did China achieve a positive equilibrium between economic growth, legal reform and stable political governance in the past two decades? And is such an achievement sustainable?

To answer these questions, scholars tend to emphasize a country's choices of reform path. Yet, in effect, the reform path could be a continuous fine-tuning process and endogenous to the transition. Consequently, the research should focus on the evolution of the transitional process, rather than a one-shot path choice. In the following, we will first analyse legal pluralism, and the diversity and complementarity between governance institutions. To do this, we will apply the theory of incomplete laws. Such incompleteness of legal systems, due to the bounded rationality of human beings and to the uncertainty in legal practice, creates the opportunity for the entry of informal institutions providing order. The nature of such co-working of official and non-official institutions is contingent on the very role of the state in presiding over its political order. Such a theoretical framework of plural governance mechanisms will be applied to China's and Russia's transitional practice and offer a legal pluralism explanation of their economic performance.

2. INCOMPLETENESS OF LAW AND THE MULTIPLE GOVERNANCE MECHANISMS

2.1 A Comparative Institutional Analysis of Transitional Governance

The pro-market cooperative order can be protected by multiple governance mechanisms. In this chapter, we discuss governance mechanisms including formal mechanisms represented by policies and laws, and informal mechanisms represented by Guanxi (interpersonal relation or connection). Under ideal conditions, there could be a complete rule of law with sound policies, well-designed laws and healthy social relationship networks that together produce a perfect cooperative economic order.

Different legal traditions may create the cooperative order in different ways. In common law countries, ideal governance may be realized under a legal system that is extremely efficient in adapting to reality and finding laws. In a competitive market, it is generally believed that the price mechanism can hardly regulate the market by itself – rather, the market operation has to be based on the legal system that will play the role of nightwatchman by setting basic incentives and restrictions favouring maximum economic efficiency. Even when disputes occur, the affected party can bring a lawsuit, and a highly efficient and fair court will make a quick response by making judgments. Case judgments become laws and such legal intervention signals clear information to market participants as to the relative prices between law-abiding and law-breaking behaviour. Consequently, such an adaptive legal system shapes individuals' utility functions, encourages compliance with contract obligations, induces cooperation and finally leads to a win–win game.

In civil law countries things are very different. Suppose that legislators are absolutely rational and perfectly informed, so as to be able to make perfect laws. Thanks to the completeness of such laws in specifying crime and punishment, judges can always make correct judgments for any possible case. What the court needs to do is to strictly enforce these laws.

Unfortunately, in the real world, the bounded rationality of judges and lawmakers and the prevalence of uncertainty preclude complete legal systems. The consequent problem is that the provision of legal order in regulating the market is less or more than desired, resulting in barriers to market innovation and cooperation. From the view of Comparative Law and Economics, policies and laws are two somewhat interchangeable official governance mechanisms.[1] Here, one solution is to rely more on governmental policies that can be ex ante, flexible and easily amendable. Governmental officials can be both rule-makers and rule-executors. In this situation, the legal functions are to some extent transferred to the executive system. Yet there is no guarantee that government regulations will not be costly, or even ineffective.[2]

The above analysis is characterized by a 'legal centrism', yet from the perspective of legal pluralism, there can be some other competing or complementary governance mechanisms. Legal pluralism notices the fact that the government is imperfect and may fail. A corollary is that, when laws are incomplete, it is not necessary to resort to governmental policies. This is especially obvious in Chinese society with a quasi-legal system under which the enforcement of contracts is, to a large extent, dependent on an informal network of relations. In fact, the incapacity of formal laws is not limited to

China.[3] Ellickson, based on his fieldwork in the US, has pointed out that rules and orders are not exclusively produced by governments.[4] He thinks that in general people make their choices, according not to a calculation of costs and benefits, but to social norms. His research shows that it is inappropriate to treat laws as the only way to settle disputes. In the real world, the governance structure is composed of multiple resources that may be substitutive and complementary. Together, these resources contribute to the preservation and evolution of the cooperative order. The non-official and official governance resources constitute a plural system of social control.

Ellickson's research indicates that various alternative social mechanisms may become active when both laws and policies are incomplete. This is obviously true for the American Shastar community that Ellickson investigated. In such a community, with closely interacting groups, there exist not only official rules, such as policies, administrative regulations and laws, but also many non-official rules that are enforced by social networks. These non-official rules include both trust-building social mechanisms, such as norms, reputation, public consensus, conventions, and tradition, but also trust-destroying social mechanisms like corruption and rent seeking.[5] They establish implicit contracts among the actors. Contrary to the official order, these rules are embedded in the network of interpersonal relations. In this chapter, we create a unified name for the non-official governance resource based on interpersonal connections – the Guanxi Rule.[6] 'Guanxi' is equal to interpersonal relation or connection. According to Coleman's definition, the Guanxi Rule can be interpreted as a kind of social capital.

2.2 Policy, Law, the Guanxi Rule and Social Capital

According to Putnam, social capital can promote efficiency by coordinating people's activities,[7] yet social capital also has counter-efficiency properties, among which boundedness and peculiarism are two important ones. It often has a functionary boundary across which different Guanxi networks may conflict. Because of China's unique cultural tradition, social capital in China often has family as the centre and extends along ties based on blood, marriage, friendship or other interpersonal ties, with marginally decreasing strength. The Guanxi Rule also bears the feature of peculiarism, rather than the universalism of laws.

So the Guanxi Rule is a double-edged sword. When in accordance with the spirit of law, it may induce social cooperation, develop trust among people and complement the legal system. We call this *the virtuous Guanxi Rule*, which cultivates social capital. When the Guanxi Rule is used by vicious forces to seek self-interest at the price of justice, legal order and social cooperation, we call it *the vicious Guanxi Rule*. In Hirshleifer's terms, they represent respectively, the 'bright side of the force' and the 'dark side of the force.'[8]

The functioning of the Guanxi Rule is heavily contingent on the stability and certainty of the political order. As can be easily understood, when the political order provides the basic level of justice and predictability, the Guanxi Rule may help to build mutual trust and cooperation as a complement to the legal system. Yet, when the formal political order cannot provide stable and reliable prediction and protection for market activities, one-shot transactions will prevail and result in all-pervasive opportunistic behaviour. To overcome the distrust towards government, market participants may develop demands for arbitration by the mafia. In that situation, the Guanxi Rule simply facilitates the counter-productive private mechanisms that reduce the general level of social efficiency. The vicious Guanxi Rule drives the virtuous Guanxi Rule away, and the virtuous social capital is dissipated.

Once the virtuous social capital is dissipated, the positive feedback mechanism may push the social order into an inefficient path. History matters. Distrust enlarges itself. In addition, virtuous social capital has the properties of public goods. Although individuals may be disgusted with the vicious Guanxi Rule and the subsequent corruption and predation, they may not be willing to resist it by themselves, knowing their personal loss will be much higher than their personal gain. Free-riding, another mechanism, also leads to compliance. Further, some individuals will emulate those who profit by bribing the mafias. Both the voluntary and forced use of the vicious Guanxi Rule exist. Consequently, corruption and mafia governance expand and enlarge social chaos and disorder. This is a typical situation of a prisoners' dilemma. All the above reasons show that it is not practical for unorganized individuals to resist the vicious Guanxi Rule. To preserve the virtuous social capital, it is a must for the government to intervene.

2.3 Legal Pluralism in Transitional Countries

The above analysis shows that the functioning of social rules depends on the protection and direction of the political order. A strong state is indispensable, yet it is also potentially destructive to social capital. It is important for a transitional country to balance the disorder resulting from a weak state with the autocracy resulting from the return of the old regime. Yet it is more important to build communication between formal and informal institutions. Policies, laws and the Guanxi Rule can be complementary, substitutive and mutually convertible. The synergy among them results in a relatively smooth transitional process in China, compared to that in Russia, at least in their early period of transition.

2.3.1 The converting mechanism

In general, policies are comparatively more exogenous, random and flexible, while laws need a relatively long process of public choice. Policies can be treated as dynamic laws, while laws can be treated as static policies. In China, successful policies are often incorporated into laws. It is also true that pervasive practices in civil society can be adopted as formal policies. Under certain conditions the Guanxi Rule may become an official rule. The household contract responsibility system, the township and village enterprise, and the private enterprise with a red-hat (Hong Mao Zi)[9] are all innovations under the Guanxi Rule, but are also recognized by the formal institutions. Conversely, formal rules may become embedded in the social belief system and continue their influence even when they are abolished. Inertia exists.

The conversion of the Guanxi Rule into an official rule constitutes one legal reform strategy that highlights the endogeneity of Chinese laws. The basic logic behind this is to adopt the successful spontaneous grassroots practice of non-state actors by using the state authority to promote, consolidate and legitimate it. Such a bottom-up reform is in sharp contrast to the top-down reform of Russia. The endogeneity of some Chinese laws makes it easier for them to be accepted and complied with.[10] It is, in some sense, a process of finding laws which are in accordance with social norms and reality. Such a process also replaces the peculiarism of the Guanxi Rule with the universalism of laws. China's legal reform largely owes its success to its conscious conversion of spontaneous social rules into official rules.

2.3.2 The substitutive and complementary effects among rules

Using cost–benefit analysis, when an actor finds that it is more cost-effective or safer to utilize another set of rules, he may shift to the new set of rules. Although this is not always true, with higher income, higher education and less reliance on local groups, people tend to treat the Guanxi Rule as inferior. Meanwhile, policies and laws can also have a strong substitutive effect. The larger the scope of policies, the bigger their crowding-out effect on laws. Under China's overwhelming centrally planned economy, laws almost entirely lost their effectiveness.

There is also complementarity among governance mechanisms. When a society experiences modernization, the operation of the Guanxi Rule also needs modernization, which can only be sustained under a favourable political order. When the transitional political order is still credible in maintaining basic social justice, the Guanxi Rule can stimulate the virtuous social capital and contribute towards good governance by supplementing the weak political order. Otherwise, the vicious Guanxi Rule may prevail and lead to economic disorder and stalemate. For example, the unlimited increase of policies can create opportunities for rent seeking, and consequently can increase the expected gain obtained from applying the vicious Guanxi Rule, such as corruption. Discretionary policies may threaten private property, distort expectations and ruin social trust.[11] Furthermore, policies and laws can be complementary in that governments can make flexible policies when laws are outdated, although the hazards of relying on policies, such as the abuse of discretion and corruption, should be avoided.

2.3.3 The ideological integration in rule enforcement

The stability of ideology will influence the accumulation and flow of social capital. Ideology constitutes the mainstream belief and the common knowledge of a society. When it is in disorder or when there is insufficient investment in it, virtuous social capital can barely span small groups and induce broad cooperation. It is very important for the state to invest in ideology. When laws and policies conflict with the Guanxi Rule, the masses, thanks to the ideological investment, will show more respect towards the former. Without a strong ideology, the costs for the government to maintain law and order, and the costs of the market to supervise transactions, will be unacceptably high.[12]

The Chinese governments have made substantial investments in ideology. They control the media in order to maintain and shape mainstream ideology. Through campaign-like propaganda, such as Three Representatives, Spirit Civilization Dissemination, Nationwide Dissemination of Basic Law, Sending Law to Villages, and so on, governments successfully manipulate the ideology and preserve a stable political order. Furthermore, Chinese governments even deem laws as ideology and incorporate them into the ideological propaganda, which helps cadres and the masses to enhance their consciousness of laws, and reduces the transaction costs of legal operation. Since 1985, the central government has initiated three major movements of nationwide legal education. Leaders of the Politburo took the lead in learning about laws.

2.3.4 Conclusion

One key problem in developing a plural social control system lies in how to preserve the virtuous social capital. It is important to enlarge the complementarity among different governing resources. The transitional experience of China and Russia indicates that a credible state and its ideological investment are of the utmost importance to the preservation of virtuous social capital and economic growth. Over-regulation, or the lack of political order, is a hotbed of the vicious Guanxi Rule.

The Chinese economic and constitutional reforms are characterized by incrementalism. These reforms created an appropriate environment for fine-tuning the relationships between multiple governance mechanisms. The capacity of a strong government to impose rewards and punishments, to make large-scale investments in ideology, and to adopt a bottom-up logic of lawmaking, helps to preserve and encourage the functioning of the virtuous Guanxi Rule. Under the synergy of policies, laws and the virtuous Guanxi Rule, the coordinative order endogenous to the real production and trading practice is maintained and promoted. This provides a fundamental institutional base for China's rapid economic growth in the past two decades.

3. EVIDENCE FROM CHINA: THE ECONOMIC REFORM UNDER A PLURAL SOCIAL CONTROL SYSTEM

Economic transition of China is characterized by decentralization and legal reform. Among various reform streams, economic reform creates the demand for legal reform and brings about challenges to the existing legal and political framework, finally inducing the leaders to acknowledge the new interest structure by making compatible legislation. New laws help to restrict governments and streamline their utility function with the market participants. Compared to Russia, the Chinese reform is gradual and smooth and has experienced several intermediate steps. Currently, all governance mechanisms coexist and work together, yet the trend is clear that laws are getting more important while the other two, policies and the Guanxi Rule, are waning. The next section applies our analytical framework to the reform history of China.

3.1 Preservation of Virtuous Social Capital and the Conversion Mechanism of Rules

3.1.1 The evolution of the household contract responsibility system (HCRS)

In early 1979, 20 villagers of the Xiaogang Village in Fengyang County, Anhui Province, non-legally utilized or, more precisely, illegally signed a contract with the village cadre. This contract not only gave them the right to use and gain from the land, but also made it an obligation for them to hand over the specified amount of corn to the government. Later their invention was followed by other rural areas and was promoted by the central government. It is worth noting that HCRS emerged within a community of acquaintances. In the beginning, HCRS was only regulated by Guanxi without being recognized by policy or law. Only in 1984, after

HCRS had greatly improved agricultural production and had reduced poverty, did the Communist Party of China (CCP) make policies to recognize and promote it, and the Supreme Court required the grass-roots courts to accept lawsuits related to HCRS contracts. The 1981 Economic Contract Law was then applicable to HCRS contracts. Such a move to legitimate HCRS is not just an effort to normalize new economic activities, but an effort of the state to re-enter rural governance. Yet law enforcement in rural areas is mainly through policy means. When courts resolve disputes, they often adopt many policy tools, such as mobilization, persuasion, education and even enticement.

Given the preferences of market actors, laws change their set of choices by influencing their opportunity cost. But the precondition is that economic actors incorporate laws into their cost–benefit function. However, this precondition can hardly be met, owing to the lack of law consciousness in rural areas, which makes the application of the Law and Economics mainstream theory not so direct or correct. Various legal practices in rural areas, such as Sending Law to Villages, Adjudicating in Villagers' households, Legal Mobilization, and Persuasion plus Education, are endogenous to China's socio-economic structure as ways of law enforcement. The involvement of grass-roots courts in HCRS disputes is not only to provide implicit prices for relevant parties, but also to change the preference structure of the relevant parties. When institutional economics is applied to HCRS, scholars treat it either as an incentive system, or as a typical case of state withdrawal, without a serious investigation into the interaction between policies, laws and the Guanxi Rule. In fact, HCRS was stabilized and protected under their multiple influences. The increasing substitution effect has made villagers more aware of their legal rights and inclined them to utilize lawsuits.[13]

3.1.2 Social capital and township and village enterprise (TVE)

The birth of TVEs is a crucial development in China's institutional transition. It not only made an important contribution to China's economic growth, but also ideologically supported China's economic reform by its public ownership. In the early stage of these enterprises, village institutions played a very active role,[14] and the Guanxi Rule also provided the virtuous social capital that helped reduce the cost of market operation. On one hand, while the market was underdeveloped, the Guanxi Rule, such as customs and traditions, was an intangible asset and created revenue inflow.[15] First, the long-term interpersonal interaction in the acquaintance community enabled those capable persons to build themselves up. These people always won the trust of the villagers and became charismatic entrepreneurs. Second, the relations based on blood, marriage, friendship and locality created the long-term stable and continuous interaction between villagers and significantly reduced the cost of cooperation. On the other hand, the Guanxi Rule managed to overcome the problem of collective ownership. TVEs belonged to the village or township governments. It was simply a myth that collective ownership led to such growth in rural areas. We explain this myth from the perspective of social capital, namely, the virtuous interaction between local governments and TVEs which, to large extent, accounted for the high efficiency of TVEs. Informal ties between local governments and TVEs encouraged the former to promote local industry. Also the workers of TVEs, being organized under the Guanxi network, could easily form trust and common goals, and thus shirking was reduced.

In the early 1990s, policies were issued to protect the autonomy of TVEs. In late 1996, the Township and Village Enterprise Law was enacted. Formal contracts could be established between TVEs and local governments. While local governments faced more restrictions regarding TVE intervention, their lasting incentive to promote TVEs nevertheless continued to exist. In fact, fiscal decentralization created the so-called 'local state' corporatism.[16] When the performance of local government was directly connected to local economic growth, local governments had to incorporate the interests of TVEs into their utility function and take a cooperative stance. The contribution of TVEs to local finance was critical in determining the attitudes of local governments. In recent years, as private firms developed quickly, market competition intensified and the performance of TVEs declined, local governments shifted their interests and even became predatory. Meanwhile, TVEs increasingly sought protection from laws and courts. As Shiding Liu analysed, the termination game emerged and various kinds of opportunist behaviour grew.[17] Clearly visible in this process is the effect of laws and policies in deconstructing the Guanxi Rule.

3.1.3 Social capital and private enterprises

In China, the status of private enterprises is a politically sensitive issue. The attitudes of governments toward private enterprises experienced a change from dislike to indifference, to support and even favour. The enlarged proportion of GDP produced by private enterprises provided an economic explanation for this change. Private enterprises are increasingly indispensable to economic growth, tax revenues and employment. This makes it not surprising that the amendments to the Constitution, CCP policies and public opinion show a common trend towards justifying their legitimacy. Yet in the early stages private enterprises faced an unfriendly environment. It is through the use of the network in a community comprising acquaintances that private enterprises grew up and grew strong. According to the investigation by Qizai Zhang,[18] about 71.2 per cent to 78.68 per cent of private enterprises are based on kinship and quasi-kinship, and about one-sixth of their funds comes from social networks. These enterprises attempt, by all means available, to establish a good relationship with local governments. For example, in order to get administrative permits or tax breaks, some private enterprises become red-hat enterprises in order to seek political shelter and patronage. These private enterprises are often affiliated to some administrative units and make themselves similar to TVEs. When the political climate and the legal environment were improved, these red-hat private enterprises 'took off their hats' and became 'private'. On some occasions, private enterprises make use of their Guanxi network to evade taxes and control. Such a practice contributes to the formation of an underground economy, where private enterprises themselves 'wear a black-hat' (Hei Mao Zi).[19] The official protection of private property rights has a great influence on the shedding or keeping of these hats. Since the political and legal environments are becoming more tolerant, it is predictable that more and more private enterprises will choose to remove their hats in the future.

3.2 The Governance Performance and the Growth of the Non-State Sector Economy

Thanks to political stability and preservation of the virtuous social capital, China's transition saw a rapid growth and dominance of the non-state sector economy, including private enterprises, TVEs and foreign-investment enterprises. The portion of GDP created by state sector economy (state-owned enterprises (SOEs) and urban collective enterprises) has decreased substantially. Within the non-state sector economy, TVEs are of primary importance. Regarding employment, TVEs absorbed a workforce of 28 million in 1978, which grew to be 135 million in 1997. In 1978, the GDP of TVEs accounted for 4–5 per cent of the national GDP, yet this figure rose to 28 per cent in 1998.[20] Since 1990, the non-state sector economy has created 73 per cent of the gross value of industrial products, 63 per cent of GDP, 100 per cent of the new jobs and 80 per cent of the economic growth.[21]

Such a transformation of the economic system induced favourable changes in CCP policies and laws, which tended to create protection for non-state property rights. These changes also created the stable expectations necessary for cooperation between private property owners. From 1978 to 1995, the average annual growth rate of national GDP was 10.83 per cent. The state sector economy contributed 9.54 per cent to this growth, the urban collective economy 13.5 per cent, while the non-state sector economy contributed up to 55.89 per cent. Furthermore, non-state economy provides handsome fiscal income at all governmental levels. In 1978, its proportion of national fiscal revenues was 13.02 per cent, yet in 1985 this went up to 28.85 per cent. In some coastal areas, non-state economy made an even greater contribution. For example, in 1994, 50.5 per cent of Fujian province's Industrial and Commercial taxation was from non-state economy. Non-state economy also has a prominent role in creating jobs. Currently, it accounts for more than 60 per cent of the workforce in the economic sector. At the same time, the state sector economy employment has decreased substantially.[22] In 1992, for the first time, the gross value of industrial products from the non-state economy surpassed that of the state economy and accounted for 52.62 per cent of the national total.

It is this structural change of the economy that established a change in direction, from discrimination to support of CCP policies and of the constitutional reform. In 1992, the 14th National Conference of the CCP was held, which adopted the socialist market economy as the general goal of economic reform. In 1993, the 3rd Plenary Meeting of the 14th CCP Central Committee and the 1st Plenary Meeting of the Eighth National People's Congress, respectively, made compatible party policy changes and amendments to the Constitution. Together, they set basic principles for utilizing market construction and property rights reform of SOEs. In the legal arena, the 1999 Amendment to the Constitution prescribes that public ownership can be achieved by various means, and multiple forms of ownership should develop side by side. The status of the private economy thus rose from being a supplement to the national economy to being an important component of the socialist market economy.

3.3 Segregate Accumulation of Social Capital

The Guanxi Rule can have negative effects. As the reform deepens, the peculiarism and boundedness of the Guanxi Rule may become an obstacle to the shift from rule of man to rule of law. Local protectionism creates conflicts at the borders of Guanxi networks. The segmentation of social capital has impeded the expansion of enterprises, the enlargement of market scope and the development of division of labour. Loopholes in laws and policies conduce to the emergence and spread of the vicious Guanxi Rule. Grey economy and black economy under the vicious Guanxi Rule have been eroding the national wealth. It is estimated that the grey economy and black economy control 20 per cent of the total national economy.[23] Although this is less than the 40 per cent of Russia, it already constitutes a serious threat to China's economic development.

3.3.1 Grey economy

In China, the grey economy is mainly induced by poorly designed reforms like the dual-track price system and the stock reform of SOEs. Qinglian He documented a number of serious and large-scale corruption cases in these areas.[24] Weiting Huang found an astonishing amount of rent[25] in the dual-track price system.[26] Corruption has become the most dangerous cancer in China's reform and development and has greatly vitiated people's trust in the government. Corrupt behaviour is opaque and tends to increase transaction costs and uncertainty in general. Judicial corruption increases litigation costs and makes individuals shift to less costly means of dispute settlement, such as arbitration by mafia gangs. This leads to the failure of the law. One research study shows that corruption is a function of the number of policies,[27] therefore it is important to impose necessary restrictions on the scope of governmental intervention. Currently, the 2000 Legislative Law has established more restrictive provisions on governments' policy making. The 2004 Administrative Licence Law has made detailed restrictions on the jurisdiction of governments for handing out administrative permits.

3.3.2 Black economy

The mafia in China is becoming more active. Gangs make use of the pervasive Guanxi network to extend their influence. Their illegal activities include smuggling, illegal drug production and trafficking, prostitution, kidnapping, underground factories, counterfeiting commodities and money, and making fake invoices and degree certificates. These activities have been recorded by Qinglian He[28] and Weiting Huang.[29] Such organized criminal activities are highly dangerous, in that they paralyse the legal system, yet their essential rule of survival depends on their penetration into the formal institutional systems through informal ways. In recent years, the mafia has become involved in commercial entities. It invests in them and then monopolizes the market. The Liu Yong case in the Shengyang Municipality and the case of Mafia's incorporation in the Zhengzhou Municipality are typical. The frequent media stories about phenomena such as private detectives and dunning companies, are clear evidence that some people choose to evade laws and shift to private relief. Although the impact of the black economy on the social justice system in China is still not as serious as on that in Russia, its potential danger in harming China's efforts to build a 'harmonious society' deserves full attention.

4. THE PERFORMANCE OF CHINA'S TRANSITIONAL GOVERNANCE: A COMPARISON WITH RUSSIA

According to the policy suggestions of Western neoclassical economists, Russia adopted a reform package of radical political liberalization and economic privatization. Because of the inability of the Russian governments to enforce their policies and laws, the reform led to political disorder and ideological disputes. Private enforcement of public and private rules became pervasive. The vicious Guanxi Rule grew to be the major governance mechanism of the economy. As a result, it is hard to attract FDI or promote domestic capital formation. The economy collapsed at Russia's early stage of reform.

After the large-scale privatization, the enforcement of private rules became popular, yet it only created an inferior institutional equilibrium based on mafia arbitration. The report issued on 17 January 1994 by the Russian Social and Economic Policy Analysis Centre pointed out that gangs owned and controlled about 40 000 enterprises, including 2000 state-owned enterprises. The journal *Economists* said, in 1994, that three-quarters of private enterprises were forced to contribute 10%–20% of their income to criminal gangs, and 150 of these gangs controlled about 40 000 private or state-owned enterprises, as well as the majority of 1800 commercial banks. In 1995, the government indicated that criminal organizations nationwide controlled over 50 per cent of economic entities, that is, about 35 000 economic entities, including 400 banks, 47 currency exchange institutes and 1500 state-owned enterprises.[30] Criminal gangs and organized crime were big social problems faced by Russians. Since the rules used by the gangs to enforce contracts and solve disputes were unable to provide stable expectations, the transaction costs for the whole society were very steep. The establishment and expansion of new enterprises was very difficult.

Meanwhile, Russia's weak central government, with insufficient provision of laws and their enforcement, could hardly set effective constraints on central government agencies and local governments in abusing their power. Governmental agencies and their agents sought rents by setting kinds of toll-gates and by changing the tax rates. Over 800 of Russia's agencies were able to halt transactions at their discretion.[31] To engage in commercial activities, individuals had to obtain the permission of many committees. The society had to use Guanxi or bribery in exchange for resources under the control of governments. As a result, the non-productive vicious Guanxi Rule constituted the fundamental order for governing the grey economy. Transparency International (TI) ranked Russia as the fourth out of 50 countries and areas as regards its corruption level.[32] Russia's radical privatization provided great opportunities for elites, either within or external to the regime, to seize public wealth.

In contrast, China's reform led by the CCP was carried out under the premise that the reform will finally strengthen rather than vitiate its rule. CCP did not open up the political market or allow the emergence of competing political parties. Instead, under its one-party regime, CCP introduced a series of economic, legal and political reforms, and managed to reduce political transaction costs. The CCP did not seek a one-shot optimization of its reform strategy. Rather, it adjusted the policies incrementally. It emphasized the political feasibility of policies and a smooth and continuous transition. Such an emphasis was demonstrated by its experiments, such as 'policy-based constitutional reform', 'dual-track legal system' and 'legal experimentalism'. These strategies of reform effectively prevented the segmentation of social capital. In the political sphere, CCP did not adopt radical political liberalization, but introduced a simulated political market. More specifically, the CCP tolerated the ideological competition between thc lcft and thc right, but maintained its final and centralized control over ideology. Ideological disputes and arguments were limited to concrete reform measures and policies, not to the basic legitimacy of the party or the political regime. As such, ideological debates found their common denominator. Fundamental conflicts between new and old ideologies were, in general, not added to the political market for debates; rather, the CCP proposed a method of 'no debates', 'experiment first', 'promulgating examples' and 'nationwide dissemination and promotion'. As discussed earlier, governments invested a lot in ideology in order to maintain the mainstream ideology and stable political order. The Chinese government not only gradually legitimated private property rights and guaranteed the enforcement of contracts, in order to advance economic development, but also compensated those who lost out under the reform, in order to enhance its legitimacy.

Although in the previous two decades China could demonstrate amazing achievements, serious problems also emerged, such as corruption, an underground economy, social distrust and the systematic dangers of the banking system. This leads to the question of the extent to which informal institutions can replace or complement formal institutions as the market gets larger and becomes more complex. Although informal institutions can be helpful in the emergence of markets, these, as formal institutions, should become more rational and impersonal during the process of expansion and complication, in order to be efficient, effective and reliable. Dixit[33] points out the diminishing marginal returns of informal institutions in such a process, due to degradation of the quality of information and the credibility of punishment. The increasing substitution of laws on Guanxi in China shows clearly that the marketization process has changed the relative price of the formal and informal institutions.

5. CONCLUSIONS

This chapter, by comparing China and Russia, shows that a successful transitional process should create a plural governance system in which policies, laws and informal institutions represented by Guanxi should work together, in order to produce a synergy effect and to provide a cooperative order. Under the incompleteness of policies and laws, the Guanxi Rule may complement the vacuum of formal institutions and accumulate the virtuous social capital that reduces transaction costs. Yet the functioning of the Guanxi Rule is, to a great extent, contingent on the role of the state in restricting the negative effects and promoting the healthy effects. Governments must provide the basic public goods, namely a stable political order, in order to avoid both state capture and state predation. Only when the functioning of the Guanxi Rule is controlled, supported and supplemented by the formal institutions can its counter-productive properties, like its boundedness and peculiarism, be overcome and its governance potential be harnessed. Overall, by understanding the substitutive, complementary and mutually convertible relations between multiple governance mechanisms, it is possible to develop appropriate institutional structures that provide effective property rights protection, contract enforcement and a base for sustainable economic growth and social stability.

There are a few generalizations that seem appropriate for our comparative analysis, as well as potential for future discussions. First, transition and reform are not equal to the retreat of state. Although state retreat is common during the transitional process, which asks for the destruction of the centrally planned economy and the introduction of the market economy, a 'self-regulating' market economy cannot be established simply by liberalization and privatization, and 'partial reform does not succeed without continued coordination through planning'.[34] The state has to remain, and even to enlarge, in many spheres, although the ways of intervention must be altered. Bringing society and the market back in can hardly succeed when the state is marginalized by this process. Yet the direct dilemma is that a strong state may prefer a partial reform and may serve as a barrier for the formation of laws and social capital.

Second, in the transitional process, the incompleteness of formal mechanisms asks for a strategy of endogenous development in policy making and law making. In other words, 'finding laws' rather than 'making laws' can be more effective in reducing transaction costs, avoiding social conflicts and promoting cooperation, although it can be incremental and time-consuming. A minimum level of social embedding of state policies and laws is necessary for a smooth and successful transition. The 'big-bang' mentality of reform should be avoided. Consequently, reform in formal institutions should never ignore the governance resources that are preserved within society. The adoption of exogenous formal institutions and endogenous local informal institutions should be balanced.

Third, while we argue that the functioning of the Guanxi Rule is quite contingent on the formal institutional environment, a further concern is to think directly about the independent effects of informal institutions on formal institutions – namely, that some informal institutions (although all informal institutions bear within them positive and negative properties) may be more market-oriented than others. So, while even the mainly positive informal institutions are in need of state regulation, the focus of state control is on those featured through the vicious Guanxi Rule. It is important to avoid undifferentiated treatment of informal institutions.

Fourth, it is still inconclusive whether incremental reform that incorporates informal institutions is optimal in the long run. It is hard to know whether such a partial reform has the momentum of continuous fine-tuning without stagnating at some certain point. Owing to the diminishing marginal returns of informal institutions in governing the market, problems may occur when the necessary removal of these institutions lacks political support. In other words, the plural governance system may lose its dynamic balance and become trapped in a low path of efficiency. Yet, although scholars may be in dispute regarding the long-term economic performance of Russia and China, our analysis makes us quite optimistic about at least the mid-term economic performance of the latter.

NOTES

1. For example, before 1900, most commercial disputes in America were solved through private litigations. Later, state and federal regulatory agencies took over the authority in policy areas like anti-trust, railway pricing, food and medicine safety and so on. See Glaeser and Shleifer (2003, pp. 401–25).
2. Pistor and Xu (2002).
3. Chow (1997, pp. 321–7).
4. Ellickson (1991, p. 286).
5. Posner (1999, pp. 13–4).
6. Zhang (2003).
7. Putnam (1993, p. 167).
8. Hirshleifer (2001).
9. Owing to the entry barrier to markets and the fear of unfair treatments, in the 1980s many privately invested enterprises registered themselves as state-owned or collective

enterprises, or affiliated themselves with some public enterprises. These private enterprises with the names of public enterprises are called 'red-hat' (Hong Mao Zi) enterprises. It is estimated that more than a quarter of all private enterprises once had a red-hat (China Private Economy Institute (2000).
10. HeGuang (2003).
11. Zhang (2001, p. 13).
12. Eggertsson (1990).
13. Zhao (2001).
14. Tan (2003).
15. Chen (2000).
16. Oi (1992, pp. 99–126).
17. Liu (1999).
18. Zhang (1998).
19. While red-hat private enterprises seek interests by manipulating the institutional symbols and gray areas, black-hat private enterprises behave in a more hazardous way by violating formal institutions. For example, black-hat private enterprises may counterfeit, occupy markets by violence, and rely on mafia arbitrage and protection.
20. Wang (2000).
21. Fang (2000).
22. Shengzhen Research Group (2000).
23. Huang (1996, p. 333).
24. He (1998, pp. 71–240).
25. The wealth created by the dual-track price system that can be collected through illegitimate use of power.
26. Huang (1996, pp. 169–70).
27. Ackerman (2000).
28. He (1998, pp. 320–44).
29. Huang (1996, pp. 24–55).
30. De Blasi (1994, p. 124).
31. Kvint (1993, p. 26).
32. Kolodok (2000, pp. 142–3).
33. Dixit (1996).
34. Murphy, Shleifer and Vishny (1992, pp. 889–906).

REFERENCES

Ackerman, B. (2000), *Corruption and Development: Corruption and the Reform of Governmental Functions*, Beijing: Zhong Guo Ji Hua Press.

Chen, J. (2000), 'The system vicissitudes and the informal village system', *Economics Research*, **1**(2).

China Private Economy Institute (2000), *Yearbook of Chinese Private Enterprises*.

Chow, G. (1997), 'Challenges of China's economic system for economic theory', *American Economic Review, Papers and Proceedings*, **87**(2), 321–7.

De Blasi (1994), *The Economic Privatization in Kremlin*, Shanghai: Fareast Press.

Dixit, A. (1996), *The Making of Economic Policy: A Transaction-cost Politics Perspective*, Cambridge, Mass.: MIT Press.

Eggertsson, T. (1990), *Economic Behavior and Institutions*, Cambridge: Cambridge University Press.

Ellickson, R. (1991), *Order Without Law: How Neighbors Settle Disputes*, Cambridge, MA: Harvard University Press.

Fang (2000), 'Dynamic process of the economic system', *Economic Research*, **1**.

Glaeser, E.L. and A. Shleifer (2003), 'The rise of the regulatory state', *Journal of Economic Literature*, **41**(2), 401–25.
He, Q. (1998), *Modernization Trap*, Beijing: China Today Press.
HeGuang, T.L. (2003), 'Exploring the legal and economic system with the endogenous legal theory', *Comparison Studies (Bi Jiao)*, **8**.
Hirshleifer, J. (2001), *The Dark Side of the Force: Economic Foundations of Conflict Theory*, Cambridge, New York: Cambridge University Press.
Huang, W. (1996), *The Shadow Economy in China*, Beijing: Chinese Business Press.
Kolodok, G. (2000), *From Shock to Therapy*, Shanghai: Fareast Press.
Kvint, V. (1993), *The Barefoot Shoemaker: Capitalizing on the New Russia*, New York: Arcade Publishing.
Liu, S. (1999), 'Embeddedness and relationship contracts', *Research of Sociology*, **4**.
Murphy, K., A. Shleifer and R. Vishny (1992), 'The transition to a market economy: pitfalls of partial reform', *The Quarterly Journal of Economics*, **107**(3) (August), 889–906.
Oi, J. (1992), 'Fiscal reform and the foundations of local corporation in China', *World Politics*, **45**, 99–126.
Pistor, K. and C. Xu (2002), 'Incomplete law', in J. Wu (ed.), *Comparative Studies*, **4**.
Posner, R. (1999), 'Constructing legal framework for the economic development', *Financial Law Forum*, **13**, 14.
Putnam, R. (1993), *Making Democracy Work*, Princeton: Princeton University Press.
Shengzhen Research Group (2000), 'Development of non-state-owned economy in China and its choice of policy', *Kaifang Dao Bao*, **4**.
Tan, Q. (2003), 'The village organizational behavior and the township and village enterprises' development in a transitional period', *Social Science in China*, **2**.
Wang, X. (2000), 'Continuability and system reform of the Chinese economic growth', *Economic Research*, **7**.
Zhang, Q. (1998), 'Distribution of social capital and resource by network', in *Social Cultural Psychology in China*, Beijing: China Social Press.
Zhang, W. (2001), *Property Right, Government and Credit*, Peking: Sanlian Press.
Zhang, J. (2003), 'Transition, Legal Reform and Law & Economics', Post-doctoral report, Peking University Law School.
Zhao, X. (2001), 'Governance by contract', *Social Sciences in China*, **2**.

PART II

Specific aspects of the Chinese legal system from an economic perspective

4. The economics of competition policy and the draft of the Chinese competition law

Roger Van den Bergh*

1. INTRODUCTION

Economic analysis has been extremely helpful in clarifying the goals of competition policy and applying the rules of competition law in the daily antitrust practice of both the United States of America (US) and the European Community (EC). It may be expected that economic analysis will play an equally important role in Chinese competition policy. Since the draft of the anti-monopoly law[1] contains an invitation for comments, this chapter will try to summarize the main insights of the economic analysis of competition law and contrast them with the text of the proposed Chinese competition law. While taking up the invitation for comments, the goal of this chapter remains modest. It is not the task of a European commentator to decide what the contents of the Chinese competition law should be. This remains ultimately a political decision to be taken by the Chinese legislator. However, sharing experiences about EC competition law, which is gradually becoming more economics based, may provide important information about the complexities inherent in developing a sound competition policy. It is hoped that this contribution will stimulate the debate in China by illuminating the tensions between economic efficiency, fairness, consumer welfare and other goals of competition policy. This may allow the Chinese legislator, who will face the highly difficult task of accommodating competing policy considerations, to make informed choices about the competition rules, which will best fit the needs of the rapidly developing Chinese economy.

The draft of the Chinese competition law prohibits three types of anticompetitive conduct: (i) agreements, decisions or other concerted actions among undertakings; (ii) abuse of dominant market positions by undertakings; and (iii) concentration of enterprises that eliminates or restricts competition. This is equivalent to the rules contained in Article 81 EC Treaty (prohibition of cartel agreements), Article 82 EC Treaty (abuse of a dominant position) and the EC Merger Regulation.[2] To the traditional list of anti-competitive practices, the Chinese draft adds 'abuse of administrative power by government agencies and their subordinate departments that eliminates or restricts competition'. This additional prohibition reflects a concern about local protectionism, which is seen as the dark side of Chinese-style federalism.[3] Local governments have created trade barriers to protect their enterprises and markets against outside competitors. Also in the European Union, governments may take decisions that lead to market partitioning. However, these public trade barriers are pulled down by applying the rules on free movement of goods, persons, services and capital. European competition law only concerns trade barriers as far as they are the consequence of agreements between private firms. This chapter does not further discuss the four fundamental freedoms of the EC Treaty. The Chinese reader who is interested in learning how public trade barriers have been eliminated in the European Union is referred to other publications.[4]

Given the similarities between Articles 81–2 EC Treaty and the EC Merger Regulation and all categories of monopolistic conduct mentioned in the Chinese draft, EC competition law offers a fruitful basis for comparison. The Chinese policy maker can learn a lot from the evolution of EC competition law from a set of rules inspired by political goals of market integration and protection of individual economic freedom (Ordoliberalism)[5] to an economically oriented interpretation of the competition rules. The choice made in this chapter to focus on EC competition law, rather than on US antitrust law, may be further supported by two additional arguments. The draft of the Chinese anti-monopoly law reveals that a choice has been made to adopt European legal concepts and techniques, such as exemptions of cartel agreements, market share thresholds and notifications of concentrations. Consequently, the European experiences with these tools of competition law may prove to be very useful for the development of Chinese competition policy. Also transition and developing economies, such as China, may prefer the fairness-tinged interpretation of abuse of dominant market position of Article 82 EC Treaty over the narrower efficiency interpretation of Section 2 of the US Sherman Act. It must be added that, at the time of writing (May 2006), a debate is taking place as to the desirability and the scope of a more economics-based interpretation of Article 82 EC Treaty.[6] In recent years, the treatment of mergers and horizontal agreements in EC competition law has been largely aligned with US antitrust law. However, it is unlikely that the old substantive rules on abuse of dominant power will be replaced entirely by economic welfare-oriented interpretations.[7] In sum, EC competition law appears to be the most useful point of reference in the discussions on the future Chinese competition law. Comparisons with US law will be made only as far as they provide additional insights with respect to the way in which decision makers cope with the conflicting goals of competition policy.

Within the confines of this chapter, a full discussion of the 58 articles of the draft of the Chinese competition law is not possible. Commentaries on EC competition law, which apply the main insights from economic analysis to the different types of prohibitions, run to several hundred pages.[8] Therefore, a choice had to be made. In our view, any discussion about the desirability and contents of a competition law should start by specifying the goals that the legal rules are willing to achieve. Only when there is clarity about the Chinese anti-monopoly law's objectives will it be possible to formulate a judgment about the effectiveness and efficiency of the concrete prohibitions it contains. Therefore, after this introduction, the second section of the chapter will discuss the different goals of the envisaged Chinese competition law and compare them with the goals of EC competition law. Besides illuminating the goals of competition policy, economic analysis is also very helpful in explaining the meaning of central legal concepts of competition law, such as 'relevant market' and 'dominant market position'. The third section of the chapter will discuss the notion of the relevant market contained in the draft of the Chinese competition law and critically assess the use of market share thresholds in judging the legality of anti-competitive practices. Given its particular importance in transition and development economies, which are facing problems of excessive prices and other abuses by (previously) public dominant firms, the fourth section will sum up the main insights from the economic analysis of exploitative and exclusionary behaviour and contrast these findings with the wording of the Chinese draft. Finally, in the fifth section, the most important conclusions will be summarized and suggestions for further research will be formulated.

2. THE GOALS OF THE CHINESE COMPETITION LAW

Article 1 of the draft of the Chinese anti-monopoly law states: 'This law is enacted for the purposes of prohibiting monopolistic conducts, safeguarding fair competition, protecting the legitimate rights of consumers, and the public interest, and to ensure the healthy development of the socialist market economy.' At first sight, this broad formulation of different goals contrasts with the current dominant view of the European Commission that the goal of competition law is to achieve allocative efficiency and enhance consumer welfare.[9] However, a closer look at EC competition law reveals that several rules or decisions in real-life cases can be explained only by other goals, such as the protection of individual economic freedom or the political goal of market integration. In addition, the laws of the EC member states contain several provisions inspired by fairness considerations, which also aim at protecting small and medium-sized businesses.[10] In sum, both real-world EC competition law and the Chinese draft show that competition policy makers are trying to attain a multitude of goals. As will be shown below, achieving different goals simultaneously is very difficult and often impossible, since the stated objectives are not always consistent with each other.

Economic analysis illuminates the relation between the different goals of competition policy and reveals that policy makers will not be able to escape from trade-offs in cases of conflicting goals. Profiting from the debate on the objectives of EC competition policy, one may contrast the following three broad categories of goals: (i) economic efficiency as a measure of total societal welfare, (ii) consumer welfare and (iii) other policy goals, such as fairness and protection of individual economic freedom. It is important to realize that the efficiency goal and the consumer welfare goal are not perfectly consistent with each other. Concerns of consumer welfare do not automatically coincide with economic welfare goals, since they may disallow profits for firms that are due to improvements in productive efficiency. The scope of potential conflicts between different goals of competition policy is much broader, however. Fairness may collide with efficiency goals, since any prohibition of unfair business conduct necessarily restricts competition. For example, outlawing low prices because they are 'unfair' goes against the main virtue of the competitive process, which is to guarantee lower consumer prices. Another source of potential inconsistencies in EC competition law is the objective of market integration, which may conflict with concerns about the efficient organization of distribution systems. The tensions resulting from the attempt simultaneously to realize different policy goals are further explained below.

2.1 The Goal of Allocative Efficiency

Microeconomic theory provides valuable insights into the economic effects of different market forms (perfect competition, monopoly, oligopoly) and types of conduct (forms of strategic interaction limiting competition). Welfare economics offers criteria to judge the desirability of these outcomes (Pareto efficiency, Kaldor–Hicks efficiency). The central insight from welfare economics is that perfectly competitive markets are Pareto-efficient, since it is no longer possible to enhance the welfare of a single individual without diminishing the welfare of another individual. When products are sold at prices covering the marginal costs of production, no consumer (producer) can be made better off without making a producer (consumer) worse off. Put differently, Pareto improvements are no longer possible in a market which is allocatively efficient. Allocative efficiency implies that firms produce what buyers want and are willing to pay for. Whereas allocative efficiency is reached in a perfectly competitive market, monopoly causes welfare losses: prices are persistently held above marginal costs and output is reduced. By combating monopolies (and cartels that achieve monopoly power) competition authorities reduce the negative consequences of monopolies and improve upon allocative efficiency.

The welfare consequences of monopoly can be summarized as follows. First, a part of the consumer surplus is redistributed to the monopolist as producer surplus or monopoly rent. This is the so-called 'price effect of monopoly': consumers pay too much. This price effect in itself is not a loss of welfare, but it may be considered as a situation with a less preferable income distribution. In a political judgment this transfer of income may be considered as socially unacceptable. Second, there is a 'deadweight loss' which lowers the welfare of the concerned economy. This is the so-called 'allocation effect of monopoly': consumers purchase less of the product in question.

Economists believed for a long time that the deadweight loss was the only social cost of a monopoly. However, when one measures the effects of market power, the costs incurred in acquiring and preserving a monopoly must also be included. Tullock (1967) has convincingly argued that all the resources which are applied to achieving monopoly profits should likewise be included in the social costs. The analysis of the welfare losses caused by a monopoly cannot be complete if the sums expended on achieving the transfer from consumers to the monopolist are excluded. Firms may compete for market power not only by incurring expenditure to influence regulatory agencies, but also by building excess capacity, excessive advertising or sales efforts coaxed from dealers through vertical restraints in distribution contracts. To the extent that these practices contribute to the creation and/or preservation of monopoly power, they should be added to the social costs of monopoly. Moreover, it should not be forgotten that one of the major benefits of a monopoly is a 'quiet life'. Once the competitive pressures have disappeared, a firm may become slower to reorganize production when that needs to be done because there are no competitors nipping at its heels. With a lazy monopolist innovative activity may also slow down. Finally, market power may also have harmful effects on factors other than price that are valued by consumers, such as product quality and variety. When these additional costs of monopoly are taken into account, the welfare losses may be quite substantial.

An intervention by the competition authority will bring an end to the allocation effect of monopoly, which causes a reduction in the production factors that are deployed. The increase in activities will result in additional demand and the extra sales will serve partially as an input into business processes throughout the economy. As explained above, monopoly causes not only negative allocation effects but also price effects that may be regarded as undesirable. The price effect is determined by multiplying the price increase as a result of monopoly power by the quantity of products sold. The estimated positive effects of antitrust supervision, measured by the deadweight loss (allocation effect) and the redistribution damage to consumers (price effect) can amount to several hundred million euros.[11]

2.2 Allocative Efficiency Versus Other Efficiency Goals

It follows from the above that allocative efficiency can be convincingly presented as a major policy goal for competition law. However, there are a number of complications that may limit the attractiveness of allocative efficiency as the universal yardstick for competition policy and law. In some cases, allocative efficiency may conflict with other efficiency goals: productive efficiency and dynamic efficiency.[12] Productive or technical efficiency implies that output is maximized by using the most effective combination of inputs; hence internal slack (also called X-inefficiency) is absent. The goal of productive efficiency implies that more efficient firms, which produce at lower costs, should not be prevented from taking business away from less efficient ones. Obviously, the achievement of productive efficiency is not a Pareto improvement since the less efficient firms are made worse off. Dynamic efficiency is achieved through the invention, development and diffusion of new products and production processes that increase social welfare. Whereas productive efficiency and allocative efficiency are static notions, progressiveness or dynamic efficiency refers to the rate of technological progress. Again, there will be losers in the dynamic competitive struggle, so that Pareto improvements cannot be achieved.

To enable policy decisions when the different efficiency goals are not consistent with each other, welfare economics offers the alternative criterion of Kaldor–Hicks efficiency. A Kaldor–Hicks improvement allows changes in which there are both gainers and losers, but requires that the gainers gain more than the losers lose. This condition being satisfied, the winners could compensate the losers[13] and still have a surplus left for them.[14] A Kaldor–Hicks improvement is also referred to as a potential Pareto improvement, since actual compensation would again satisfy the Pareto criterion. The central value judgement underlying Kaldor–Hicks efficiency is that an exchange of money has a neutral impact on aggregate well-being, which may not be the case when the incomes of gainers and losers differ. By using the Kaldor–Hicks criterion, total welfare is maximized. The use of this welfare notion has far-reaching consequences for competition policy. The Kaldor–Hicks criterion may make it possible to clear mergers that enable the merging firms to achieve important scale economies and thus improve productive efficiency, but at the same time enable previously independent firms to collude and raise prices above competitive levels. In terms of total welfare, it is irrelevant that producers rather than consumers capture the surplus produced by achieving efficiencies, as the monopoly overcharge paid by purchasers to stockholders is treated as a transfer from one member of society to another and so is ignored in the balance.

There is also a possible trade-off between market power and technological progress. So far the analysis has been limited to issues of allocative efficiency and possible trade-offs with productive efficiency. In a static analysis, Pareto improvements occur when firms realize cost efficiencies and pass on (a part of) these benefits to consumers. Besides cost efficiencies, there are efficiencies in the form of new or improved products. Dynamic efficiency (in a broad sense: including both productivity increases and product innovation) raises additional issues. The relationship between market power and innovation is highly debated. The dispute was initiated by the seminal contribution by Schumpeter (1943), who argued that monopolists and large firms are better equipped to generate innovation, since they can more easily finance costly research and, thanks to their size, can fully exploit the innovation achieved. This idea was contested by Arrow (1962), who showed that, theoretically, a monopolist has less incentive to innovate than a new entrant or a firm in a competitive industry. In the absence of unambiguous theoretical conclusions, the relationship between market power and innovation is ultimately an empirical matter. Empirical evidence, however, still fails to demonstrate any definite relationship between firm size, market concentration and the pace of innovation. The individual circumstances of the industry under scrutiny weigh heavily on the final outcome.[15]

2.3 Consumer Welfare

Clearly, textbook criteria of welfare economics have not been the driving force of EC competition policy and law. The rules of EC competition law cannot be easily economically 'rationalized' by referring to the notions of Pareto efficiency and Kaldor–Hicks efficiency (total welfare). Instead, a pragmatic concern for consumer welfare dominates current EC competition policy and law. The goal of a competition policy that is primarily intended to increase economic welfare can be defined in terms of consumer surplus, producer surplus and total welfare. Consumer surplus is a concept used to describe the difference between what a consumer is willing to pay for a good and what the consumer actually pays when buying it. Producer surplus refers to the variance between the price in the market that producers collectively receive for their products and the sum of those producers' respective marginal costs at each level of output. Total surplus then is the sum of producer surplus and consumer surplus. Total welfare is a notion designed to take into account the welfare effects on the entire economy, bypassing the markets directly involved in the analysis of a particular industry.

The total welfare view asserts that the chief objective of antitrust is increasing total welfare by allocating resources through the price system to those users who value these most. Using the Kaldor–Hicks criterion, total welfare will be maximized. In this way, competition authorities may clear mergers that enable the merging firms to achieve important scale economies and thus improve productive efficiency, but at the same time enable previously independent firms to collude and raise prices above competitive levels. The total welfare standard accepts an 'efficiency defence', which allows producers to capture the surplus as long as their gains are higher than the losses of consumer surplus. Policy makers may object to this criterion because of the undesirable effects on the distribution of income. However, if an actual Pareto improvement is required (benefits to firms without any harm to consumers) the 'efficiency defence' will fail in the vast majority of cases.

A number of theoretical papers have investigated how large the size of the efficiency gains should be to allow for Pareto improvements. In a Cournot model,[16] the size of the compensating marginal cost reduction will depend on the firms' market share and the price elasticity of market demand. Modest marginal cost reductions may prevent price increases following mergers of modest size. However, the cost reductions will need to be large to prevent large mergers from raising price. By way of example, if the merging firms' market shares are 20 per cent each, a 0.5 elasticity of demand would require a 66.67 per cent compensating marginal cost reduction, while a higher elasticity, say 1, would require a lower 25 per cent reduction in marginal costs.[17] Another paper investigated the case of differentiated good markets under Bertrand price competition.[18] The compensating marginal cost reduction required to offset the anti-competitive effects induced by mergers will depend on pre-merger product prices, diversion ratios[19] among products, and profit margins. By estimating the compensating marginal cost reduction for different levels of pre-merger profit margins and diversion ratios, the conclusion was reached that, 'if the products are highly differentiated and the merging firms compete intensively, large typically implausible cost reductions are necessary to restore pre-merger prices'. For example, for a 25 per cent diversion ratio and 0.7 profit margin, the compensating marginal cost reduction is 77.78 per cent.[20] In sum, the conclusion from these papers seems to be that, under a Pareto efficiency standard, the scope for an efficiency defence is (very) limited.

The important insight is that allocative efficiency (assessed in terms of total welfare, which is total surplus in the entire economy) and consumer welfare (defined as maximization of consumer surplus) are conflicting concepts and that policy makers cannot escape from trade-offs if these goals are to be pursued simultaneously. Unlike the total welfare approach, the consumer welfare model views redistribution in the form of wealth transfers from consumers to producers as harmful rather than neutral.[21] Competition policy may be more inspired by equity considerations concerning the distribution of resources than by efficiency criteria. In the view of the European Commission, cost reductions which result from reductions in output cannot be considered as efficiencies benefiting consumers. Even if total welfare increases, there is still an unlawful restriction of competition if the agreement (or the merger) reduces consumer surplus. The Commission thus seems to have endorsed a pragmatic consumer welfare standard, by requiring that the net effect of an agreement (or merger) at least be neutral from the point of view of consumers affected by the agreement. Even though this benchmark is much less demanding than insisting on price decreases, it is not perfectly in line with an efficiency-based approach. The requirement that consumers in the relevant market are not made worse off excludes increases in total welfare. The latter may result either from gains of producers (shareholders) exceeding consumers' losses or from balancing negative effects in one relevant market against positive effects for consumers in different geographic or product markets. In sum, the use of consumer welfare criteria in competition law requires efficiency–equity trade-offs. The rejection of the Kaldor–Hicks criterion implies that more weight is given to competitive prices for consumers than to cost savings for efficient firms or profits for shareholders. Not efficiency considerations but wealth transfers thus seem to be the driving force for formulating general rules and deciding hard cases. Competition authorities should be fully aware of these underlying value judgements and policy choices. Making these trade-offs explicit, rather than paying lip service to efficiency arguments, can improve the quality of the decision making.

2.4 Market Integration

Besides distributional concerns about consumer welfare, EC competition law has been inspired by other policy goals. These include market integration, protection of freedom of business decisions, and goals of fairness (protection of small and medium-sized traders) and social equity. This third category of goals creates further tensions with the objectives of allocative efficiency and consumer welfare discussed above. In European competition law, freedom of individual competitors is seen as an important benefit of preserving competition. The European Commission has held that 'effective competition preserves the freedom and right of initiative of the individual economic operators and it fosters the spirit of enterprise'.[22] The Article 81(3) Notice states that 'a general principle underlying Article 81(1) which is expressed in the case law of the Community Courts is that each economic operator must determine independently the policy which he intends to adopt on the market'.[23] The emphasis on freedom of action may explain why the Commission often objects to contracts limiting the freedom of parties to take independent decisions (for example, vertical restraints in distribution agreements). The tension between the goal of market integration and other policy goals lies at the heart of many heavily debated issues in EC competition policy. The achievement of market integration may entail losses in terms of total welfare. In addition, it cannot be excluded that consumer surplus will be reduced, so that market integration conflicts also with a consumer welfare standard. The conflicts between the goals of allocative efficiency and the protection of freedom of business decisions and goals of fairness are best illustrated in the EC case law on abuse of a dominant position (Article 82 EC Treaty);[24] they are discussed in the third section of this chapter. Below, the focus will be on the tension between the objective of market integration and goals of allocative efficiency and consumer welfare.

2.4.1 Conflicting policy goals and the regulation on vertical restraints

The goal of market integration has put a heavy legacy on EC competition law. Until today, it has kept prohibitions in place (such as the ban on absolute territorial protection) which may cause substantial inefficiencies in the organization of production and distribution. Traditionally, EC competition rules have been used as instruments to avoid firms partitioning the internal market along national borders. In this way, EC competition law was a logical complement to the prohibitions of the EC Treaty addressed to the member states not to maintain or enact regulations hindering the free movement of goods, services, persons and capital.[25] The emphasis on the market integration goal of European competition law has created rules which are difficult to reconcile with goals of allocative efficiency and consumer welfare.

The Regulation on vertical restraints in distribution agreements may serve as an example to illustrate the tensions between the market integration goal and other objectives of EC competition policy. In this 'new-style' block exemption,[26] the European Commission works with two parameters: the nature of the vertical restraint and the level of market power involved. The new Regulation introduces a presumption of legality (a so-called 'safe harbour') to the benefit of manufacturers with a market share not exceeding 30 per cent, provided they do not include a number of blacklisted clauses in their distribution agreements. The Block Exemption does not apply to hardcore restraints, such as minimum resale price maintenance and absolute territorial protection. Both may lead to market segmentation across national borders, which fly in the face of the market integration goal. Even though the Commission has claimed that the new Regulation is based on economic insights, there still remain many inconsistencies with a purely economic approach. Economic theory offers no justification for distinguishing between different types of vertical restraints, since they can all be substitutes for each other. Both price and non-price restraints may have two effects: they may achieve efficiencies in the organization of distribution networks and they may restrict competition. A real economics-based approach would require a case-by-case investigation to assess which of the two explanations is the more convincing.

By using the example of vertical minimum price fixing, it can be shown that a strict ban is in conformity neither with a welfare economics standard (since minimum retail prices may improve allocative efficiency) nor with a consumer welfare standard (since minimum prices may increase the variety of goods offered on the market). There are three efficiency explanations for resale price maintenance: the need to cope with free-riding if pre-sales services are important, the wish to guarantee after-sales services and the desire to achieve an optimal density of retail stores. If minimum retail prices were used only to realize such efficiencies, rather than to restrict competition, there would be no reason to prohibit them if the goal of law was the maximization of total welfare. Obviously it must be added that minimum prices may also serve anti-competitive purposes since they may make collusion between traders easier. However, an efficiency-oriented competition policy would require a clear proof of such conspiracies and prohibit minimum price fixing only as far as its costs exceed the efficiency gains.

If the goal of competition law is consumer welfare, the analysis becomes even more complicated. Firms and consumers may disagree on the optimal amount of retail services or, more precisely, on the right mix between retail services and prices. The divergence between the objectives of the manufacturer and distributor, on the one hand, and the objectives of the consumers, on the other hand, is likely to be important when the vertical structure enjoys substantial market power. If consumers can easily switch to alternative solutions, vertical minimum price fixing is unlikely to hurt consumers. In the other case, the relevant considerations under a consumer welfare standard are the following. Manufacturers are interested in the marginal consumers they can attract through increased sales efforts and they tend to neglect the impact of their decisions on inframarginal consumers. Whereas the former are just willing to pay for the product at its prevailing price, the latter are willing to pay significantly more, including a compensation for the services offered. The marginal consumers will purchase more products only if the value they derive from the services is higher than the increase in price. By contrast, inframarginal consumers are relatively insensitive to a price increase caused by the provision of retail services, and will continue to buy the product even if the additional services are valued less than the increase in price. As a result, manufacturers will profit from imposing minimum resale price maintenance when the marginal consumers value the additional services more than their costs, regardless of the inframarginal consumers' preferences. If marginal consumers are willing to pay more to benefit from additional services whereas inframarginal consumers would prefer to have lower services and prices, then it may be in the interest of the vertical structure to increase the level of effort and the retail price, even though it hurts the majority of consumers. However, this is not a necessary outcome. It is also possible that the losses of inframarginal consumers are small, so that the total group of consumers benefits. Minimum retail prices leading to increased demand may thus generate both additional profits for the manufacturer and an increase in consumer surplus.[27] Consequently, a flat prohibition of minimum retail prices may conflict with the goal of improving consumer welfare.

Another inconsistency of the new block exemption is the prohibition of absolute territorial protection. Together with minimum resale price maintenance, such arrangements are put on the blacklist with practically no chance of being exempted from Article 81(1) EC Treaty. In a passage of the Guidelines, the European Commission states that it is not required to assess the actual effects on the market of the hardcore restrictions.[28] This amounts to a formulation of per se prohibitions, which is not hospitable to economic analysis. It is easy to see how the distributor's incentives to make investments for the promotion of the manufacturer's products would be undermined if distributors in other EC member states, where the brand has already been introduced, could free-ride on those investments. To avoid free-riding, distributors active in other markets should then be restrained from selling in the new market. The Commission is aware of the problem,[29] but remains reluctant to accept its consequences to their full extent. On the positive side, a manufacturer may appoint an exclusive distributor in certain territories, provided that 'passive sales' to such territories are permitted.[30] This means that distributors must be free to sell and deliver goods in response to unsolicited requests from individual consumers, including generally over the Internet. In addition, the Guidelines on Vertical Restraints do not consider it to be anti-competitive if, in the case of entering a new geographic market, restrictions on active and passive sales to intermediaries in the new market are imposed on the direct buyers of the supplier located in other markets over a period of two years.[31] On the negative side, an absolute territorial protection excluding equally active and passive sales to consumers without time limitation cannot be organized. Given the growth of Internet trading and website marketing, direct orders by consumers may gain in importance. If the protection from free-riding is not watertight, distributors may be discouraged from launching products in new geographic markets. In addition, free-riding is not necessarily a time-limited problem; temporary territorial protection is thus no guarantee that distribution efficiencies will be preserved. It is to be deplored that the existence of a trade-off between market integration and competition is not explicitly acknowledged. At best, the current Guidelines may be seen as an unspoken compromise between the conflicting objectives of market integration and the desirability of enhancing vertical restraints.

To judge the effects of territorial restrictions under the consumer welfare standard, the relevant criteria are the same as in the case of resale price maintenance. The first issue to be investigated is the effect on output in the entire internal market. If firms circumvent the prohibition by withdrawing products from certain parts of the market, thus making parallel imports impossible, overall output may decrease. Another question relates to the valuation of the services, guaranteed through territorial exclusivity, by consumers. Again, this valuation may be different across groups of consumers. The important point is that it cannot be excluded that a flat prohibition will come at the expense of a loss in terms of consumer welfare.

In sum, EC competition law may sacrifice efficiency on the altar of the internal market. It is to be expected that EC competition law will become more hospitable to efficiency arguments as European economic integration reaches its stage of completion. It may be expected, though, that practices that are thought of as prone to undoing the effects of market integration will continue to be subjected to strict prohibitions.

2.4.2 Lessons for China

For the Chinese legislator it should be clear that copying rules of EC competition law may be inappropriate if the prohibition is inspired by market integration goals. In this respect, doubts arise with respect to Article 8(vi) of the draft of the Chinese competition law, which outlaws limitations on fixing resale prices. Economic theory has shown that resale price maintenance may generate several economic advantages. Maximum prices avoid double monopoly mark-ups in cases where market power exists at both the upstream and downstream level of the distribution chain.[32] Minimum prices prevent free-riding among dealers and may guarantee an optimal provision of services to consumers (see above). For this reason, a rule making it possible to justify resale price maintenance in cases of substantial efficiency savings is preferable. Therefore it is suggested that maximum and minimum resale prices may benefit from the exemption provided for in Article 9 of the Chinese draft, if the conditions thereto required are satisfied.

The most important lesson for the Chinese legislator is that he should be cautious not to transplant EC competition rules, inspired by market integration objectives, into the Chinese legal order when a similar concern about geographic market partitioning by private firms does not exist. Trade barriers which are the consequence of decisions of governmental agencies (local protectionism) cannot be combated by rules of competition law but need separate rules which guarantee free movement of goods, persons, services and capital across the Chinese provinces.

On top of this, it may also be questioned whether competition law should really be concerned with market partitioning. The objectives of market integration are perfectly legitimate but may be pursued better by other legal instruments. It is highly questionable whether competition law is an appropriate instrument to further market integration.[33] This goal is largely impeded by factors such as fiscal disparities and different regulatory interventions by governmental agencies, which are external to concerns of competition policy. An illustrative example from Europe is the car industry, where price differences are caused by differences in tax levels, and the pharmaceutical industry, where price differences are the consequence of differences in the health policies of the Member States (varying between the two extremes of a single buyer and a competitive health insurance market). Prohibiting companies active in the European Union from adapting their sales policies to heterogeneous local conditions is nothing other than combating effects without reaching the causes of the existing disparities. Using rules of competition law to bring about price convergence by means of the arbitrage of parallel trade comes down to imposing the costs of non-Europe on companies, whereas the primary responsibility of persisting price differences lies with the governments of the Member States.

3. MARKET DEFINITION, MARKET SHARES AND MARKET DOMINANCE

In EC competition law, a common way of establishing market dominance is a calculation of market shares on the so-called 'relevant market'. If the market share held by the undertaking is very high (50 per cent or more, provided that rivals hold a much smaller share of the market), this may indicate a dominant position.[34] By contrast, undertakings holding market shares no higher than 25 per cent are not likely to enjoy a dominant position on the relevant market.[35] The Draft of the Chinese Anti-Monopoly Law adopts the concept of a relevant market and introduces a number of presumptions of dominant market position based on market shares. The relevant market is defined as 'the territorial area within which the undertakings compete against each other during a time period for relevant products' (Article 4). The following market shares lead to a presumption of a dominant market position: (i) the market share of a single undertaking accounting for at least one-half or more of the relevant market; (ii) the joint market share of two undertakings occupying the first two positions in terms of market share and accounting for at least two-thirds or more of the relevant market; and (iii) the joint market share of three undertakings occupying the first three positions in terms of market share and accounting for at least three-quarters or more of the relevant market. Undertakings with a market share of less than one-tenth are not presumed to occupy a dominant market position (Article 15). These Articles invite two sets of comments. First, the Chinese legislator could consider embracing explicitly the so-called 'SSNIP test', which is the theoretical economic foundation for defining relevant markets, and adapt the wording of Article 4 accordingly. Second, the use of presumptions of dominant market position may be criticized, since it reflects a strong structuralist approach to problems of identifying market dominance. This view, based on the structure–conduct–performance paradigm[36] has been rejected in the most recent Law and Economics literature. Both points will be further elaborated below.

3.1 The SSNIP Test

To determine the relevant market in both its product and geographic dimension, it is necessary to identify the immediate competitive constraints faced by an undertaking. According to the traditional legal definition, a relevant product market comprises all those products which are regarded as interchangeable or substitutable by the consumers, by reason of the product's characteristics, their prices and their intended use.[37] The relevant geographic market is defined by assessing whether the conditions of competition in a given region are sufficiently homogeneous. Conversely, the SSNIP test defines the relevant market as a product or group of products and a geographic area in which it is sold so that a hypothetical profit-maximizing firm, that was the only present and future seller of those products in that area, would impose a profitable small but significant and non-transitory increase in price above prevailing or likely future levels. In contrast with the traditional legal definition, the SSNIP test gears the delineation of the market to the crucial question of market power. It takes into account three forces that simultaneously may discipline market power: demand substitution, supply substitution and potential competition. The SSNIP test also defines the product market and the geographic market simultaneously instead of sequentially.

The old-style definition based on product characteristics has a number of drawbacks. The criterion of functionable interchangeability does not carry as its central aim the ultimate task of identifying market power, as the attributes of products and regions are only relevant inasmuch as they influence the extent of competition between commodities and locations. A comparison of product characteristics does not allow one to judge whether products belong to the same relevant market. Products with different characteristics may constitute the same relevant market (for example, beer and wine, trains and buses or small and large trucks).[38] Conversely, products having the same characteristics may constitute different relevant markets (for example, branded products and non-branded products that are physically identical). The same criticism applies to products in the same price range[39] or products with a similar intended use. Consequently, a market definition based upon irrelevant product characteristics, similarity of price levels or intended uses may lead to distorted conclusions in the firms' market power.[40] What competition authorities should be figuring out instead is whether the companies under investigation can significantly and lastingly raise their prices because buyers do not enjoy substitutes they can turn to. Further, if it is thought that a price increase of 5 to 10 per cent as compared to the competitive price is unacceptable, then the regulators have to determine which products and geographic areas the hypothetical monopolist has to control in order to be able to sustain such a price increase profitably, as it is precisely those products and areas that its buyers would transfer to in response to the increase in price. That way, reasonable judgments become possible on the potential exercise of market power. To avoid ill-conceived decisions on market definition and inconsistencies resulting from the mixed use of old-fashioned legal definitions and modern economic insights,[41] the Chinese legislator may thus be advised to endorse the SSNIP test explicitly.

There is one important *caveat*, however. The SSNIP test was launched in US antitrust law as a way to define relevant markets in merger cases. In markets not yet highly concentrated, pre-merger prices may be an appropriate point of reference for the SSNIP test. By contrast, if market concentration is high and collusion is already a problem, this approach to market definition will be biased in favour of permitting mergers. To counter such an effect, Section 1.11 of the 1997 US Merger Guidelines specifically states that the prevailing price will be used 'unless pre-merger circumstances are strongly suggestive of coordinated interaction'. In Article 82 EC Treaty investigations (abuse of dominant position) the problem is pervasive. The prevailing price may already have been substantially increased. If this fact is not taken into account, the market will be defined too widely. In *Du Pont*, the US Supreme Court argued that cellophane is only one of a number of products making up the market of flexible packing materials, as a high level of cross-price elasticity of demand was determined between cellophane and other wrapping materials. Cellophane could thus not constitute a separate market, as, obviously, consumers would switch to substitute products when confronted with monopoly prices for cellophane. The key issue remaining untouched, however, is whether consumers treat the products as close substitutes under competitive prices. Du Pont, being the sole producer of cellophane, had already set prices at levels where alternative products provided an effective competitive constraint on the pricing of its product, implying, in fact, that the high cross-price elasticities indicated Du Pont was exercising monopoly power. One method to avoid this so-called 'Cellophane fallacy' is to estimate the competitive price and use that price for the purposes of applying the SSNIP test. If this is not possible, the SSNIP test is likely to be inadequate in abuse of dominance cases and additional tools are required to check whether no false substitutes have been included.

3.2 Market Shares: Only a Proxy for Market Dominance

At the outset it should be made clear that defining relevant markets is an indirect way of assessing market power. Market shares are only a proxy for market power. Economists agree that figures about firms' residual demand elasticities are immediately relevant for defining their degree of market power. Conversely, calculating market shares on a previously determined relevant market is only an indirect approach for assessing market power. For example, if it is possible to calculate the price increases caused by a merger in a differentiated goods market, the exercise of market definition may be superfluous. Calculating market shares is an indirect way of assessing market power when the relevant data are not available. Quite regularly the use of an indirect approach leads to focusing attention on market definition, not on the fundamental question of the effects of market power. If market definition becomes the goal of the assessment by the competition authority, rather than an instrument to better understand the antitrust problems at hand, decisions in real-life cases may be biased. This risk is particularly severe when the old-fashioned legal definition focusing on product characteristics is used. The policy problems which may then arise are numerous: lack of transparency leading to large discretionary powers of competition authorities, danger of regulatory capture (the regulator becomes dependent on information provided by the industry under investigation) and lack of objectivity (how much substitution is necessary?).

The relevance of market shares and concentration indices is not only dependent upon the objectivity of the definition of the market in question. It also depends on the type of the anti-competitive effects encountered. Market shares may give reliable indications as to whether markets for homogeneous goods which are under scrutiny are conducive to collusion, but will be less reliable indicators of antitrust worries when unilateral effects in differentiated product markets arise. Market share analysis which shows low market shares may overestimate the competitive constraints between products. In merger control cases, antitrust intervention is not only needed in an environment of fewer competitors, which is more favourable to collusion (giving rise to oligopolistic or collective dominance). The concept of unilateral effects makes it clear that, after a merger, firms can increase prices also without taking into account competitors' responses or co-ordinating behaviour. The loss of localized competition may make post-merger price increases profitable. Also, when mergers do not lead to high market shares, competitive constraints may thus be substantially weakened and necessitate antitrust intervention to avoid lasting supranormal profits. This has been acknowledged by the European Commission in its Horizontal Merger Guidelines. Indeed, while the structuralist approach based on market shares may bring forth convincing conclusions in markets distinguished by homogeneous goods, this no longer holds when goods are differentiated or branded[42] and market shares do not confer trustworthy information on the market's competitive situation.[43]

Market shares not only entail the risk of market power being underestimated in differentiated goods markets. There is also the risk of overestimation of market power. The theory of contestable markets has made clear that market power can be exercised only in the absence of entry and exit barriers. Even a monopolist cannot profitably increase prices if newcomers can easily enter the market (without incurring a cost disadvantage compared to the incumbent firm) and leave the market without impediments (absence of sunk costs). If markets are contestable, dominant firms will be vulnerable to hit-and-run competition. If the barriers to entry faced by potential rivals are low, a high market share may not be indicative of dominance. Any attempt to increase prices above the competitive level will attract new entry or expansion by rivals and make the price increase unprofitable.

Empirical developments in the US have initiated an evolution that decreases the emphasis on the role traditional methods of market definition play in determining the market players' positions and, ultimately, market power. Initially cultivated as a means of assessing merged companies' incentives to raise differentiated goods' prices post-merger, the unilateral effects theory mentioned above comprehensively diminishes the need for delineating relevant markets. As noted by Stigler and Sherwin (1985), the hypothetical monopolist test coupled with a judgement concerning the level and changes in concentration is not in any way easier than asking directly whether the merger under investigation will result in an increased price. Hereinafter, two of the more commonly applied techniques for directly assessing market power will be briefly discussed: price-concentration analysis and simulation analysis.

Price-concentration analysis, which explores the relationship between concentration and prices, may provide important information about the likely effects of a merger. This econometric technique is particularly useful in a cross-section analysis (for example comparison of price levels in different geographic markets) where one market is under scrutiny. If higher concentration levels are associated with higher prices, this suggests that a merger will lead to higher prices. One example is the investigation of the American Federal Trade Commission into the effects of the merger between Staples and Office Depot, two superstores selling office products. The FTC collected data on concentration and prices in different geographic areas and used different econometric studies, which tried to assess market power directly. It resulted from these studies that Staples and Office Depot could charge significantly higher prices in the monopolized markets than in markets with two or three competitors (respectively 13 and 15 per cent). These results were an important factor in the ultimate decision to reject the merger.[44] Price concentration analysis can also be a useful instrument in dominance cases. If there is no price-concentration relationship in a given market, this suggests that a high market share does not confer market power. In Article 82 EC cases, the need for market definition also diminishes if the challenged conduct itself proves both the existence of a dominant position and its abuse.

An alternative technique is direct assessment of market power through a structural oligopoly model describing the conduct of consumers and producers. On the basis of information on observed prices and sales, price elasticities and the intensity of competition can be estimated. Through simulation analysis the market power may be deduced or the change in market power through a merger may be calculated.[45] A case example is *Volvo/Scania*.[46] The direct identification of market power has several benefits. It is no longer necessary to make the detour of the SSNIP test with its inherent complexities to reach a decision. Another advantage is that other factors can also be incorporated in the analysis. A simulation analysis may allow an answer to the question of whether the cost savings resulting from a merger will be sufficiently passed on to consumers, which allows the competition authority to judge whether the anti-competitive effects will be compensated. Also in this way, decisions can be reached without going first through the market definition exercise.

It may be concluded that in recent years market shares have lost a lot of their importance in establishing dominance. This is also recognized by the European Commission in recent documents, where it is stated that market shares provide 'useful first indications' of the market structure and of the competitive importance of various undertakings active on the market and only a proxy for market power. Particularly in merger control cases, the framework for the assessment of market power under EC competition law – as in the US – now constitutes a healthy balance between indirect and direct methodologies, drawing from both qualitative and quantitative evidence. From a Law and Economics perspective, this important development is to be appreciated. It is by no means fully accepted, however. For example, in German competition law, the indirect approach is actually taken one step further, as market power may be assumed on the mere basis of a market share test. If market shares reach a certain threshold, the German competition authority may intervene, unless the firms demonstrate that substantial competition will be preserved after the merger (Section 19(3) of the German competition law). Moreover, the German concept of a market-dominating position deviates from the European approach. Besides dominance, German competition law also includes the notion of 'superior market position' (*überragende Marktstellung*, see Section 19(2) nos. 1 & 2). This is interpreted in a static and very structured manner, so that according to the majority view it may even apply to situations in which substantial competition does not come into question.[47] Also the Draft of the Chinese Competition Law has endorsed market shares as presumptions of market dominance. Given the recent criticisms of a structuralist approach and the rapid development of econometric techniques allowing a direct identification of market power, the Chinese legislator might wish to reconsider his choice.

4. ABUSE OF A DOMINANT POSITION

Chapter 3 of the draft of the Chinese competition law bans both exploitative and exclusionary abuses. An undertaking with a dominant market position shall not abuse its power to sell or buy products at unfair (high or low) prices (Article 16). Without valid reasons, an undertaking enjoying a dominant position shall not, for the purpose of impairing competition, sell products at prices below cost (Article 17). Also applying dissimilar prices or other transaction terms to equivalent trading partners, so as to put some of them at a competitive disadvantage, is qualified as an abuse (Article 18). The fourth prohibition relates to refusals to deal, which is likewise outlawed in the absence of valid reasons and proof of a competitive disadvantage of purchasers or harm to the legitimate interests of consumers (Article 19). Furthermore, an undertaking with a dominant market position shall not require its distributors to sell exclusively its own products or impose other exclusive or forced transactions (Article 20). Also tying shall be prohibited as well as requiring the acceptance of additional obligations that are irrelevant to the subject of the contract (Article 21). Finally, the draft prohibits refusal of access to a network at unreasonable prices. However, this prohibition will not apply if the dominant firm can prove that it is impossible or unreasonable to grant access on account of technology, security or other justifiable reasons (Article 22). Readers familiar with both US antitrust law and EC competition law will notice that the Chinese draft is much closer to the latter than to the former legal regime. Excessive prices are not really an issue under American antitrust law and the formulation of the prohibitions of predatory pricing, discrimination, tying and refusals of access to a network closely resemble the prohibitions of Article 82 EC Treaty and the relevant case law of the European Court of Justice. Obviously, within the limited frame of this chapter, a full discussion of the very complex provisions on abuse of a dominant market position is not possible. The most useful lessons for the Chinese legislator seem to be the following: (i) the difficulties arising from the use of an abuse statute as a covert instrument of price regulation, (ii) the tension between the goal of allocative efficiency and the protection of individual competitors, and (iii) the ambiguous consequences of so-called 'exclusionary abuses', such as refusals to deal and tying.

4.1 The Problem of Excessive Prices

An important historical difference between Section 2 of the US Sherman Act and Article 82 EC Treaty concerns the greater importance of public firms in the EC. Whereas American antitrust law was originally dominated by concerns about rapid expansion of private economic power, European competition law was enacted in a period of state monopolies and powerful public enterprises. The stricter substantive rules under Article 82, such as the prohibition of unfair prices and refusals to deal, can be explained by the fact that many monopolies and dominant positions were created by government regulations rather than by innovation and internal growth of the most efficient firms.[48] In many European countries, price regulation was seen as necessary to protect consumers until competition had developed more fully.[49] A similar historical context may explain why transition and developing economies, such as China, may wish to use the prohibition of abuse of dominance as a mechanism to control prices.

The condemnation of 'unfair purchase or selling prices' under Article 82 EC Treaty contrasts sharply with the rejection of excessive pricing claims by the US courts. Establishing whether prices are too high is not an easy task, however. A number of methodologies can be used for gauging whether or not prices charged are excessive. These include a comparison of the selling price of the product or service with (i) its cost of production and the resulting revenue/profit margin[50] (comparison A); (ii) the selling price of the same products or services sold by competitors (comparison B); and/or (iii) prices charged on similar markets which are open to competition (either in closely related product areas, or in different geographic markets)[51] (comparison C). In *Deutsche Post*, the European Commission applied the above methodologies cumulatively, expressly stating, however, that it did not intend to act as a price regulator for dominant firms. The Commission also wanted to avoid any finding implying that prices of a dominant company would need to go beyond cost and some reasonable mark up.[52] In fact, the Commission's decisions in this area reveal that only truly exorbitant pricing has triggered regulatory intervention. The following two examples are illustrative. In *General Motors*, up to 400 times the 'actual cost' was deemed excessive while up to eight times the 'effective cost' was held acceptable.[53] In *Deutsche Telekom*, price comparisons showed differences up to 100 per cent, but the Commission decided that this may be remedied by price reductions between 38 per cent and 78 per cent.[54]

Also the decision practice of competition authorities of the EC Member States shows the typical difficulties that arise from attempts to control excessive prices charged by dominant firms. Under German competition law, an *Als-Ob* argumentation (comparison C) was used to conclude that prices charged by a dominant firm deviated substantially from so-called 'normal' prices in competitive markets. To make comparisons between prices in the latter market and those charged in a monopolized market, a lot of factors that influence prices (differences in consumer preferences and market characteristics) must be discounted; it must equally remain possible for the dominant firm to justify price differences on economic grounds (cost savings). The *Als-Ob* method was largely unsuccessful because of the difficulty of finding a similar market, where prices are not above competitive levels and the large number of adjustments that must be made when comparing competitive with non-competitive prices.[55] In the United

Kingdom, the level of pricing and profitability in directories services (*Yellow Pages* and the like) was recently investigated by the Office of Fair Trading.[56] In its review of the profitability levels[57] of the two UK directories suppliers, Yell and Thompson, the OFT compared the two companies' profitability (comparison B). However, since there was a risk that prices in this already highly-concentrated market would not be at a competitive level, the OFT benchmarked the profitability levels against those of 'comparator firms' in other industries, chosen either because they were involved in the similar activity of newspaper publishing and advertising, or because they had a similar ratio of tangible assets to turnover to Yell (comparison C).[58] The most aggressive application of the abuse of dominance provision in prohibiting excessive prices can be found in the Netherlands. The Dutch Competition Authority has gone further than the European Commission but has been criticized for having acted as a price regulator.[59]

In marked contrast to Article 82 EC, excessive pricing claims have been rejected in principle under Section 2 of the Sherman Act.[60] Several arguments underlie the more liberal US approach. First, it is feared that prohibiting excessive prices may penalize dominant firms that have reached that position through efficient means, thus reducing the incentives to compete and hurting dynamic efficiency. As forcefully stated by Judge Learned Hand: 'The successful competitor, having been urged to compete, must not be turned upon when he wins.'[61] Second, it is expected that monopoly profits attract new competitors whose entry will drive prices back to competitive levels. Finally, in practice it is very difficult to determine the borderline between a reasonable and an abusive price. The US authorities seem more concerned with over-deterrence (type II errors, false negatives) and less concerned with under-deterrence (type I errors, false positives) than their European counterparts.[62] This is neatly reflected in the recent *Trinko* case, where the Supreme Court has stated: 'The mere possession of monopoly power, and the concomitant charging of monopoly prices, is not only not unlawful; it is an important element of the free-market system. The opportunity to charge monopoly prices – at least for a short period – is what attracts "business acumen" in the first place; it induces risk taking that produces innovation and economic growth.'[63]

4.2 Protection of Competitors Versus Consumer Welfare

A well-known criticism of competition law is that rules may be (ab)used to protect competitors from competition. The criticism is widely accepted in the field of rules on unfair competition, but is equally relevant in the domain of competition law *sensu stricto*. The tension between consumer welfare and protection of competitors is acknowledged by the European

Commission. In its Notice on the appraisal of horizontal mergers, the Commission mentions various factors to determine the extent of the merged entity's economic power: economies of scale and scope, privileged access to supply, a highly developed distribution and sales network, access to important facilities, and other strategic advantages, such as the ownership of the most important brands, a well-established reputation, or an extensive knowledge of the specific preferences of consumers. The Commission argues that some of these factors are likely to benefit the customers of the paramount firm, but adds: 'However, they may also make it difficult for competitors, either individually or in the aggregate, to effectively constrain the paramount firm to a sufficient degree.'[64] This tension also manifests itself when practices of individual firms have to be controlled. In the field of unfair competition, the prohibition of sales at loss prices (or with an unreasonable small profit margin) serves as the clear example of a rule protecting competitors at the expense of competition (and consumer welfare). In the area of competition law, the treatment of discounts under Article 82 EC Treaty provides a nice example.

Firms may wish to offer incentives to their customers to buy more of their products. Loyalty rebates are considered normal business practice but they may be declared illegal if practised by a dominant firm. The case law of the European Court of Justice has evolved from a prohibition of exclusive purchasing for (a large part of) all requirements to objections against rebate schemes practised by dominant firms. In its investigation of Hoffmann La Roche, the European Commission held that the discounts granted constituted an abuse, since, inter alia, customers were 'bound by an exclusive or preferential purchasing commitment in favour of Roche for all or a very large proportion of their requirements' and because the discounts were not based 'on the differences in costs borne by Roche in relation to the quantities supplied'.[65] The Commission's decision was approved by the European Court of Justice in its *Vitamins* judgment.[66] In the *Michelin* case, the Court went one step further by raising objections against rebate schemes based on a previous period's purchases by an individual retailer. The rebate system was held to be abusive because of the long period of reference (one year) and its lack of transparency (repeated changes, no written confirmation of the awarded bonus).[67] Another case under Article 82 EC Treaty centres on a travel agency commission scheme used by British Airways. For seven years, this airline company had offered travel agents extra commission payments for meeting or exceeding the previous year's sales of British Airways tickets in the United Kingdom. In the European Commission's view the extra sales commissions were not related to distribution costs savings. Instead, by rewarding customer loyalty, they made the travel agents loyal to British Airways and discouraged them from providing services to other airlines; a substantial fine of 6.8 million euros was imposed.[68]

The principles which may be derived from the above case law and the outcomes of the individual proceedings may be criticized for several reasons. First, a rule requiring that discounts be based on cost differences is ill-conceived. Discounts are offered not only to reflect cost savings, but also to gain more customers. The latter goal tells nothing about the impact of the discount scheme on competition. On the one hand, discount schemes may enliven competition and benefit consumers; on the other hand, they may exclude rival suppliers (for example, because shelf space in stores is limited) and lead to market foreclosure. Only a case-by-case approach is able to distinguish competitive and anti-competitive uses of discount schemes. The European Commission may be criticized for not carrying out a market effect test determining whether discount schemes enable dominant firms to exclude rivals and raise prices afterwards. A necessary condition for a finding of exclusionary pricing behaviour is that rival firms have been induced to exit the market or that their market share is in decline, so that their continued existence as effective rivals is in doubt.[69] Second, the requirement that rebate schemes to dealers reflect savings in distribution costs or increases in the value of services provided by the distributor is too simplistic. Not only distribution costs, but also production costs, matter. In addition, price discrimination may be objectively justified in industries where there are large fixed costs and low marginal costs.[70] For firms with high fixed costs, it is important to be able to offer high discounts on incremental sales to recoup the fixed cost investments. Even if the price–cost margin on sales to inframarginal consumers substantially exceeds the margin earned on the incremental sale, this does not mean that the latter sale is abusive or that the former sales were made at an excessive price. From a viewpoint of economic efficiency, large price rebates are cost-justified if they are intended to increase sales with the purpose of recouping large fixed costs, as long as they exceed the marginal costs of supply. The European Commission's approach is overinclusive since it omits a market effect test to demonstrate market foreclosure.[71] Such a rule protects competitors rather than the competitive process. Under a consumer welfare standard, the current assessment of discount schemes practised by dominant firms should be criticized: it may limit price competition and reduce output. Protection of competitors necessarily entails losses in terms of consumer welfare.

4.3 Ambiguous Effects of So-called Exclusionary Practices

Chapter 3 of the draft of the Chinese competition law mentions several types of exclusionary behaviour by dominant firms: predatory pricing, discrimination, refusals to deal, tying and refusal of access to networks or other infrastructures. The welfare effects of these practices are inherently difficult to assess. All forms of so-called 'exclusionary behaviour' may also generate efficiencies and benefit consumers. This leaves competition authorities and judges who take economic analysis seriously with a difficult task: they have to analyse carefully the reasons why firms engage in such practices and assess their effects on allocative efficiency and consumer welfare in real-life markets. In most cases, the Chinese draft leaves sufficient scope for such an assessment, since the prohibitions apply only in the absence of 'valid reasons'.

Article 17 of the draft states that 'without valid reasons, an undertaking with a dominant position shall not, for the purpose of impairing competition, sell products at prices below cost'. Low prices practised by dominant firms may be a sign both of healthy competition and of predation. The stylized story of predatory pricing goes as follows. A dominant firm uses price reductions (below some measure of cost) to induce the exit or deter the entry of an efficient competitor, or to discipline a rival firm. Afterwards, it increases prices in order to reap supranormal profits. Authors of the Chicago School argued that such a strategy is irrational, because of the high costs it entails for the predator, the possibility of new entry after the elimination of the target and the availability of a profitable alternative strategy, namely a merger.[72] Subsequently, game theorists have shown that predatory pricing strategies cannot totally be excluded. Smaller rival suppliers may be excluded from the market if the dominant firm is able to profit from imperfections in capital markets (financial predation),[73] establish a reputation of aggressive behaviour,[74] or signal that market entry will not be profitable.[75] An economically sound competition law should carefully analyse whether anti-competitive effects (exclusion) really may materialize. The current EC case law on predatory pricing is overtly restrictive. In its most recent policy document, the European Commission states that, once it has been established that the price is below AAC,[76] it is not necessary to investigate any further the actual or likely exclusion of the target firm (prey). In contrast with US antitrust law,[77] the Commission (closely following the case of the European Court of Justice)[78] does not consider it necessary to provide a separate proof of recoupment 'as dominance is already established which implies that entry barriers are sufficiently high'.[79] Finally, an efficiency defence is rejected.[80] The Chinese legislator might consider an approach that is more in line with economic analysis, since he is not bound by the restrictive case law of the European Court of Justice. This would imply an integration of the game-theoretic insights, making it possible to establish predation irrespective of whether the prices of the dominant firm are below some measure of cost[81] and a broader scope for defences, such as meeting the competition of a rival, price-fighting firm and efficiency reasons. The latter include below-cost prices to induce sufficient demand in the case of network externalities, sales of perishable goods and sales of a good below cost to induce the purchase of a complementary good.

Also tying and bundling may both cause competitive harm and serve legitimate business goals which enhance efficiency. The traditional story is that a dominant company may use tying to expand its monopoly power in an adjacent market. Chicago economists criticized this view, arguing that it is impossible to charge monopoly profits twice, since buyers may react by reducing the purchases of the package.[82] Even though the single monopoly profit theorem of the Chicago School has limited the relevance of the leverage theory, it cannot be totally excluded that firms make a strategic use of bundling and tying to prevent entry in the market either of the tying or of the tied product. Conversely, bundling and tying may be used to increase efficiency: the practice may allow a firm to achieve cost savings, guarantee quality or enable price discrimination (and increase output). Again, an effects-based analysis is necessary to distinguish beneficial and harmful instances of bundling and tying. In this respect, it may be deplored that (in contrast to the other prohibitions contained in Chapter 3) Article 21 of the draft outlaws tying unconditionally. The Chinese legislator may, therefore, be advised explicitly to allow the dominant firm to also provide 'valid reasons' for tying.

The draft of the Chinese competition law does not contain unqualified prohibitions of refusals to deal and refusals to grant access to a network or other infrastructures owned by a dominant undertaking. In the first case 'valid reasons' may justify the refusal and in the second case it may be shown that 'it is impossible or unreasonable to grant access to the network or other infrastructures to other undertakings on account of technology, security or other justifiable reasons'. This balanced approach of the draft competition law must be welcomed. To assess the effects of refusals to deal, a trade-off between short-term and long-term competition is needed. This need is particularly acute in cases where small competitors require access to facilities of the dominant firm deemed to be 'essential'. An example is the electricity market, where a monopoly owns essential facilities, such as transmission and distribution grids, whose reduplication is technically infeasible or economically undesirable. On the one hand, stepping in to guarantee a small firm's dealings may be justified by the need to protect short-term competition in the relevant market. In the given example, competition in the generation and sale of electricity, which are not themselves natural monopolies but require access to essential facilities, may be enhanced. On the other hand, if firms have to fear that they might be coerced to give competitors access to their assets, such as the facilities they have built, the incentive to engage in useful economic activities (innovation) might be reduced in the first place. Therefore competition authorities should carefully balance the costs and benefits of granting access. There is also a further complication that is worth mentioning. If access must be granted, a logical next question concerns the pricing of the essential facilities. It falls outside the scope of traditional competition policy to supervise continuously prices charged for access to a network or other infrastructures owned by dominant firms. This task is best entrusted to a specialized regulatory agency.

5. CONCLUSIONS

The draft of the Chinese competition law mentions a multitude of goals, ranging from the elimination of monopolistic conduct (allocative efficiency) to consumer welfare and fairness. This is not different from EC competition law, which emphasizes allocative efficiency and consumer welfare as the main objectives, but also includes concerns about protection of individual economic freedom and market integration. Competition policy makers should realize that these different goals are partly inconsistent with each other. Allocative efficiency may convincingly be presented as a major goal of competition policy, since it allows reducing the negative price and allocation effects of monopolies. However, allocative efficiency may conflict with productive efficiency (the classic example being a merger increasing prices but at the same time reducing costs) and dynamic efficiency (optimal degree of innovation). If the goal of competition policy is consumer welfare, efficiency–equity trade-offs may become unavoidable. Allocative efficiency defined in terms of total welfare contrasts with the maximization of consumer surplus and prevents balancing countervailing effects on economic welfare in different product and geographic markets. In the European Union, the picture is further complicated since EC competition law has been used as an instrument of market integration. The main lesson for the Chinese legislator is that different goals may conflict with each other and that a consistent competition policy requires a clear hierarchy of policy objectives.

With respect to the definition of dominance, the Chinese draft adopts a structuralist approach based on the calculation of market shares on a relevant product and geographic market. Modern economic literature has criticized an exclusive reliance on market shares, since they are merely a proxy for market power. The traditional legal definition focusing on product characteristics is not geared to the relevant question whether the firm under investigation is able to increase prices above competitive levels. Consequently, differences in product characteristics or geographic entities may be decisive in defining the relevant market even if these characteristics have no impact on the competition between commodities and regions. The Chinese legislator may therefore be advised explicitly to adopt the SSNIP test, which defines the relevant market as the smallest set of products and regions that is worth monopolizing. Moreover, the use of presumptions of market dominance may be criticized. High market shares are not a reliable indicator that market power may be exercised; abuses will not be possible if markets are sufficiently contestable. Low market shares do not make it possible to conclude with confidence that there will be no antitrust worries; for example, a merger may lead to anti-competitive unilateral effects in differentiated goods markets. Modern econometric techniques, such as price concentration analysis and simulation analysis, may allow defining market power directly and overcoming the shortcomings of the market share approach. The Chinese legislator may, therefore, also be advised to endorse explicitly these modern techniques and abandon a merely structuralist approach.

The provisions on abuse of dominant position reflect the particular concern of the Chinese legislator to prevent exploitative abuses by dominant firms. However, European experience shows that competition law is not a good instrument to cope with excessively high prices and that competition authorities should avoid acting as a price regulator. Counterproductive effects also occur when the prohibition is (ab)used to protect individual competitors rather than the competitive process. This risk is inherent in outlawing discounts practised by dominant firms without requiring proof of negative anti-competitive effects. Finally, this chapter has shown that the welfare consequences of exclusionary abuses are ambivalent. Therefore the possibility provided in the draft of advancing 'valid reasons' to justify those practices must be welcomed.

Within the confines of this chapter, it was not possible to discuss the entire draft of the Chinese competition law. There thus remains ample scope for further research. The control of mergers is the area of competition law where the impact of an economics-based approach has become most prominent. Some of the most relevant insights have been presented in the second section on market definition and market dominance. Other problems remain, such as the question as to the best suitable criterion for judging anti-competitive effects (creation of dominance, substantial lessening of competition or substantial impediment to effective competition) and the procedural framework for assessing mergers. Besides merger control, attention should equally be focused on problems of enforcement. What is the optimal level of sanctions for infringement of the competition rules? Can detection of cartels be furthered by way of a leniency policy? Should enforcement of competition law remain the exclusive domain of public authorities or is there also a role for private parties? These and other questions guarantee that the debate on the future Chinese competition law will remain a lively topic in the years ahead.

NOTES

* The author wishes to thank Thomas Eger for useful comments on a previous draft. The usual disclaimer applies.

1. Anti-Monopoly Law of the People's Republic of China, Draft for Comments, 8 April 2005.
2. Council Regulation (EC) No. 139/2004 of 20 January 2004 on the control of concentrations between undertakings, OJ L 24, 29.01.2004, pp. 1–22.
3. See Chapter 1 of this volume.
4. Craig and de Burca (2003).
5. Ordoliberalism is a German school of thought that was very influential in the period 1930–50 (see, for an overview, Gerber (1988, pp. 46 et seq.)). The ordoliberal view of society was distinguished by a search for a third way between capitalism (market economy) and socialism (command economy), which became known under the term of 'social market economy'. This term is remarkably close to the wording of Article 1 of the draft of the Chinese anti-monopoly law, which uses the term 'socialist market economy'. The ordoliberals accepted the main idea of classical liberalism, viewing economic freedom as the corollary of political freedom and competition as the main instrument to realize a free society. However, a legal framework was deemed necessary to protect individual economic freedom not only against governmental interference but also against private economic power. The ordoliberal ideas had a clear impact on the formulation of Article 82 EC Treaty, which mentions exploitative abuses of a dominant position and thus stresses goals of fairness and protection of individual economic freedom. This is different from Section 2 of the Sherman Act, which uses a formulation (prohibition of 'monopolizing'), which focuses above all on exclusionary conduct harming allocative efficiency and consumer welfare. Given these different perspectives and the objectives stated by Article 1 of the draft, the Chinese legislator may find the European experience more useful than the American one, for the purposes of developing rules on abuse of dominance that are best suited for the Chinese socialist market economy.
6. See DG Competition discussion paper on the application of Article 82 of the Treaty to exclusionary abuses, <http://europa.eu.int/comm/competition/antitrust/others/article_82_review.html>. See also EAGP, 'An economic approach to Article 82', downloadable from the same website address.
7. Contrary to the rules on cartel agreements and merger control, which are contained in Regulations, most of the rules on abuse of a dominant position have been laid down in judgments of the European Court of Justice (ECJ). Hence the status quo will probably remain since the ECJ case law takes precedence over Commission decisions. A decisive move towards an economics-based interpretation of Article 82 EC cannot come from the European Commission but must be made by the European Court of Justice.
8. Bishop and Walker (2002); Van den Bergh and Camesasca (2006).
9. Guidelines on the application of Article 81(3) of the Treaty, OJ C 101, 27.04.2004, at no. 13.
10. Examples include the German law on unfair competition (Gesetz gegen den unlauteren Wettbewerb) and the Belgian law on trade practices and the information and protection

of the consumer (Wet betreffende de handelspraktijken en de voorlichting en bescherming van de consument). For a comment on the German law, see Köhler and Piper (2006). For a brief comment on the Belgian law, see Dirix, Montangie and Vanhees (2005, pp. 346–404).

11. For example, the Dutch competition authority estimates the effects of enforcement of the Dutch competition law as high as 900 million euros for the period 2002 to 2004. See *Measuring the harm caused by cartels and assessing the benefits of competition enforcement – Analysing economic damage at the Netherlands Competition Authority (NMa)*, OECD Document DAF/COMP/WP3/RD (2005, p. 5).
12. Brodley (1987).
13. The relevant criterion is potential compensation, since actual compensation would again satisfy the Pareto criterion.
14. Compare Kaldor (1939) and Hicks (1941).
15. For a survey of numerous studies, see Scherer (1992). Recent empirical work arguing a positive correlation between competition and innovation includes Geroski (1990). Other authors found that large firms tend to innovate more, but industry concentration has a counteracting effect (Blundell, Griffith and Van Reenen, 1995).
16. The Cournot model assumes that firms produce a homogeneous product and that each firm chooses the quantity of output that maximizes its profits, taking competitors' output as given.
17. Froeb and Werden (1998, pp. 367–9).
18. The Bertrand model describes the competitive scenario in markets where firms produce non-homogeneous (differentiated) products, and therefore, compete in prices rather than quantities. In this model, firms fix the price for their products in order to maximize profits. In equilibrium, each firm cannot, by changing its price, increase its profits, given the prices of competitors.
19. The higher the demand substitutability among products, the smaller will be the anti-competitive effect.
20. Werden (1996, pp. 409–13).
21. Roberts and Salop (1995) and Lande (1982).
22. European Commission, *XV. Annual Report on Competition Policy 1985*, Brussels (1986).
23. Guidelines on the application of Article 81(3) of the Treaty, cited footnote 6, no. 4.
24. Another example, which shows that EC competition law is also still permeated by rules aiming at the protection of the individual economic freedom of market players, is the Regulation on distribution of cars, which lays down several requirements to protect the commercial freedom of the 'weak' car dealer against supposedly abusive behaviour by the 'strong' car manufacturer. See Commission Regulation (EC) No 1400/2002 of 31 July 2002 on the application of Article 81(3) of the Treaty to categories of vertical agreements and concerted practices in the motor vehicle sector, OJ L 203 (01.08.2002, pp. 30–41).
25. For an overview, see Craig and De Burca (2003, pp. 580–823).
26. This Regulation is qualified as a 'new-style' document since, contrary to the old Regulations, the emphasis is less on technical legal distinctions and more on the economic effects of certain practices. However, the safe harbour for manufacturers occupying a market share not higher than 30 per cent is not in perfect harmony with the criticisms in modern economic writings on structuralist approaches towards competition law (see section 2.2 of this chapter).
27. For graphical presentations, see Scherer and Ross (1990, pp. 541–8) and Utton (2003, pp. 235–8).
28. EC Commission Notice – Guidelines on Vertical Restraints, OJ C 291 (13.10.2000, no. 7).
29. EC Commission Notice – Guidelines on Vertical Restraints, OJ C 291 (13.10.2000, no 116 (2)).
30. Article 4(b) Commission Regulation (EC) No 2790/1999 of 22 December 1999 on the application of Article 81(3) of the Treaty to categories of vertical agreements and concerted practices, OJ L 336, 29.12.1999.

31. EC Commission Notice – Guidelines on Vertical Restraints, OJ C 291 (13.10.2000, no 119 (10)).
32. Spengler (1950).
33. Pardolesi (2001).
34. Case 85/76 *Hoffmann-La Roche & Co. AG* v. *Commission* [1979] ECR 461, paragraph 41.
35. Recital 32 of Council Regulation (EC) No 139/2004 of 20 January 2004 on the control of concentrations between undertakings (the EC Merger Regulation) OJ L 24 (29.01.2004, pp. 1–22).
36. See on the structure–conduct–performance paradigm and rival economic approaches to competition policy: Van den Bergh and Camesasca (2006, ch. 2).
37. A leading case in EC competition law is United Brands, in which it was held that there is a separate relevant market for bananas, given the specific characteristics of this product that make it especially valuable for particular groups of consumers (the very young and the very old) and not substitutable by other types of fruit. See Case 27/76 *United Brands Company and United Brands Continentaal BV* v. *Commission* [1978] ECR 207. This decision is criticized in Camesasca and Van den Bergh (2002).
38. In *Mercedes-Benz/Kässbohrer*, the European Commission distinguished different markets according to the loading capacity of trucks: between five and six tons and above 16 tons (Case IV/M 477, Decision of 14.02.1995, *Mercedes-Benz/Kässbohrer*, OJ L 211/1 (06.09.1995)).
39. In *Orkla/Volvo*, the European Commission argued that the price of beer is only one-fourth of the price of a similar quantity of wine and distinguished two separate markets accordingly (Case IV/M 582, Decision of 20.09.1995 *Orkla/Volvo*, OJ L 66/17 (16.03.19960)). This decision may be criticized, since the relevant question is whether a sufficient number of consumers would switch to beer in the case of a 5–10 per cent increase in the price of wine, so that the price increase would be unprofitable.
40. Van den Bergh (1996) and Desai (1997). Section 36 of the 1997 Notice does contain a nuance on the importance of product characteristics in that 'product characteristics and intended use are insufficient to show whether two products are demand substitutes'. If this statement is accepted at face value, the question remains why the traditional definition was not scrapped completely.
41. This is the main weakness of the EC Commission's Notice on market definition. For an elaboration of the relevant criticisms, see Camesasca and Van den Bergh (2002).
42. Products can be differentiated in any number of ways, including characteristics relating to the product itself (such as by brands, physical characteristics, or utility for the end user), or relating to how and to whom the product is sold (such as by channel of distribution, customers, or being sold as a cluster). See, for an overview, Keyte (1995).
43. Compare Chamberlin (1950) and Schmalensee (1982).
44. See, for further discussion: Van den Bergh and Camesasca (2006, pp. 348–75).
45. Examples of simulation analyses include the telecommunications industry (Hausmann and Leonard, 1997) and the trucks market (Ivaldi and Verboven, 2000).
46. Case COMP/M. 1672 *Volvo/Scania* [2001] OJ L 143/74.
47. Bechtold (1992, p. 352).
48. Geradin (2004).
49. See also Gal (2004).
50. On option (i) in particular, see Case IV/26.699 *Chiquita* [1976] O.J. L 95/1; Case 27/76 *United Brands* v. *Commission* [1978] E.C.R. 207; and Case 66/86 *Ahmed Saeed* [1989] E.C.R. 803.
51. On options (ii) and (iii) in particular, see Case 395/87 *Ministère Public* v. *Tournier* [1989] E.C.R. 2521; Joint Cases 110/88, 241/88 and 242/88 *Lucazeau* v. *SACEM* [1989] E.C.R. 2811; and Case 30/87 *Bodson* v. *Pompes Funèbres* [1988] E.C.R. 2479.
52. *Deutsche Telekom, 27th Annual Report on Competition Policy*, 77 (1997).
53. Case IV/28.851 *General Motors* [1975] O.J. L 29/14.
54. *Deutsche Telekom, 27th Annual Report on Competition Policy*, 77 (1997).
55. See, e.g., BGH, Wuw/E, BGH, 1454; BGH, *WRP*, 1980, 259.
56. See OFT Report (2005), *Classified Directories Advertising Services*.

57. The OFT measured profitability based on Return on Sales (ROS). ROS was found to be a more accurate indicator of profitability than Return on Capital Employed (ROCE) because ROS excludes goodwill (which is potentially high in this market but is also very difficult to value). In 2003, Yell's ROS was 37 per cent (for print directories only), whereas Thompson in the same year had a ROS of 27 per cent but covering all lines of business; however, the OFT viewed confidential information and reported that Thompson's Return on Sales on print alone did not change the OFT's view on its overall profitability.
58. See OFT Report (2005), cited above at note 56, at para. 34 *et seq*.
59. Pijnacker Hordijk (2002).
60. For a comparison of EC and US law, also from an economic perspective, see generally: Gal (2004).
61. *United States* v. *Aluminium Co. of America*, 148 F.2d 416 (2d Cir.,1945) at 430.
62. Evans and Padilla argue in favour of no *ex post* intervention, given the size of the error costs (Evans and Padilla, 2005).
63. *Verizon Communications Inc*. v. *Law Offices of Curtis V. Trinko, LLP*, 124 S. Ct. 872, 879 (2004). For a critical comment, see Gavil (2004).
64. At 21–2.
65. OJ, 1976, L 223/27 (Vitamins).
66. Case 85/76, 13 February 1979, ECR (1979, 535–51).
67. Case 322/81, 9 November 1983, ECR, 1983, 3518, at para. 83.
68. Case IV/D – 2/34.780, Virgin/British Airways. An appeal to the European Court of Justice was unsuccessful (Case T-219/99 *British Airways plc* v. *Commission*, 17 December 2003, not yet reported.
69. In British Airways no evidence supporting exclusionary behaviour was furnished. By contrast, British Airways' market share was in constant decline (from around 46 per cent to less than 40 per cent). The counter-argument that competitors had been able to gain market share was discarded by the European Commission, arguing that 'It can only be assumed that competitors would have had more success in the absence of these abusive commission schemes' (para. 107). The latter statement is typical of the Commission's lack of understanding of the relevant economics.
70. Office of Fair Trading, *Assessment of Individual Agreements and Conduct* (1999).
71. The recent discussion paper of the European Commission is largely based upon the existing case law of the European Court of Justice and does not really allow an effects-based approach. Efficiency considerations may justify a rebate system, but the burden of proof lies on the dominant firm. The requirements that a rebate system is indispensable to obtain cost advantages and that these benefits must be passed on to consumers seem to exclude a justification merely based on the need to recoup fixed costs.
72. McGee (1958) and Bork (1993, pp. 144–60).
73. See Bolton and Sharfstein (1990).
74. Milgrom and Roberts (1982).
75. Roberts (1986).
76. In its recent policy document (cited note 4) the European Commission states that the relevant question is whether the dominant company, by charging a lower price for its output over the relevant time period, incurred losses that could have been avoided by not producing that output. Average avoidable costs (AAC) are thus suggested as the relevant benchmark for assessing whether prices are predatory.
77. *Matsushita Elec. Indus. Co*. v. *Zenith Radio Co*., 475 U.S. 574 (1986); *Brooke Group* v. *Brown & Williamson Tobacco*, 125 L Ed 2d 168 (1993).
78. Case 62/86, *AKZO* v. *Commission*, ECR, 1991, I-3359; case T-83/91 *Tetra Pak International Sa* v. *Commission*, ECR (1994, II-755).
79. EC Commission Discussion Paper on Article 82, cited note 4, p. 35, no. 122.
80. Ibid., p. 38, no. 133.
81. In the game-theoretic models, the costs of the prey (not those of the predator) are the relevant benchmark.
82. See, for further discussion, Van den Bergh and Camesasca (2006, pp. 265–70).

REFERENCES

Arrow, K.J. (1962), 'Economic welfare and the allocation of resources for invention', in R. Nelson (ed.), *The Rate and Direction of Inventive Activity*, New York: Princeton University Press, p. 609.

Bechtold, R. (1992), 'Antitrust law in the European Community and Germany – an uncoordinated co-existence?', in B. Hawk (ed.), *Fordham Corporate Law Institute*, New York: Juris Publishing, p. 352.

Bishop, S. and M. Walker (2002), *The Economics of EC Competition Law*, 2nd edn, London: Sweet and Maxwell.

Blundell, R., R. Griffith and J. Van Reenen (1995), 'Dynamic count data models of technological innovation', *Economic Journal*, **105**, 333.

Bolton, P. and D.S. Scharfstein (1990), 'A theory of predation based on agency problems in financial contracting', *American Economic Review*, **80**, 93.

Bork, R.H. (1993), *The Antitrust Paradox. A Policy at War With Itself*, New York: Free Press.

Brodley, J.F. (1987), 'The economic goals of antitrust: efficiency, consumer welfare, and technological progress', *New York University Law Review*, **62**, 1025.

Camesasca, P.D.N. and R.J. Van den Bergh (2002), 'Achilles uncovered – revisiting the European Commission's 1997 market definition notice', *Antitrust Bulletin*, **46**, 146.

Chamberlin, E.H. (1950), 'Product heterogeneity and public policy', *American Economic Review*, **40**, 86.

Craig, P. and G. De Burca (2003), *EU Law. Text, Cases, and Materials*, 3rd edn, Oxford: Oxford University Press.

Desai, K.S. (1997), 'The European Commission's draft notice on market definition: a brief guide to the economics', *European Competition Law Review*, **18**, 476.

Dirix, E., Y. Montangie and H. Vanhees (2005), *Handels-en Economisch Recht in Hoofdlijnen*, Antwerp: Intersentia.

Evans, D.S. and A. Padilla (2005), 'Excessive prices: using economics to define administrable legal rules', *Journal of Competition Law and Economics*, **1**, 97.

Froeb, L.M. and G. Werden (1998), 'A robust test for consumer welfare-enhancing mergers among sellers of a homogeneous product', *Economics Letters*, **58**, 367.

Gal, M. (2004), 'Monopoly pricing as an antitrust offense in the U.S. and the EC: two systems of belief about monopoly?', *Antitrust Bulletin*, 343.

Gavil, A.I. (2004), 'Exclusionary distribution strategies by dominant firms: striking a better balance', *Antitrust Law Journal*, **72**, 3.

Geradin, D. (2004), 'Limiting the scope of Article 82 EC: what can the EU learn from the US Supreme Court's judgment in Trinko in the wake of Microsoft, IMS and Deutsche Telekom?', *Common Market Law Review*, **41**, 6.

Gerber, D.J. (1988), *Law and Competition in Twentieth Century Europe*, Oxford: Clarendon Press.

Geroski, P. (1990), 'Innovation, technical opportunity and market structure', *Oxford Economic Papers*, **42**, 586.

Hausmann, J.G. and G. Leonard (1997), 'Econometric analysis of differentiated products mergers using real world data', *Antitrust Law Journal*, 889.

Hicks, J.R. (1941), 'The rehabilitation of consumer's surplus', *Review of Economic Studies*, **9**, 108.

Ivaldi, M. and F. Verboven (2000), *Quantifying the Effects from Horizontal Mergers in European Competition Policy*, London: CEPR.

Kaldor, N. (1939), 'Welfare propositions in economics', *Economic Journal*, **49**.

Keyte, J.A. (1995), 'Market definition and differentiated products: the need for a workable standard', *Antitrust Law Journal*, **63**, 701.
Köhler, H. and H. Piper (2006), *Gesetz gegen den unlauteren Wettbewerb (UWG)Kommentar*, 4th edn, Munich: Beck.
Lande, R.H. (1982), 'Wealth transfers as the original and primary concern of antitrust: the efficiency interpretation challenged', *Hastings Law Journal*, **34**, 65.
McGee, J.S. (1958), 'Predatory price cutting: the Standard Oil (N.J.) Case', *Journal of Law and Economics*, 37.
Milgrom, P. and J. Roberts (1982), 'Predation, reputation and entry deterrence', *Journal of Economic Theory*, **27**, 280.
Pardolesi, R. (2001), 'Ritorno dall'isola che non c'è. Ovvero: l'intesa malintesa e l'integrazione del mercato come obiettivo dell'antitrust comunitario', *Mercato Concorrenza Regole*, 561.
Pijnacker Hordijk, E. (2002), 'Excessive pricing under EC Competition Law: an update in the light of Dutch developments', in B.E. Hawk (ed.), *2001 Fordham Corporation Law Institute*, 463.
Roberts, G.L. and S.C. Salop (1995), 'Dynamic analysis of efficiency benefits', *World Competition*, **19**, 5.
Roberts, J. (1986), 'A signalling model of predatory pricing', *Oxford Economic Papers (supplement)*, **38**, 75.
Scherer, F.M. (1992), 'Schumpeter and plausible capitalism', *Journal of Economic Literature*, **30**, 1416.
Scherer, F.M. and D. Ross (1990), *Industrial Market Structure and Economic Performance*, 3rd edn, Boston: Houghton Mifflin.
Schmalensee, R. (1982), 'Another look at market power', *Harvard Law Review*, **95**, 1800.
Schumpeter, J. (1943), *Capitalism, Socialism and Democracy*, New York: Harper Collins.
Spengler, J. (1950), 'Vertical integration and antitrust policy', *Journal of Political Economy*, **58**, 347.
Stigler, G. and R. Sherwin (1985), 'The extent of the market', *Journal of Law and Economics*, 555.
Tullock, G. (1967), 'The welfare costs of tariffs, monopolies and theft', *Western Economic Journal*, 224.
Utton, M. (2003), *Market Dominance and Antitrust Policy*, 2nd edn, Cheltenham, UK and Northampton, MA, USA: Edward Elgar.
Van den Bergh, R.J. (1996), 'Modern industrial organisation versus old-fashioned European competition law', *European Competition Law Review*, **17**, 82.
Van den Bergh, R. and P. Camesasca (2006), *European Competition Law and Economics. A Comparative Perspective*, 2nd edn, London: Sweet and Maxwell.
Werden, G.J. (1996), 'A robust test for consumer welfare enhancing mergers among sellers of differentiated products', *Journal of Industrial Economics*, **44**, 409.

5. The law and economics of professional regulation: what does the theory teach China?

Niels J. Philipsen*

1. INTRODUCTION

This chapter will address the economic theories of regulation with respect to professional services (such as those provided by lawyers, notaries, accountants, pharmacists, engineers and architects), as well as an application of these traditional theories to the People's Republic of China. In Europe and the United States, many professions are subject both to public regulation and to self-regulation by professional bodies. On the one hand this regulation may improve the quality of professional services, while on the other hand it may restrict entry into the profession and limit competition within the profession. For this reason, regulation of professional services has been a topic receiving much attention in the theoretical law-and-economics literature. In addition, questions about regulatory reform and deregulation in the professions have become important in practice, particularly in competition policy. In Europe the topic has been high on the political agenda for several years now. In 2003, the European Commission started an extensive investigation into the effects of regulation in the professions. The central question in this ongoing research by the European Commission is whether this kind of regulation serves the interests of users of professional services. In addition, national competition authorities in Europe such as the OFT in the United Kingdom, the Irish Competition Authority and the Dutch NMa, have shown a great interest in the (de)regulation of professional services.[1]

The structure of the discussion in this chapter is as follows. Section 2 contains a summary of the economic theories of regulation, as developed mainly (but not only) in the United States. Why do we need to regulate professional services in the first place and what regulatory instruments would be most suitable, according to law-and-economics theory? The famous public interest argument, which looks at regulation as a means to cure information asymmetry and externalities, will be explained first (section 2.1), as well as the private interest approach to regulation, which is rooted in public choice and Stigler's 'economic theory of regulation' (section 2.2). After that some of the different regulatory instruments are presented briefly (section 2.3). Some authors have attempted to test the economic theories empirically for individual professions in specific countries (again: mainly in the United States), but the number of such studies is limited because there has always been a problem of acquiring good empirical data (section 2.4). In section 3, subsequently, an overview is given of the current state of affairs in Europe regarding the regulation of professions and the actions taken by the European Commission within the framework of its professional services project. This will provide us with some interesting background information before moving to the application of economic theories of regulation to China, which is the subject of the following section. Indeed, in section 4, the question will be addressed to what extent the framework presented in section 2 also applies to China. And when it does not apply, what can we still learn from it, or how can the traditional model be tailored to the special situation in China? I will discuss the regulation of two professions in China in more detail: lawyers (section 4.2) and accountants (section 4.3). Before that, the 2003 Administrative Licensing Act of the People's Republic of China will be discussed (section 4.1). Finally, in section 5, I will present some concluding remarks.

2. ECONOMIC THEORIES OF REGULATION[2]

The views on regulation as found in the economic literature can broadly be divided into two (opposing) approaches: the public interest approach and the private interest approach. The former looks upon regulation as a possible remedy for so-called 'market failure'. The latter stresses the danger of rent-seeking behaviour by interest groups via lobbying or self-regulation. Both of these approaches, which have been discussed extensively in the economics literature (also in relation to professional services) will be recapitulated in this section.[3] After that I will address some regulatory forms that could be used to regulate the quality of professional services. Especially interesting in that respect are the advantages and disadvantages of self-regulation as opposed to public regulation. Finally, I will discuss some empirical literature on the effects of regulation of professional services.

2.1 The Public Interest Approach

The public interest approach presents a number of (potential) grounds for regulation. These have in common that they are derived from perceived shortcomings of the market system itself to deal with certain problems preventing an economically efficient outcome in a market.[4] Four kinds of market failure are generally discerned: (1) information problems, (2) externalities, (3) the presence of public goods, and (4) market power.[5] Intervention in the market, either by the government or by means of self-regulation, may be necessary to cure these problems. Such intervention could consist of (changes in) liability rules, taxes and subsidies, or some form of regulation, depending of course on the particular market failure. Moreover, liability rules can be used jointly with regulation.[6] The public interest approach to regulation assumes that regulatory intervention is always directed towards gaining an improvement in social welfare. However, one has to be careful in choosing the optimal form (instrument) of regulation, as regulation may generate costs that can outweigh the benefits.

Of the four kinds of market failure mentioned above, most important here is information problems. Markets for professional services are usually characterized by information asymmetry between professionals and clients. There are two main reasons for the existence of this information asymmetry: firstly, professional services generally involve application of the professional's human capital in order to judge individual cases; and secondly, evaluation of the quality of the service itself may be extremely difficult.[7] In addition, the provision of such services generally does not occur on a regular basis, so learning by repeat buying and reputation have only limited impact. Indeed, professional services are experience goods, the quality of which can only be determined after having consumed or used them, or trust goods, the quality of which cannot be assessed correctly even after consumption of the good.[8] The information asymmetry may give rise to a famous problem analysed by Akerlof: quality deterioration resulting from adverse selection.[9] If clients cannot evaluate the quality of professional services provided by individual professionals, but can only discriminate on price, professionals have no incentives to provide high-quality services. After all, as a result of the information asymmetry they cannot signal relative differences in the quality of their services. Bad professionals (quacks) will drive those who provide high-quality services out of the market and some form of quality regulation might be needed to convert the market outcome of low quality and low price into one characterized by high(er) quality and reasonable price. In addition to adverse selection, information asymmetry could lead to a moral hazard problem: demand generation. This occurs when additional services are provided by the professional, which consumers would not have wanted if they were fully informed.[10]

One needs to take into account, however, that the information asymmetry problem will be much smaller when users of professional services are not individual consumers (households) but business clients or public sector users. Big business users and public sector users can often be considered expert users, requiring services that are tailored to their needs. They want flexibility; and contracts with service providers are usually large and complex. Small business users may not have such expertise, but may nonetheless be repeat users of professional services. So in markets for professional services such as auditing, accountancy, architecture and engineering, information problems are likely to be less severe than in, for example, the market for medical services (pharmacists, physicians). The legal services market probably lies somewhere in-between, depending on the type of client. One thus needs to be careful in making generalizations: the specifics of the market under review should always be considered.[11]

A second possible public interest justification for regulation arises from the presence of externalities.[12] In the professions externalities appear if the quality of rendered services is poor and affects third parties. For example, a poorly designed or constructed building may collapse and cause casualties (architects or engineers). Or bad auditing services (auditors or accountants) may negatively affect decisions made by shareholders. Or, in the medical professions (physicians, pharmacists), the negative consequences of poor advice may affect others than the patient him/herself, for example, in the case of contagious diseases. Although the Coase theorem[13] teaches us that, in a market with no or very low transaction costs, parties could 'internalize the externality' by means of bargaining (by including a risk premium in the prices for professional services), this seems to have little relevance here. Indeed, in the market for professional services transaction costs are very high, mostly because of the high information costs. Another solution to the externality problem offered in the economic literature is to introduce a (Pigou) tax equal to the amount of the external costs, but again this solution does not seem practical for professional services. Quality regulation and liability rules[14] are likely to be better solutions to cure negative externalities in the professions.

The third market failure, the presence of public goods,[15] is less important here. Although it can be argued that some professional services serve a public goal (such as promoting public health, facilitating the good functioning of the judicial system, and so on) and may generate positive externalities, a 'free-rider problem' does not seem to occur in the market for professional services. The solutions offered in the economic literature to solve a pure public good problem, that is, production by the government or providing subsidies to public good providers, do not seem to be relevant for the professions.

Market power, the last kind of market failure mentioned above, results either from the existence of monopolies (possibly protected by law) and related market structures, or from cartel-like behaviour by a group of firms/suppliers. Naturally, market power is not always a problem: in the case of a so-called 'natural monopoly' it will be optimal to only have one or a few firms in a market. As far as the markets for professional services are concerned, we need regulation in the form of competition law to combat any cartel-like behaviour and abuse of dominant positions by, for example, professional associations. However, this is not the focus of this chapter.

The costs of correcting market failure by means of regulation have to be smaller than the efficiency gains from the regulation. Moreover, regulation should not go further (in limiting market entry or restricting competition) than is necessary to cure the prevailing market failure. The most efficient regulatory instruments should be chosen, taking into account the effects of regulation on consumer surplus, producer surplus and the deadweight welfare loss. For example, one should not use restrictive instruments such as price regulation or licensing systems when simple information regulation or certification systems work also. In practice, unfortunately, the choice between the many different regulatory instruments is hardly ever easy. The type of regulation to be used depends very much on the specific circumstances of a market. I will come back to this issue below (section 2.3).

2.2 The Private Interest Approach

The private interest approach, which has originated from public choice theory, the capture theory and the so-called 'economic (Chicago) theory of regulation',[16] stresses the influence of interest groups in the formation of regulation. The basic idea of this approach, formulated in a somewhat simplified form here, is that interest groups are continually influencing political decisions in order to seek rents for themselves, which is unproductive from a social welfare point of view.[17] After all, resources are devoted to capturing a wealth transfer from consumers to producers. Interest groups may have such a powerful influence on politicians that their efforts to obtain regulatory failures override general preferences. Professional associations are often small relative to the public at large, single issue-oriented and well organized. These are precisely the criteria that are likely to make an interest group successful in lobbying according to Olson (1965), particularly when information costs for the public at large (of finding out about the detrimental effects of rent seeking) are large. Politicians can be seen as the brokers of the wealth transfers that take place from the public to the interest groups.[18] Naturally, the danger of rent-seeking behaviour arises also in the case of self-regulation.[19]

According to Stigler (1971), regulation is acquired by the industry and is designed and operated entirely for its benefit.[20] He stated that every branch of industry which is powerful enough to do so will lobby the government for the erecting of entry barriers such as obligatory training or apprenticeships, product requirements, taxes, import quotas, and so on. Naturally, such rules are favourable to the insiders in a market. Likewise, a prohibition to advertise would lead to a less transparent market where the prices asked can and will be higher than in a market without advertising bans.[21] Becker (1983) later pointed to the fact that regulation can be the result of competition for political influence among many different interest groups. He unifies the view that governments correct market failures with the view that they favour the politically powerful. In Becker's model both are produced by the competition for political favours.[22]

2.3 Public Regulation and Self-Regulation

Examining the various types of regulation, one could make a distinction between entry regulation (also called market structure regulation) and conduct regulation. Entry regulation defines the conditions that have to be fulfilled by potential service providers in order to be allowed to practise the profession. Examples include educational requirements (in combination with registration, certification or licensing), an 'economic needs test' and a *numerus clausus* on the number of practitioners in the market. Conduct regulation covers all rules that directly regulate the conduct of professionals. These may range from, for example, advertising rules, restrictions on incorporation and interprofessional cooperation[23] and geographical and other restrictions on the exercise of the profession, to price regulation[24] in its various forms (minimum prices, maximum prices, fee schedules, advisory prices, and so on). Most of those rules can be in the form of either public regulation or self-regulation. Clearly, it would be impossible to discuss each regulatory instrument here. Instead I will only address, very briefly, the basic forms of quality regulation (as opposed to price regulation), as well as self-regulation.

2.3.1 Quality regulation

As far as quality regulation of professional services is concerned, several different forms of regulation could be used. Least restrictive of competition would be simple forms of information regulation such as mandatory information disclosure (product labels, websites and so on), passive regulation of advertising (including the prohibition to use misleading advertising) and certification. However, to disclose information on the quality of professional services is a complicated matter because it concerns experience goods or trust goods. Labels cannot be used for services and the information found on websites or elsewhere may be difficult to interpret for the average consumer. Certification may provide a better solution to information problems if consumers can recognize the value of the particular certificate or special title. However, professionals might be inclined to invest too much in education in order to signal high quality levels.[25] More restrictive than information regulation are various forms of entry regulation that exclude certain professionals from the market, such as mandatory registration and title protection (which may effectively exclude service providers without a title from the market) and licensing,[26] both of which are usually tied to specific requirements of education and practical experience. Such entry regulation may better insure risk-averse consumers against possible harmful consequences of bad services, provided there is a positive relationship between education level and service quality (which is not self-evident). Unfortunately, such regulation can be used as an entry barrier by interest groups, and it may incite consumers to substitute licensed services by alternatives.[27] Therefore, quality regulation should not limit market entry more than is necessary to cure the prevailing market failure. In other words, the regulation should be both *justified* (in order to cure the problem at hand) and *proportional*. The specific circumstances of the market (the level of information asymmetry, the extent of the externality problem, the 'public good' nature of the service, the risk of rent-seeking behaviour) must all be considered.

A related topic is that of the concepts of integrity and independence of profession members, often mentioned in professional codes and rules of conduct and used by professionals to justify all kinds of competition-restrictive behaviour. Indeed, in some cases these concepts may to some extent be related to service quality. However, one should be careful in using integrity and independence as a justification for regulation. It is, for example, not clear how a prohibition to advertise truthful information would be linked to a better quality of service. And although a lawyer should do his/her work independently and with integrity, this does not mean that the prices of legal services need to be regulated or that all cooperation with other professions should be prohibited.

Finally, a note on the combination of quality and price regulation. In some professions prices/fees or profit margins are fixed. A notable example is the pharmaceutical profession, where generally profit margins for pharmacists are determined by law (for example, a fixed fee per prescription), in addition to the regulated prices of medicines. In such a situation, where price competition is totally excluded, pharmacists would only be able to compete in quality, for example by offering individual advice to patients on medicine use, home-delivery, longer opening hours, providing pharmacotherapeutic information and advice to physicians, and so on. If, however, in such cases quality competition is restricted as well (as a result of either public regulation or self-regulation), all possibilities for competition in the market may be eliminated, which is not likely to be a proportional cure for market failure.[28]

2.3.2 Self-regulation

Many professions are subject to self-regulation[29] by professional bodies (such as the Bar, Order or any other professional association). These professional bodies are often drawn exclusively or predominantly from members of the profession itself. Thus, while public regulatory bodies are usually independent of the interests they regulate (or at least should be), this independence is totally absent in the professions. Although professional groups themselves argue that by means of self-regulation they aim for higher quality of services, self-regulation may also restrict competition and serve private interests rather than the public interest.

At first sight self-regulation seems to have some advantages as opposed to public regulation. Miller (1985) makes a case for more government reliance on self-regulation.[30] He argues that private parties (1) have more or better information on quality and risks than the government (or can get it at lower cost); (2) are less bureaucratic, which is especially valuable in dynamic markets where innovation is important and/or where consumer preferences change regularly; and (3) are better able to minimize the costs of regulation, including both enforcement and compliance costs. However, only the information argument has remained undisputed in the literature. The other arguments put forward by Miller may or may not be refuted on the basis of a private interest analysis: professions may lack appropriate incentives to control and enforce quality standards. In addition, one could argue that professional associations lack democratic legitimacy to do so. As stated above (section 2.1) one needs to consider the specifics of the market for each professional service and each country separately, by looking for qualitative and quantitative evidence of rent-seeking behaviour, and one should refrain from making generalizations on this point.[31]

2.4 Empirical Research[32]

In order to be able to analyse the extent to which regulation in a particular profession serves public or private interests (or none at all), it is often inevitable to do a quantitative (empirical) analysis in addition to the qualitative (theoretical) analysis. Although there are definitely some indications in the (mostly US-based) empirical literature backing up the private interest approach and its rent-seeking hypothesis, there is no real consensus in this literature on the actual incidence and consequences of rent-seeking behaviour in the professions. There seems to be a relative lack of empirical results as opposed to the amount of theoretical literature. In many papers and research reports that attempt to analyse the regulation of professions from a quantitative point of view, lack of data (especially on earnings, but also on prices and costs as a time-series) excludes the proper use of statistical and econometric models to assess the effects of restrictive regulation.[33] To some extent this can be explained by the difficulty in gathering data with respect to prices, tariffs, costs and incomes. Such data may be hard to obtain because of non-disclosure policies or (worse) because sometimes these data are just not available. Moreover, high incomes do not necessarily correspond to high rents; it is necessary to distinguish between supra-competitive profits and high incomes. A high income may also be – at least to some extent – an effect of investments in long training or a compensation for greater responsibilities. With respect to other indicators, such as quality of services, finding suitable ways of defining and measuring the indicators may be the main problem.

In some cases solutions to the data availability problem may be found in defining new indicators, such as amounts of goodwill paid (which may incorporate rents) as a proxy for incomes. Philipsen (2003) attempts to measure rents obtained by pharmacists by means of an analysis of takeover prices of pharmacies, because rents might be incorporated in the goodwill and the takeover price of the pharmacy.[34] Sometimes valuable empirical information (albeit less firm) may be found in defining 'indirect' indicators, such as the number of professionals and the number of practices. The latter indicators will especially be of interest when related to cases of changes in regulation and deregulation to answer questions such as 'do changes in regulation lead to more competition in the market?' and 'do changes in regulation have an effect on availability of services for consumers?' In the light of the current debate, especially in Europe,[35] it is necessary to continue research in this direction. In the remainder of this section I will present some key results of past empirical studies, focusing on the effects of entry regulation and advertising restrictions, respectively.

2.4.1 Entry regulation

According to economic theory, entry regulation, such as licensing (linked to a long and difficult educational track) and establishment restrictions, can give rise to significant restrictions of competition: the supply of a particular service may decline (because the number of professionals decreases) and mobility of professionals may be restricted, both leading to higher fees. In addition, consumers lose access to low-quality services and the earnings of professionals are likely to increase with restrictive licensing policies. On the other hand, licensing could of course lead to an increase in service quality.

Shapiro (1986) has proved formally that, if the relationship between human capital and high quality is indeed positive and if suppliers can build reputations over time by providing high quality, consumer welfare can be increased by licensing (or certification). However, Shapiro's model shows that this holds only if consumers value high quality significantly compared to the marginal costs of providing quality for suppliers. Moreover, licensing will never lead to a Pareto-improvement, because there will always be consumers who would rather have bought low quality goods or services at a lower price.[36]

There is a large body of literature on the effects of entry regulation on fees and quality of service. Cox and Foster (1990), in a US Federal Trade Commission report, review several of these studies. They conclude that, 'while a few studies indicate that higher quality levels may result from business practice restrictions, a majority of the studies finds quality to be unaffected by licensing or business practice restrictions associated with licensing'. Kleiner and Kudrle (2000) use data on the dental health of incoming Air Force personnel to analyse the effects of varying licensing restrictions among US states. The authors find that tougher licensing raises prices and profits (measured by hourly earnings per dentist) while it does not improve overall dental health (measured by complaints to dental licensing boards and malpractice premiums). In addition to these studies, the *Encyclopedia of Law and Economics*[37] refers, inter alia, to studies by Pfeffer (1974: on insurance agents and brokers, real estate brokers, salesmen and plumbers), White (1978: on clinical lab personnel), Perloff (1980: on the construction industry), Muzondo and Pazderka (1983: Canada) and Van den Bergh and Faure (1991: attorneys, architects, physicians and pharmacists in a number of European countries). All these studies have shown a positive relation between measures of licensing strictness and either costs, prices or earnings.

Price increases due to licensing may also lead to substitution effects, when consumers decide to do without the service, or decide to do the service themselves. Such substitution effects can be quite dangerous: for example, if consumers, rather than hiring an electrician, do their own electrical repair work. Carroll and Gaston (1981) found that stricter entry requirements for electricians, leading to lower per capita availability of electricians, are significantly associated with a rise in the rate of death from accidental electrocution.[38]

2.4.2 Advertising restrictions

Advertising of truthful information regarding price or service quality should not be restricted by regulation, unless the advertising is misleading. In practice, however, advertising bans are common in many professions.

Rather than decrease the information asymmetry on the market, advertising bans do just the opposite. Justifications for advertising bans given by the professional associations themselves, such as 'protecting the integrity of the profession' and 'respect for the profession's ethical standard', are not particularly convincing. Advertising bans as such do not increase the quality of the service. Moreover, as an instrument to prevent quality degradation that results from adverse selection, advertising restrictions seem to be disproportional.[39]

Economists have often analysed the effects of advertising restrictions for professional services and what happens to fee levels when such restrictions are relaxed. As early as 1975, Benham and Benham published a landmark paper on advertising restrictions concerning the US eyeglasses market. The authors found that prices were significantly higher in state markets with greater professional control on information. The increase in price as a result of advertising restrictions was estimated to be between 25 and 40 per cent.[40] Five years later, Bond et al. (1980) found that the average price for certain eye care services in the US was approximately 33 per cent higher in cities where restrictions prevent both advertising and commercial practice. Stephen and Love (2000) refer to an earlier study from 1996, where they review 17 studies on advertising and come to the conclusion that 'the general thrust of this empirical literature is that restrictions on advertising increase the fees charged for the profession's services and that the more advertising there is the lower the fees'.[41]

3. REGULATION OF PROFESSIONAL SERVICES IN EUROPE

In March 2000, the European Council adopted an economic reform programme with the aim of making the European Union (EU) the most competitive and dynamic knowledge-based economy in the world by 2010. This led inter alia to an extensive new research project on competition in professional services, conducted by Directorate-General (DG) for Competition. After all, professional services have an important role to play in improving the competitiveness of the European economy.[42] It is interesting to address briefly the progress of this research project here (before moving to the regulation in China), as it teaches us about the current state of affairs of regulation in Europe and the discussions about that.[43]

The first (public) step in the investigation of DG Competition concerned the publication in January 2003 of an independent study carried out by the Institute for Advanced Studies (IAS) in Vienna. This study includes a schematic overview of the regulation in the then 15 EU Member States for lawyers, notaries, accountants (including tax advisors), architects, engineers and pharmacists. For each of these professions IAS presents an overview of rules restricting the entry into the market and rules affecting market conduct. IAS also computes a so-called 'regulation index' for each profession and for each Member State,[44] which indicates the degree of regulation, with a value between 0 and 12. In order to compute the index, weights are assigned to each form of regulation. For instance, concerning market entry regulation, distinction is made between licensing, requirements in education and quota (such as a *numerus fixus* or an economic needs test), but the authors assign a relatively low weight to quota. Conduct regulation is subdivided into regulations on prices and fees, advertising, location, diversification, form of business and interprofessional cooperation, all having different weights, the highest being assigned to price and fee regulation. However, this does not alter the fact that the regulation indices generally provide a reasonable indication of the *level* of regulation in EU Member States, because a relatively large shift in the weights often leads only to a relatively small change in the value of the index.[45]

What catches the eye immediately is that the level of professional regulation differs widely from country to country. IAS presents (for each profession) a list of most and least regulated countries. Countries that are regulated the most, that is, those having a high regulation index for all or most professions, are Austria, Germany, Italy and Luxembourg (and possibly Greece). The middle group comprises Belgium, France, Spain and Portugal. The lowest regulation indices were found for Denmark, Finland, Ireland, the Netherlands, Sweden (except for pharmacists: all pharmacies are owned by the government) and the United Kingdom. Additionally, IAS observes that most rules can be found in the pharmaceutical profession, while architects and engineers are relatively unregulated.[46]

In Chapter 5 of its report, IAS gives the initial impetus to an empirical analysis at EU level. On the basis of data on – among other things – numbers of professionals and turnover related to population size and GDP (profit data are often not available), the authors come to two carefully formulated conclusions. Firstly, IAS concludes that there is no indication of malfunctioning of markets in relatively less regulated countries. This might suggest that some rules are unnecessary. Secondly, the authors state that less regulated countries have relatively lower revenues per professional, but a proportionally higher number of active professionals who generate a relatively higher overall turnover. This would suggest that more freedom in the professions is not a hindrance but rather a spur to overall wealth creation.[47] Some economists have criticized the empirical analysis in the IAS study because it uses turnover figures as an indication of profits. Also the assumption made in the study that the quality of professional services in the various EU Member States can be compared has been criticized. The results have to be interpreted very carefully, which is emphasized by the European Commission. However, if one considers that the empirical analysis in the IAS study is actually an impetus to further research at a comparative (European) level, it certainly offers interesting points of departure.

Right after the publication of the IAS report a stocktaking exercise started. Interested parties – that is, both profession members, their clients (companies, consumer associations and individual consumers) and public bodies – were invited to comment on the report by means of a questionnaire. All approximately 250 responses received by the Commission have been summarized and – if not confidential – made public via the Internet in October 2003.[48] The majority of the submissions concerned responses by individual profession members or their associations, trying to justify certain forms of regulation. Profession members often claim regulations are 'necessary to ensure the quality of the services' without giving any further explanations. Other common justifications for restrictive regulations are 'independence', 'integrity' and 'respect for the profession's ethical standard' – all rather hazy concepts. The Commission received relatively few submissions from consumer associations and businesses, which can roughly mean two things: (1) users of professional services are generally satisfied with the price and quality of services offered, or (2) these users are hardly capable of judging the quality of services offered and the content of (potentially) restrictive and price-boosting regulation, for example because they lack information or are not well organized. Anyway, even if in some cases (1) would be closer to the truth than (2), users apparently are not inclined to inform the Commission about that.

Simultaneously with the summary of responses the Commission published a second document, which offers an overview of the regulation of accountants, notaries, architects, engineers and pharmacists in the then 15 EU Member States.[49] This overview document has been composed on the basis of the IAS study and the responses to that. Both documents also served as background information for a conference on the regulation in the liberal professions, held on 28 October 2003 in Brussels and hosted by DG Competition. At this large-scale conference various interested parties were represented, including a large number of European associations of liberal professions, the European Commission, a number of national competition authorities and ministries, some consumer associations and some academics (lawyers and economists). Details regarding the speeches and discussions of this conference, among than a closure speech by then Commissioner Monti, are available at the website of DG Competition.

Monti's closing speech did not contain many new or surprising elements. Again, professional associations and individual Member States were called on to review critically the existing (public and self-) regulation and to reform or eliminate rules if need be, especially those concerning price fixing, recommended prices and advertising bans. Rules on business structure and multidisciplinary practices should according to Monti be decided on a case-by-case basis. These messages are also central in the Report on Competition in Professional Services, published by the Commission in February 2004.[50] That report also includes an overview of the *legal* state of affairs, that is, concerning the application of competition law to the liberal professions and the greater role assigned to national competition authorities and courts in enforcing competition law as of May 2004. A follow-up report was published in 2005, discussing the progress in eliminating restrictive and unjustified rules. Apparently, most progress is being made in Denmark, the Netherlands and the United Kingdom, which are countries 'where there is a structured programme of pro-competitive or regulatory reform in place. [. . .] In other countries the reform process has not yet got underway, or can best be described as haphazard'. However, overall, 'there has been some substantive progress in refining and eliminating disproportionate restrictions to competition in legislation and in the rules and regulations of professional bodies during 2004/05'.[51]

4. REGULATION OF PROFESSIONS IN CHINA

When applying 'western' theories of competition and regulation to fast developing countries in the east, such as China, one has to bear in mind that there may be huge differences between legal systems. Some traditional law-and-economics theories may simply not apply to fast developing countries, or need to be adapted to some extent to take account of, for example, particularly large information asymmetries and law enforcement differences. However, as Williams (2005) put it: 'a one size fits all mentality is often apparent, that demonstrates either a bias towards the foreign consultants' own familiar but complex system and/or a lack of knowledge of the realities of government and law enforcement in eastern countries'.[52] In the case of competition law, for example, often comprehensive competition law systems have been adopted by developing countries throughout the world that did not have the appropriate infrastructure to support their effective implementation.

Clarke (2003b) discusses such problems for the specific case of the Chinese legal system. He argues that understanding the Chinese legal system is very difficult for western researchers just because it is so very different from their own legal system. Hence particular characteristics of the Chinese system are easily overlooked. Often a so-called 'Ideal Western

Legal Order' approach is used (explicitly or implicitly) that leaves unstated and unjustified its most crucial component: the ideal against which the Chinese legal system is identified and measured, which may in many cases be an ideal that does not even exist in western states.[53]

The rather modest goal of this section is to look at some laws and regulations that have been implemented in China with respect to entry regulation (in the form of licensing) generally and with respect to the regulation of two specific professions: lawyers and accountants. Although I will attempt to relate the Chinese regulation to the economic framework discussed in section 2, in doing so I will take into account the special characteristics of China. The analysis in this section will necessarily be brief and, moreover, it will be practically impossible to discuss some specific but important issues such as the actual enforcement of laws and regulations. Nonetheless, this section should present a handy picture of some developments in professional regulation in China, and I will give some indications as to how the 'traditional' theories of regulation could be tailored to China.

4.1 The Licensing Act

Before discussing the specific regulation of lawyers and accountants, it is interesting to examine the more general conditions applying to licensing in China, in particular because the relevant law is a very recent one. On 1 July 2004 the *Administrative Licensing Act of the People's Republic of China* of 27 August 2003[54] (*zhong hua ren min gong he guo xing zheng xu ke fa*; hereinafter: Licensing Act) entered into force. This act includes general guidelines as to the question whether a licensing system may or may not be established by public bodies. Following Zhang (forthcoming, 2007), I will make a distinction between 'positive guidelines' and 'negative guidelines'. According to Article 12 of the Licensing Act, which contains the positive guidelines, the following activities, products, or occupations may be governed by licensing:

a. any activity that directly affects national security, public safety, macroeconomic control, ecological environment protection, human health, and safety of life and property, which shall be approved according to the legal requirements;
b. the development and utilization of limited natural resources, the allocation of public resources, and market entry to special industries directly related to the public interest, which shall be entitled with special rights;
c. any vocation or trade that provides services to the public or is essential to the public interest, and requires a high reputation, special talents and skills;

d. any product, equipment or facility that directly affects public safety or human health and property safety, which shall be examined or inspected in accordance with specific technical conditions or norms;
e. any establishment of enterprises and other institutions; and
f. other activities or products that may be subject to licensing controls in accordance with laws and regulations.[55]

Obviously, item (c) refers to the professions. I noted in section 2 that, according to economic theory, regulation in the form of licensing or otherwise may be necessary to solve particular forms of market failure in professional services markets, notably information asymmetry (which may be low or high, depending on the type of client and the specific professional service), negative externalities and possibly some public good justification (such as public health). Chinese law, in the form of the 2003 Licensing Act, apparently shares this mode of thought and, although I will not discuss items (a), (b) and (d) here, at first sight they seem to be justifiable – at least to some extent – from a public interest point of view. However, the public interest justifications for items (e) and (f) are far less clear. Business licensing (mentioned in Article 12 under item (e) has been discussed in a recent paper by Ogus and Zhang (2005). They argue that the provision of information by means of *registration* reduces the administrative costs of regulation (for example, the costs of levying taxes). And, if necessary, such registration will also facilitate law enforcement.[56] But *licensing* of course goes further than registration and may be disproportional. Thus there might be other explanations for including business licensing in Article 12, such as potential revenue-raising explanations or private interest explanations (in particular with regard to the private interests of politicians and public officials). A related issue is corruption: there is empirical evidence of a causal relationship between excessive regulation and corruption, including evidence on corruption in public offices dealing with business licences in China.[57] Item (f), finally, leaves open the possibility to use licensing in any situation, even if none of the criteria mentioned under (a) to (e) have been fulfilled. The inclusion of item (f), which supposedly was meant to catch any omissions from the list of positive guidelines, could also have been a result of (and can still give rise to) rent-seeking behaviour, for example by those formulating the legislation. Unfortunately it is difficult to make firm statements, as there is only limited information on the issue of rent seeking in China. Moreover, the law-making process itself is quite untransparent: much information is treated as sensitive by the government.[58]

If a (potential) licensing regime meets one of the criteria (a) to (e) defined in Article 12, it may not be established if it does not meet also the negative guidelines. The negative guidelines can be found in Article 13 of the

Licensing Act. Any aforesaid activity or product may not be subject to licensing control if (a) it can be decided upon by citizens, legal persons or other institutions themselves, (b) it can be regulated effectively by market competition mechanisms, (c) it can be regulated effectively by self-regulatory bodies, or (d) it can be governed successfully by ex post regulatory controls or through other administrative methods.[59]

Of special interest for this chapter are subsections (b) to (d). Article 13(b) broadly states that competition is preferred to public regulation. In the light of the economic theories discussed in section 2,[60] this sounds promising. In writing at least, here the Chinese lawmakers seem to follow the western models based on neoclassical economics and the belief that the market is able to solve many problems itself – a belief that is often associated with the Chicago School of economics, but is central in many economic schools of thought and in industrial economics generally. Of course, this Chinese 'trust' in western economic models of competition can also be found in the recent proposal for a Chinese competition law: the 2004 Draft Anti-Monopoly Law (which followed the 1999 draft version and modifications to that draft in 2001). One may, however, pose the question to what extent this proposal has resulted from pressure by transnational organizations, but I will not address this question here.[61] Article 13(c) of the Licensing Act states that, as a rule, self-regulation is preferred to public regulation. As discussed above,[62] this is not always obvious: it depends on the question whether or not there is a risk of rent-seeking behaviour by special interest groups. But again, it shows China's willingness to adopt market-based economic strategies.

Article 13(d) deals with the issue of the choice of regulatory instruments. This provision states explicitly that ex post measures are preferred to ex ante control (prior approval) such as licensing, provided that ex post regulatory measures can offer a solution to the problem at hand. Indeed, we noted above that the least interventionist regulatory instrument should be chosen: regulation should both be justified and proportional.[63] However, the costs of regulation, both administrative and social, are not mentioned at all in Article 13(d), which makes this provision somewhat vague. Obviously the costs have to taken into account as well in choosing the optimal regulatory instrument. And what about private law remedies? In some cases liability rules might offer an even better solution to particular problems than both ex post and ex ante regulation, but this possibility is not mentioned in Article 13.[64] Then again, private law remedies may be less effective in China than in western economies. I will come back to this issue below.

The following Articles of the 2003 Licensing Act contain some provisions on who is allowed to pass licensing laws and, thus implicitly, who is not allowed to do so. Article 14 holds that, at national level, only the National People's Congress and its Standing Committee (which together exercise the legislative power of the state)[65] have the authority to pass licensing laws, regulations and rules affecting all territories in China. Article 15 holds provisions regarding the local level. There are three levels of local People's Congresses and their Standing Committees (provincial, provincial capital cities and other relatively large cities),[66] and they have somewhat limited authority to pass licensing regulations governing their local affairs. In the case of an immediate need to impose a licensing control, local governments are allowed to pass a licensing regulation that is valid for one year only.[67]

Summarizing, although the central government has the final say in allowing or not allowing licensing regimes, the provisions in the Licensing Act (especially Article 13) generally seem to follow a market-based approach. Article 12(f) creates opportunities for rent seeking by the government, but there is no empirical evidence of this actually occurring, considering the very recent introduction of this Act and the fact that in general there is limited information on rent-seeking behaviour in China. The fact that professions are included in the Licensing Act seems only natural, following both economic theory and the current regulations in European countries, where most professional services are regulated by some kind of licensing or title protection regime.

4.2 Regulation of Lawyers

In Imperial China, and until the early decades of the People's Republic of China, there were relatively few lawyers compared to the number of lawyers in the western world. This may to some extent be explained by Chinese people having sought to address their problems mainly through reliance upon morality, custom, kinship or politics, rather than legal formality.[68] However, in the period 1980–93, the Chinese legal profession multiplied more than twenty-fold from a base of 3000 members (which it had also in 1957) to well over 60 000.[69] Clarke (2003a) reports two different sources stating, respectively, that at the end of 1998 there were 80 000 full-time lawyers and 20 000 part-time lawyers; and that in 2000 there were 110 000 lawyers in total.[70] Alford (1995) noted that these changes were 'not merely a matter of numbers. Individuals who once toiled for the state at modest, officially prescribed rates are now serving the people – provided the people can afford the going hourly rate – over portable phones and power lunches through co-operative law firms [. . .] with nation-wide and international ambitions that bear more than a faint resemblance to their private foreign counterparts'.[71] Indeed, some more general changes that influenced the legal profession eventually gave rise to the introduction of new legislation in 1996, which will be described below. First, however, let us take a quick glance at the development of the legal profession in the period 1980–95.[72]

The *Interim Regulations of the People's Republic of China on Lawyers* (*zhong hua ren min gong he guo lü shi zan xing tiao li*), which were adopted in August 1980 and became effective as of 1 January 1982,[73] provided that lawyers are 'state legal workers' (*guo jia fa lü gong zuo zhe*). State legal workers have an obligation to protect socialism and the state. Their task is 'to give legal assistance to state organs, enterprises and institutions, public organisations, people's communes and citizens in order to ensure the correct implementation of the law and protect the interests of the state and collectives as well as the lawful rights and interests of citizens.'[74] 'Legal advisory offices' (*fa lü gu wen chu*) were owned and run by the government, under the supervision of the Ministry of Justice and its affiliates.[75] Prices were fixed at low levels for the state's enterprises and people, but were different for the occasional foreign companies seeking legal advice. In addition, in rural areas, special 'legal service offices' (*fa lü fu wu chu*) were opened, staffed largely by relatively unqualified lawyers, that is, paraprofessionals. The fact that lawyers were considered 'state legal workers' in the early and mid-1980s is no surprise: they were involved mainly in facilitating the accomplishment of administratively directed undertakings. Indeed, in a planned economy all important industrial enterprises are owned by the state, which also determines what those enterprises are to do, with whom, on what terms, and remedies for failure to comply.[76] However, this situation started to change soon after that, in the wake of the opening up of economic markets and the growing number of private enterprises in China, which required far more extensive and complex legal rules and led to a growing number of legal disputes. The first reaction of the state to these developments was to allow more and more 'state legal workers' on the market. But changes in the organizational structure (and notably licensing) of the legal profession followed soon, with the introduction of national bar examinations (in 1986) in addition to the previous stress on experience and education as a measure of expertise.[77] However, lawyers were still lacking professional independence from the Chinese Communist Party.

The *Law of the People's Republic of China on Lawyers* (*zhong hua ren min gong he guo lü shi fa*; hereinafter: Lawyer's Act)[78] was adopted on 15 May 1996 and later amended in December 2001. The introduction of this Act in 1996 was a reaction to the changes mentioned above, in particular to the growing number of disputes, not only between private parties but also between private parties and the state. With regard to the latter, Chinese lawyers (being 'state legal workers') were of course likely to experience conflicts of interest and therefore they were looking for more independence from the state. According to Article 2 of the Lawyer's Act, a lawyer is no longer a 'state legal worker' but instead 'a practitioner who has acquired a lawyer's practice certificate pursuant to law and provides legal services to the public'. Also, 'to practise law, a person shall acquire the qualifications of a lawyer and a practice certificate'.[79] Both Articles have remained unchanged by the 2001 amendments. The 2001 amendments did, however, make entry into the All-China Lawyers' Association (the Bar) more difficult, by adopting a uniform national judicial examination.[80] Foreigners apparently are excluded from taking the exam – and hence from becoming a lawyer in China.[81] Article 8 of the Lawyer's Act contains some additional requirements, such as the condition that each applicant must be a person of good character and conduct and must uphold the Constitution, and also specifies that each applicant must have had a practice training in a law firm for one year. There are quantitative limits to the number of people receiving a licence, determined by the Ministry of Justice together with the Supreme People's Court and the People's Prosecuting Authority. This limit should (in theory) be based on the actual demand for judges, prosecutors and lawyers.[82]

Chapters 5 and 7 of the 2001 Lawyer's Act make it clear that the All-China Lawyers' Association and the local lawyers associations do not have the power of self-regulation. However, they have to perform the following (general) duties:

1. Ensuring that lawyers practise in accordance with the law and protecting lawyers' lawful rights and interests;
2. summarizing and exchanging lawyers' work experiences;
3. organizing professional training for lawyers;
4. conducting education in, inspection of, and supervision over, the professional ethics and practice disciplines of lawyers;
5. making arrangements for exchanges between Chinese and foreign lawyers;
6. mediating disputes arising in lawyers' practice activities; and
7. other duties prescribed by law.[83]

Access to the All-China Lawyers' Association is still controlled by the Ministry of Justice and its affiliates. Every lawyer must join his local association and, after joining the local association, he is at the same time a member of the All-China Lawyers' Association.[84] The All-China Lawyers' Association is funded by mandatory fees levied on law firms by the Ministry of Justice.[85] Article 45 of the Lawyer's Act describes the situations in which the 'judicial administration department of the people's government of the province, autonomous region, or municipality directly under the Central government' shall revoke the licence of a practitioner: for example, in case of divulging state secrets, bribing and providing false evidence.[86] Also, lawyers have to register their licence once a year and pay the corresponding fee; unregistered licences are not valid.[87] All of this creates opportunities for rent-seeking behaviour by public officials in the Ministry of Justice and its affiliates, although there is no empirical evidence of this.

The professional monopoly and the title 'lawyer' are protected by Article 14 of the Lawyer's Act, which states that, without a practice certificate, no-one is allowed to use the title 'lawyer', nor may such persons act as an agent *ad litem* or defend an entrusting party 'for the purpose of seeking economic benefit'. However, Zhang (forthcoming, 2007) states that, according to the Criminal Procedure Law, the Civil Procedure Law and the Administrative Procedure Law, laypersons who are *not* making a profit from it are indeed allowed to act as a defending advocate in criminal cases or an agent *ad litem*. And, moreover, anyone is allowed to provide other legal services such as legal advice.[88]

Other important provisions in the Lawyer's Act are those on the establishment of law firms. Article 12 contains a geographical restriction in that lawyers are allowed to practise in one law firm only. As regards such firms, lawyers are allowed to establish cooperative law firms or partnership law firms,[89] but there is one important condition: they need a separate 'law firm practice certificate', issued by the people's government at or above the level of the province, autonomous region or municipality directly under the Central Government.[90] Article 15 defines a minimum capital requirement (100 000 RMB) for establishing a law firm, whereas two other requirements are laid down in the 2004 *Partnership Law Firms Regulations* (*he huo lü shi shi wu suo guan li ban fa*): there must be at least three full-time lawyers and each of them must have more than five years' working experience.[91] Individual lawyers are prohibited from undertaking business with clients and to collect fees from them; only law *firms* are allowed to do so.[92] Clearly, these regulations on the establishment of law firms constitute a second 'level' of licensing in China, which may hamper entry into the market. The high level of state intervention in the legal profession has been criticized in the literature, but there has been no response to such criticism.[93]

In December 1993 (before the introduction of the Lawyer's Act) the Ministry of Justice had already issued a *Guide to Lawyers' Professional Ethic and Practicing Discipline* (*lü shi zhi ye dao de he zhi ye ji lü gui fan*). Article 15 of this regulation, which deals with fair competition between lawyers, includes a prohibition to advertise via public media (subsection 5) and a prohibition to 'lower the prices competitively or even charge nothing' (subsection 2).[94] Article 12 states that lawyers are not allowed to charge their clients privately or accept money or things of value from them, which is comparable to the provisions on law firms in the Lawyer's Act. The *Code of Ethics and Practice Discipline for Lawyers* was adopted by the All-China Lawyers' Association in 1996 and contains similar provisions. However, according to the Institute of Developing Economies (2001), moral hazard by lawyers is not uncommon:

> The practice of Chinese lawyers in reality is, generally speaking, highly recommendable, although violation of professional ethics and discipline by lawyers is not a rare phenomenon in China. Engaging in unfair competition by various means, such as soliciting business by paying middleman's fees and kickbacks and exerting unjust influences on judicial personnel are relevantly widespread phenomena in China. Incidents of lawyers squandering the money of clients, accepting or asking for unjust payment from clients, catering for the unjust demands of clients and maliciously collaborating with others to harm the interests of clients are also common in China. [. . .] Therefore, strengthening the professional ethics and practice discipline of lawyers remains an important task in the construction of the lawyer's system in China.[95]

Applying the 'western' economic theories presented in section 2, we can find various potential justifications for regulation of legal services. Leaving out all details here,[96] there are broadly three arguments for regulation of lawyers: (1) legal services may be considered 'credence goods', leading to the information asymmetry problems of adverse selection and moral hazard (this argument will not apply for commercial clients who are repeat buyers of legal services); (2) low-quality legal services provided by incompetent professionals and improper behaviour by lawyers may give rise to negative externalities affecting either third parties, the court system, or the public at large; and (3) regulation may be needed in the (rather unlikely) case that there is an undersupply of legal services because of positive externalities. In China, the information asymmetry problem is probably more serious than in the west. Many people in China are insufficiently educated about the law and the availability of legal services, at least more so than people in the west,[97] whereas the Chinese government even discourages lawyers from disclosing information about their services. The introduction of some kind of minimum quality standard, as in the current Chinese regulation (and in all western countries),[98] therefore seems warranted. However, one should be careful not to define too strict entry requirements, and in that respect one should be aware also of the risk of rent-seeking behaviour by insiders on the market.[99] The latter risk could be reduced in theory if certificates were used instead of licences; but then consumers should be able to judge the quality of the different certificates. This is not likely to be the case in the Chinese legal services market. An alternative to regulation might be tort law. However, tort law has some shortcomings here, considering the information problem in identifying the quality of legal services and the often diffuse nature of the possible harm caused by low-quality services.[100] In addition, Zhang (forthcoming, 2007) refers to a distinct feature of traditional Chinese culture: 'shame at litigation'.

Furthermore, while the professional monopoly of lawyers in acting as agents *at litem* might have resulted in a situation where the many poor people do not have access to legal services, this problem has been reduced to some extent by allowing the above-mentioned 'local legal workers' on the market in rural areas – which is actually contrary to Article 14 of the Lawyer's Act. Zhang (forthcoming, 2007) reports that in 2001 there were 115 816 of those para-professionals on the market, which is comparable to the number of lawyers.[101] On the other hand: one may wonder whether the (presumably lower-quality) services provided by these para-professionals increase the risk of negative externalities; and if they do not, one may wonder why Article 14 is still there. It will be impossible here, within the limits of this chapter, to make a further assessment of the entry restrictions in the legal profession in China. Further qualitative and (if possible) quantitative research into the effects of the Chinese legislation would be necessary to formulate hard conclusions about the public or private interest nature of this regulation.[102]

In that respect it is important to make one (rather obvious) final remark here: one needs to be careful in making generalized statements about the legal profession in China or about the application of the law by Chinese judges and courts. Apart from being controlled by the Ministry of Justice, the roles of lawyers, judges and courts are very different from the roles they have in traditional common law and civil law countries.[103] For example, Chinese courts still have a tradition of inquisitorial legal procedure instead of the common law tradition of adversarial legal procedures, and hence the role of lawyers may be smaller (compared to the judge) than it is in western countries such as the United States and the UK.[104] Clarke (2003a and b) discusses some of these differences between China and western states in more detail, but also notes that 'at the moment, only some very basic information is known about lawyers [in China], and very little is known about the financial structure and internal workings of law firms'. And, with respect to courts, 'They have a larger, more complex role to play [in China]. We may misunderstand a key feature of court functioning if we measure their activity using indices designed for institutions with a different mission.'[105]

4.3 Regulation of Accountants

As a second case study of professional regulation in China, I would like to turn briefly to the accountancy profession. In general, the accountancy profession conducts a wide range of activities such as auditing, accountancy and bookkeeping, and tax consultancy. Even within Europe the structure of the accounting profession and dividing lines between these activities vary quite considerably between the Member States.[106] With regard to China, I will focus on the so-called 'certified public accountants'. Following economic theory, that is, the public interest approach to regulation as discussed above,[107] regulation of accountants may be necessary to cure negative externalities: indeed, bad auditing or accounting may generate severe losses for third parties. Furthermore, a uniform accounting system can be considered a public good and this requires some (general) legislation regarding accounting services. However, information problems such as moral hazard and adverse selection may be relatively small in this specific market: clients are mostly public or private enterprises that require accounting or auditing services on a regular basis and 'demand generation' for accounting services is not very likely. Finally, accountants should be independent of their clients and should be reliable, but this does not mean they have to be subject to strict regulations.

The Chinese accounting market is developing rapidly because of the fast economic developments that have taken place since the early 1980s (the development of many private enterprises, investments by foreign companies, the development of the capital market, and so on). However, China also has more than 170 000 state-owned enterprises (numbers relate to 2004), among them some very large enterprises. These require a large amount of human and financial resources to be audited. Given that China resumed the development of the accountancy profession only in 1980, the number of firms that can audit such gigantic state-owned enterprises is still relatively small, according to Chen Yugei, Secretary General of the public professional body for Certified Public Accountants CICPA.[108] Nonetheless, at the moment (numbers relate to 2005), the CICPA has over 5000 organizational members and over 130 000 individual members.[109]

Liu (2005) states that 'the Chinese government and the CICPA have implemented a series of reform measures to promote standardization of the profession, rectify order of the accounting market, promote development of professional integrity and upgrade public credibility of the profession'.[110] Indeed, with regard to accountancy, there is, firstly, a more general law called the *Accountancy Law of the People's Republic of China (zhong hua ren min gong he guo kuai ji fa)*. This law was approved on 21 January 1985, amended twice (29 December 1993 and 31 October 1999), and became effective as of 1 July 2000.[111] Article 1 states that the Accountancy Law 'is stipulated to standardize accountancy, guarantee real and complete accounting data, strengthen economic and financial management, enhance economic results and maintain the order of the socialist market economy'.

The Accountancy Law provides that accountancy nationwide is supervised by the finance department of the State Council,[112] whereas at local level the finance departments of the local people's governments are in charge of accountancy within their administrative areas (Article 7). There is a unitary accounting system, formulated by the State Council, which is laid down in Chapters 2 and 3 of the Accountancy Law. The responsible finance department shall supervise the procedures used by accounting firms to issue audit reports, as well as, among other things, the content of their audit reports (Articles 31 and 32). Provisions with regard to accounting organs and accounting personnel are laid down in Chapter 5. All accountants must have a qualification certificate, and 'chief accountants'[113] must also have the professional title of at least an accountant or over three years of experience in accountancy (Article 38). Professional ethics must be observed by all accountants, and their education and training shall be improved (Article 39). Furthermore, Article 36 provides that 'large and medium-sized state-owned enterprises, as well as large- and medium-sized enterprises whose state-owned assets control the stocks or play a leading role in them, shall employ a general accountant, whose qualifications for the post, appointment and dismissal procedures, and responsibilities and powers shall be stipulated by the State Council'. There is thus direct supervision from the central government over accounting in these enterprises.

Secondly, a number of more detailed provisions have been incorporated in the *Law of the People's Republic of China on Certified Public Accountants* (*zhong hua ren min gong he guo zhu ce kuai ji shi fa*) of 31 October 1993, which became effective on 1 January 1994.[114] Article 2 defines a CPA as a 'practising accountant who has lawfully received the certificate of CPA and accepts assignments for auditing, accounting consultation, or other accounting-related service'. According to Articles 3 and 16, all CPAs must be members of an accounting firm and accept assignments only via that firm, which is comparable to the situation for lawyers discussed in the previous subsection. The establishment of an accounting firm is subject to some conditions included in Articles 23 (on partnerships), 24 (conditions for a legal entity with limited liability)[115] and 25 (a list of documents that must be submitted to the finance department of the State Council). Also the establishment of branch offices must be approved by the responsible local finance department (Article 27). Articles 7–13 contain provisions on examination and registration of CPAs. There is a national uniform system of examinations, regulated by the State Council and administered by the above-mentioned professional body, CICPA (Article 7). Next, 'those who have passed the national uniform examination of CPAs and have been engaged in the auditing services for more than two years can apply to the institutes of CPAs of provinces, autonomous regions, and municipalities directly under the central government for registration as CPAs'.[116] Some reserved tasks for CPAs are defined in Article 14; these include issuing an auditing report for enterprises, issuing a capital verification report, and performing audits related to a merger, splitting or liquidation of an enterprise.

Thirdly, there is a specific law on auditors called the *Audit Law of the People's Republic of China* (*zhong hua ren min gong he guo shen ji fa*) of 31 August 1994, which for reasons of space will not be discussed here. According to the Audit Law, government audit institutions are responsible for auditing state-owned enterprises, state-owned monetary organizations, social security funds, and so on.[117]

The accounting market is one of the first markets that was opened up by China to the outside world. The market has already been liberalized since the 1980s, especially by permitting foreign accounting firms to set up their representative offices in China,[118] by permitting them temporarily to carry out audits in China,[119] and by permitting them to identify their member firms there.[120] Also overseas members of CICPA have been allowed since the 1980s to apply for the Chinese CPA certificate.[121] There are, however, some conditions that need to be fulfilled by foreign applicants in order to become a CPA in China, that is, in order to receive a professional qualification. Apart from having passed the national uniform CPA exam, applicants should be working in a Chinese accounting firm and have accumulated at least two years of experience in independent auditing – as is also the case for Chinese applicants. In addition, he or she should have a fixed domicile or a fixed liaison domicile in China and have a residence record there of at least one year. According to CICPA President Liu Zhongli, in 2005 several hundred overseas candidates passed CICPA exams and over 30 of them succeeded in applying for the Chinese CPA qualification.

As in the legal services market, there is only limited room for self-regulation by accountants in China. Although the CICPA has published a *Charter of the Chinese Institute of Certified Public Accountants*[122] (*zhong guo zhu ce kuai ji shi xie hui zhang cheng*), this professional body is not at all independent from the central government. The CICPA has been founded in accordance with the Law on Certified Public Accountants and is subject to the supervision of the Ministry of Finance and the Ministry of Civil Affairs.[123] Moreover, the publication of the Charter is a direct result of Article 34 of the Law on Certified Public Accountants. Notwithstanding this, the CICPA has many functions and responsibilities of its own, which have been defined in Article 5 of the Charter. These include examining and approving applications for CICPA membership, drawing up and monitoring professional standards and rules,[124] organizing national uniform exams, organizing and promoting training activities, and quite a few more. Membership is mandatory both for individuals and for accounting firms, and 'membership dues have to be paid in accordance with regulations'.[125] The latter of course creates opportunities again for rent seeking, as was also discussed above, in the subsection on lawyers.[126] If a member fails to perform his or her duties, or becomes no longer qualified, the Council of the institute may request him or her to leave the CICPA (Article 10). Lin (2004) found that 'the majority of audit beneficiaries and auditors are supportive of improving auditor independence by reducing governmental control of intervention and moving towards self-regulation of the professions'.[127] Furthermore, the CICPA published some specific rules focused on the development of professional integrity – the so-called *Guidance on Codes of Professional Ethics* – designed partly as a reaction to the worldwide scandals concerning quality of accounting information. And according to CICPA President Liu Zhongli, efforts are still made by the profession to reinforce self-regulation as well as to reform and improve the examination and training systems of CPAs.[128]

Evidently, much more detailed research needs to be done with regard to the regulation of the Chinese accountancy market before any real conclusions can be formulated. This short overview presents just some of the basics of the regulatory framework and does not contain any information about the *enforcement* of the Accountancy Law, the Law on Certified Public Accountants, the Audit Law and the CICPA Charter in China.[129] Nonetheless, it seems at first sight that the entry regulation of accountants in China is not much stricter than it is in some European countries, although there is indeed a lot of governmental control. And, naturally, more information should be gathered on conduct regulation, for example, price regulation, advertising restrictions and rules on interprofessional cooperation, if there are any.

4.4 Application of Traditional Theory of Regulation to China

The case studies of legal services and accountancy services show that the regulation of professional services in China generally seems to be quite similar to the regulation found in some of the more heavily regulated European countries,[130] at least on paper. In both professions there is regulation of entry tied to educational requirements and practical experience, and in both professions some tasks have been reserved for those owning a licence. Concerning lawyers there are, however, also quantitative limits to the number of professionals, which are determined each year by the state. All of these rules have been incorporated in legislation. Furthermore, in both cases there is a professional body that defines rules on professional ethics and 'fair competition', albeit that in both cases these bodies are directly supervised by the central government. Moreover, there are probably additional regulations applying to lawyers and certified public accountants that have not been discussed here, as my focus has been on entry regulation especially. It is impossible to say to what extent the regulatory framework in China serves public or private interest goals, because empirical evidence, on quality of service, prices, earnings and so on, is very hard to obtain. And, as stated above, one needs to take into account that there are huge differences between the Chinese legal system and western legal systems, which also influence the actual enforcement of legislation. One should know the specifics of China's legal system and its functioning in practice as regards professional services before drawing any conclusions.

Notwithstanding that, one could say a few words about the application of the public interest theory of market failure to China. Of course the problems of externalities and abuse of market power by cartels and monopolies exist in similar forms in China.[131] However, the question what is a public good – and, more importantly, the related question as to what products or services should be produced or controlled by the government – has long been answered in a different way by the Chinese government,[132] although this situation is changing slightly. Considering the regulation of lawyers and accountants, we found that there is much interference in the market by the Chinese government. As regards the fourth kind of market failure, information asymmetry between professionals and clients, the problem (and hence the justification for regulation of professionals) is probably much greater in China than in most western countries. With respect to our case studies, this applies in particular to lawyers and, to a lesser extent, to accountants. Compared to western people, many Chinese, in particular those living in one of the many remote and rural areas in China, have only limited knowledge of the law and are less organized in consumer associations. Many farmers living in the west and the central areas are poor and generally have little or no education. These considerable differences in China between poor and rich people and between educated and insufficiently educated people may even provide some paternalistic justifications for intervention in the market, in addition to the justifications that would also apply to western countries, such as the information asymmetry between service providers and client and negative externalities.[133] Also a relatively high share of insufficiently educated and/or poor people would imply that private law remedies are less effective. The costs of taking legal action against suppliers are simply too high. And, apparently, there are huge difficulties in receiving full compensation for victims through private law.[134] Instead, one would have to turn more quickly to a different form of intervention in the market system, such as regulation.

While regulation may indeed provide a better solution than tort law under these circumstances, a problem to be solved then is the monitoring (administration) and enforcement of such regulation. It is beyond the scope of this chapter to discuss these important topics here,[135] but they should at least be mentioned, considering the fact that China is to some extent still working on the improvement of enforcement, although we have already noted in section 4.2 that the legal profession and the court system are developing very fast. Also we noted that, according to economic theory, regulation should not go further than is necessary to cure the market failure, in order to avoid efficiency losses and rent seeking; regulation should be both justified and proportional. With respect to rent seeking in China, we noted that there are probably few possibilities for rent-seeking behaviour by profession members such as lawyers and accountants themselves, but that the current regulations (in theory) leave room for rent-seeking behaviour by public officials and those designing the regulations. However, there is little empirical evidence of this actually occurring.

5. CONCLUDING REMARKS

This chapter started by recapitulating the main points of the well-known public and private interest approaches to regulation and by presenting some empirical evidence on the effects of restrictive regulation. In addition I addressed some developments in the actual regulation of professions in Europe. With regard to the latter, a trend towards deregulation of professional services could be noted in most European countries. What does all of this teach China? First, of course, that the same public interest arguments for regulation in principle apply also to China. Externalities, market power, public goods and information asymmetry between providers and clients may all provide justifications for intervention in the market, in addition to non-economic arguments (for example, paternalistic or distributive arguments) that have not been discussed in this chapter. The information asymmetry problem is probably much greater in China than in western countries because of the presence of large groups of relatively poor and insufficiently educated people, although the seriousness of the information problem depends also on the nature of the professional service under review. Liability rules may not (yet) be a good alternative for or supplement to quality regulation in China, which hence makes a stronger case for regulation. On the other hand, there is a risk of rent-seeking behaviour by public officials and those designing the regulation, because government bodies in China are directly involved in designing, administrating and monitoring all professional regulation. We noted this for both of our case studies, lawyers and accountants. Finally, the economic theory taught us also that there may be a more general risk that regulation is disproportionate in going further than necessary in order to cure the market failure at hand.

Of course, much more research, including empirical research (if possible), will have to be carried out before one can judge the public or private interest nature of the Chinese regulation of professional services and future developments of this regulation. The analysis in this chapter was only a first, modest attempt to do so. In subsequent research, the following points (as mentioned above and in other parts of this chapter) should always be taken into account: larger information asymmetries, a different notion of public goods, less back-up via liability rules, the risk of rent seeking and disproportionate regulation, a (probably) different definition of specific professional services, and the different legal system.

NOTES

* I am grateful to Michael Faure for commenting on a first version of this paper; and to Qing Zhang, Hui Wang and Lili Wang for tracing and translating Chinese legal texts. I would also like to thank Wenjing Liu and other conference participants for commenting on this paper at the China-Europe conference on Law and Economics in Shanghai, 16–17 March, 2006.

1. I will not go into detail here about activities of national competition authorities. For the UK, see OFT (2001), which identifies restrictions to competition in the professional rules of accountants, architects, solicitors and lawyers. OFT (2003) studies the pharmaceutical profession in the UK. For Ireland, see Indecon and London Economics (2003), which contains an overview and analysis of the regulation of eight distinct professions. In the Netherlands, the competition authority NMa has already dealt with many cases involving (self-) regulation in the professions. For actions taken by the Dutch government and a report written by the Ministry of Economic Affairs, see MDW (2003) and Van den Heuvel Rijnders, Lackner and Verkerk (2004), respectively, and Philipsen (2005). For other countries, see e.g. OECD (2000).
2. This section draws heavily on Philipsen (2003, pp. 9–45), and Philipsen and Faure (2002, pp. 155–82).
3. The discussion of the public and private interest approach to regulation will be brief here in order to prevent too much repetition. For more elaborate summaries and analyses of the public and private interest approach, see e.g. Posner (1974), Faure et al. (1993), Hägg (1997), Den Hertog (2000) and Philipsen (2003). Hantke-Domas (2003) questions the existence of the public interest theory of regulation.
4. I will leave out other possible justifications for regulation, such as those resulting from distributive purposes or paternalistic arguments.
5. For a brief discussion of economic efficiency and market failure, see, e.g., Cooter and Ulen (2004, pp. 43–8), and Varian (1984, pp. 190–209, 253–62).
6. Shavell (1984) discusses four criteria that determine the choice between tort law and regulation as instruments for controlling risky activities: information, insolvency risk, the threat of a liability suit and administrative costs. He concludes (p. 365) that 'a complete solution to the problem of control of risk evidently should involve the joint use of liability and regulation, with the balance of them reflecting the importance of the determinants'.

7. Arruñada (2006, p. 52).
8. Nelson (1970) introduced the concept experience good. Darby and Karni (1973) discuss trust goods.
9. Akerlof (1970) himself presented the example of the used cars market (the market for 'lemons').
10. For the sake of completeness, I should mention another information problem that may be an argument for regulation of professional services: *bounded rationality* of consumers. For a short discussion, see, e.g., Philipsen (2003, pp. 16–17).
11. See also Stephen (2006) and European Commission (2005, pp. 3–5).
12. Externalities are benefits or costs imposed on third parties. In other words, they are (positive or negative) side-effects of production or consumption. For an economic analysis of externalities see, e.g., Varian (1984, pp. 259–63), and Cooter and Ulen (2004, pp. 44–6). See also Ogus (1994, pp. 18–19, 35–8).
13. The general version of this theorem states that, in the absence of transaction costs, an optimal allocation of resources (efficiency) will always follow, irrespective of the initial distribution of property rights (irrespective of the prevailing liability rule). It is based on Coase (1960). For a general description of the Coase theorem, I refer to Cooter and Ulen (2004, pp. 85–96), and Philipsen (2003, pp. 17–18).
14. Shavell (1984).
15. Public goods have two special characteristics that distinguish them from private goods: nonrivalrous consumption and nonexcludability. If a product is a public good, the market sometimes does not (or not sufficiently) generate the product. For a brief discussion of public goods and free-riding behaviour, see, e.g., Cooter and Ulen (2004, pp. 46–7), Ogus (1994, pp. 33–5) and Varian (1984, pp. 253–6).
16. The leading papers of the Chicago theory of regulation are Stigler (1971), Peltzman (1976) and Becker (1983). For additional information, see the literature mentioned in the introduction, *supra*, notes 2 & 3.
17. Buchanan, Tollison and Tullock (1980) present a selection of leading papers on rent-seeking behaviour.
18. See also Van den Bergh (1997, p. 32).
19. *Infra*, section 2.3.
20. Stigler (1971, p. 3).
21. *Infra*, section 2.4.
22. Becker (1983, p. 384).
23. In this respect it is interesting to mention the famous case *Wouters (C-309-99)*, which dealt with multidisciplinary partnerships between accountants and lawyers. In 2002, the European Court of Justice concluded in this case that the specific prohibition on multidisciplinary partnerships between accountants and lawyers is necessary in order to ensure the proper practice of the (*in casu* Dutch) legal profession. However, similar restrictions on interprofessional cooperation are still studied by, among many others, the European Commission (within the context of its project on competition in professional services markets; *infra*, §3).
24. Price fixing is obviously the most restrictive regulatory instrument, especially when the government implements it or when it is backed by a declaration of 'generally binding'.
25. Shapiro (1986, p. 855).
26. A formal–economic analysis of licensing can be found in Leland (1979). He concluded that professional groups are likely to set quality standards too high from a social welfare point of view. Shaked and Sutton (1981) extended Leland's analysis, but addressed also the specific problem of the suppliers that are excluded from the primary market by licensing. Permitting the entry of a 'para-profession' on the market can be welfare improving.
27. *Infra*, §2.4.
28. For a discussion of this problem in the pharmaceutical market, see Philipsen (2003).
29. Self-regulation exists in many forms, which differ in legal force and in the degree of autonomy from the government. See in particular Ogus (2000, pp. 588–9).
30. Miller (1985, pp. 897–8).

31. For a longer discussion, including a discussion of some formal–economic papers on self-regulation, see Philipsen (2003, pp. 35–41). See also Van den Bergh (1997, pp. 28–30), and Van den Bergh (2006). In the latter paper two alternative systems are analysed: co-regulation (which is based on cooperation between the state and self-regulating bodies) and competitive self-regulation.
32. This subsection is partly based on research I conducted during a working period at the European Commission in 2003. Part of my responsibilities concerned making an overview of available empirical academic literature: see speech by N.J. Philipsen, 'Overview of the Commission's Stocktaking Exercise (Part II)', Liberal Professions Conference, 28 October 2003 (available at <http://europa.eu.int/comm/competition>).
33. Paterson, Fink, Ogus et al. (2003, pp. 126–7).
34. See Philipsen (2003, pp. 147–50).
35. *Infra*, §3.
36. Shapiro (1986, p. 856).
37. Svorny (2000, p. 312).
38. Carroll and Gaston (1981, p. 965). The authors claim (p. 973) that their study, which mostly covers electricians, dentists and plumbers, is 'the first broad exploratory empirical investigation on the effect of the received quality of services from state-licensed occupations'.
39. For more on the economic analysis of advertising, see Rubin (2000) and Stephen and Love (2000, pp. 996–7).
40. Benham and Benham (1975, p. 446).
41. Stephen and Love (2000, p. 997).
42. European Commission (2004, p. 8).
43. Currently (2006) an additional study is running with the European Commission, DG Internal Market, concerning regulatory restrictions in the field of pharmacies in the EU25.
44. Information is not complete as far as Greece and Portugal are concerned. Moreover, the regulation overview is not complete down to the smallest detail because of the relative time pressure under which the report has been drawn up and non-availability of some data.
45. Nevertheless, a critical note must be made here: the indices seem to ignore self-regulation to a certain extent.
46. Paterson, Fink, Ogus et al. (2003, ch. 3).
47. See also European Commission (2004, p. 9).
48. European Commission (2003a) (available at <http://europa.eu.int/comm/competition>).
49. European Commission (2003b) (available at <http://europa.eu.int/comm/competition>).
50. European Commission (2004).
51. European Commission (2005, p. 24).
52. Williams (2005, p. 24).
53. Clarke (2003b, p. 9).
54. The text can be found here: (<http://news.xinhuanet.com/zhengfu/2003–08/28/content_1048844.htm >) in Chinese, 20 January 2006. See <http://www.fdi.gov.cn/ltlaw/lawinfodisp.jsp?id=CENSOFT0000000009603&appId=1> for an English translation. An alternative English translation of the title of this Act used there is *Administrative License Law of the People's Republic of China*.
55. Translation obtained from <http://www.fdi.cn> (*supra*, note 54) and Zhang (forthcoming, 2007).
56. Ogus and Zhang (2005, p. 131).
57. Ogus and Zhang (2005, pp. 138–41). The authors analyse revenue-raising explanations and private interest explanations for business entry controls in developing countries, in addition to public interest explanations. For more on these issues, see Chapter 6 of this volume and Williams (2005, pp. 103–6).
58. See also Clarke (2003a, p. 26), and Williams (2005, pp. 19, 57,127–9).
59. Translation obtained from <http://www.fdi.cn> (*supra*, note 54) and Zhang (forthcoming, 2007).

60. *Supra*, §2.1.
61. For a discussion of existing and proposed Chinese competition provisions, see in particular Williams (2005, pp. 153–221). See also Jin and Luo (2002) and Chapter 4 of this volume.
62. *Supra*, §§2.2–2.3.
63. *Supra*, §2.3.
64. See also Zhang (forthcoming, 2007).
65. According to the Constitution of the People's Republic of China (adopted 4 December 1982, and amended four times), Article 57: 'The National People's Congress of the People's Republic of China is the highest organ of state power. Its permanent body is the Standing Committee of the National People's Congress.' See, furthermore, Articles 58–78 of the Constitution. The executive body of the National People's Congress is called the State Council. Article 85 of the Constitution reads as follows: 'The State Council, that is, the Central People's Government of the People's Republic of China, is the executive body of the highest organ of state power; it is the highest organ of state administration.' See, furthermore, Articles 86–92.
66. Article 7 of the 1979 Law of the People's Republic of China on the Organization of Local People's Congresses and Local People's Governments at Various Levels (fourth modification 27 October 2004; *quan guo ren min dai biao da hui chang wu wei yuan hui guan yu xiu gai <zhong hua ren min gong he guo di fang ge ji ren min dai biao da hui he di fang ge ji ren min zheng fu zu zhi fa> de jue ding*) provides that the provinces, municipalities and special cities (administrated directly by the national government) can enact local laws. The text can be found here: <http://www.gov.cn/ziliao/flfg/2005-06/21/content_8297.htm> (in Chinese, 20 January 2006).
67. See also Zhang (forthcoming, 2007).
68. Which does not mean that Imperial China did not have a substantial body of public, positive law, because of course it did have one. However, 'legal professionalism' as such (including concepts such as independence and autonomy) did not exist at the time, although individuals were active in advising others in the field of law. See Alford (1995, p. 26).
69. Alford (1995, pp. 22, 27).
70. Clarke (2003a, p. 10). See also Institute of Developing Economies (2001, p. 41, 52–3).
71. Alford (1995, p. 23).
72. For a much longer description of regulation of lawyers in this period and the development of the legal profession in China, see, e.g., Alford (1995, pp. 26–32) and the references mentioned therein, and Institute of Developing Economies (2001, pp. 38–53), which also includes an overview of the historical development from 1900 to 1980.
73. The text can be found at: <http://www.wzsf.com.cn/lawchxun/law/renda/sifa/lvshi/dgd.htm> (in Chinese and in English, 1 February 2006). The promulgation and implementation of these Interim Regulations marked the restoration of the lawyer's system after many years of setbacks.
74. Article 1 of the Interim Regulations on Lawyers of the PRC.
75. Article 13 of the Interim Regulations on Lawyers of the PRC.
76. Alford (1995, p. 29).
77. Nonetheless, many older legal workers were (and still are) trained mainly in a period of a centrally planned economy and most of them do not have university law degrees. Additional legal training offered by the state in the early 1990s has remedied this situation to some extent.
78. English translation obtained via <http://www.lawinfochina.com>.
79. Article 5 of the Lawyer's Act.
80. Article 6 of the Lawyer's Act. The All-China Lawyers' Association was established already in 1986. The examination itself has been criticized by (among others) Williams (2005, p. 133), for being 'essentially a memory test of multiple-choice questions. [. . .] To become a lawyer merely requires an excellent memory and a good knowledge of orthodox political thought, which is also an integral part of the examination'.

81. See the *Implementing Rules for the National Judicial Exam (guo jia si fa kao shi shi shi ban fa (shi xing))*, issued in October 2001, which list some conditions for applicants.
82. See again the Implementing Rules, *supra*, note 81, and the *Regulation on Awarding a Lawyer's Qualification without Reference to a Lawyer's Examination*, issued in October 1996. See also Zhang (forthcoming, 2007).
83. Article 40 of the Lawyer's Act.
84. Article 38 of the Lawyer's Act.
85. Alford (1995, p. 35).
86. Article 44 contains 11 scenarios where this 'judicial administration department etc.' shall impose disciplinary warnings, a penalty of cessation of practice for no less than three months but no more than one year; and any illegal proceeds shall be confiscated.
87. See also Ministry of Commerce, 'Lawyer System', 24 October 2005. That short text contains a summary of the regulation of lawyers and can be obtained from the website of the Ministry of Commerce: <http://www.mofcom.gov.cn> (26 January 2006).
88. Zhang (forthcoming, 2007).
89. Articles 17 and 18 of the Lawyer's Act.
90. Article 19 of the Lawyer's Act.
91. The text can be found here: <http://www.law-star.com/cac/2332.htm> (in Chinese, 26 January 2006). Article 6 presents four requirements for setting up a law firm: (1) it must have its own firm name, residence and articles of association; (2) it must have the written partnership contract; (3) it must have more than three partners; (4) it must have more than 100 000 RMB of assets. Article 11 states three requirements for the partners: (1) They must have acquired the official practice certificates; (2) their experience as a lawyer must exceed five years; (3) they have not experienced any administrative punishment (which is more serious than suspending the lawyer profession) during the former three years before they become the partners.
92. Article 23 of the Lawyer's Act.
93. See Institute of Developing Economies (2001, pp. 46–7), Williams (2005, pp. 133–4), Zhang (forthcoming, 2007).
94. The text can be found here: <http://www.cer.net/article/20010101/3045338.shtml> (in Chinese, 26 January 2006).
95. Institute of Developing Economies (2001, pp. 50–51).
96. I refer to Stephen and Love (2000) and Barton (2001) for an extensive discussion of regulation of the legal profession. The latter also criticizes 'professionalism' as a non-economic justification for entry regulation in the market for legal services. See also Zhang (forthcoming, 2007). For general public interest arguments: *supra*, §2.1.
97. See also *infra*, §4.4.
98. For the EU15, see Paterson, Fink and Ogus et al. (2003, pp. 45–7), and European Commission (2003b).
99. Although, as noted, the power of lawyers and lawyer's associations themselves is limited compared to the power of the Ministry of Justice and its affiliates.
100. Shavell (1984): *supra*, note 6.
101. Also *supra*, note 70.
102. *Supra*, §2.4.
103. For an extensive analysis of China's judicial system and judicial reform since the early 1980s, see Institute of Developing Economies (2001). Williams (2005, pp. 129–38), examines the past and present of the Chinese legal system, its courts and its lawyers.
104. Zhang (forthcoming, 2007).
105. Clarke (2003a, pp. 10, 12–13). See also (Clarke, 2003b).
106. European Commission (2003b, p. 4).
107. *Supra*, §2.1.
108. Chen Yugei, 'Opportunities and Opening-up of China's Accounting Market', speech made at the International Conference hosted by ICAI at Jaipur, India, 13 March 2004. See <http://www.cicpa.org.cn> (1 February 2006).
109. Liu Zhongli, 'China's Capital Market and Accountancy Profession: Advance amidst Reform', speech given at the Conference hosted by the Institute of Chartered

Accountants in England and Wales, 13 April 2005. See: <http://www.icaew.co.uk> (1 February 2006). NB: over 60 000 of the individual members are practising members while over 70 000 are non-practising members.

110. Liu Zhongli (2005), *supra*, note 109.
111. English translation obtained from Foreign Languages Press (Beijing, 2001, first edition). The text can also be found here: <http://www.law-lib.com/law/law_view.asp?id=103>, or here: <http://www.xjb.ac.cn/text/kjf2.htm> (both in Chinese, 1 February 2006).
112. *Supra*, note 65.
113. A chief accountant is the head of the accounting organ of a unit. A unit, in turn, can be a state organ, mass organization, company, enterprise, institution or other organization (Article 2 of the Accountancy Law).
114. The text can be found here: <http://www.cicpa.org.cn/English/zckjsf20040322.htm> (in English, 7 February 2006). This Law replaced the Regulations on CPAs of 1986.
115. These conditions include a condition that the accounting firm must have a registered capital of not less than RMB 300 000 and must have a number of full-time professional staff and at least five of them are CPAs.
116. Article 9 of the Law of the People's Republic of China on Certified Public Accountants. Some general conditions for rejection of such registration applications are formulated in Articles 10 and 11. See also Articles 33 and 34.
117. For more information, see the website of the National Audit Office of the PRC at <http://www.cnao.gov.cn>. See also Article 43 of the Law of the People's Republic of China on Certified Public Accountants.
118. Provisional Regulations on Representative Offices of Foreign Accounting Firms of 4 January 1994 (*jing wai kuai ji shi shi wu suo chang zhu dai biao ji gou guan li zan xing ban fa*). An English version was obtained from the CICPA website:<http://www.cicpa.org.cn> (7 February 2006).
119. Provisional Rules on Temporary Performance of Audit Services in China by Foreign Accounting Firms of 6 December 1993 (*wai guo kuai ji shi shi wu suo zai zhong guo jing nei lin shi zhi xing shen ji ye wu de zan xing gui ding*). An English version was obtained from the CICPA website: <http://www.cicpa.org.cn> (7 February 2006).
120. Notice Concerning Permission for International Accounting Firms to Identify Member Firms in China of 22 January 1996 (*guan yu yun xu guo ji kuai ji shi shi wu suo zai zhong guo jing nei fa zhan duo de cheng yuan suo de tong zhi*). An English version was obtained from the CICPA website: <http://www.cicpa.org.cn> (7 February 2006).
121. Chen Yugei (2004), *supra*, note 108.
122. The text of the 2004 version can be found here: <http://www.cicpa.org.cn/English/charter20031226.htm> (in English, 7 February 2006). The discussion here has been kept brief for reasons of space.
123. Articles 1 and 4 of the Charter.
124. See also Article 35 of the Law on Certified Public Accountants.
125. Articles 6 and 8 of the Charter.
126. *Supra*, §4.2.
127. Source: <http://papers.ssrn.com/sol3/papers.cfm?abstract_id=499383>. Unfortunately, the whole article could not be obtained. The reference is Z.J. Lin (2004).
128. Liu Zhongli (2005), *supra*, note 109.
129. It is a well-known fact that in China there is (still) a sharp discrepancy between laws on paper and their enforcement by courts. See, for example, Institute of Developing Economies (2001, p. 3).
130. *Supra*, §3, for a brief overview of regulation in the EU15.
131. As regards the latter, the discussion about new competition rules is still going on: *supra*, note 61 and accompanying text.
132. That is, different as opposed to the answers given by the economic (public interest) theory of market failure.
133. Williams (2005, pp. 106–8), discusses unemployment and poverty in China. An additional and related problem is that the growing inequalities in income and wealth risk incurring the wrath of the dispossessed and creating social instability.

134. See, for example, Zhang (forthcoming, 2007), and Institute of Developing Economies (2001, p. 3).
135. Williams (2005, pp. 425–7), who discusses these topics in the context of the draft competition law, is critical of the current administration and enforcement of laws in China. Clarke (2003a, 2003b), however, is more positive.

REFERENCES

Akerlof, G. (1970), 'The market for lemons: quality, uncertainty and the market mechanism', *Quarterly Journal of Economics*, **85**, 488–500.

Alford, W.P. (1995), 'Tasselled loafers for barefoot lawyers: transformation and tension in the world of Chinese legal workers', *China Quarterly*, **141**, 22–38.

Amato, G. and L.L. Laudati (eds) (2001), *The Anticompetitive Impact of Regulation*, Cheltenham, UK and Northampton, MA, USA: Edward Elgar, pp. 1–143.

Arruñada, B. (2006), 'Managing competition in professional services and the burden of inertia', in C.D. Ehlermann and I. Atanasiu (eds), *European Competition Law Annual 2004: The Relationship between Competition Law and (Liberal) Professions*, Oxford, UK and Portland Oregon, US: Hart Publishing, pp. 31–71.

Barton, B.H. (2001), 'Why do we regulate lawyers? An economic analysis of the justifications for entry and conduct regulation', *Arizona State Law Journal*, **33**, 429–90.

Becker, G.S. (1983), 'A theory of competition among pressure groups for political influence', *Quarterly Journal of Economics*, **98**(3), 371–400.

Benham, L. and A. Benham (1975), 'Regulating through the professions: a perspective on information control', *Journal of Law and Economics*, **18**, 421–7.

Bond, R., J. Kwoka, J. Phelan and I. Whitten (1980), *Effects of Restrictions of Advertising and Commercial Practice in the Professions: The Case of Optometry*, report by the Federal Trade Commission, Washington: FTC.

Buchanan, J.M., R.D. Tollison and G. Tullock (eds) (1980), *Toward a Theory of the Rent-Seeking Society*, College Station, Texas: Texas A&M University Press.

Carroll, S.L. and R.J. Gaston (1981), 'Occupational restrictions and the quality of service received: some evidence', *Southern Economic Journal*, **47**(4), 959–76.

Clarke, D.C. (2003a), 'Empirical research into the Chinese judicial system' (<http://ssrn.com/abstract=412660>).

Clarke, D.C. (2003b), 'Puzzling observations in Chinese law: when is a riddle just a mistake?', in C.S. Hsu (ed.), *Understanding China's Legal System*, New York: New York University Press, pp. 93–121. (<Http://ssrn.com/abstract=293627>).

Coase, R. (1960), 'The problem of social cost', *Journal of Law and Economics*, **3**, 1–44.

Cooter, R. and T. Ulen (2004), *Law and Economics*, 4th edn, Boston: Pearson/Addison Wesley.

Cox, C. and S. Foster (1990), *The Costs and Benefits of Occupational Regulation*, report by the Federal Trade Commission, Washington: FTC.

Darby, M. and E. Karni (1973), 'Free competition and the optimal amount of fraud', *Journal of Law and Economics*, **16**, 67–88.

Den Hertog, J. (2000), 'General theories of regulation', in B. Bouckaert and G. De Geest (eds), *Encyclopedia of Law and Economics, Volume III: The Regulation of*

Contracts, Cheltenham, UK, and Northampton, MA, USA: Edward Elgar, pp. 223–70.
European Commission (2003a), *Invitation to Comment. Regulation in Liberal Professions and its Effects: Summary of Responses*, Brussels: Competition DG.
European Commission (2003b), *Stocktaking Exercise on Regulation of Professional Services: Overview of Regulation in the EU Member States*, Brussels: Competition DG.
European Commission (2004), *Communication from the Commission: Report on Competition in Professional Services*, COM(2004) 83 final, Brussels: Competition DG.
European Commission (2005), *Commission Staff Working Document: Progress by Member States in Reviewing and Eliminating Restrictions to Competition in the Area of Professional Services*, COM(2005) 405 final / SEC(2005) 1064, Brussels: Competition DG.
Faure, M., J. Finsinger, J. Siegers and R. Van den Bergh (eds) (1993), *Regulation of Professions: A Law and Economics Approach to the Regulation of Attorneys and Physicians in the U.S., Belgium, the Netherlands, Germany and the U.K.*, Antwerp: MAKLU.
Hägg, P.G.T. (1997), 'Theories on the economics of regulation: a survey of the literature from a European perspective', *European Journal of Law and Economics*, **4**, 337–70.
Hantke-Domas, M. (2003), 'The public interest theory of regulation: non-existence or misinterpretation?', *European Journal of Law and Economics*, **15**, 165–94.
Indecon and London Economics (2003), *Indecon's Assessment of Restrictions in the Supply of Professional Services*, prepared for the Competition Authority by Indecon International Economic Consultants – London Economics, Dublin–London.
Institute of Developing Economies (IDE-JETRO) (2001), *China's Judicial System and its Reform*, IDE Asian Law Series No. 2, Beijing: Institute of Law, Chinese Academy of Social Science.
Jin, C. and W. Luo (2002), *Competition Law in China*, Buffalo: William S. Hein and Co.
Kleiner, M.M. and R.T. Kudrle (2000), 'Does regulation affect economic outcomes? The case of dentistry', *Journal of Law and Economics*, **43**, 547–82.
Leland, H.E. (1979), 'Quaks, Lemons and Licensing: A Theory of Minimum Quality Standards,' *Journal of Political Economy*, **87**, 1328–46.
Lin, Z.J. (2004), 'Auditor's responsibility and Independence: Evidence from China', *Research in Accounting Regulation*, **17**, 169–92.
Liu, Z. (2005), 'China's capital market and accountancy profession: advance amidst reform', speech given at the conference hosted by the Institute of Chartered Accountants in England and Wales, 13 April, http://www.icaew.co.UK.
MDW (2003), *Eindrapport MDW*, The Hague: Marktwerking Deregulering en Wetgevingskwaliteit.
Miller, J.C. (1985), 'The FTC and voluntary standards: maximizing the net benefits of self-regulation', *The Cato Journal*, **4**, 897–903.
Muzondo, T.R. and B. Pazderka (1983), 'Income-enhancing effects of professional licensing', *Antitrust Bulletin*, **28**, 397–415.
Nelson, P. (1970), 'Information and consumer behavior', *Journal of Political Economy*, **78**, 311–29.

OECD (2000), *Competition in Professional Services*, Paris: Committee on Competition Law and Policy.
OFT (2001), *Competition in Professions: A Report by the Director General of Fair Trading*, London: Office of Fair Trading.
OFT (2003), *The Control of Entry Regulations and Retail Pharmacy Services in the UK: A Report of an OFT Market Investigation*, Vols 1–3, London: Office of Fair Trading.
Ogus, A.I. (1994), *Regulation: Legal Form and Economic Theory*, Oxford: Clarendon Press.
Ogus, A.I. (2000), 'Self-regulation', in B. Bouckaert and G. De Geest (eds), *Encyclopedia of Law and Economics, Volume V: The Economics of Crime and Litigation*, Cheltenham, UK and Northampton, MA, USA: Edward Elgar, pp. 587–602.
Ogus, A. and Q. Zhang (2005), 'Licensing regimes East and West', *International Review of Law and Economics*, **25**, 124–42.
Olson, M. (1965), *The Logic of Collective Action: Public Goods and the Theory of Groups*, Cambridge: Harvard University Press.
Paterson, I., M. Fink, A. Ogus et al. (2003), *Economic Impact of Regulation in the Field of Liberal Professions in Different Member States: Regulation of Professional Services*, Study for the European Commission, Vienna: Institute for Advanced Studies.
Peltzman, S. (1976), 'Toward a more general theory of regulation', *Journal of Law and Economics*, **19**, 211–40.
Perloff, J.M. (1980), 'The impact of licensing laws on wage changes in the construction industry', *Journal of Law and Economics*, **23**, 409–28.
Pfeffer, J. (1974), 'Some evidence on occupational licensing and occupational incomes', *Social Forces*, **53**, 102–11.
Philipsen, N.J. (2003), *Regulation of and by Pharmacists in the Netherlands in the Netherlands and Belgium: An Economic Approach*, Antwerp/Groningen: Intersentia.
Philipsen, N.J. (2005), 'Vrije Beroepen, Concurrentie en Regulering in Nederland: Zijn We op de Goede Weg?', *SEW Tijdschrift voor Europees en Economisch Recht*, **53**, 54–9.
Philipsen, N.J. and M.G. Faure (2002), 'The regulation of pharmacists in Belgium and the Netherlands: in the public or private interest?', *Journal of Consumer Policy*, **25**, 155–201.
Posner, R.A. (1974), 'Theories of economic regulation', *Bell Journal of Economics and Management Science*, **5**, 335–58.
Rubin, P.H. (2000), 'Information regulation (including regulation of advertising)', in B. Bouckaert and G. De Geest (eds), *Encyclopedia of Law and Economics, Volume III: The Regulation of Contracts*, Cheltenham, UK and Northampton, MA, USA: Edward Elgar, pp. 271–95.
Shaked, A. and J. Sutton (1981), 'The self-regulating profession', *Review of Economic Studies*, **48**, 843–62.
Shapiro, C. (1986), 'Investment, moral hazard and occupational licensing', *Review of Economic Studies*, **53**, 843–62.
Shavell, S. (1984), 'Liability for harm versus regulation of safety', *Journal of Legal Studies*, **13**, 357–74.
Stephen, F.H. (2006), 'The market failure justification for the regulation of professional service markets and the characteristics of consumers', in C.D. Ehlermann

and I. Atanasiu (eds), *European Competition Law Annual 2004: The Relationship between Competition Law and the (Liberal) Professions*, Oxford, UK and Portland Oregon, US: Hart Publishing, pp. 143–54.

Stephen, F.H. and J.H. Love (2000), 'Regulation of the legal profession', in B. Bouckaert and G. De Geest (eds), *Encyclopedia of Law and Economics, Volume III: The Regulation of Contracts*, Cheltenham, UK and Northampton, MA, USA: Edward Elgar, pp. 987–1017.

Stigler, G.J. (1971), 'The theory of economic regulation', *Bell Journal of Economics and Management Science*, **2**, 3–21.

Svorny, S. (2000), 'Licensing, market entry regulation', in B. Bouckaert and G. De Geest (eds), *Encyclopedia of Law and Economics, Volume III: The Regulation of Contracts*, Cheltenham, UK and Northampton, MA, USA: Edward Elgar, pp. 296–328.

Van den Bergh, R. (1997), *Self-Regulation of the Medical and Legal Professions: Remaining Barriers to Competition and EC-Law*, Diskussionsbeiträge Recht und Ökonomie no. 31, Hamburg: Universität Hamburg.

Van den Bergh, R. (2006), 'Towards efficient self-regulation in markets for professional services', in C.D. Ehlermann and I. Atanasiu (eds), *European Competition Law Annual 2004: The Relationship between Competition Law and the (Liberal) Professions*, Oxford, UK and Portland Oregon, US: Hart Publishing, pp. 155–76.

Van den Bergh, R. and M.G. Faure (1991), 'Self-regulation of the professions in Belgium', *International Review of Law and Economics*, **11**, 165–82.

Van den Heuvel Rijnders, J., I.J.M. Lackner and H.C. Verkerk (2004), *Publieke Belangen en Marktordening bij Vrije Beroepen*, The Hague: Ministerie van Economische Zaken, Kenniscentrum voor Ordeningsvraagstukken.

Varian, H.R. (1984), *Microeconomic Analysis*, 2nd edn, New York: Norton.

White, W.D. (1978), 'The impact of occupational licensure of clinical laboratory personnel', *Journal of Human Resources*, **13**, 91–102.

Williams, M. (2005), *Competition Policy and Law in China, Hong Kong and Taiwan*, Cambridge: Cambridge University Press.

Zhang, Q. (forthcoming, 2007), *An Economic Analysis of Regulatory Licensing Systems with Implications for Chinese Laws*, draft version, University of Manchester School of Law; Oxford, UK and Portland, Oregan, US: Hart Publishing.

6. Regulatory arrangements and incentives for opportunistic behaviour

Anthony I. Ogus

1. PROBLEMS OF OPPORTUNISTIC BEHAVIOUR

'Opportunism is a subtle and pervasive condition of human nature with which the study of economic organization must be actively concerned.'[1] In general, we tend to think most about opportunism in a contractual setting, in particular where one party (say A) has power in relation to the other party (say B) either as a result of a monopoly relationship or because of significant information asymmetry.[2] That power can induce B to agree to terms of the contract, for example regarding payment, which would not otherwise have been agreed to. It can also make it difficult for B to monitor and evaluate the conduct of A to ensure faithful performance of obligations that have been undertaken, either because A lacks sufficient information about what is necessary for A to fulfil his contractual obligations or because, as a result of the monopoly, it is futile for B to complain because no alternative is available in the market.

A variety of legal principles serve to restrain opportunistic behaviour of this kind.[3] The law can can impose specific obligations regarding price or quality of performance on the contractual relationship; it can classify the A–B relationship as giving rise to a fiduciary duty (by A), with the array of obligations which flow from that; and it can subject A's conduct to the general obligation of good faith. The inherent difficulty of solutions of this kind is that they rely on legal initiatives being taken by the very party (B) who is disadvantaged by the circumstances of the relationship and from whom, therefore, remedial action is relatively unlikely.

An alternative is to use the law to prevent or control the excessive power of A. In relation to monopolies, this can be done by competition law or antitrust law; and in relation to information asymmetries, in part at least, by forcing disclosure on A or, in other ways, enhancing the information available to B. Note, too, that legal interventions of this kind can be achieved by public law instruments, thus using public agencies, rather than private individuals to enforce the law.

The connection between opportunistic behaviour by individuals within a contractual context and by public officials within a regulatory context has not been often noticed, but there are important parallels.[4] Regulatory arrangements which require a decision to be made on, for example, the granting of a trading licence, the awarding of a public franchise or whether there has been a contravention of some imposed standard, necessarily confer power on the decision maker (say C) relative to the individual or firm (say D) subject to the regulatory arrangements. The situation mirrors that of the contracting parties insofar as the C position is likely to be monopolistic (D cannot normally decide to have the case dealt with by another official), and C's knowledge of the rules governing the situation is likely to be far superior to that of D.

Unlike the contractual situation, there are not many ways in which C, within a regulatory context, can exploit the power to acquire *lawful* financial and other advantages. Nevertheless, and obviously, there is the possibility of securing *unlawful* financial and other gains. And the same policy question arises: to what extent should the law aim directly to restrain behaviour of this kind and to what extent should it rather aim at preventing the opportunities for such behaviour by reducing the power which C has in relation to D?

2. DIRECT RESTRAINTS OF REGULATORY OPPORTUNISTIC BEHAVIOUR

In Western, industrialized societies, the primary legal instruments for directly restraining regulatory opportunistic behaviour are those available in criminal and administrative law. By means of the criminal law unlawful opportunistic behaviour can be punished and thus deterred; and administrative law may control such behaviour through the accountability of decision makers, both to their superiors and (ultimately) to independent tribunals. However, the effectiveness of these instruments in dealing with the problem may be doubted.

Take, first, the criminal law. The receipt of an unauthorized payment, for example a bribe, in relation to a regulatory decision is invariably a criminal offence. What conditions must be satisfied for this form of restraint to be effective? The law-and-economics literature[5] adopts variants of the standard Becker economic model of crime, requiring the cost to the offender arising from conviction, when discounted by the probability of apprehension and conviction, to exceed the utility to be derived from the criminal act.[6] In the present context, this suggests that the size of the penalty should, after discounting for the probability of escaping detection, be related to the amount of the unlawful payment.[7] By itself that might not seem to be problematic. However, account must also be taken of the level of detection and conviction. In many countries this will be very low as a consequence of insufficient resources being available for monitoring and/or the fact that the problems of opportunism may have seriously infiltrated the law enforcement and criminal justice processes themselves. If, under such conditions, the deterrent effect is to be preserved, the formal sanctions consequent on conviction must be of such a draconian severity that few courts will be willing to impose them.[8]

To combat the lax enforcement problem, some[9] argue that there should be a special agency, independent of the police, and it has been suggested[10] that the existence of such an agency in Singapore contributed significantly to the reduction of the problem in that jurisdiction. However, as the experience of other countries[11] suggests, the creation of a special agency can actually exacerbate the problem by creating more opportunities for unlawful payments.[12]

Moreover 'networks' of opportunistic behaviour may arise.[13] There are likely to be increasing returns to making unauthorized payments to officials, relative to productive investment. This is because, as the level of opportunistic behaviour grows, so the returns on productive investment decline, thus reducing the opportunity cost of further opportunistic behaviour – an argument derived from the rent-seeking literature.[14] The reasoning is independent of another set of arguments which have been used to explain the same phenomena.[15] Just as the level of demand for network commodities (for example, fax machines) is crucially dependent on expectation as to the demand from others, so the likely gains from opportunistic behaviour depend on the expectation of the number of others also behaving opportunistically. The more such behaviour is anticipated, the greater will be the perceived need to engage in it. The vicious circle then becomes difficult to break.[16]

To combat phenomena of this magnitude by means of the criminal law is clearly extremely difficult: there must be sufficient political will, perhaps through a combination of domestic interests and pressure from foreign institutions.[17] In its absence, a virtuous circle will not emerge.[18]

In some jurisdictions, the person making, or offering to make, the unauthorized payment is also subject to criminal liability. Although notions of fairness might inhibit that approach, at least where the initiative in seeking the payment was taken by the official, the existence of joint criminal liability might seem to improve the efficacy of the deterrence regime. Nevertheless, the resource and infiltration problems already referred to suggest that such a policy is unlikely to be any more successful. What about rewarding 'whistle blowing?' For example, those, including bribers, reporting unlawful transactions might become entitled to a certain proportion of the penalties levied, or at least have their costs reduced, by ensuring anonymity.[19] Such an approach is likely to be most effective where the whistle-blowers are potential victims of the opportunistic behaviour, as with attempted cases of extortion,[20] but it can also plausibly be applied to bribers who defect from the deal and expose the transaction. Indeed, adopting a game-theoretical perspective, Cooter and Garoupa (2000) have argued that a most effective (and relatively cheap) solution is to undermine the spirit of cooperation between parties to such a transaction and thereby establish a 'virtuous circle of distrust'.

The argument is compelling but there are grounds for believing that compensating whistle-blowers may actually induce more opportunistic behaviour. First, it gives the briber a sanction, should the bribee fail to comply with the agreement, thus overcoming the problem that unlawful transactions are not enforceable in the courts. Secondly, it may encourage gamekeepers to become poachers, by enabling bribers to threaten to frame innocent officials, and thus extort payments from them.[21]

What then of administrative law? Policies can be adopted directed towards reforming bureaucracies by reference to traditional, Weberian administrative and process values. These might include depoliticizing the civil service; removing conflicts of interests; raising the quality of public officials recruited; increasing transparency by insisting on clear procedural steps and articulated reasons for decisions; improving internal auditing and monitoring systems; and extending external powers of appeal and review.[22] Insofar as these developments require a strong and impartial judiciary, a proactive citizenry, adequate resources for auditing and monitoring behaviour, and effective procedures for implementing as well as formulating the principles of administrative law, they will in many countries have to overcome deeply embedded cultural attitudes and the cost will be simply too large. Experience in some Latin American jurisdictions provides a good illustration of this.[23]

We can nevertheless envisage more modest measures which, at the margins, may significantly improve procedures and thus prove to be cost-effective. In South Korea, for example, resources have been invested in information technology which provides citizens with more information, automatically records transactions, thus rendering decision making more transparent, and in some cases enables transactions to be made electronically, thus depersonalizing the process.[24] The computerization of the customs services in the Philippines is reported to have reduced the average period of processing a cargo from eight days to about two hours, with an assumed significant reduction in unlawful payments.[25]

Taken as a whole, what emerges from the above analysis is that conventional strategies to constrain regulatory opportunistic behaviour are likely to be less effective in jurisdictions where such behaviour significantly infiltrates the criminal justice and law enforcement systems, where the resources available for monitoring the conduct of officials are relatively modest, or where the political will to adopt a robust and all-embracing approach to the problem does not exist. We now turn to policies dealing with the design of regulatory regimes. We need to see how institutional arrangements may be organized so as to limit opportunistic possibilities or to render them less profitable.[26]

3. DESIGN OF REGULATORY INSTITUTIONS AND PRINCIPLES

As with the contractual context, the main alternative to direct control of bureaucratic opportunistic behaviour is to limit the possibilities of its occurrence. Now, the appropriate design of regulatory institutions and principle is a subject of much current interest. It features prominently, alongside promotion of the rule of law and the constraint of corruption, in the agenda for developing countries articulated by the World Bank and other financial sponsors (World Bank, 2002). And Western models of regulatory arrangements are often, with insufficient consideration of their applicability, proffered as ideals which developing countries are advised to follow.[27]

Some of the possible reforms to regulatory structures to combat opportunism correlate well with developments and tendencies occurring in industrialized countries;[28] others point in the opposite direction. Some remain ambiguous. For a good example of the latter, take first the issue of privatization, perhaps the most salient feature of regulatory reform in industrialized countries. A study of a number of transitional economies in Eastern Europe and Central Asia found that the replacement of public ownership by private ownership reduced the amount of bribes paid, since the owners of the privatized companies had more incentives than officials managing a public company to control it.[29] Nevertheless, other studies of these phenomena have shown that the process of privatization may make the disease worse before it becomes better. This has been particularly true of Eastern Europe.[30] One reason is that a temporary combination of controlled 'public' prices and market prices creates opportunities for highly profitable arbitrage;[31] another is that the sale of assets can be used to benefit vested groups, the process being facilitated where insiders have discretion and information not available generally.[32]

Another, much-debated, though largely unresolved, question is whether a policy of decentralization, again associated with Western regulatory thinking, facilitates or hinders regulatory opportunistic behaviour. On the one hand, it is argued that decentralized decision making must by its nature be more transparent than when carried out at a distance from the subjects affected (local information flows being more rapid) and therefore corruption is, in such circumstances, more difficult to conceal.[33] On the other hand, if law enforcement is largely in the hands of a centralized authority, the very distance of the formal audit systems from the subject of investigation may limit its effectiveness: in remoter areas the authority of the law may simply not be recognized.[34] Moreover, the 'once-for-all' payment necessary to secure the cooperation of the central official may distort the economy less than the variety of payments at other levels: the bribee can control deviations from typical behavioural patterns and render its effects less uncertain.[35]

Related to the question of decentralization is that of competition between regulatory offices and officials. We have already identified monopolistic power as a key determinant of opportunistic behaviour. Promoting some such form of competition would thus seem to offer a plausible, and not too costly, means of combating it or at least reducing its level.[36] There is some empirical evidence to support this: the overlap in the power of local, state and federal authorities to control illegal drugs has been thought to reduce police corruption in the USA,[37] and a statistical study of corruption among the judiciary in Latin America suggests that this is less prevalent where there are viable alternative procedures for settling disputes.[38]

However, care must be taken over the way competition is introduced: a series of alternative individuals or offices providing the same service, or perhaps overlapping services, would meet the objective,[39] but adding further layers of bureaucratic decision making would simply exacerbate the problem.[40] Also a lack of clarity in the demarcation of public services can increase bureaucratic discretion, leading to more opportunism.[41] Suggestions linked to the competition argument include using committees instead of single decision makers and regularly moving bureaucrats between various offices,[42] although of course both of these increase the costs of administration.

Deregulation is a major theme in Western regulatory developments and an obvious, though not necessarily significant, point is that, since many opportunities for regulatory opportunistic behaviour arise from regulation, a reduction in the amount or intensity of regulation should reduce its level.[43]

The legalization of off-course betting in Hong Kong is a well-known instance of a simple deregulatory measure leading to a significant fall in unlawful payments to police,[44] but that very example should alert us to the risk of reaching superficial conclusions on deregulation. The control of gambling is a relatively peripheral form of social regulation and, as such, should not be the basis of broad generalizations about the undesirability of large areas of health and safety, and environmental and financial protection in developing countries. Given also that in many jurisdictions private law is ineffective to deal with many types of market failure, there is a strong *prima facie* case for regulatory intervention. It is, then, a question of exploring how an excess of possibilities for regulatory opportunism may be dismantled.[45]

A prime example here is that of registration and licensing systems which, as controls on business entry, are particularly prone to unauthorized transactions.[46] They have tended to proliferate in developing countries, with adverse economic consequences.[47] There are public interest justifications for the existence of such systems. The registration of firms prior to their lawful activity may significantly reduce costs of subsequent routine administration.[48] And, in some circumstances, licensing may be the optimal regulatory instrument for dealing with certain forms of information failure and negative externalities, particularly where the potential losses are very large and/or ex post enforcement of regulatory standards is particularly costly.[49] But these arguments do not justify multiple registration requirements where the information supplied to one authority is identical to that provided to others ('one-stop shops', enabling one registration application to serve for other applications, have been successfully introduced in some developing countries).[50] Nor do they justify systems imposing licence requirements on ordinary business entrants whose activities do not give rise to significant failure of the kind described.

A second possibility for positive deregulatory reforms arises from the use of the criminal law to enforce regulatory regimes.[51] In industrialized countries, the heavy cost of securing a conviction in the criminal courts may reduce its effectiveness as a deterrent, and for this reason administrative sanctions may be preferable.[52] In developing countries, use of the criminal process has the added disadvantage that it creates a further opportunity for unlawful payments. Evidence suggests that the level of bribes increases significantly when courts are involved in law enforcement.[53]

In other respects, the need to constrain regulatory opportunism suggests strategies which do not lie easily with reforms taking place in industrialized countries. According greater discretion to regulatory rule makers has there, alongside decentralization, enabled interventionist measures to be better aimed at local and diverse circumstances.[54] But, particularly in a developing country context where instruments of accountability may be weak, it also creates more opportunities for regulatory opportunism than where the requirements are the subject of clear and precise rules.[55] This is illustrated by Indonesian legislation on procurement systems which requires simply a standard of 'fair competition' between firms of 'equal standing' and, as such, creates much leeway for discretionary, and therefore opportunistic, decision making, depending on how the concepts of 'fair competition' and 'equal standing' are interpreted.[56] This is not to imply that discretion should be removed from regulatory systems; that would, indeed, be an impossibility. The suggestion is rather that, in developing countries, the design of regulatory systems should err on the side of having less discretion, rather than more.

A similar argument applies to the choice between formal and informal rules. In industrialized countries, there has been a perception that the traditional command-and-control sets of formal rules are often too prescriptive and too rigid, firms often knowing better than regulators what can best meet the regulatory goal at lowest cost. There has therefore been a movement to replace formal rules with guidelines.[57] The experience with informal rules in transitional economies and developing countries[58] has not been a happy one. Individuals have often been faced with a multitude of highly specific regulatory rules and procedures, knowing that in practice these may not be adhered to, and that informal rules, built into informal relationships with those who are to be favoured, will prevail. Those unwilling to submit to the conditions of the informal rules, and their financial implications, can still be subjected to the, often unreasonable, exigencies of the formal rules. The policy implication seems to be fewer and simpler formal rules, but not informal rules.

Next, and perhaps more controversially, there is the question of consultation processes. Within the Western tradition there has been an increasing emphasis on regulatees and third parties contributing to, and participating in, regulatory policy making and rule making. The potential benefits, in terms of improved information flows, better transparency and greater accountability are substantial, but direct access to regulatory officials does of course increase the opportunity for unlawful transactions. In the USA, efforts to maximize consultation and, at the same time, to limit the opportunities of private manipulation of the policy-making processes have led to the introduction of some important transparency measures. These include the principle that private meetings and private communications between officials and third parties are to be placed on the official record.[59] However, adequately defining and policing the requirement of a 'private' meeting, and maintaining in an accessible and transparent form the official record, may not in practice be achievable in many jurisdictions. If that is the case, some compromising on the ideals of consultation may be the price to be paid for reducing regulatory opportunistic behaviour.

4. CONCLUSIONS

In this chapter I have sought to draw parallels between opportunistic behaviour in a contractual and in a regulatory context. In both contexts it is possible to constrain the phenomenon directly by rendering the conduct subject to ex post sanctions or robust principles of accountability. However this approach requires, in the contractual context, enforcement by the victims of the opportunism who, because of their disadvantaged situation, are unlikely to be sufficiently proactive, and, in the regulatory context, by systems of criminal and administrative justice which, in some developing countries, may be insufficiently powerful and independent.

The alternative is to adopt policies which restrict the possibilities for opportunism. In the second half of the chapter I have shown how this policy goal can influence the design of regulatory institutions and principles. One of the intriguing implications of the analysis is that the models of regulatory systems urged on developing countries by Western commentators and sponsors may not always be apt for this purpose; and in consequence some trade-off will have to be made. For example, centralized, rule-based systems may, relative to the regulatory goals, be over-rigid and cumbersome, but they may reduce the possibilities for opportunistic behaviour to which flexible, discretionary systems give rise.

NOTES

1. Williamson (1985, p. 6).
2. Williamson (1998).
3. Kostritsky (2004).
4. Aviram (2003).
5. Bowles (2000).
6. Becker (1968).
7. Rose-Ackerman (1999).
8. Cooter and Garoupa (2000); Polinsky and Shavell (2001).
9. E.g. Doig (1995); World Bank (2003).
10. Quah (2001).
11. E.g. Georgia: Corruption Research Centre (Georgia) (2000).
12. Kaufmann (1997).
13. Bardhan (1997, pp. 1327–34).
14. E.g. Murphy, Shleifer and Vishny (1993).
15. Andvic and Moene (1990).
16. Tirole (1996).
17. Lindsey (2002).
18. See, for example, the experience in Cambodia, Laos and Vietnam: Wescott (2003).
19. Bardhan (1997, p. 1338).
20. Alam (1995).
21. Polinsky and Shavell (2001, pp. 19–20).

22. Rose-Ackerman (1999, ch. 5); World Bank (2003).
23. Buscaglia (1997).
24. Seoul Metropolitan Government (2001).
25. Ables (2001).
26. Ogus (2004).
27. Minogue (2004).
28. Vogel (1996).
29. Clarke and Xu (2001).
30. Kaufmann and Siegelbaum (1996); and for Latin America, Manzetti and Blake (1997).
31. Bardhan (1997, p. 1329).
32. Huther and Shah (2001).
33. Lederman, Loyaza and Soares (2001).
34. Green (1997, p. 67).
35. Shleifer and Vishny (1993).
36. Rose-Ackerman (1978).
37. Bardhan (1997, p. 1337).
38. Buscaglia (1997).
39. Bowles (2000).
40. Lederman, Loyaza and Soares (2001).
41. Wescott (2003, p. 261).
42. Klitgaard (1988, ch. 3).
43. Lederman, Loyaza and Soares (2001, p. 6).
44. Klitgaard (1988, p. 116).
45. Platteau (1996).
46. For China, see Manion (1996).
47. Djankov et al. (2002) who report inter alia that in Mozambique an entrepreneur must complete 19 procedures involving at least 149 business days.
48. Bureau of Industrial Economics Australia (1996, pp. 17–18).
49. Ogus and Zhang (2004).
50. Morisset and Neso (2002).
51. Australian Law Reform Commission (2002).
52. Ogus and Abbot (2002).
53. Green (1997, pp. 66–7).
54. Majone (1996, pp. 68–74).
55. Seidman and Seidman (1994, p. 178).
56. World Bank (2003, p. 33).
57. Baldwin (1995).
58. E.g. Zimbabwe: Goredema (2000).
59. Breyer and Stewart (1985, pp. 663–71).

REFERENCES

Ables, A.C. (2001), 'Making Philippine customs services e-ready', paper presented at the First Workshop of the APEC–OECD Cooperative Initiative on Regulatory Reform, Beijing (available at <http://www.oecd.org/dataoecd/46/19/2506438.pdf>).

Alam, M.S. (1995), 'A theory of limits on corruption and some applications', *Kyklos*, **46**, 419–35.

Andvic, J.-C. and K.O. Moene (1990), 'How corruption may corrupt', *Journal of Economic Behavior and Organization*, **13**, 63–76.

Australian Law Reform Commission (2002), *Principled Regulation: Civil and Administrative Penalties in Australian Federal Regulation*, report no. 95.

Aviram, A. (2003), 'Regulation by networks', *Brigham Young University Law Review*, 1179–1238.

Baldwin, R. (1995), *Rules and Government*, Oxford: Clarendon Press.

Bardhan, P. (1997), 'Corruption and development: a review of issues', *Journal of Economic Literature*, **35**, 1320–46.

Becker, G.S. (1968), 'Crime and punishment: an economic approach', *Journal of Political Economy*, **76**, 169–217.

Bowles, R. (2000), 'Corruption', in B. Bouckaert and G. De Geest (eds), *Encyclopedia of Law and Economics*, vol. 5, Cheltenham, UK and Northampton, MA, USA: Edward Elgar, pp. 460–91.

Breyer, S. and R. Stewart (1985), *Administrative Law and Regulatory Policy*, 2nd edn, Boston: Little, Brown.

Bureau of Industrial Economics Australia (1996), *Business Licences and Regulation Reform* (Report 96/10), Canberra: Australian Government Publishing Service.

Buscaglia, E. (1997), 'Corruption and judicial reform in Latin America', *Policy Studies Journal*, **17**, 273–95.

Clarke, G.R.G. and L.C. Xu (2001), 'Ownership, competition and corruption: bribe takers versus bribe players', World Bank Working Paper 2783.

Cooter, R. and N. Garoupa (2000), *The Virtuous Circle of Distrust: A Mechanism to Deter Bribes and Other Cooperative Crimes*, Berkeley Olin Program in Law and Economics, working paper 32.

Corruption Research Centre (Georgia) (2000), *Independent Anti-Corruption Agencies: Basic Trends and Implementation in International Practice* (available at <http://crc.gateway.ge/crc.html>).

Djankov, S., R. La Porta, F. Lopez De Silanes and A. Shleifer (2002), 'The regulation of entry', *Quarterly Journal of Economics*, **117**, 1–38.

Doig, A. (1995), 'Good government and sustainable anti-corruption strategies: a role for independent anti-corruption agencies?', *Public Administration and Development*, **15**, 151–65.

Goredema, C.T. (2000), 'Policy reforms needed to combat corruption in Zimbabwe', public lecture (available at <http://www.kubatana.net/tiz/docs/reform000229.pdf>).

Green, R.H. (1997), 'Bureaucracy and law and order', in J. Faundez (ed.), *Good Government and Law: Legal and Institutional Reform in Developing Countries*, London: Macmillan, chapter 3.

Huther, J. and A. Shah (2001), 'Anti-corruption policies and programs: a framework for evaluation', World Bank Working Paper 2501.

Kaufmann, D. (1997), 'Corruption: the facts', *Foreign Policy*, **107**, 114–31.

Kaufmann, D. and P. Siegelbaum (1996), 'Privatization and corruption in transition economies', *Journal of International Affairs*, **50**, 419–98.

Klitgaard, R. (1988), *Controlling Corruption*, Berkeley, CA: University of California Press.

Kostritsky, J.P. (2004), 'Taxonomy for justifying legal intervention in an imperfect world: what to do when parties have not achieved bargains or have drafted incomplete contracts?', *Wisconsin Law Review*, 323–78.

Lederman, D., N. Loyaza and R.R. Soares, (2001), 'Accountability and corruption: political institutions matter', World Bank Working Paper 2708.

Lindsey, T. (2002), 'History always repeats? Corruption, culture and "Asian Values"', in T. Lindsey and H. Dick (eds), *Corruption in Asia: Rethinking the Governance Paradigm*, Sydney: Federation Press, chapter 1.

Majone, G. (1996), 'The European Commission as regulator', in G. Majone (ed.), *Regulating Europe*, London: Routledge, chapter 4.

Manion, M. (1996), 'Corruption by design: bribery in Chinese enterprise licensing', *Journal of Law, Economics and Organization*, **12**, 167–96.

Manzetti, L. and C. Blake (1997), 'Market reforms and corruption in Latin America: new means for old ways', *Review of International Political Economy*, **3**, 662–97.

Minogue, M. (2004), 'Public management and regulatory governance: problems of policy transfer to developing countries', in P. Cook, C. Kirkpatrick, M. Minogue and D. Parker (eds), *Leading Issues in Competition, Regulation and Development*, Cheltenham, UK and Northampton, MA, USA: Edward Elgar.

Morisset, J. and O.L. Neso (2002), 'Administrative barriers to foreign investment in developing countries', World Bank Policy Research Working Paper 2848.

Murphy, K.M., A. Shleifer and R.W. Vishny (1993), 'Why is rent-seeking so costly to growth?', *American Economic Review*, **83**, 409–14.

Ogus, A. (2004), 'Corruption and regulatory structures', *Law and Policy*, **26**, 329–46.

Ogus, A. and C. Abbot (2002), 'Pollution and penalties', *Research in Law and Economics*, **20**, 493–512.

Ogus, A. and Q. Zhang (2004), 'Licensing east and west', *International Review of Law and Economics*, **25**, 124–42.

Platteau, J.P. (1996), 'The evolutionary theory of land rights as applied in Sub-Saharan Africa', *Development and Change*, **27**, 29–86.

Polinsky, A.M. and S. Shavell (2001), 'Corruption and optimal law enforcement', *Journal of Public Economics*, **81**, 1–24.

Quah, J.S.T. (2001), 'Combating corruption in Singapore: what can be learned', *Journal of Contingencies and Crisis Management*, **9**, 29–35.

Rose-Ackerman, S. (1978), *Corruption: A Study in Political Economy*, New York: Academic Press.

Rose-Ackerman, S. (1999), *Corruption and Government: Causes, Consequences and Reform*, Cambridge: Cambridge University Press.

Seidman, A. and R. Seidman (1994), *State and Law in the Development Process: Problem-solving and Institutional Change in the Third World*, Basingstoke: Macmillan.

Seoul Metropolitan Government (2001), 'Seoul anti-corruption symposium 2001: the role of on-line procedures in promoting good governance', (available at <http://unpan1.un.org/intradoc/groups/public/documents/un/unpan001019.pdf>).

Shleifer, A. and R. Vishny (1993), 'Corruption', *Quarterly Journal of Economics*, **108**, 599–617.

Tirole, J. (1996), 'A theory of collective reputation', *Review of Economic Studies*, **63**, 1–22.

Vogel, S.K. (1996), *Freer Markets, More Rules: Regulatory Reform in Advanced Industrialised Countries*, Ithaca and London: Cornell University Press.

Wescott, C. (2003), 'Combating corruption in South-East Asia', in J.B. Kidd and F.J. Richter (eds), *Fighting Corruption in Asia: Causes, Effects and Remedies*, Singapore: World Scientific Press, chapter 7.

Williamson, O.E. (1985), *The Economic Institutions of Capitalism: Firms, Markets, Relational Contracting*, New York: Free Press.

Williamson, O.E. (1998), 'Opportunistic behaviour in contracts', in P. Newman (ed.), *The New Palgrave Dictionary of Economics and the Law*, London and Basingstoke: Macmillan, vol. 3, pp. 410–17.

World Bank (2002), *Initiatives in Legal and Judicial Reform*, Washington DC: World Bank.

World Bank (2003), 'Combating corruption in Indonesia: enhancing accountability for development', (available at <http://wbln0018.worldbank.org/_>).

7. Special treatment (ST) firms and administrative governance of capital markets in China

Julan Du,[1] Lucy Liu Yajun and Sonia M.L. Wong

1. INTRODUCTION

In the past two decades, the remarkable development of China's financial markets was associated with poor formal legal institutions.[2] This puts China in sharp contradiction to the Washington Consensus which holds that strong property rights and investor rights protection are a central prerequisite for financial market development. The influential law and finance literature on cross-country studies demonstrates the importance of legal institutions for the emergence and development of financial markets such as formal minority shareholder,[3] formal mandatory disclosure rules and their enforcement,[4] the effectiveness of legal institutions,[5] and the legacy of legal development in countries being studied.[6]

When we turn to transition economies, including China, we find that they typically suffer from severe enforcement failures, which include deterrence failure and regulatory failure. The consequences of enforcement failures for financial market development have been identified in the literature.[7] If we were to apply the conventional logic of law and finance to the transition economies, we would predict with much confidence that financial market development in transition economies would be severely retarded. However, it seems that China defies the above prediction. As the most populous and the fastest-growing country in the world, China is too large to ignore or treat as a negligible outlier. Then why and how did China manage to develop its financial markets on the basis of weak legal institutions?

Pistor and Xu (2005)[8] and Du and Xu (2004)[9] suggest that the administrative governance institutions deployed in China's financial markets may explain this paradoxical phenomenon. In their view, the quota system is the core mechanism of the administrative governance system. The central government controls the aggregate amount of stock issuance in the initial public offering (IPO) and seasoned equity offering (SEO) stages, and allocates stock issuance quotas to different provinces. Their evidence suggests that the allocation of quotas to each region was determined by the earlier aggregate performance of the listed firms from the region. This naturally implies that the regional governments that selected better performing firms at the stock issuance stage in previous periods were rewarded by gaining more quotas at a later stage; and vice versa. By doing so, this administrative governance system which was largely inherited from the pre-reform central planning era has mitigated deterrence and regulatory failure. Although currently the rigid quota system has been replaced by the approval or 'approbation' system, the administrative control of corporate listing and stock issuance still remains to a large extent.

The accumulated evidence suggests that the quota and the approval system effectively utilized the pre-existing institutions of state and party governance in the selection of companies for listing on a stock exchange. It was built upon existing regional competition, and it created further competition among regions for access to centrally controlled equity market entry. It successfully tapped into the insider knowledge about state-owned firms possessed by state bureaucrats working for companies and/or local governments. Its reputation and incentive effects encouraged local governments to pick better performing state-owned enterprises under their jurisdiction to be listed. It effectively reduced adverse selection in the IPO stage.

The quota system and the approbation system can also improve the post-listing corporate governance to some extent by allocating the amount of seasoned equity offerings and rights issued according to regional listed company performance. However, as shown by Pistor and Xu (2005)[10] and Du and Xu (2004),[11] the quota system or the approbation system still cannot effectively curb the moral hazard problem in the post-listing stage. It has been found that more than 90 per cent of all violations by firms listed in the Shanghai and Shenzhen stock exchanges were related to violation of continuous – that is, post-listing or post-issuing – disclosure, of which 64 per cent concerned violations of ad hoc disclosure requirements.[12] The deteriorating corporate governance in the post-listing stage reflects that the market forces of the stock market, that is, the individual investors' voting through their buying and selling of shares, seems insufficient to monitor the listed companies effectively.

Furthermore, the post-listing regulation of listed companies also meets the problem of lack of credible commitment to punishing poorly performing companies. As the listing quota is the result of bargaining between the central government and the local governments, delisting a poorly performing company may meet a lot of resistance from the local government, as well as the company itself. In order to make the delisting threat credible, the central government started to implement the special treatment system in May 1998. According to the 'delisting mechanism' introduced by the China Securities Regulatory Commission (CSRC), a listed company will be labelled as a Special Treatment (ST) firm if the firm experiences one of the following: (1) there are negative net profits for two consecutive fiscal years; (2) the shareholders' equity is lower than the registered capital (the par value of the shares); (3) while auditing a listed firm's financial report the auditors issue negative opinions or declare that they are unable to issue opinions; (4) a company's financial condition is considered abnormal by the stock exchanges or CSRC. The designation of the ST status should have negative impacts on a listed firm because its interim report must be audited and the daily fluctuation of its share price is limited to 5 per cent. More importantly, if an ST company continued to make losses for one more year, it would have been further downgraded to a particular transfer (PT) firm before the abolition of the PT mechanism in 2002, and since 1 January 2002 will now directly face the danger of being delisted. While the daily price increase of a PT share cannot be more than 5 per cent to prevent insider manipulation, the price of a PT share is allowed to drop without limit. Furthermore, PT shares can only be traded on Fridays.

By announcing a company with continuous unsatisfactory performance as an ST firm, the central regulatory authorities put themselves under public scrutiny for the fulfilment of their promise to delist a company once the company's operational performance keeps deteriorating. This helps strengthen the credibility of the delisting threat.

More importantly, the ST system sends a strong signal to the local governments indicating that some listed companies under their jurisdiction have met serious operational problems. By threatening to delist ST firms and reducing future quota allocation or tightening future approval of listing for that region, the central government alerts and motivates the local governments to rescue and restructure the ailing ST firms.

This study examines the effects of ST designation on ST-listed firms. Specifically, we investigate the stock price performance as well as the impact on the likelihood of ST decapping and the ST companies' operational performance changes from corporate restructuring activities, such as share restructurings, CEO changes and largest shareholder changes, and government rescue activities, such as government subsidies to ST firms in particular and local government expenditure in general. We find significant negative abnormal returns (ARs) in the 20-day period surrounding ST announcements, but a positive cumulative abnormal return during a ten-month period after ST events. Furthermore, our results show that government subsidies as well as various restructuring activities help ST firms to improve corporate performance. Overall, our study demonstrates the partial effectiveness of the ST system as an administrative governance mechanism in maintaining the operation of China's stock markets and protecting minority shareholders.

Our research is also related to a lot of studies exploring the impact of corporate restructuring activities on financially distressed firms. For example, Gilson, John and Lang (1990),[13] and Asquith, Gertner and Scharfstein (1994)[14] examine debt restructuring of distressed firms. Brown, James and Mooradian (1993)[15] examine asset sales by distressed firms. Khanna and Poulsen (1995)[16] examine the actions of managers prior to filing for Chapter 11 bankruptcy protection. Hotchkiss and Mooradian (1996)[17] investigate the relationship between vulture investors and the market for the control of distressed firms. However, very few studies have been carried out to analyse the corporate restructuring activities of ST firms in China. Zhang (2003, in Chinese)[18] conducts a comprehensive case-study analysis of around 20 typical ST and PT firms in China's financial market, which provides a rich collection of real-world restructuring examples. Li (2003, in Chinese)[19] gives a theoretical analysis of the restructuring activities of China's ST companies. Ning and Zhang (2004)[20] believe that the ST system helps financially distressed firms to improve their corporate governance. Bai et al. (2002)[21] estimate the value of corporate control by examining the stocks' cumulative abnormal return surrounding an ST event. Ning and Zhang (2004)[22] analyse 26 public firms that were specially treated in 1998 and conclude that 'Special Treatment' policy is not as useful for corporate governance as it is supposed to be. But there have been no studies so far that examine the impact of both corporate restructurings and local government support on ST companies' accounting and market performance. Thus, our work fills this gap.

The rest of the chapter is organized as follows. Section 2 provides a detailed description of the ST mechanism in the Chinese stock market. Section 3 describes our data and provides some descriptive statistics on ST firms. Section 4 displays the methodology for event study. Section 5 studies the market reaction to ST events in the short and long term. The relationship between CAR and corporate restructuring activities is studied in Section 6. Section 7 analyses how restructuring activities affect the exit from ST status. In Section 8, we examine how restructuring activities affect the operational performance of ST firms. Section 9 concludes the chapter.

2. THE ST SYSTEM IN CHINA

The ST system was introduced in 1998. Until August 2003, there were altogether 165 firms falling into the ST firm category, among which 135 stocks were labelled as ST, 30 stocks as *ST,[23] in order to indicate their special risks; 64 stocks were once ST stocks but had their ST 'hat' successfully removed, while 101 companies were downgraded to PT or finally were delisted from the stock market after one year since they were 'specially treated'.

When a company is labelled as an ST firm, it will usually face pressure from both insiders and outsiders of the companies which aim to pull the firm's business operations and performance back onto the right track as soon as possible. Pressure normally comes from various sources, such as provincial or municipal governments, large shareholders within the firm, and potential outside bidders for corporate control.

Firstly, local governments have strong incentives to initiate corporate restructurings for ST firms. Until now, access to listing in China's stock market has been strictly administered by the central government through the 'quota' system (before March 2000) and the 'approbation' system (after March 2000). The listing quota, which is a precious and scarce resource, was allocated to each province on the basis of certain criteria, such as location, development level, liaison with central government, and past performance of listed stocks from this province.

Hence, when a listed firm becomes an ST firm, the local government, out of concern that it may 'lose face' and, more importantly, fearing the possible adverse effects on the listing opportunities that it can obtain from the central government, will be actively involved in the rescue activities. The regional competition created by the quota allocation system motivates local governments to improve listed company performance. This positive side of regional competition has been extensively documented in the literature.[24] It is widely viewed as an important reason for China's success in incremental economic reforms. In this study, we may show how regional competition encourages local governments to rescue ST firms and improve their performance.

Usually, the local government will force the incumbent controlling shareholder either to present a credible restructuring plan, often requiring substantial resource commitment, or to give up its control to another party whose restructuring plan is more convincing.

Local governments will sometimes employ political power and allocate resources under their control to rescue the ST firms. For example, some local governments act as intermediaries to initiate and arrange acquisition deals; some put administrative pressure on major creditors or state banks to write off the debts of ST firms; some use fiscal revenues to purchase the products of ST firms as a disguised form of fiscal subsidy; and some directly grant more subsidies to ST firms.

Hypothesis 1 Local governments have strong incentives to rescue ST firms. They may initiate restructuring plans by putting pressure on parties; they may directly subsidize ST firms to help prevent them from making further losses.

Secondly, the stringent quota and quantity restrictions that the central government imposed on the stock market created huge economic rents for incumbent listed firms, which are called 'shell' value. This shell value is primarily attributable to the access to the costless post-IPO equity financing. Therefore large shareholders of ST firms would like to keep this shell value by restructuring the firm.

As Bai et al. (2002) point out, the abnormal market return following the designation of ST reflects the shell value; that is, the external agents would like to pay this premium price to obtain control of the firm. Most ST firms will be restructured shortly after being labelled as such. According to Zhang (2003),[25] the restructuring plan could be divided into two camps: asset restructurings and share restructurings. Asset restructurings refer to the restructuring activities involving asset swapping, asset acquisition and asset disposal.[26] Asset restructurings, in most cases, are implemented on a large scale, mainly driven by the incentives of the controlling shareholders. The swapping includes selling inferior assets to large shareholders and in the meantime purchasing an equal amount of superior assets from them. Value differences of the superior assets over the inferior ones are always exempted by their large shareholders. This means the ST companies usually could obtain the superior assets free of charge. Take ST Zhang Jia Jie (000430), which became an ST firm in 2002, as an example. It replaced 148 million Yuan of bad assets such as accounts receivable, other receivables, prepayments and investment securities with 227 million Yuan of superior assets without paying the price difference to its largest shareholder. Furthermore, 20 million Yuan of debt burden was relieved. Hence, Zhang Jia Jie obtained 17.38 million Yuan of net profits with earnings per share (EPS) of 0.095 Yuan to get rid of the ST 'hat' in 2003.

In addition to asset restructuring, the other restructuring strategy adopted by the listed firms is share restructuring, which refers to those activities associated with share transfers and share acquisitions. Share restructuring is the most frequently used measure in all restructuring cases, which means the incumbent shareholders sell their shares to another company that wants to go public in the stock market by capturing the 'shell' resources. According to statistics from the CSMAR database, from 1998 to 2003, 1063 firms (70 per cent) of all companies listed on the Shanghai Stock Exchange had share transfers and share acquisitions, whereas only 458 had asset restructurings. A similar ratio exists in the Shenzhen stock market, where there were 586 cases of share restructurings. This indicates that share restructurings are more frequently used by listed firms. Share restructurings are frequently accompanied by mergers and acquisitions (M&A), CEO changes, large shareholder changes, business line changes, the introduction of private buyers and so on.

> *Hypothesis 2* Share restructurings and asset restructurings as well as corporate governance improvement activities such as CEO changes can help ST firms to improve market and operational performance and exit ST status.

3. SAMPLE SELECTION AND DATA DESCRIPTION

In this study, we have used several databases for different purposes. To identify firms that have been designated 'special treatment' (ST) firms from 1998 to 2003 we use the WIND Information System provided by Shanghai Wind Co. Ltd. The WIND Database covers all companies listed on the Shanghai and Shenzhen stock exchanges and includes information on stock prices and important economy-wide or firm-specific news events. From the ST announcements made in the period from 1998 to August 2003 that are contained in the WIND dataset, we identify 165 ST firms, among which 135 stocks were labelled with ST and 30 with *ST to indicate their extraordinary risks.

From the Sinofin and CSMAR databases we identified the subset of companies that underwent restructuring activities within two years of the ST announcement. Sinofin is a financial and economics database developed by the China Center for Economic Research (CCER) of Peking University, and CSMAR is a financial database developed by Shenzhen Guo Tai An Information Technology Co. We can find 125 companies out of 165 ST firms that undertook restructuring activities within two years of being labelled as ST. We can also find a lot of information related to restructurings, such as restructuring methods, CEO changes, largest shareholder changes, and large shareholders' province affiliation changes.

In addition, the firms' operational performance data come from Bloomberg, which is a leading database providing real-time and archived financial and market data and pricing information. Stock quotation data and market index quotation data come from Yahoo.com.

Table 7.1 documents the industries which ST firms are mainly engaged in and the local provinces they belong to. Using the industry classification in the CSMAR database, we divide the companies into six large industry categories: industrials, conglomerates, finance, commerce, properties and utilities. Of the 165 ST firms, most are industrials (108/165, 65.5 per cent), 27 are conglomerates (16.4 per cent), 14 are commerce (8.5 per cent);

Table 7.1 Companies entering ST status during 1998–2003

Geographical distribution			Industrial distribution			Distribution over shares type		
Province	Total	%	Industrials	Total	%	Shares type	Total	%
Guangdong	34	20.6	Commerce	14	8.5	A	140	84.8
Sichuan	14	8.5	Conglomerates	27	16.4	B	25	15.2
Shanghai	20	12.1	Industrials	108	65.5	Grand total	165	100.0
Liaoning	13	7.9	Properties	9	5.5			
Shandong	11	6.7	Utilities	7	4.2			
Hainan	10	6.1	Grand total	165	100.0			
Jilin	6	3.6						
Jiangsu	5	3.0						
Hebei	5	3.0						
Fujian	5	3.0						
Tianjian	4	2.4						
Hubei	4	2.4						
Henan	4	2.4						
Heilongjiang	4	2.4						
Chongqing	4	2.4						
Tibet	3	1.8						
Others	19	11.5						
Grand total	165	100.0						

Notes: By searching the WIND Database provided by Shanghai WIND Co. Ltd, we identify 165 ST firms during 1998–2003. This table summarizes the geographical distribution of ST firms, the industrial distribution of ST firms, and the distribution of ST firms between A and B share types.

nine are properties (5.5 per cent), seven are utilities (4.2 per cent) and none are financials (0 per cent).

Of all the provinces in China, Guangdong has the largest number of ST firms (34/165, 20.6 per cent), apparently because Guangdong has the largest number of listed firms. Other provinces which have at least ten ST firms are Shanghai (20), Sichuan (14), Liaoning (13), Shandong (11) and Hainan (10). Interestingly, Beijing just had one ST firm during the period 1998–2003.

Table 7.2 shows the causes of the ST designation. According to the ST mechanism, there are four main reasons for a firm to be labeled: (1) negative net profits for two consecutive fiscal years; (2) the shareholders' equity is lower than the registered capital (the par value of the shares); (3) while auditing a listed firm's financial report, the auditors issue negative opinions or declare that they are unable to issue opinions; (4) a firm's operation has been stopped, and there is no hope of its being restored within three months owing to a natural disaster or serious accident or if the firm is involved in a damaging lawsuit or arbitration and so on. We saw that reason (1) is most common (95/165, 57.6 per cent), followed by reason (2) (62/165, 37.6 per cent). In addition, 24 firms (14.6 per cent) are dragged into ST because the auditors issue negative opinions or claim that they are unable to issue opinions, and 17 firms (10.3 per cent) have ST status because their financial conditions are considered abnormal by the stock exchanges or CSRC. Note that there is an overlap between the different categories, since some companies were labelled as ST for more than one reason.

Among the 165 ST firms, 64 (38.8 per cent) succeeded in having their ST hats removed within one year and 101 firms were kept in ST status or delisted from the market after one year. Among ST firms with reason 1,

Table 7.2 Distribution of ST firms based on the ST reasons

ST reasons	Still ST after 1 year	Exit ST after 1 year	Delisted after 1 year	Number of firms
Type 1	8	30	24	62
Type 2	12	11	9	32
Type 3	8	5	8	21
Type 4	6	6	5	17
Type 1 & 2	6	12	12	30
Type 1 & 3	0	0	3	3
Total	40	64	61	165

Notes: We map the distribution of ST firms based on their ST reasons, and also investigate their ST status after one year. Note that some stocks were labelled as ST for multiple reasons.

about 50 per cent were finally relieved of the ST hat. They have a higher likelihood of taking off the ST hat than the overall sample average. ST firms with reasons 3 and 4 seem to have the most serious problems and are more likely to be delisted.

Based on the information available in the Sinofin and CSMAR databases, 125 firms (76 per cent of the sample) have had restructuring activities within two years of ST events. According to our earlier restructuring classification, we find that, of 125 firms, 75 (60 per cent) have share restructurings, which are defined as share transfers and share acquisitions, while 50 (30.3 per cent) have asset restructurings, that is, asset swapping, asset acquisition and asset disposal.[27] No company has debt restructuring activities within the period under our investigation.

Table 7.3 displays the detailed information about the ST firms undergoing share restructurings. Share restructurings may well induce related changes to the corporate governance structure of the ST firms, such as the change of the largest shareholder and CEO, the change of the province to which the largest shareholder belongs, the change of industry of the ST firms, and whether the buyers or controllers are private firms or not. Of the 75 firms in our sample with share restructurings, 23 ST firms have experienced a change in their largest shareholders and 30 firms changed their CEOs. As many as 45 firms have share transfers between two large shareholders located in different provinces, and just a small proportion (7/75) of ST firms change industries. In 21 cases of share restructurings, buyers are privately owned firms; in 14 cases, buyers finally become the controlling shareholders of the firms.

To figure out the factors that can help ST firms successfully exit ST status, we compare the number of successfully decapped firms under different conditions. Firstly, we divide the sample into two parts, one with share restructurings and the other without these, to see whether share restructuring plans affect the likelihood of removing the ST hat. Table 7.4 reports the statistical results. There are only 140 firms left in the sample since we exclude B shares that lack restructuring information. Among the 75 (54 per cent) ST firms with share restructuring activities, only 24 firms (32 per cent) exit ST status successfully after one year. The ratio is lower than that for non-share-restructured firms (31/65=47.7 per cent). However, this does not necessarily mean share restructurings have a negative impact on likelihood of exiting ST status. We still need to control other variables to get a clearer picture.

Secondly, in Table 7.4, we also investigate whether the likelihood of leaving ST status depends on the induced corporate governance activities measured by the following dummy variables: change of CEO, change of the largest shareholder, change of province which the firm's largest shareholder belongs to, and whether buyers are private or becoming controlling shareholders. Specifically, for share restructuring activities with CEO

Table 7.3 Summaries of the share-restructuring ST firms

Distribution of STOFF			Distribution of Ind_change			Distribution of CEO_change		
STOFF	Total	%	Ind_change	Total	%	CEO_change	Total	%
0	20	27	0	44	59	0	28	37
1	24	32	1	7	9	1	30	40
2	31	41	3	24	32	3	17	23
Grand total	75	100	Grand total	75	100	Grand total	75	100
Distribution of buyer control			Distribution of private buyer			Distribution of Largest_change		
Buyer control	Total	%	Private buyer	Total	%	Largest_change	Total	%
0	60	80	0	44	59	0	52	69
1	14	19	1	21	28	1	23	31
3	1	1	3	10	13			
Grand total	75	100	Grand total	75	100	Grand total	75	100
Distribution of Province_change								
Province_change	Total	%						
0	30	40						
1	45	60						
Grand total	75	100						

Notes: Using the information available in the CSMAR and Sinofin databases, we find 75 ST firms that have share restructurings. Several variables are designed to describe the detailed characteristics of the restructuring plans. STOFF depicts the status of the ST firms after one year, where it takes value one if 1 the ST firm exits ST status, 2 if the ST firm is delisted, and 0 if the ST firm keeps the ST hat. Ind_change, Largest_change, CEO_change, and Province_change are dummy variables that take value one if the ST firm changes its industry, its largest shareholder, its CEO through restructurings, the provincial affiliation of its largest shareholder, respectively, and take value zero otherwise. Buyer_control equals one when the buyer finally controls the firm and zero otherwise. Private_buyer equals one when the buyer is a privately-owned company and zero otherwise. Note that, for all variables, value three means there is no public information about them and they will be ticked off as missing data.

Table 7.4 Characteristics of ST firms with share restructurings

	Obs	Firms exiting ST after one year
Share_res after ST	75	24
Share_res* CEO change	30	8
Share_res* Ind change	7	1
Share_res* buyers are private	23	12
Share_res* province change	45	14
Share_res* largest shareholder change	23	10
Share_res* buyers are controllers	14	6
Non share_res after ST	65	31
Total	140	55

Notes: This table compares the descriptive statistics of share restructuring firms with those of non-share-restructuring firms. Note that there are only 140 firms in the sample. The sample does not include the B shares since we have no information about their restructuring plans. Share_res * CEO change means there is a CEO change in the course of the restructuring activities, and the same for other indicators.

changes, eight out of 30 firms successfully took off the ST hat after one year. Only one out of seven companies with industry changes during the restructuring is successfully decapped. As for the province affiliation change, only 14 of 45 firms exit ST status after one year. The result shows that changes of CEO, industry and province are not particularly useful for improving ST firm performance, judging by the descriptive statistics at least. However, if the buyer is a private entity, more than half (12/23) of the firms successfully exit ST status after one year. Meanwhile, if the largest shareholder changes and if buyers are controlling shareholders, success probabilities are higher, at 10/23 and 6/14, respectively, showing that a change in the management team of a company has a greater impact on the company's performance.

4. METHODOLOGY FOR EVENT STUDY

Picking an ST announcement as a signalling event, we can use a standard event study approach to calculate the abnormal return. We adopt the market model to calculate the normal return as follows:

$$R_{it} = \alpha_i + \beta_i R_{mt} + \eta_{it}, \tag{7.1}$$

where α_i is the intercept measuring the mean return over the period not explained by the market, β_i is the slope coefficient, which measures the risk of a firm relative to the market, η_{it} is the error term at time t, which has a mean of zero and constant variance σ_i^2.

The abnormal returns (AR) are the actual stock return over the event window minus the normal return of the stock over the same event window, in which the normal return is the expected return if no event occurs. It can be expressed as follows:

$$AR_{it} = R_{it} - E[R_{it} | X_t], \tag{7.2}$$

where AR_{it}, R_{it} and $E[R_{it}|X_t]$ are abnormal, actual and normal returns for firm i at time t. X_t is the conditioning information for the normal performance model.

Let $t=0$ denote the announcement date. The OLS coefficients of the market model regression are estimated over the estimation window: $t = -120$ to $t=-21$. After estimating the parameters, we begin to calculate ARs within the event window. We choose the period from -20 to 20 as the event window.

To cancel out the 'noise' for individual stock returns, the residuals are averaged across firms for each day t in the designated period to produce the average abnormal return of the day $\overline{AR}_t$ as

$$\overline{AR}_t = \frac{1}{N}\sum_{i=1}^{N} AR_{it}. \tag{7.3}$$

N is the number of the firms in the sample, and $t=-20$ to $+20$.

If we want to reveal the average total effect of a merger announcement over the specified period, we calculate the cumulative abnormal return, which is expressed thus:

$$\overline{CAR}_{T1T2} = \sum_{t=T1}^{T2} AR_t,\ [T_1, T_2] \subset [-20,20]. \tag{7.4}$$

We use a statistical test similar to that of Dodd and Warner (1983) and Travlos (1987) to see whether the null hypothesis of no abnormal returns holds.

H_0: the average AR of day t is zero, i.e., $AR_t=0$
H_1: the average AR of day t is unequal to zero, i.e., $AR_t \neq 0$

We also want to test whether there is a significant cumulative abnormal return:

H_0: the cumulative average AR over event window $[T_1,T_2]$, i.e., $\overline{CAR}_{T1T2} = 0$
H_1: the cumulative average AR over event window $[T_1,T_2]$, i.e., $\overline{CAR}_{T1T2} \neq 0$

The test statistics of AR_t and $\overline{CAR}_{T1T2}$ are based on the average standardized AR ($\overline{SAR}_t$) and average standardized cumulative AR ($\overline{SCAR}_{T1T2}$).

$$\overline{SAR}_t = \frac{1}{N}\sum_{i=1}^{N}\frac{AR_{it}}{S_{it}},\ t = -20,\ldots,20 \qquad (7.5)$$

$$\overline{SCAR}_{T1T2} = \sum_{t=T_1}^{T_2}\overline{SAR}_t,\ [T_1,T_2]\subset[-20,20] \qquad (7.6)$$

Here, S_{it} is the square root of firm i's estimated forecast variance calculated by

$$S_{it} = \sqrt{S_i^2 + \frac{1}{L}\left(1 + \frac{(R_{mt} - \overline{R}_m)^2}{\sum_{j=1}^{L}(R_{mj} - \overline{R}_m)^2}\right)} \qquad (7.7)$$

where $S_i^2 = (1/(L-2))\Sigma_{j=1}^{L}(R_{ij} - \hat{\alpha}_i - \hat{\beta}_i R_{mj})$ is the residual variance for firms from the market-model regression; L is the number of days in the estimation window; R_{mj} is the daily market return for the jth day in the estimation window; R_{mt} is the daily market return for day t in the event window; $\overline{R}_m$ is the average daily market return for the entire estimation window.

We can define the statistic Z_1 as

$$Z_1 = \sqrt{N} \times \overline{SAR}_t,\ t = -20,\ldots,20 \qquad (7.8)$$

to test the hypothesis that $\overline{SAR}_t$ is equal to zero.
We can also define the statistic Z_2 as

$$Z_2 = \sqrt{\frac{N}{T_2 - T_1 + 1}} \times \overline{SCAR}_t \qquad (7.9)$$

to test whether $\overline{SCAR}_{T1T2}$ equals zero.

If we assume that the individual abnormal returns are normally distributed and independent through time t and across firms, Z_1 follows a normal distribution.

5. MARKET REACTION TO ST EVENTS: EVENT STUDY

We examine in this section the market reactions to ST events by calculating the short-term and long-term abnormal returns and the cumulative abnormal returns surrounding the ST announcements. As mentioned in section 3, we have obtained a sample of 165 ST firms. However, before calculating the abnormal returns within the event window, we need to make a further examination of the stock price data. We require that the sample companies have complete stock quotation data for two years surrounding the ST announcement date. We drop some firms according to the following criteria: firstly, those stocks with a long period of non-trading days before or after the ST announcement event and those stocks issued less than one year before the ST event will be eliminated from the sample because we cannot get accurate abnormal returns; secondly, a few firms were delisted after the transactions so that we cannot find their stock prices around the event.[28] This produces a final sample of 130 firms.

The market return is expressed as the market index return. We choose the Shanghai Composite Index and the Shenzhen Component Index as proxies for market performance because of their long history and wide use. Historical index data are collected from Yahoo as well. We mainly examine the short-term and long-term market reaction to ST events. To see the short-term reactions, we calculate the abnormal returns during a short window, that is, between 20 days before ST events and 20 days after the events. The estimation window (for model parameters) is −120 days to −21 days. Date 0 is the ST announcement day. Table 7.5 depicts clearly the average abnormal returns, the standardized abnormal return and their statistical test results. We find negative daily standardized abnormal returns in most of the days during the event window [−20,20], which have significant Z-statistics. It is noteworthy that on the announcement date (day 0) not only does the abnormal return fall to the lowest level (−1.5 per cent) during the period, but also the Z-statistics are most significant at the 1 per cent level (−16.64). This means that the ST firms have the most significantly negative abnormal return at the announcement day. The mean of the abnormal return for the whole event window is −0.24 per cent, with a standard deviation of 0.47 per cent. Thus we cannot reject the hypothesis that the average abnormal return is zero. In this sense, the short-term market reaction to ST designation is similar to the negative reactions to delisting firms in the Western developed markets.

However, when we take a longer event window, there is a positive valuation effect for ST firms. Just as Bai et al. (2002)[29] did in their paper, weekly return data are used to calculate the cumulative abnormal return. The event

Table 7.5 Abnormal return for the short event window

Date	ARbar 1	SARbar 1	Z1
−20	0.0006	−0.01	−0.15
−19	0.0028	0.11	1.44
−18	0.0040	0.08	1.13
−17	0.0017	0.07	0.89
−16	−0.0016	−0.08	−1.08
−15	0.0040	0.05	0.61
−14	0.0003	−0.48	−6.55***
−13	−0.0051	−0.75	−10.13***
−12	−0.0049	−0.78	−10.54***
−11	−0.0034	−0.68	−9.23***
−10	−0.0005	−0.49	−6.60***
−9	−0.0010	−0.55	−7.40***
−8	−0.0020	−0.52	−7.01***
−7	−0.0036	−0.62	−8.40***
−6	−0.0045	−0.70	−9.44***
−5	−0.0010	−0.49	−6.66***
−4	−0.0035	−0.64	−8.67***
−3	−0.0063	−0.80	−10.86***
−2	−0.0078	−0.82	−11.14***
−1	−0.0087	−0.08	−1.03
0	−0.0148	−1.23	−16.64***
1	−0.0150	−0.83	−11.28***
2	−0.0131	−0.38	−5.11***
3	−0.0092	−0.34	−4.64***
4	−0.0014	−0.24	−3.22***
5	0.0014	0.04	0.50
6	−0.0040	−0.05	−0.62
7	0.0042	0.11	1.50
8	−0.0022	−0.17	−2.25**
9	0.0039	0.18	2.49**
10	−0.0010	−0.04	−0.55
11	0.0044	0.06	0.78
12	−0.0007	−0.10	−1.38
13	0.0016	0.16	2.17**
14	−0.0002	−0.07	−0.94
15	−0.0045	−0.14	−1.91
16	0.0010	−0.02	−0.28
17	−0.0010	−0.02	−0.33
18	−0.0026	−0.20	−2.64***

Table 7.5 (continued)

Date	ARbar 1	SARbar 1	Z1
19	−0.0014	−0.36	−4.81***
20	−0.0041	−0.31	−4.13***

Notes: This table reports the abnormal return during the short event window of [−20,+20] days around the ST announcement date; *ARbar1* is the average abnormal return adjusted by the market index for date *t*; *SARbar1* is the standard abnormal return; and *Z1* shows the Z-test statistics to see whether the abnormal return is significant or not. Owing to limited data availability, 130 observations are included: * significant at 10%; ** signifiicant at 5%; *** significant at 1%.

Table 7.6 Summary statistics for the long-term cumulative abnormal return

	Obs.	Mean (%)	Standard deviation (%)	Minimum (%)	Maximum (%)
Whole sample	130	9.67	36.20	−38.5	150.6
1998–2000	42	35.9	42.1	−28.7	150.6
2001–2003	88	−2.9	24.78	−38.5	75.2
A-shares	111	6.8	33.75	−38.5	66.3
B-shares	19	26.38	45.8	−24.3	150.6
Share restructuring	75	10.28	36.79	−38.1	116.9
Non-share restructuring	55	9.07	35.83	−38.5	65.77

Notes: This table summarizes the ten-month cumulative abnormal return after ST announcement events. We also break down the whole sample by time, share type and restructuring events. Non-share restructuring is defined to describe the firms with no restructuring plans and restructuring other than share restructuring plans (asset restructuring).

window is about ten months long, from the tenth week after the ST announcement day to the forty-eighth week after the day, i.e. [+10,+48]. The estimation window is −sixtieth week to +tenth week, i.e. [−60,+10].

Table 7.6 summarizes the results. The mean of the cumulative abnormal return for the whole sample during the ten-month period after the ST event is as high as 9.67 per cent, with a median of 10.1 per cent. There is a big variation in CARs, with the standard deviation equal to 36.2 per cent. The lowest cumulative abnormal return is −38.5 per cent, while the largest is 150.6 per cent.

To identify the factors affecting the cumulative return, we also examine the cumulative abnormal returns (CARs) for ST firms in different categories. We first calculate the CARs in two time periods: the first period is from 1998 to 2000, and the second one is from 2001 to 2003. The mean cumulative abnormal return in 1998–2000 is 35.9 per cent. This result is consistent with that of Bai et al. (2002).[30] However, the second period produces an average CAR of −2.9 per cent.

We also compare the CARs for A shares and B shares. The mean abnormal return for A shares is 6.8 per cent, while that for B shares is as high as 26.38 per cent. Foreign investors seem to give a larger positive response to ST events than domestic investors do. Perhaps companies with B shares are more inclined to undertake proactive rescuing activities to prevent the stocks from being delisted, given that the company or local government do not want to be humiliated in front of foreign investors.

Finally, we compare the mean CARs for ST firms with different restructuring methods. According to the last two rows of the table, the average CAR for ST firms with share restructurings is 10.28 per cent, while the mean CAR for non-share-restructuring firms is 9.07 per cent. It is not very easy to assess from the descriptive statistics whether these two camps of restructuring methods affect the market reaction differently.

6. RELATIONSHIP BETWEEN CUMULATIVE ABNORMAL RETURNS AND RESTRUCTURING ACTIVITIES

This section provides a cross-sectional analysis of the CARs. There are basically two questions we are trying to address. Firstly, we want to investigate whether or not corporate restructuring activities following ST events will affect the stocks' market performance. We include two dummy variables, *Share_restructuring* and *Asset_restructuring*, in the regression analysis. They are equal to one when there are share and asset restructurings taking place in the ST firm, respectively, and zero otherwise.

Secondly, we examine whether corporate governance restructurings such as CEO or largest shareholders changes affect CARs. These activities may reshuffle the corporate management team and improve corporate performance. Meanwhile, these activities are often initiated or administrated by provincial or local governments since listing quota is a scarce and, thus, valuable resource for each province and local governments normally do not want to lose any listed company unless no better solutions could be found.

If corporate control changes hands from one shareholder in one province to another shareholder in another province, it is also an important signal. Local governments normally have strong incentives to arrange the restructuring activities among the companies under their jurisdiction so as to keep the listing quota and financing channel. Only when they cannot find a suitable buyer within their own provinces will they allow interprovincial share transfers to take place.

As privately owned enterprises are widely agreed to be more profit-maximization-oriented, corporations under their control are likely to perform better than state-controlled ones. We thus include ownership status in the regressions, which takes the value one when the buyer is private and zero otherwise.

In addition, we also control for factors such as ST reasons (*ST_reason*) and industry (*Industry*). To control for the potential effects of regional characteristics, we include provincial GDP (*GDP*), provincial government expenditure (*GE*), provincial unemployment rate (*Unemploy_rate*) and so on. We also put provincial dummy variables into the regressions to control for other immeasurable provincial factors.

Moreover, we control for the listing quota of each province in the regressions. We use the ratio of the number of listed companies to the total number of firms of each province to proxy for the quota. In this sense, we assume that each province will make full use of its listing quota so that the number of listed companies from each province is approximately equal to the maximum quota allocated to each province. Since the listing quota is closely associated with the number of companies or the financing demands of each province, we divide it by the total number of companies in this province.[31]

Direct subsidies from local governments to ST firms are a central approach to rescuing ST companies. To assess the effects of government subsidies, we introduce two variables: *Subsidy_ST_yr* and *Subsidy_1yr_after*, which refer to the government subsidy shown in the Income Statement in the year of, and the year after, the ST event.

Panel (a) of Table 7.7 shows the regression results on asset restructurings. We find that asset restructurings do not significantly affect the market performance of ST firms. However, in Panel (b) of Table 7.7, we obtain a significantly positive estimated coefficient (0.159 with p-value 0.043) for *Share_restructuring*, which indicates that the stock market reacts positively to the share restructuring activities of ST firms. This confirms our hypothesis that share restructurings have positive effects on the market valuation of the ST firms.

The statistically significant and positive coefficient (0.06 with p-value 0.046) on the *CEO_change* shows that the ST firms with CEO changes can generally gain a larger cumulative abnormal return. This demonstrates how managerial turnover may improve corporate performance. The dummy variable indicating largest shareholder changes has a positive but insignificant coefficient, implying that largest shareholder changes do not have as great an impact as CEO changes do. The positive but insignificant estimated

Table 7.7 Regression results on cumulative abnormal return

Notes: The dependent variable is the long-term (ten-month) cumulative abnormal return (CAR) for each individual firm. The regressors include dummy variables for related restructuring methods (*Asset_restructuring* and *Share_restructuring*) and other dummy variables for the ST reasons, industries, change of CEO and largest shareholder change etc. To control for the governments' influence, we include provincial dummy variables and province-level economic indicators in the regressions, such as GDP (*GDP*), Government Expenditure (*GE*) and unemployment rate (*Unemploy_rate*). We also see the effects of a government subsidy in the year of, and one year after, ST events (*Subsidy_ST_yr* means the government subsidy level in the year the ST occurs; and *Subsidy_1yr_after* refers to government subsidy level one year after ST events). Meanwhile, to control for the effect of the listing quota for each province, we define the variable *Quota* as the number of listed companies over the total number of firms for each province, which measures the listing pressure of quota for each province.

Panel (a) Regression results with asset restructurings

	Estimated coefficients	Standard deviation	t value	Pr(>|t|)
Asset_restructuring	−0.046	0.081	−0.572	0.569
ST_reason1&2	0.104	0.109	0.955	0.343
ST_reason1&3	−0.185	0.359	−0.515	0.608
ST_reason2	0.109	0.104	1.054	0.296
ST_reason3	−0.023	0.126	−0.179	0.859
ST_reason4	0.054	0.181	0.298	0.767
Subsidy_ST_yr (mn Rmb)	−0.021	0.062	−0.329	0.743
Subsidy_1yr_after (mn Rmb)	0.062	0.038	1.569	0.122
CEO_change	0.060	0.040	1.640	0.110
Largest_change	0.028	0.071	0.402	0.689
Buyer_private	0.040	0.088	0.490	0.630
Industry_Conglomerates	0.044	0.152	0.290	0.772
Industry_Industrials	0.053	0.129	0.414	0.680
Industry_Properties	−0.017	0.208	−0.082	0.935
Industry_Utilities	−0.107	0.278	−0.385	0.701
GDP (mn Rmb)	0.002	0.001	1.660	0.100*
Quota	13.410	57.140	0.240	0.820
Unemploy_rate (%)	0.010	0.012	0.860	0.400
GE (mn Rmb)	0.010	0.005	2.270	0.030**
Province_Beijing	0.191	0.477	0.402	0.689
Province_Chongqing	0.244	0.388	0.630	0.531
Province_Fujian	0.341	0.396	0.861	0.392
Province_Gansu	0.187	0.424	0.441	0.661
Province_Guangdong	0.091	0.346	0.264	0.793
Province_Guizhou	−0.235	0.481	−0.490	0.626

Panel (a) (continued)

	Estimated coefficients	Standard deviation	t value	Pr(>|t|)
Province_Hainan	0.189	0.359	0.526	0.600
Province_Heilongjiang	−0.006	0.413	−0.015	0.988
Province_Henan	0.095	0.392	0.242	0.810
Province_Hubei	−0.024	0.379	−0.063	0.950
Province_Hunan	−0.010	0.407	−0.023	0.981
Province_Jiangsu	0.325	0.407	0.798	0.428
Province_Jilin	−0.007	0.376	−0.019	0.985
Province_Liaoning	0.282	0.358	0.787	0.434
Province_Inner Mongolia	−0.108	0.428	−0.253	0.801
Province_Ningxia	−0.164	0.420	−0.391	0.697
Province_Shandong	0.052	0.360	0.146	0.884
Province_Shanghai	0.022	0.349	0.062	0.951
Province_Shanxi	0.499	0.480	1.039	0.303
Province_Sichuan	0.258	0.350	0.736	0.465
Province_Tianjin	0.061	0.551	0.112	0.912
Province_Xinjiang	0.661	0.499	1.326	0.189
Province_Xizang	0.276	0.387	0.712	0.479
Province_Zhejiang	0.056	0.499	0.113	0.910

Residual standard error: 0.3275; adjusted R-squared: −0.1174; F-statistic: 0.7053, p-value: 0.8712, Number of observations: 130

Notes: This table examines the impact of asset restructurings on the stocks' long-term cumulative abnormal returns by controlling other factors; * significant at 10%; ** significant at 5%; *** significant at 1%.

Panel (b) Regression results with share restructurings

	Estimated coefficients	Standard deviation	t value	Pr(>|t|)
Share_restructuring	0.159	0.077	2.061	0.043**
ST_reason1&2	0.088	0.106	0.825	0.412
ST_reason1&3	−0.276	0.351	−0.788	0.434
ST_reason2	0.113	0.100	1.129	0.263
ST_reason3	−0.015	0.120	−0.126	0.900
ST_reason4	0.065	0.173	0.374	0.710
Subsidy_ST_yr (mn Rmb)	−0.021	0.031	−0.650	0.518
Subsidy_1yr_after (mn Rmb)	0.061	0.036	1.799	0.077*

Panel (b) (continued)

	Estimated coefficients	Standard deviation	t value	Pr(>|t|)
Industry_Conglomerates	0.081	0.148	0.543	0.589
Industry_Industrials	0.079	0.125	0.632	0.530
Industry_Properties	0.022	0.200	0.110	0.913
Industry_Utilities	0.027	0.278	0.097	0.923
CEO_change	0.060	0.030	2.009	0.046**
Largest_change	0.032	0.039	0.84	0.42
Buyer_private	0.040	0.090	0.490	0.630
GDP (mn Rmb)	0.002	0.001	1.660	0.100*
Quota	13.41	57.14	0.240	0.820
Unemploy_rate (%)	0.002	0.002	0.900	0.400
GE (mn Rmb)	0.006	0.003	2.030	0.040**

Residual standard error: 0.3181; Adjusted R-squared: −0.05411;
F-statistic: 0.856, p-value: 0.6894, Number of observations: 130

Notes: All regressions include provincial dummies. This table examines the impact of a share restructuring on the stocks' long-term cumulative abnormal return by controlling other factors; * significant at 10%; ** significant at 5%; *** significant at 1%.

Panel (c) *Regression results with share restructurings and asset restructurings*

	Estimated coefficients	Standard deviation	t value	Pr(>|t|)
Share_restructuring	0.158	0.077	2.044	0.045**
Asset_restructuring	−0.044	0.079	−0.565	0.574
ST_reason1&2	0.084	0.107	0.787	0.434
ST_reason1&3	−0.296	0.354	−0.835	0.407
ST_reason2	0.109	0.101	1.074	0.287
ST_reason3	−0.03	0.123	−0.247	0.806
ST_reason4	0.047	0.177	0.268	0.79
Subsidy_ST_yr (mn Rmb)	−0.021	0.032	−0.690	0.493
Subsidy_1yr_after (mn Rmb)	0.062	0.035	1.784	0.079*
Industry_Conglomerates	0.084	0.149	0.566	0.573
Industry_Industrials	0.092	0.127	0.711	0.483
Industry_Properties	0.044	0.205	0.214	0.831
Industry_Utilities	0.035	0.28	0.125	0.901
CEO_change	0.033	0.042	0.811	0.421

Panel (c) (continued)

	Estimated coefficients	Standard deviation	t value	Pr(>|t|)
Largest_change	0.019	0.212	0.092	0.910
Buyer_private	0.004	0.112	0.043	0.972
GDP (mn Rmb)	0.072	0.041	1.660	0.10*
Quota	13.41	57.14	0.240	0.82
Unemploy_rate (%)	0.003	0.003	0.861	0.42
GE (mn Rmb)	0.052	0.021	2.271	0.03**

Residual standard error: 0.3198; Adjusted R-squared: −0.06527;
F-statistic: 0.8327, p-value: 0.723, Number of observations: 130

Notes: All regressions include provincial dummies. This table puts share restructuring and asset-restructuring together into one regression and examines the impact of both restructuring methods on the stocks' long-term cumulative abnormal return, by controlling other factors; * significant at 10%; ** significant at 5%; *** significant at 1 %.

coefficient on the dummy variable *Buyer_private* does not support the prediction that private firms bring better market reactions.

Subsidy_ST_yr, which stands for the government subsidy level in the ST announcement year, has a negative but statistically insignificant estimated coefficient (−0.021 with p-value 0.518). Interestingly, *Subsidy_1yr_after*, that is, the government subsidy level in the year following the ST announcement year, produces a positive estimated coefficient which is significant at the 10 per cent level (0.061 with p-value 0.077). This depicts a positive relationship between government subsidies and stock market performance, and implies that government subsidies play a pivotal role in covering operational losses and injecting new capital into the ST firms, which in turn help revive corporate performance and boost investors' confidence in the ST firm.

Now let us turn to the province-level economic variables. Government expenditure (*GE*) has a positive coefficient that is significant at the 5 per cent level (0.006 with p-value 0.04). This reinforces our conclusion that government subsidies, as part of government expenditure, help improve the market performance of ST firms. The provincial GDP level (*GDP*) has a positive impact on market reaction, which is statistically significant at the 10 per cent level (0.002 with p-value 0.1). This illustrates that investors are more optimistic about ST firms from provinces with a larger economy and thus potentially larger fiscal resources to rescue the ST firms.

In Panel (c) of Table 7.7, we include both restructuring methods in the regressions. *Share_restructuring* still has a positive and significant effect (0.158 with p-value 0.045) on stock market performance while *Asset_restructuring* does not show significant impacts (−0.044 with p-value 0.574). Government subsidy level in the year following the ST announcement year (*Subsidy_1yr_after*), provincial GDP level (*GDP*) and government expenditure (*GE*) still show significantly positive impacts on stock market performance. In our results, the listing quota of each province (*Quota*), industry (*Industry*) and ST reasons (*ST_reason*) do not exhibit significant influences.

Overall, the cross-sectional analysis adds to the evidence that share restructurings after ST events and government subsidies play a vital role in improving the performance of ST firms.

7. RELATIONSHIP BETWEEN ST STATUS AND RESTRUCTURING ACTIVITIES

When a firm enters ST status, both the local government and the controlling shareholders have strong incentives to rescue the firm because of the appealing 'shell' value. Moreover, as state and state legal person shares dominate the shareholding structure in most listed companies in China, regional or local governments representing the state owner have an obligation to rescue the companies. Government subsidy is commonly used to improve the financial performance of those ST firms, although sometimes this could be pure window dressing.

In this section, a Probit model is adopted to see what factors help ST firms successfully remove their ST 'hats'. We use STOFF as the dependent variable, which equals one if the firm gets decapped from ST in one year's time and zero otherwise.[32] Similarly, the variables that explain the magnitude of CARs can also explain the strength the incentives of the largest shareholders or the local governments have to take off the firm's ST 'hat', and how likely they would be eventually to succeed.

As to the regressors, we also employ the dummy variables *Share_restructuring* and *Asset_restructuring* to see if the likelihood of ST decapping is associated with the restructuring methods. As in the previous section, we include a host of other variables such as *CEO_change*, *Largest_change*, *Buyer_private*, *ST_reason*, *Industry*, *Subsidy_ST_yr*, *Subsidy_1yr_after*, *Quota* and province-level economic variables (*GDP, Unemploy_rate, GE*) in the regression to examine whether they affect the likelihood of exiting ST status.

Panel (a) of Table 7.8 shows the Probit model regression results with asset restructurings. We find that the asset restructuring activities have slightly positive but insignificant effects on the likelihood of ST de-capping. This result is consistent with the insignificant effects of asset restructurings on the CAR of ST firms in Table 7.7.

Table 7.8 Probit model regression for ST status and restructuring plans

Notes: This series of tables presents the empirical results on the factors explaining the relationship between restructuring activities and the likelihood of ST decapping. The dependent variable is a dummy variable, STOFF, which equals one when a ST firm exits ST status after one year and zero otherwise. The regressors include dummy variables for related restructuring methods (*Asset_restructuring* and *Share_restructuring*) and other dummy variables for the ST reasons, industries, change of CEO and largest shareholder change etc. To control the governments' effect, we include provincial dummy variables and province-level economic indicators in the regressions, such as GDP (*GDP*), Government Expenditure (*GE*) and the unemployment rate (*Unemploy_rate*). We also examine the effects of a government subsidy in the year of, and one year after, ST events (*Subsidy_ST _yr* means the government subsidy level in the year the ST occurs; and *Subsidy_1yr_after* refers to the government subsidy level one year after ST events). Meanwhile, to control for the effect of the listing quota for each province, we define the variable *Quota* as the number of listed companies over the total number of firms for each province which measures the listing pressure of the quota for each province.

Panel (a) Probit model regression result with asset restructurings

	Estimated coefficients	Standard deviation	Z value	Pr(>|Z|)
Asset_restructuring	1.117	0.607	1.342	0.167
ST_reason1&2	−0.386	0.606	−0.637	0.524
ST_reason1&3	−5.709	23.220	−0.246	0.806
ST_reason2	1.979	1.400	1.413	0.158
ST_reason3	−2.216	0.772	−2.870	0.004***
ST_reason4	−2.382	0.997	−2.390	0.017**
Subsidy_ST_yr (mn Rmb)	−0.020	0.008	−2.442	0.015**
Subsidy_1yr_after (mn Rmb)	0.041	0.020	2.035	0.042**
Industry_Conglomerates	0.701	0.823	0.852	0.394
Industry_Industrials	−0.430	0.801	−0.537	0.591
Industry_Properties	0.062	1.217	0.051	0.959
Industry_Utilities	3.246	16.300	0.199	0.842
CEO_change	−0.628	1.415	−0.444	0.657
Largest_change	−0.474	1.624	−0.292	0.771
Buyer_private	−0.321	1.523	−0.221	0.791
GDP (mn Rmb)	−0.018	0.011	−1.648	0.099*
Quota	−457.800	484.800	−0.944	0.345
Unemploy_rate (%)	0.002	0.015	0.135	0.892
GE (mn Rmb)	0.023	0.021	1.041	0.298

AIC: 150.94
Null deviance: 142.546 on 102 degrees of freedom
Residual deviance: 77.287 on 60 degrees of freedom
Number of observations: 130

Notes: All regressions include provincial dummies. This table examines the impact of asset restructurings on the likelihood of ST decapping, by controlling for other factors;
* significant at 10%; ** significant at 5%; *** significant at 1%.

Panel (b) Probit model regression result with share restructurings

	Estimated coefficients	Standard deviation	Z value	Pr(>|Z|)
Share_restructuring	1.065	0.548	1.963	0.050**
ST_reason1&2	−0.276	0.622	−0.444	0.657
ST_reason1&3	−4.734	23.230	−0.204	0.839
ST_reason2	1.366	1.367	1.000	0.317
ST_reason3	−1.917	0.710	−2.701	0.007***
ST_reason4	−1.973	0.900	−2.191	0.028**
Subsidy_ST_yr (mn Rmb)	−0.023	0.011	−2.153	0.031**
Subsidy_1yr_after (mn Rmb)	0.043	0.021	2.164	0.030**
Industry_Conglomerates	0.660	0.812	0.813	0.416
Industry_Industrials	−0.067	0.769	−0.087	0.931
Industry_Properties	−0.012	1.267	−0.010	0.992
Industry_Utilities	3.510	15.200	0.231	0.817
CEO_change	0.24	0.119	2.076	0.038**
Largest_change	−0.156	0.597	−0.261	0.794
Buyer_private	−0.435	1.542	−0.281	0.771
GDP (mn Rmb)	−0.010	0.010	−1.006	0.315
Quota	−560.800	486.600	−1.152	0.249
Unemploy_rate (%)	0.002	0.008	0.211	0.833
GE (mn Rmb)	0.002	0.004	0.446	0.656

AIC: 237.57
Null deviance: 142.55 on 102 degrees of freedom
Residual deviance: 65.75 on 60 degrees of freedom
Number of observations: 130

Notes: All regressions include provincial dummies. This table examines the impact of share restructurings on the likelihood of ST de-capping, by controlling for other factors; * significant at 10%; ** significant at 5%; *** significant at 1%.

Panel (c) Probit model results with share restructurings and asset restructurings

	Estimated coefficients	Standard deviation	Z value	Pr(>|Z|)
Share_restructuring	1.642	0.504	3.260	0.001***
Asset_restructuring	0.518	0.449	1.154	0.248
ST_reason1&2	0.054	0.570	0.094	0.925
ST_reason1&3	−3.730	23.220	−0.161	0.872

Panel (c) (continued)

	Estimated coefficients	Standard deviation	Z value	Pr(>|Z|)
ST_reason2	−1.482	0.598	−2.478	0.013**
ST_reason3	−1.342	0.715	−1.877	0.061*
ST_reason4	1.137	1.221	0.931	0.352
Subsidy_ST_yr (mn Rmb)	−0.041	0.021	−1.978	0.048**
Subsidy_1yr_after (mn Rmb)	0.054	0.024	2.332	0.020**
Industry_Conglomerates	0.751	0.839	0.895	0.371
Industry_Industrials	−0.180	0.786	−0.229	0.819
Industry_Properties	−0.238	1.165	−0.205	0.838
Industry_Utilities	3.725	15.450	0.241	0.809
GDP (mn Rmb)	−0.004	0.007	−0.599	0.549
Quota	−414.0	392.8	−1.054	0.292
Unemploy_rate (%)	0.004	0.005	0.829	0.407
GE (mn Rmb)	−0.003	0.006	−0.484	0.629

AIC: 149.7
Number of observations: 130

Notes: All regressions include provincial dummies. This table puts share restructuring and asset restructuring together into one regression and tries to examine the impact of both restructuring methods on the likelihood of ST decapping, by controlling for other factors; * significant at 10%; ** significant at 5%; *** significant at 1%.

Panel (b) of Table 7.8 displays the Probit model regression results with share restructurings. We see that share restructurings can help companies remove the ST hat. This result is reasonable and consistent with the positive relationship between share restructuring activities and CARs of ST firms in Table 7.7. This suggests that share restructurings, usually accompanied by share acquisitions, business line changes and CEO changes and the rest, have improved the ST firms' operational performance so that they are more likely to exit ST status.

We find a positive and significant coefficient on the dummy variable *CEO_change* (0.24 with p-value 0.038), which indicates that ST firms are more likely to exit the ST status if they reshuffle their management team. *Subsidy_ST_yr* produces a negative coefficient (−0.023 with p-value 0.031), while *Subsidy_1yr_after* has a positive coefficient significant at the 5 per cent level (0.043 with p-value 0.03). It shows that the higher the government subsidy level in the year after firms are being ST-ed, that is, the greater the efforts by the local governments to rescue the ST firms, the more likely it is that the companies can get rid of the ST hat. The coefficients of *ST_reason3* and *ST_reason4* are both significantly negative (−1.917 with p-value 0.007, and −1.973 with p-value 0.028, respectively). In other words, those firms labelled as ST for non-operating reasons, such as because auditors issue negative or no opinions (ST reason 3) or business operations stopped because of serious accidents or legal issues (reason 4) have a smaller probability of getting rid of ST caps. The results are reasonable since non-operational problems are usually more difficult to solve than operational performance problems, since the latter can be solved through restructurings, earnings management or government subsidies, and so on.

Panel (c) of Table 7.8 includes both restructuring methods, and the results reiterate our conclusion that share restructurings can help ST firms get out of the ST status, while asset restructuring has no significant effect.

8. OPERATIONAL PERFORMANCE BEFORE AND AFTER SHARE RESTRUCTURING ACTIVITIES OF ST FIRMS

In this section, we will examine whether share restructurings contribute to the improvement in ST firms' operational performance so as to help them remove the ST hat. We compare the pre- and post-restructuring measures of profitability. Accounting measures of profitability are used by Hotchkiss (1995)[33] to describe performance subsequent to the Chapter 11 bankruptcy protection reorganizations. Similar variables are considered here for ST firms. Among the 75 ST firms with share restructurings, 68 firms do not have missing data and are used in this study.

In this study we consider five financial indicators: total revenue, operating income, total assets, operating cash flow, and net debt to the shareholder's equity, that is, leverage ratio. Operating cash flow is measured as the cash flow generated from the company's operating activities. Operating income is defined as total sales minus cost of goods sold (COGS) and selling, general and administrative expenses (SG&A) before deducting depreciation and amortization. We normalize the operating income by either total revenue or total assets, in order to exclude the bias generated by company size. The return on sales measure is less directly affected by asset write-downs or divestitures and by differences in accounting treatments between the sample firms and their industry counterparts which are used to calculate the industry-adjusted term. All related variables are reported on an industry-adjusted basis by subtracting the mean of the industry portfolio that consists of all other comparable firms.[34]

Table 7.9 reports the descriptive statistics of the absolute and industry-adjusted mean values of the accounting variables in three full fiscal years surrounding the share restructuring events. The three-year time period is from the year before the share restructuring event until two years after the restructuring.

Table 7.9 Performance of ST firms before and after share restructuring activities

		Operating income/ total sales		Operating income/ total assets	
	Obs	Mean	Industry-adjusted mean	Mean	Industry-adjusted mean
			Year −1		
All restructured firms	68	−0.167	−0.055	−0.06	−0.014
		(1.63)	(1.62)	(0.26)	(0.26)
Restructured with CEO changes	25	−0.37	−0.28	−0.038	−0.0004
		(1.07)	(1.04)	(0.066)	(0.07)
Restructured with private buyers	19	−0.11	0.014	−0.026	0.027
		(0.26)	(0.29)	(0.057)	(0.07)
Restructured with largest shareholder changes	22	−0.10	0.011	−0.023	0.024
		(0.35)	(0.33)	(0.061)	(0.064)
Restructured with largest shareholders' province changes	37	−0.18	−0.069	−0.02	0.025
		(0.55)	(0.55)	(0.067)	(0.079)
			Year +1		
All restructured firms	68	−0.48*	−0.37*	0.0004*	0.045*
		(3.65)	(3.65)	(0.18)	(0.17)
Restructured with CEO changes	25	0.032*	0.17*	0.033*	0.036*
		(0.99)	(0.89)	(0.11)	(0.10)
Restructured with private buyers	19	0.039*	−0.129	0.008	0.059*
		(0.91)	(0.11)	(0.065)	(0.066)
Restructured with largest shareholder changes	22	−0.13	−0.02	0.016	0.063
		(0.61)	(0.58)	(0.08)	(0.085)
Restructured with largest shareholders' province changes	37	0.1*	0.22*	0.034*	0.079
		(1.0)	(0.97)	(0.104)	(0.097)
			Year +2		
All restructured firms	68	0.16	0.28*	0.038	0.082
		(2.31)	(2.31)	(0.32)	(0.32)

Table 7.9 (continued)

	Obs	Operating income/ total sales		Operating income/ total assets	
		Mean	Industry-adjusted mean	Mean	Industry-adjusted mean
Restructured with CEO changes	25	0.18	0.28	0.046	0.084
		(0.91)	(0.92)	(0.147)	(0.15)
Restructured with private buyers	19	0.4*	0.576*	0.005	0.05
		(1.61)	(1.63)	(0.068)	(0.083)
Restructured with largest shareholder changes	22	0.33	0.45	0.06	0.11
		(0.79)	(0.81)	(0.12)	(0.127)
Restructured with largest shareholders' province changes	37	0.18	0.298	0.021	0.066
		(1.64)	(1.65)	(0.101)	(0.11)

Notes: Standard deviation value in parentheses; number of observations: 68. This table shows accounting measures of operational performance for a sample of 68 ST firms that have share restructurings after ST announcements. Year −1, year +1 and year +2 are the previous full fiscal year, the first and the second fiscal year following restructuring activities, respectively. Industry categorization is based on the CSMAR database; * denotes 5% significant level based on two-tailed Wilcoxon signed rank tests.

The negative industry-adjusted operating income over total sales (−0.167) and total assets (−0.014) in the year preceding the share restructuring event shows that most ST firms perform worse than the industry mean. Here we use the Wilcoxon Signed Rank test to see whether or not operational performance has improved over time. The operating income normalized by total assets improved from year −1 to +1 (mean value turns from −0.014 to 0.045, significant at the 5 per cent level). However, the industry-adjusted operating income normalized by total sales deteriorates (mean value from −0.055 to −0.37).

We then take CEO changes, largest shareholder changes, private buyers and the largest shareholder's province change into consideration, and obtain the results by categories. From Table 7.9, we can obviously observe that restructuring activities accompanied by CEO changes, largest shareholder's province changes and privately-owned buyers will be helpful for the improvement of operating performance (with mean values of industry-adjusted operating income normalized by total sales or total assets, all turn from negative numbers to positive numbers with 5 per cent significance).[35]

When comparing the operating income between year +1 and year +2, the mean values in all categories in the second year after share restructurings (year +2) are better than those in year +1, although some of them are significant and some are not. Operating income normalized by total sales of all firms with share restructurings changes significantly from year +1 to +2 (mean values increase from −0.37 to 0.28 with 5 per cent significance). All in all, by combining the mean value changes from year −1 to year +2, we can draw the conclusion that share restructuring plans help improve the operational performance within two years of restructuring activities.

To examine further the factors affecting the operational performance during the share restructuring process, we also conduct an Ordinary Least Squares (OLS) regression on operating income. The dependent variable is the industry-adjusted performance in the first fiscal year after the share restructuring, measured as operating profits normalized by total assets of ST companies (which is significantly positive according to Table 7.9) subtracted by the mean for all counterpart firms in the same industry in the same year.

As to the regressors, total assets, leverage ratio and pre-restructuring industry-adjusted performance are measured in the last full fiscal year prior to restructuring (*Pre_asset*, *Pre_leverage, Pre_operating_income*).

Table 7.10 exhibits the results. We find that the change of CEO has a positive effect (significant at the 10 per cent level) on the operational performance measured as industry-adjusted operating income/total assets. This result implies that the new managers will usually try their best to manage the firms and their efforts do pay off.

On the other hand, the variable *Pre_operating_income* produces positive and significant estimated coefficient (0.42 with p-value 0.0017), that is, the better the ST firms performed before the restructurings, the better they will perform after the restructurings. The negative coefficient of the leverage measure (−0.00034 with p-value 0.04) also supports the theoretical prediction that, the higher the firm's leverage ratio, the more difficult it will be to reorganize the company and produce a better operational performance. Finally, it is worth noting that both the R-square and the adjusted R-square are high enough for this type of regression.

Overall, the cross-sectional analysis demonstrates the positive role played by share restructurings in improving the operational performance of ST firms.

9. CONCLUSION

As a warning signal of stock delisting, the Special Treatment (ST) system is a unique mechanism that only exists in the Chinese stock market. In the Western literature, there are many empirical studies showing that delisting stocks or to-be-delisted stocks are facing heavy selling pressure in stock

Table 7.10 Ordinary Least Squares (OLS) regression results on the relations between operational performance and corporate restructurings

	Estimated coefficients	Standard deviation	t value	Pr(>|t|)
Pre_operating_income	0.419	0.123	3.398	0.002***
Pre_asset[a]	0.129	0.194	0.664	0.511
Pre_leverage	−0.0003	0.0002	−2.129	0.040**
CEO_change	0.423	0.280	1.66	0.10*
Province_change	0.274	0.308	0.89	0.379
Private_buyer	−0.443	0.351	−1.261	0.216
Largest_change	−0.676	0.326	−2.075	0.045**

Residual standard error: 0.89 on 67 degrees of freedom
Multiple R-Squared: 0.4213, Adjusted R-squared: 0.3055
F-statistic: 3.64 on 7 and 67 DF, p-value: 0.00473
Number of observations: 68.

Notes: [a] in the form of a logarithm. The dependent variable is the industry adjusted performance in the first fiscal year after a share restructuring, measured as operating cash flow/assets minus the mean for all counterpart firms in the same industry and the same year. Total assets, leverage and pre-restructuring industry-adjusted performance are measured in the last full fiscal year prior to restructuring (*Pre_operating_income*, *Pre_asset*, *Pre_leverage*). The dummy variables for CEO changes (*CEO_change*), largest shareholders' province changes (*Province_change*), private buyers (*Private_buyer*) and largest shareholder changes (*Largest_change*) equal one when there are changes and zero otherwise;
* significant at 10%; ** significant at 5%; *** significant at 1%.

markets. However, the Chinese stock market presents a surprisingly different picture. We often see that the prices of many ST firms' stocks, after experiencing a short-term drop, soar in the long term. How to explain this positive market response?

This study tries to shed light on the positive cumulative abnormal return by investigating the role of the restructuring activities following ST announcements. Share restructurings and government rescue are the main focus of our study. Finding a positive correlation of share restructurings with long-term CAR and the likelihood of ST decapping, respectively, we show that share restructurings can help ST companies exit ST status. Then, by comparing the operational performance before and after restructuring activities of ST firms, we further demonstrate that share restructuring activities do improve the companies' operational performance within two years of restructuring, thus they help the companies leave ST status. This constitutes the underlying rationale for the positive market response in the long term.

However, this study does not intend to prove that the ST mechanism is a good or efficient institution. Under the institutional constraints in China's transition from a central planning economy to a market economy, the ST mechanism serves as an administrative governance tool. It motivates local governments that have a large political and economic interest in listed firms under their jurisdiction to help rescue those ailing ST firms, and it is true that some ST firms successfully improved their operational performance after restructurings under the auspices of local governments. However, the ST system is far from a panacea, as many other ST firms were unable to conduct successful restructurings and finally were delisted from the stock market. We thus conclude that the ST system plays a limited role in tackling the post-IPO moral hazard problem.

Some people may argue that the improvement in ST firms' operational performance may have resulted from earnings management rather than the real enhancement of corporate governance and productivity. Though we cannot completely rule out this possibility, we still believe our research methodology is reasonable, for the following reasons. First, the literature provides sufficient justification for using accounting variables as a proxy for companies' operational performance, such as Hotchkiss and Mooradian (1996).[36] Second, given that all ST firms have quite similar incentives to manage their earnings, earnings management could cause the whole ST firm sample to have a similar degree of earnings inflation. Since we are mainly interested in the variation of ST firm performance in response to various corporate restructuring and government rescue activities, we can still detect what determines the cross-firm variation in corporate performance even if they have a common tendency to inflate earnings. On the basis of these considerations, we believe our results are not overly biased.

NOTES

1. We are grateful to Jeffrey Law for his research assistance and are indebted to Terence Chong, Eric Chou, Jun Zhang, one anonymous referee and participants of the China–Europe Conference on Law and Economics at Fudan University for their helpful discussion, comments and suggestions. An earmarked research grant (CUHK4112/04H) from the Research Grants Council of Hong Kong Government is gratefully acknowledged.
2. Allen et al. (2004); Pistor and Xu (2005).
3. La Porta et al. (1997); La Porta et al. (1998).
4. La Porta et al. (2002).
5. Pistor et al. (2000).
6. Berkowitz et al. (2003).
7. Xu and Pistor (2004).
8. Pistor and Xu (2005).

9. Du and Xu (2004).
10. Pistor and Xu (2005b).
11. Du and Xu (2004).
12. Du and Xu (2004).
13. Gilson, John and Lang (1990).
14. Asquith, Gertner and Scharfstein (1994).
15. Brown, James and Mooradian (1993).
16. Khanna and Poulsen (1995).
17. Hotchkiss and Mooradian (1996).
18. Zhang (2003, in Chinese).
19. Li (2003, in Chinese).
20. Ning and Zhang (2003, 2004).
21. Bai et al. (2002).
22. Ning and Zhang (2003, 2004).
23. 'Special Treatment Warning System' commenced implementation on 12 May 2003. Stocks with significant delisting risks are labelled '*ST' to disclose their special risks to investors. These stocks suffer (1) two consecutive years of negative net profits; (2) significant accounting errors or false accounting records in financial reports, which fail to be revised in the specified period of time, or two years of negative profits which arise after correcting the mistakes. Since the difference between the ST and *ST is not the major concern in our study, we take them as identical.
24. See for example Qian and Xu (1993).
25. Zhang (2003).
26. Debt disposal could be seen as another restructuring method besides share restructuring and asset restructuring. However, only 16 stocks had debt disposal in the Shanghai and Shenzhen stock markets from 1998 to 2003. We therefore do not treat debt disposal as a separate category of corporate restructuring.
27. We consider more than one company restructuring activity as one single restructuring if the subsequent restructurings are made within one year and only the first announcement date is recorded in the sample, because we believe it is most highly associated with the ST rescuing purpose.
28. Note that the firms are just dropped from our sample in this specific event study of ST.
29. Bai et al. (2002).
30. In Bai et al. (2002), the mean cumulative abnormal returns of their ST sample during the 22-month period surrounding ST data is as high as 28.99 per cent, with a median of 31.32 per cent. There is a big variation in CARs, the standard deviation being equal to 39.45 per cent.
31. Number of companies in each province is obtained from the China Statistical Yearbook.
32. For some firms, we cannot find any information about their status after one year. These firms are dropped from the sample because of the missing data.
33. Hotchkiss (1995).
34. The adjusted terms are the mean of the related variables for all firms in the same industries. We categorize all companies into six industries according to the CSMAR database: commerce, conglomerate, property, industrials, utility and finance. Note that there are no finance industry firms in our ST sample. We calculate their mean during the period 1998 to 2004.
35. For example, the mean value of industry-adjusted operating income over total sales of restructured firms with CEO changes increases from −0.37 in year −1 to 0.032 in year +1 with 5 per cent significance.
36. Hotchkiss and Mooradian (1996).

BIBLIOGRAPHY

Alexander, G., C. Eun and S. Janakiraman (1988), 'International listings and stock returns: some empirical evidence', *Journal of Financial and Quantitative Analysis*, **23**(2), 35–151.

Allen, F., J. Qian and M. Qian (2004), 'Law, finance, and economic growth in China', *Journal of Financial Economics*, **77**, 57–116.

Asquith, P., R. Gertner and D. Scharfstein (1994), 'Anatomy of financial distress: an examination of junk bond issues', *Quarterly Journal of Economics*, **109**(3), 625–58.

Bai, C.E., Q. Liu and F. Song (2002), 'The value of corporate control: evidence from Chinese ST firms', working paper, University of Hong Kong.

Berkowitz, D., K. Pistor and J.F. Richard (2003), 'Economic development, legality and transplant effect', *European Economic Review*, **47**(1), 165–95.

Brown, S.J. and J.B. Warner (1985), 'Using daily stock returns: the case of event studies', *Journal of Financial Economics*, **14**, 3–31.

Brown, D., C. James and R. Mooradian (1993), 'The information content of distressed restructurings involving public and private debt claims', *Journal of Financial Economics*, **33**, 93–118.

Chen, X., C.W. Lee and J. Li (2003), 'Chinese tango: government assisted earnings management', working paper.

Dodd, P. and J.B. Warner (1983), 'On corporate governance: a study of proxy contests', *Journal of Financial Economics*, **11**(1), 401–38.

Du, J. and C. Xu (2004), 'Law, finance and administrative governance: evidence from Chinese stock markets', working paper, Chinese University of Hong Kong and London School of Economics.

Edelman, R.B. and H.K. Baker (1984), 'The effects of delisting on the price behavior of common stocks', working paper, U.S. Securities and Exchange Commission.

Foerster, S.R. and G.A. Karolyi (1993), 'International listings of stocks: the case of Canada and the U.S.', *Journal of International Business Studies*, **24**, 763–84.

Gilson, D., K. John and L. Lang (1990), 'Trouble debt restructuring: an empirical study of private reorganization of firms in default', *Journal of Financial Economics*, **16**, 315–54.

Grammatikos, T. and G. Papaioannou (1986a), 'Market reaction to NYSE listing: tests of the marketability gains hypothesis', *Journal of Financial Research*, **9**, 215–27.

Grammatikos, T. and G. Papaioannou (1986b), 'The information value of listing on the New York stock exchange', *The Financial Review*, **21**, 485–99.

Guo, Z. and P. Yang (2004), 'The status quo and perfection of China's listed companies delisting mechanism', *Value Engineering*, **9** (in Chinese).

Han, Z.G. and Q. Duan (2002), 'Delisting mechanism' (a book written in Chinese).

Han, Z.G. and Q. Duan et al. (2002), 'Delisting mechanism: market repression or repressing market?', *Economic Science Publishing House* (in Chinese).

Hotchkiss, E.S. (1993), 'Investment decisions under Chapter 1 bankruptcy', Ph.D. dissertation, New York University.

Hotchkiss, E.S. (1995), 'Post-bankruptcy performance and management turnover', *Journal of Finance*, **50**, 3–21.

Hotchkiss, E.S. and R.M. Mooradian (1996), 'Vulture investors and the market for control of distressed firms', *Journal of Financial Economics*, **43**, 401–32.

Jarrell, G.A. (2004), 'The stock price effects of NYSE de-listing for violating corporate governance rules', working paper, U.S. Securities and Exchange Commission.

Khanna, N. and A. Poulsen (1995), 'Managers of financially distressed firms: villains or scapegoats?', *Journal of Finance*, **50**, 919–40.

La Porta, R., F. Lopez-de-Silanes and A. Shleifer (2002), 'Government ownership of banks', *Journal of Finance*, **LVII**(1), 265–301.

La Porta, P.R., F. Lopez-de-Silanes, A. Shleifer and R.W. Vishny (1997), 'Legal determinants of external finance', *Journal of Finance*, **52**, 1131–50.

La Porta, P.R., F. Lopez-de-Silanes, A. Shleifer and R.W. Vishny (1998), 'Law and Finance', *Journal of Political Economy*, **106**(6), 1113–55.

Li, B. (2003), 'Studies of strategic restructuring of China's ST listed companies following their financial distress', *Management Modernization* (in Chinese).

Lu, S. and X. Zhiwei (1998), 'Market adjustment and government intervention – insights from enterprise merger, acquisition and asset restructurings', *Operations and Management*.

Merjos, A. (1963), 'Stricken securities', *Barron's*, **44** (4 March), 9.

Ning, X.D. and H.W. Zhang (2004), 'Is "special treatment" policy useful for corporate governance?', working paper, Tsinghva University.

O'Donnell, J.L. (1969), 'Case evidence of the value of a new stock exchange listing', Michigan State University Business Topics, **17**, 15–21.

Pistor, K. and C. Xu (2004), 'Incomplete law', *Journal of International Law and Politics*.

Pistor, K. and C. Xu (2005), 'Governing stock markets in transition economies' lessons from China', *American Law and Economics Review*, **7**(1), 184–210.

Pistor, K., M. Raiser and S. Gelfer (2000), 'Law and finance in transition economies', *The Economics of Transition*, **8**(2), 325–68.

Qian, Y. and C. Xu (1993), 'Why China's economic reform differs: the M-form hierarchy and entry/expansion of the non-state sector', *The Economics of Transition*, **1**(2), 135–70.

Sanger, G.C. and J.J. McConnell (1986), 'Stock exchange listing, firm value, and security market efficiency: the impact of NASDAQ', *Journal of Financial and Quantitative Analysis*, **21**, 1–25.

Sanger, G.C. and J.D. Peterson (1990), 'An empirical analysis of common stock delistings', *Journal of Financial and Quantitative Analysis*, **25**(2), 261–72.

Sun, Q., Y.K. Tang and W.H.S. Tong (2002), 'The impact of mass delisting: evidence from Singapore and Malaysia', *Pacific-Basin Financial Journal*, **10**, 333–51.

Travlos, N. (1987), 'Corporate takeover bids, methods of payment, and bidding firms' stock returns', *Journal of Finance*, **42**(4), 943–63.

Wilconxon, F. (1945), 'Individual comparisons by ranking methods', *Biometrics Bulletin*, **1**, 80–82.

Xu, C. and K. Pistor (2004), 'Enforcement failure under incomplete law', mimeo, London School of Economics.

Yang, D.Y. (2002), 'The study on earnings management of the ST listing companies', graduation thesis, Wuhan University of Technology.

Ying, L.K., W.W.G. Lewellen, G.G. Schlarbaum and R.C. Lease (1977), 'Stock exchange listings and securities returns', *Journal of Financial and Quantitative Analysis*, **12**, 415–32.

Zhang, N.Q. (2003), *Cases of ST, PT and Delisting Companies Economic Daily Press*, pp. 23–5 (written in Chinese).

Zhang, N. et al. (2003), 'ST, PT and delisting cases – interpreting stock market phenomena with Chinese characteristics', *Economic Daily Press*, 23–5.

8. Monitoring problems versus fiduciary duties in Chinese stock companies: an economic and comparative analysis on corporate governance

Qing-Yun Jiang[1]

1. INTRODUCTION

Corporate governance plays a very important role in a nation's economy with respect to product development, marketing and finance. Excessive managerial discretion could cause many problems, such as high monitoring costs (agency costs) and breach of fiduciary duties (fraud, cheating investors) and therefore it is inefficient and harmful to the economy. The debate on corporate reform in China in recent years has focused on how to solve the problem of business structure and reduce excessive discretion by the board in state-owned companies. The newly effective Chinese Corporate Law has stressed the importance of fiduciary duties in the management and protection of small shareholders through the introduction of many Western practices, such as 'piercing the corporate veil', accumulative voting and derivative lawsuits.[2]

As is well known, most Chinese stock companies have been transformed from large state-owned firms. In these corporations, the State has dominant control, with more than 51 per cent or even up to 80 per cent of the shares. Under such a structure the directors and officers are nominated by the State as the largest shareholder, and they represent the interests of the State. This kind of dominant control is often referred to as 'insider control' in the literature and is thought to be the reason behind the dysfunction of the board and self-dealing between the corporation and the large shareholder. As a result, the conflict of interest between large shareholders and other small investors is unavoidable.

Furthermore, such a structure leads to many other legal problems, such as abuse of managerial discretion and financial fraud. In recent years, people have been shocked by the fraud practices in some cases, such as *Yin Guang Xia* and *Lan Tian Holding*.[3] These cases involved millions in losses to the corporation and small investors and consequently seriously damaged the confidence of investors in the stock market. The breach of fiduciary duties further exposes high risks in corporate finance which could ruin corporate assets and result in heavy loss by small investors. Breaches of fiduciary obligations lead to loss of confidence of the investors in the stock market, contribute to the collapse of the Chinese stock market and hinder the development of a capital market.[4]

To improve fiduciary duties in corporate governance, the concept of independent directorship is introduced to Chinese law[5] as a means to tackle the problem of 'insider control'. Thus, the board of directors, the supervisory board and the independent directors are seen as a solution to resolving the monitoring and principal–agent problem in Chinese public corporations. In this context, this chapter will examine whether the current monitoring model will be efficient in overseeing management and consequently reduce agency costs. Furthermore, the chapter will address the importance of stricter enforcement of fiduciary duties as stipulated in the new Chinese Corporate Law, such as allowing derivative lawsuits, accumulative voting and 'piercing the corporate veil', as well as stricter implementation of accountancy like the US model GAAP or IAS.

2. OWNERSHIP AND CONTROL IN CHINESE STOCK COMPANIES

In the legal conception, the principal has the power to control and direct the activities of the agent.[6] In this relationship, the principal sets the ultimate objective and general strategy for the agent to pursue, 'occasionally specifies details of the agent's behaviour, and stands ready to countermand specific acts of the agent'.[7]

However, the central dilemma of corporate law is the separation of ownership and control in public corporations. On the one side are the shareholders, as 'the ostensible owners'; on the other side are corporate managers/officers, as 'the shareholders' ostensible fiduciaries'. The shareholders select and delegate power to the board to manage the corporation.[8] Though the corporate law does not explicitly answer the question of whose interest the board and the officers should serve, lawyers, judges and economists usually assume that the board/the officers, as fiduciaries, should make and maximize profits for its shareholders as an ultimate purpose of public corporations.[9] In this model, ownership and control are not materially separated, 'the officers are subservient to the directors and the directors are responsible to the shareholders'.[10]

The traditional legal conception might only apply to the ordinary principal and agent. In stockholder and director relationships, this might not be the case. The Berle and Means theory demolished the traditional theory.[11] In their thesis, the authors argued that, in large public corporations, managers had seized control from the shareholders, 'the ostensible owners'. The separation is a result of the pattern of stock ownership in public companies. 'Each shareholder owned few shares and lacked the means or inclination to participate actively in electing directors.'[12] Their attitude is often referred to as 'rational apathy'.[13] The managers, meanwhile, having both the means and the motive, can easily induce the shareholders to elect a board subservient to the managers.[14] As a consequence, monitoring or overseeing management becomes difficult simply because directors (or outside directors) are subordinate to management.[15]

Not fully coinciding with Western firms, the modern corporate system in China is based on the reform of state-owned companies. These stock companies were mostly transformed from large state-owned companies. In general, the State holds the dominant proportion of the shares in these stock companies, ranging from 51 per cent up to 80 per cent.[16] These state-owned shares and the so-called 'state legal person shares' are not transferable on the stock market. Unlike the Western public firms, especially the American firms, Chinese stock companies are controlled by the State, while in Western companies, like those in the US and Britain, even the five largest shareholders hold on average a sum of 20 per cent to 25 per cent of the shares. The shares of the firms are widely dispersed among the investors. After two decades of corporate reform in China, the goal to establish good corporate governance in Chinese state-owned firms is still far from the expectations of the reformers: the president of the board has the position of general manager, and the director members are managers of the companies. 'In these companies, owing to the absence of an independent board of directors, the discretion of the president of the board is almost unrestricted. Although theoretically the State as the sole largest shareholder has full control over these stock companies, the ownership of the State cannot be materialised due to its non-personality and absence of effective monitoring of its directors.'[17] Therefore, the study of corporate governance must distinguish between the corporate structures of these regimes. The Western theory on corporate governance might not apply to the Chinese model. Specifically, the dominant control of shares by the State creates severe monitoring problems with respect to agency costs and fiduciary obligations.

3. MONITORING PROBLEMS IN CHINESE STOCK COMPANIES

Corporate governance in China is a mixed product of continental corporate law and American corporate law. On the one hand, like German Corporate Law, Chinese Corporate Law stipulates a basic model of the board, management and the supervisory board as a governance model. On the other hand, it also introduces outside directors to deter the abuse of managerial discretion and oversee the management.[18] The introduction of outside directors is supposed to cure the weakness of the supervisory board. Will such corporate governance be efficient?

Agency costs are defined as 'the sum of monitoring expenditures by the principals (i.e. shareholders or institution investors); bonding expenditures of the agent (the owner–manager) and residual loss from uncontrollable deviation of the agent from his promise'.[19] Agency costs are thought to be optimal in shareholder-controlled firms. The rationale behind this is that, in shareholder-controlled firms, the problem of information asymmetry can be more effectively avoided; shareholders have an interest in selecting more professional and knowledgeable managers to direct the corporation. As the shareholders are generally risk-neutral, the problem of risk aversion of managers can be curbed and the firm may have a better chance to grow. Additionally, under an efficient proxy system, the shareholders or institutional investors can select their own directors and therefore can cure the major problems resulting from the separation of ownership and control, such as risk aversion of the managers, fraudulent behaviour, self-dealing, insider information and so on.[20]

In most of Chinese stock companies, state shares have a dominant proportion. The managers are very often both directors and managers. They enjoy almost full discretion to manage the firms. Meanwhile, the remaining investors, who comprise numerous small shareholders, lack the incentive to attend the general meeting to vote simply because of the shareholders' collective action problem. The State as the largest shareholder can select its own representatives to direct and manage the firms as it likes. Small shareholders have no opportunity to participate in management and most of them are short-term speculators in the stock market. The existence of the State as the largest and dominant shareholder causes monitoring problems: the board of directors is selected by the relevant governmental bodies, while the rest of the shareholders cannot influence or select directors.

3.1 Incompetence of Shareholder Meeting

The Chinese Corporate Law stipulates that shareholder meetings enjoy managerial discretion.[21] Shareholder meetings have the discretion to set the goal of the company and the investment plan, as well as review the board's report and decide dividends; they also have the discretion to agree on separation, mergers and acquisitions or liquidation of the company, if it is necessary.[22] Shareholder meetings can also supervise and influence the board through selecting or dismissing the directors and deciding the level of their compensation.[23] However, under the current structure of the organizational setting, it would be difficult for shareholder meetings to supervise and influence the board. In Chinese corporate law, the board is entrusted with exclusive discretion on whether to hold a shareholder meeting or not. Even the supervisory board and shareholders with more than 10 per cent of the company share can suggest or call for a shareholder meeting,[24] but the decision is still subject to the board. Though the new Chinese Corporate Law has provided a legal remedy for the supervisory board and shareholders in case of the board's refusal to hold a shareholder meeting,[25] the phenomenon of 'insider control' is still difficult to eliminate. The local administrative bodies, normally represented by the state-owned Assets Management Committee,[26] control shareholders' meetings and select the directorial members. In most of these stock companies, managers are both directors and representatives of the state-owned Assets Management Committee. Accumulating a 10 per cent share is a tough task in the Chinese stock market, as normally over 51 per cent of shares are controlled by the State. Considering the collective action problem and high cost of organizing a lawsuit, it is difficult for the shareholders to bring a case to the court.

3.2 Regulatory Intervention in Corporate Governance

Though one aspect of corporate reform in China is to separate the administrative influence from the companies, administrative bodies still have the legitimate right to intervene in the management of the corporation in the name of the largest shareholder. For example, they can hinder the efforts of mergers and acquisitions, reassigning directors and managers in the corporation. In fact, most of the members of the board of directors, the supervisory board and the shareholder representatives are nominated and assigned according to the personnel of the original firms, but not according to their professional knowledge. As a consequence, the corporations are often subject to the interference of the local administrative bodies and small shareholders have no means to participate in important corporate decision making. Ironically, the State as the largest shareholder does not have personality and is absent from the daily business operations of the company.[27] In other words, the State as the largest shareholder cannot monitor the directors it sends to the company. Though the administrative bodies can replace the board and officers when they are found financially guilty or commit corruptive behaviour, at this time, a company very often faces heavy losses due to mismanagement or the corruption of the directors or managers. The CAOHC case[28] reveals the important problem of corporate governance in state-owned firms, in which the directors and managers enjoy almost unrestricted discretion in decision making.[29] This undemocratic decision-making process in Chinese stock companies incurs high agency costs: first, small shareholders' interests are not well protected, as they are absent from voting for their representative on the board. Secondly, the State as the largest shareholder controls shareholder meetings as a tool for sending its representatives to the board. This results in excessive discretion by the board and officers. But the worst is that it cannot supervise the board and managers effectively because of its nature of non-personality. The absence of the State as the largest shareholder in management causes serious monitoring problems: directors and managers enjoy excessive discretion without effective monitoring from large shareholder(s).[30]

3.3 Dysfunction of the Supervisory Board

Additionally, within the corporation, the members of the supervisory board are normally chosen by the board from the personnel already in the corporation. Unlike the employee representatives in Germany, Chinese employee representatives on the supervisory board are subordinate to the board and managers. As a result, the corporation articles and the ultimate objective of the corporation are not respected; the interests of small investors are not well protected. In this relationship, a shareholder meeting, the board and managers may act passively because of the vagueness of executive power and conflict of interest. Under the dominant control of the State, small investors lack interest in the long-term performance of the corporation. They would rather focus on the short-term benefits from speculation than on long-term savings or investments.[31]

Therefore, under current corporate governance, neither shareholder meetings nor the largest shareholder (the State) and the supervisory board can effectively monitor or oversee the board and officers.

3.4 Do Outside Directors Play a Role?

As a remedy to these shortcomings, especially to the weakness of the supervisory board in Chinese corporate governance and as a means to deter the excessive discretion of the directors and the corporate managers, outside directors are introduced into the company to oversee and monitor management. They include various professionals such as lawyers, accountants, university professors, bankers and suppliers. Their task is to oversee the firm's audit, executive compensation and director nominations. Outside directors are supposed to perform a valuable service by overseeing or monitoring management, though they do not manage the firm.[32] However, it is sceptical to suggest that the problems of corporate governance can be solved by the introduction of outside directors, since it is thought that outside directors normally go along with management; otherwise they either choose to resign or to decline the position.[33] Many directors are subordinate to management and are only nominally independent.[34] Even if outside directors have enough time for the firms they work for, they have limited knowledge about their workings, and they lack independent sources of information about the company's affairs. They obtain most of the information from the managers and directors whom they are supposed to oversee,[35] and consequently they follow the opinion of management. Furthermore, the compensation for outside directors is a small fraction of their income and is not tied to the corporation's or their own performance – as a result, they lack the incentive to 'assert independence and maximize profits'.[36] Outside directors are more risk-averse than managers because they want to avoid mistakes, so that they will 'not be held liable or at least subjected to an unpleasant lawsuit'.[37] Therefore monitoring or overseeing the firm's business by outside directors seems implausible. The function of outside directors is very limited.[38]

In general, the current monitoring model in Chinese stock companies is structured to tackle the problem of supervision in corporate governance. The idea is good, but this monitoring model cannot work effectively because of excessive discretion of the board and managers that represent the State as the largest shareholder. Shareholder meetings do not function simply because they are a tool controlled by the large shareholder(s) for selecting the board and managers. It is difficult for small shareholders to participate in management because of the lack of democracy in voting and legal means to sue the managers in the case of their failure to fulfil their legal obligations. Members of the board often hold managers' positions in Chinese public firms, and it is naïve to expect them to serve the interests of small shareholders. The supervisory board lacks the ability to oversee the board and officers because its members are normally corporate personnel and they are selected by their managers and directors. Outside directors' influence is very limited in curing the weaknesses of the supervisory board in the same way, owing to the problems of dominant control of the State's shares and 'insider control'; they lack the necessary information to supervise management even if they oppose the decision making of the board and managers. In short, the current model of monitoring therefore cannot function well, considering the current corporate structure and the dominant position of large shareholder(s) in corporate governance.

These are the shortcomings existing in corporate governance in Chinese public corporations. Bad corporate governance not only results in high monitoring cost and low efficiency of corporate performance, but also damages economic development.

3.5 Solution: Empower the Supervisory Board and Tackle the Problem of 'Insider Control'

There have been some reforms aiming to solve these problems, such as the introduction of an independent supervisor instead of outside directors, mandatory disclosure and further legislature to improve corporate governance. But the fundamental shortcomings existing in corporate governance cannot be solved only by these technical remedies. The problem of 'insider control' resulting from the dominant position of the state-owned shares should be tackled so as to create a good social environment for managers, and allowing for the participation of the shareholders in overseeing and monitoring directors and managers.

The most effective way is to reduce the proportion of the state-owned shares. This might involve a privatization scheme, but the issue concerns the fairness of the stock market. As the state-owned shares are not transferable at the time of issuing and were obtained at very low prices, to allow these shares to be sold at current high prices would mean unfairness to the numerous shareholders who purchased the shares from the stock market at higher prices. Because of this dilemma, the reform of the stock market, with respect to reducing the proportion of state-owned shares, remains hesitant.

If reduction of the proportion of state-owned shares under a privatization scheme is not feasible at the moment, another way to deter excessive discretion of the board is to increase the discretion of the supervisory board, since outside directors simply cannot play the role of overseeing and supervising the board of directors and management. The experiences of other countries are valuable to the Chinese monitoring model. In the Netherlands, the supervisory board is an obligatory organ and an important power shift from the shareholders' meeting to the supervisory board. It is the same in Germany, where the supervisory board has the discretion to select directors and decide the compensation scheme,[39] and even lodge a claim against directors for damage compensation. The new Chinese Corporate Law has already learned from Western practices and corrected some missing regulations in the law.[40] The implementation of the law and the functioning of the supervisory board are very decisive, since otherwise the law loses its meaning and is only worth the paper it is written on. Before this more effective new corporate law, there has been no real improvement in the supervisory mechanism. The members of the supervisory board are not selected, but are chosen by the corporate managers. Therefore, it is not surprising that the supervisory board is only nominal and that it does not function as it should. As a result, a subservient supervisory board will not challenge the board of directors. This is quite similar to the selection of outside directors in China. The outside directors should be qualified and recommended by a third party like the association of outside directors and, in the end, selected by the shareholders' meeting. While outside directors in Chinese stock companies are selected by the management, it cannot exclude the private relationship factor. Generally, the management will not select independent directors who do not share the common view of the board of directors. Consequently, outside directors cannot act independently. The mechanism of outside directors does play a significant role in overseeing and monitoring under a well-designed legal system. Even in the US, where the mechanism of outside directors plays an important role, there are still pros and cons concerning the introduction of outside directors. Considering these factors, the role of the supervisory board should be reconsidered and strengthened. As there is no real implementation of the mechanism of the supervisory board in China,[41] it is too early and unreasonable to replace the function of the supervisory board by the introduction of the American monitoring mechanism of independent directors, which does not conform to the legal tradition and the reality in China. The reform might be in vain and incur the cost of corporate reform.[42] *The question is: if we can improve monitoring by improving the function of the supervisory board, why should we opt for outside directors?*

Very similarly to German corporate law, in which the employees participate in monitoring the board of directors,[43] Chinese Corporate Law also stipulates that at least one-third of the members of the supervisory board should come from the employees.[44] The German model of the supervisory board can be a good reference for improving the supervisory board in China. The revision of Chinese Corporate Law has shifted much of the power from shareholder meetings to the supervisory board, such as appointment and dismissal of board members, in order to allow the latter to be well informed about corporate management and corporate decisions. Besides, the supervisory board can oversee and monitor the directors by bringing lawsuits to the court. A further consideration is to introduce *independent supervisors* to the supervisory board. Like the practice of outside directors, independent supervisors can be selected from amongst small shareholders, or be recommended by small shareholders (but not by the large shareholders). Specifically, the number of independent supervisors should be increased, and they should have a fixed compensation plus bonus or another incentive scheme. And they should be liable for any breach of their obligations. If the current regulations on independent directors are transplanted into the design of the supervisory board, it is not necessary to introduce independent directors.

As mentioned before, either independent directors or the supervisory board have limited influence over directors, because of the problems of the dominant control of the State, as the largest shareholder. If more than 60 per cent of the stock companies hold 50 per cent of the shares of individual companies, the problem of 'insider control' is inevitable and cannot be solved. As far as a dominant shareholder exists, independent directors or the supervisory board will be controlled by the large shareholder, and the interests of small investors cannot be protected. And it is pointless to discuss whether to introduce independent directors or to improve the supervisory board for effective monitoring if the reform of the structure of shares, and the fact that the State is the largest shareholder, are ignored.

4. FIDUCIARY DUTIES AND THE SCOPE OF LIABILITY OF BOARD MEMBERS

4.1 The Fiduciaries

Another important aspect of corporate law is to discipline the managers to act 'with care' in daily business, and to therefore reduce agency costs. Many cases of fraudulent accounting happened a few years ago, severely damaging the confidence of investors. For example, in the American and European stock markets, the representative cases include Enron, World Com and Xerox; in China, as mentioned before, the cases of *Hong Guang Enterprises*, *Zheng Bai Wen* and *Yin Guang Xia*[45] shocked investors and led to troublesome civil and criminal litigations. These cases raise a fundamental question: how to improve fiduciary duties by improving corporate governance and, consequently, reducing the agency costs?

Fiduciary duties are self-discipline standards that can restrict managerial discretion and reduce agency costs from an economic viewpoint. These fiduciary duties include 'affirmative duties to disclose', 'open-ended duties to act', 'closed-in rights to positional advantages' and 'moral rhetoric'.[46] Corporate managers' fiduciary status requires them to disclose full or necessary information to the investors. They are required to act in accordance with a 'duty of care', with skill, diligence and open-ended loyalty to the company. The fiduciary duty of loyalty further requires managers or directors not to conduct self-dealing transactions, insider trading or to abuse their positional advantage to buy or develop corporate opportunities for themselves, 'unless the corporation is unable to do so or its disinterested decision makers expressly agree to the director's doing so'.[47]

In China, the problem of information asymmetry in stock companies and the problem of 'insider trading' are two major obstacles to a sound development of the stock market. Typically, in the earlier stages of the stock market, some companies in China conducted fraudulent accounting so as to meet the requirements of issuing shares in the stock market. In addition, management might also consider a fraudulent financial scheme to avoid collapse of the company in a situation of financial distress. Furthermore, management may use a fraudulent financial scheme to attain satisfactory performance, so as to have better compensation. According to some statistics, there are more than 90 cases involving penalties imposed by the China Security Supervision and Management Committee. About ten companies and their boards were charged and found guilty under criminal law from 1997 onwards. And, since the issuing of a judicial notification[48] by the People's Supreme Court in 2002, the courts in China have dealt with several hundred civil cases relating to damage compensation, and most of the cases were resolved by mediation, reconciliation or dismissal.[49] The cost of breach of fiduciary duties is high: the discouraged investors will vote by getting out of capital markets because of the uncertainty and risk of being cheated. That is why the number of Chinese shareholders sharply reduces and the same happens with their enthusiasm in the capital market. This contributes partly to the roaring prices of real estate and unhealthy economic development in China: private money does not go to industrial development but is excessively concentrated in real estate. Also litigation is costly. Resources invested in litigation could be immense, since settlements are harder to strike and judgments are difficult to enforce in China. The investments in litigation are often wasteful.

4.2 Information Disclosure and Accountancy

Information asymmetry increases agency costs as the shareholders might not be fully informed about the business risk. On the one hand, management obtains more detailed information than shareholders; on the other hand, information asymmetry reflects the advantage of the division of work between the shareholders and management. Professional managers need more information to manage the company, while shareholders do not. To cure the problem of information asymmetry, many courts have regulated mandatory disclosure in their security laws,[50] in an effort to enhance *information transparency*. However, information processing and disclosure incur costs, while shareholders do not need all the information; they only need the necessary information for monitoring and risk control. As shareholders are residual claimants, they are the bearers of these costs. Cost and benefit analysis should not only focus on the comparison of the benefits from cost reduction and the costs of an unqualified management, but also on the costs of information disclosure and processing.[51] The solution in corporate law to save costs is to establish a standardized and routine information disclosure procedure. Therefore, it is not necessary to solve the problems of information asymmetry; rather, a mechanism should be set up to guarantee that the shareholders obtain the necessary information, enough to assess the business risk, so as to the reduce the agency costs.

Experiences in Western countries indicate that an efficient solution is to establish a standardized accountancy and reporting standard to enhance information transparency. Unlike corporate law, which is compulsory to the parties, accountancy and reporting standards belong to 'soft' law, and its implementation is not assured by the State. However, its implementation can be realized through other means. For example, compulsory issuing standards can be imposed by security authorities; specific criteria of accounting and reporting standards must be met if a firm intends to be listed on the stock market. Another measure is to integrate these norms (accounting and reporting standards) into the code of corporate governance so that the 'soft' law becomes compulsory and enforceable. For instance, the German Code of Corporate Governance has integrated IFRS into its accounting standard, requiring that the annual report and mid-term report should be made in accordance with 'internationally recognized accounting principles', namely IAS, IFRS and GAAP.[52] The Code stipulates the obligation of issuing auditing reports; the auditor must report to the supervisory board his important findings in auditing.[53] The Code recommends 'an internationally recognized standard' to ensure availability of sufficient information for the shareholders.[54] Furthermore, the Code requires the corporation to disclose necessary information to the relevant parties. Such information disclosure shall satisfy the minimum requirements of the relevant laws with respect to financial reports and information disclosure. More importantly, the corporation shall establish an internal information system which can provide reliable and accurate information to shareholders, and through which the shareholders can check the corporation's documents.[55] Such normative integrity of accounting and reporting standards provides an effective remedy to avoid fraud. At the EU level, the European Commission has also required all *Konzerne* in its member states to apply IAS and IFRS in annual financial reports from 2005 onwards.[56] Through legislative procedure these 'soft' laws have become compulsory for the corporations. The purpose of this normative integrity is to establish a strict and effective standard for informational disclosure and protect the shareholders in general.

In recent years, corporate scandals in Europe and the US, in particular the case of Enron, have shocked investors. These scandals were detrimental to the trust in financial markets and existing commercial systems. The accounting regulations appeared incapable of delivering the assurance they should have delivered to the various shareholders, and the collapse of the markets and systems threatened. This is relevant to the case of the Chinese stock market. Accounting scandals in China have caused the Chinese stock market to become troubled. The practice of fraudulent financial schemes in recent years has discouraged investors and hindered the development of the capital market in China. In an effort to deter fraud, the China Security Authority has invited international accounting firms like KPMG, Price Waterhouse Coopers and Deloitte to engage in a so-called 'supplementary auditing' or 'dual auditing' and deter the collusive practices of the domestic accounting firms and stock companies. However, such measures have not realized the deterrent effect. Price Waterhouse Cooper and Deloitte are charged with breach of accounting obligations in the cases of *Jin Zhou Port* and *Kelong Electronics*.[57] Although it is the stock companies who are blamed in the first stage, the difference in the domestic accounting system and international accounting standards is being questioned. In the past 13 years, there has been no unified accounting system in China. Different standards, such as branch accounting standards, corporate accounting standards and corporate accounting regulations, apply simultaneously; besides, different uses of accounting standards cause inaccuracies when the firm is listed in the foreign stock market or when the firm is listed in a domestic stock market and this firm is involved with foreign investment. The newly enacted Chinese Corporate Accounting Standards (2006),[58] which came into effect on 1 January 2007, are an effort to make these different Chinese accounting standards consistent with international accounting standards. In fact, the new standards have adopted the essential contents from IAS. In particular, the new standards provide a good chance for the Chinese stock companies to refurbish their image by stricter and standard information disclosure. Whether these new standards can be an effective solution to deter fraud depends very much on the development of stricter enforcement of personal liability to the directors and officers.

4.3 The Need of Stricter Enforcement of Personal Liability

4.3.1 Corporate liability in Chinese security law

The goal of standard and mandatory disclosure is clear: anti-fraud. Chinese civil law, corporate law, security law and criminal codes have stipulated legal liability against breach of fiduciary duty.[59] However, there are some shortcomings in the relevant laws like the Security Act, especially on civil liability. First, even in the newly amended Security Act,[60] there are many articles concerning administrative penal sanctions (fines) and criminal liability, but only a few articles governing civil liability.[61] In Chapter 11 of legal liability, the law only stipulates administrative liability and criminal liability in terms of inside trading and manipulation of portfolio prices, while civil liability is hardly even addressed.[62] As an international practice, the law does not exclude imposing liability for fines or damage compensation upon board members or other parties, 'provided the general conditions of criminal liability set forth in the Criminal Code are fulfilled, in particular that the party in question has committed the contravention either wilfully or negligently'.[63]

For example, the American Securities Exchange Act stipulates that the manipulator shall be liable for damage compensation. Similar regulations can be found in the Japanese Security Act and the Hong Kong Security Act.[64] Also some of the articles in the Chinese Security Act are too harsh and not practical enough in calculating damage compensation.[65] Of course, the missing regulations can be remedied through legal interpretation by the Supreme People's Court or by improving the relevant regulations with regard to civil liability by, for example, adding the articles of civil liability and the calculation of damage compensation. Secondly, the Security Act stipulates that civil litigation for damage compensation must be subject to administrative or criminal rulings. Such a precondition restricts the right of small investors and increases their litigation costs. Very often, shareholders choose to give up the litigation because of the cost consideration. Thirdly, collective action incurs high litigation costs in China. Though the law stipulates that individuals or groups can bring lawsuits in the court, it lacks practical measures, such as legal remedies, with respect to relief of litigation costs and the reverse burden of proof. Therefore, further integrity of practical measures is needed. For example, the American practices are valuable with respect to the (reverse) burden of proof, and the burden of litigation cost.[66] Only with practical and enforceable measures can the law provide legal remedies to small shareholders.

4.3.2 Personal liability for the board of directors

The introduction of international accounting firms is being considered by the Ministry of Finance, in order to set up a good model for domestic auditing firms which have encountered a crisis of trust in recent years. The qualification of the auditing firm Zhong Tian Qing was revoked in the famous *Yin Guang Xia* case. These scandals in recent years have severely damaged the image of Chinese auditing firms and, on the other hand, strengthened the existence of international firms in China. The breach of fiduciary duties is attributed partly to the low cost of the breach and the high profit in auditing, and the failure of legal sanctions against directors and auditors. The newly amended Corporate Law and Security Law now give the shareholders and the supervisory board more rights to protect their interests. Besides, there is an increasing tendency in Chinese law firms to engage in derivative lawsuits and even to sue the auditors for breach of fiduciary duties in auditing.[67] In public corporations, the directors and independent auditors are seen as fiduciaries of the corporation and must serve the best interest of the corporation. Of course, the burden of proof is decisive in identifying whether the auditor is liable, namely, whether the auditor breaches his professional duty or not. In the *Kelong Electronics* case, the law firm not only sued the auditing firm Deloitte China and the responsible auditor for breach of professional duty and personal liability, but also sued the directors of Kelong Electronics for damage compensation. This new development in the concept of personal liability in China may exert a positive effect on the stock market. As directors may be held liable for breach of fiduciary duties, they are thought to act with 'care' in business decisions.

In principle, the board is not liable for damage compensation so long as the decision making is within its discretion. The difficulty for the law is how to define a reasonable and acceptable level of care, since business decisions always face risks. The board may escape the liability by applying 'the rule of commercial judgment'. Therefore, good corporate law should also establish a mechanism of risk management and control, as well as a democratic decision-making procedure. Under such a mechanism, the board should examine the decision making with care and make it conform to the best interests of the corporation. Additionally, the set-up of the business organization and decision-making process should be improved, in order to avoid mistakes in decision making. The supervisory board should have the right to examine and approve big business, as with mergers and acquisitions. If the board violates the obligations under such a mechanism and this leads to a loss which is avoidable, it should be held liable.[68] In general, within the firms, a workable mechanism with a well-defined scope of discretion should be established through the improvement of the decision-making process and corporate structure, and facilitate the judgment as to whether the board member has violated his duty of care. As to Chinese stock companies, this is much more meaningful since the board and managers enjoy excessive discretion.

Another aspect of good corporate governance is the imposing of sanctions on a breach of duties by enforcement of damage compensation. Current Chinese corporate law allows shareholders to claim damage compensation in cases where the decisions of shareholder meetings or the board of directors have violated the law and regulations, and consequently damage the interests of the shareholders.[69] In addition, the newly amended law has also given the right to the supervisory board and shareholders with a certain proportion of the shares to sue the directors if fiduciary duties are violated.[70] In comparison, the law and court decision[71] in Germany even allows a minority of the supervisory board to sue the board in a case where the board of directors has damaged the interests of the corporation.[72] Furthermore, German corporate law, like many other European corporate laws, extends legal rights to the shareholders with 10 per cent or 500 000 euros, to claim damage compensation in the name of the company. In practice, the law tries to avoid possible abuse of litigation rights if the proportion is set too low, since unnecessary lawsuits may disturb the normal operation of the company. Therefore derivative lawsuits should be based on adequate facts as a precondition and must prove material breach of duties by the board. In a country with weak legal remedies, civil litigation, including derivative lawsuits, will have a positive influence on deterring the abuse of managerial discretion in Chinese stock companies. As most of the stock companies are controlled by the State, the design of a workable mechanism is important in order to enhance fiduciary duties of the board. The direction of the reform should focus on how to deter the abuse of (excessive) managerial discretion of the board of directors through stricter enforcement of civil liability besides criminal and administrative sanctions.

5. GENERALIZATIONS

Many cases have shown that business structures in Chinese public firms lead to excessive discretion of the board of directors and officers. Overseeing and monitoring the board and managers becomes difficult, owing to the problem of information asymmetry and undemocratic decision making in management. Therefore reform is necessary to enhance corporate governance in China; in particular, the State as the sole largest shareholder should reduce its share of state-owned companies, so as to optimize the structure of shareholders. For example, the proportion of State shares should not exceed 50 per cent and the total proportion of the second and third largest shareholders should exceed the proportion of the State's share.[73]

With respect to monitoring and overseeing the board of directors, as outside directors do not attain their goal of monitoring, a power shift from the shareholder meetings to the supervisory board, as set forth in the new Chinese Corporate Law, gives a good opportunity to re-establish a monitoring mechanism. An impartial supervisory board with sufficient discretion can call for general meetings and influence the meetings with respect to the appointment and dismissal of board members. By bringing derivative lawsuits against dishonest or disloyal directors and officers on behalf of the corporations, the supervisory board and shareholders can put pressure on the board and managers to abide by their fiduciary obligations.[74] Through better monitoring and overseeing of the directors and officers, agency costs can be reduced and corporate governance can be improved as well.

The scandals which occurred in China in recent years severely damaged the sound development of the capital market and led to a crisis of trust amongst shareholders. Accounting regulations in China cannot deliver the assurance they should deliver to the investors. An effective remedy is to integrate IAS into Chinese accounting standards. The new Corporate Accounting Standards is seen as an effort to unify different criteria and standards existing in different laws and regulations. The normative integrity is to enhance transparency in information disclosure. A further consideration is to introduce the American practice of an auditing committee in each stock company for selection of public accountants, oversight of corporate financial information disclosure, internal and external auditing, moral norms of the company, risk management and so on.[75]

Corporate governance in China should be strengthened by the further development of the concept of personal liability. In particular, directors, managers and auditors should be liable for damage compensation in cases of breach of their fiduciary duties. This is significant in delivering a warning to fiduciaries not to engage in fraudulent financial schemes. In this regard, the newly amended Chinese Security Law should be further interpreted so as to provide practical legal remedies in collective lawsuits.

To summarize, corporate governance is very important to a nation's economy. Better corporate governance can reduce the transaction costs of firms and thus enhance economic efficiency. The business structure in Chinese public firms results in monitoring problems and thus incurs high agency costs. Externally, owing to excessive discretion of the board and managers in state-owned firms, the mechanism of the supervisory board and outside directors does not function well in overseeing and monitoring the board and managers. Internally, fiduciary obligations of the board and managers are often in question, and the fiduciary rules are often violated. In this context, corporate governance in China should focus on how to improve the monitoring mechanism and protect the interest of small investors. Specifically, a mandatory information disclosure should enable the directors to obtain information about the managers' business activities, and the supervisory board should have the right to obtain information from the board of directors and the managers. Additionally, the supervisory board should obtain regular financial reports from the board of directors.[76] Furthermore, the board and managers should be loyal to the company and should manage the corporation with 'duty of care'. Small shareholders have the right to select their directors under a mandatory accumulative voting system and can also bring derivative lawsuits against directors or managers on behalf of the corporation if they breach their fiduciary obligations.[77] These means can partly deter the current excessive discretion of the board. Also, to deter abuse of managerial discretion, some missing regulations with respect to civil liability (damage compensation) should be restored. Most importantly, as this chapter reveals, the reduction of the large proportion of State shares in stock companies seems imminent, since the existence of the State as the sole largest shareholder hinders the improvement of corporate governance. Without changing the structure of shares, the reform effort to improve the discretion of the supervisory board will be in vain. The purpose of changing the business structure is obvious: by changing the business structure, the interests of private investors can be better protected and thus stimulate investment.

NOTES

1. I would like to thank Prof. Michael Faure, Dr Niels Philipsen (University of Maastricht), Prof. Zhang Naigen (Fudan University), Prof. Gao Xujun (Tongji University), Prof. Thomas Eger (University of Hamburg), Susan Schneider and Prof. Pierre Garello (University of Aix-Marseille) for their valuable comments and help. Thanks also to Tongji University, Faculty of Law and Chinesisch-Deutsches Hochschulkolleg, Shanghai.
2. See Art. 20 III ('piercing the corporate veil'), Art. 106 (accumulative voting), Art. 54 V and Art. 152 (derivative lawsuit) of the new Chinese Corporate Law. The new corporate law is effective beginning 01.01.2006. Besides the new registration, capital is reduced to 30 000 Yuan (approximately equal to US$3700) and a one-man company is allowed to encourage private investment.
3. These cases are related to a fraudulent financial scheme which incurred heavy losses to numerous small investors.
4. The prices of the stocks fell sharply from their highest level of 2000 points to the current low level of *ca.* 1100 points since 2001 in the Shanghai Stock Exchange Market. As a result, many investors shift their investments into real estate which can yield high returns.
5. On 16 August 2001 the China Security Authority issued a directive called *Directive to Establish Independent Directors in Public Corporations.*
6. This leading definition can be found in *American Law Institute, Restatement [Second] of Agency*, sec. 1(1): '"Agency": the fiduciary relation which results from the manifestation of consent by one person to another that the other shall act on his behalf and subject to his control, and consent by the other so to act.'
7. Clark (1995, pp. 55–79).
8. Eisenberg (1976, p. 1).
9. Clark (1986, p. 17).
10. Dent (1989, p. 883).
11. Berle and Means (1932, pp. 4–5, 84–8, 114).

12. Berle and Means (1932).
13. Clark (1979, pp. 776, 807).
14. Berle and Means (1932, pp. 4, 47–63, 84–9).
15. Dent (1989, pp. 892–903). There are also many arguments supporting separation of ownership and control. This 'managerialist' view is based on the argument that large corporations are not private enterprises, but social institutions accountable not only to shareholders but to many constituencies, including creditors, consumers, employees, suppliers and the communities in which the firms operate. Managers have a broader perspective that balances the needs of the firms' many policies. Compare Manning (1958, p. 1477) and Dodd (1932, p. 1145).
16. Liang (2000, p. 173).
17. Liang (2000, pp. 143–4).
18. Besides the introduction of outside directors, the American legal practice of 'piercing the corporate veil' is also incorporated into the new Corporate Law which is effective as of 1 January 2006.
19. Jensen and Meckling (1976, p. 305). Also see Fama (1980, p. 288). Alchian and Demsetz (1972, p. 777).
20. For detailed analysis of different views on agency costs and optimal level of agency costs, see Clark (1985, pp. 65–8).
21. Art. 38 and Art. 100 of Chinese Corporate Law (2006).
22. *Supra*, note 21.
23. *Supra*, note 21.
24. Art. 101 III, V of Chinese Corporate Law (2006).
25. Art. 102 and Art. 152 of Chinese Corporate Law (2006). Shareholders with 10 per cent of the share (including accumulative share) can call for shareholder meetings or bring lawsuits against members of the board of directors in the case of misbehaviour.
26. The State-owned Assets Management Committee is established in all levels of the local government to represent the State in management of the State assets. Directors and managers in large state firms are assigned by the committee.
27. Gao (2003, p. 71).
28. Abbreviation for China Aviation Oil (Singapore) Corporation Ltd.
29. CAOHC (Singapore) lost US$5.5 billion in its speculative activities in the oil market in 2005 owing to 'unacceptable and careless' decision making of the Managing Director of the company. This raises the question about corporate governance of Chinese public firms. Directors or managers enjoy excessive discretion in business. Even the board cannot monitor managing directors. The result is often tragic: the managers are fired and the company faces heavy financial distress. The interest of shareholders is severely damaged (<http://finance.news.tom.com/zhuanti/zhy.html>).
30. Many lawsuits (e.g. *Jiu Zhou*, *Yin Guan Xia*) reveal the problem of dictatorship of managing directors in Chinese public-going corporations and the lack of monitoring by shareholders and other directors. They get involved in fraud, disclosure of false information and careless decision making due to the lack of supervision and monitoring.
31. The small shareholders are dispersed in the country and would not like to bear the cost of travelling to attend the shareholder meetings.
32. Eisenberg (1976, pp. 162–70). Also see Dent (1981, pp. 623, 629).
33. According to Art. 4.1. and 7.5. of *the Guidelines about Outside Directors*, issued by the China Security Supervision Committee, shareholders who accumulate 1 per cent of the total share can propose their own representative on the board. But large shareholders can veto the proposal without any difficulty. In general, the candidate can be approved only with support from large shareholders and based on the same consideration. The board of directors or the supervisory board will not propose a candidate who will not have the support of the large shareholders. As a result, outside directors are supposed to be inclined to the interest of large shareholders.
34. Compare Dent (1989, p. 898).
35. Eisenberg (1976, pp. 141–3).
36. Dent (1989, p. 899).

37. Dent (1989, p. 899). This happens very often when a firm is considering a big business proposal or risky business venture; outside directors are more conservative and risk-averse. Sometimes a good business opportunity might be lost owing to opposition by the outsiders.
38. The function of outside directors overlaps with the supervisory board. Besides, as with the supervisory board, outside directors cannot assert independence from the board of directors and corporate officers. See Gao and Tang (2003, p. 232). For further comments, see Hu (2003, pp. 54–61).
39. Art. 84 of AG.
40. Art. 54, 55 and Art. 118, 152 of Chinese Corporate Law (2006).
41. Members of the supervisory board are appointed by the board of directors and are subservient to the board; as a result, they cannot oversee the directors.
42. Hu (2003, pp. 54–61), Eisenberg (1976, pp. 141–3).
43. Art. 95–116 AG Recht.
44. Art. 52 of Chinese Corporate Law (2006).
45. All these firms conducted fraudulent financial schemes in order to be listed in the stock market or for financial purposes.
46. Clark (1995, pp. 71–8).
47. Clark (1995, pp. 73–4).
48. See 'Notification about Civil Disputes Arising from Fraudulent Statement in Stock Market', the People's Supreme Court, 15 January 2002.
49. See Gu (2003, p. 128).
50. Art. 10b-5d, 16b of American Securities Exchange Act, Art. 6, 7 of German Code of Corporate Governance (Deutscher Corporate Governance Kodex), Art. 63, 177, 181, 202 of Chinese Security Law.
51. Easterbrook and Fischel (1984, pp. 695–6).
52. Art 7.1 of German Code of Corporate Governance (Deutscher Corporate Governance Kodex): '. . . the consolidated Financial Statements and interim reports shall be prepared under observance of internationally recognized accounting principles'. See Peltzer (2003, p. 102–5).
53. Art. 7.2 of German Code of Corporate Governance (Deutscher Corporate Governance Kodex).
54. Art 7.3 of German Code of Corporate Governance (Deutscher Corporate Governance Kodex).
55. Art. 6.1 of German Code of Corporate Governance (Deutscher Corporate Governance Kodex).
56. Verordnung Nr. 1606/2002 vom 19.07.2002, Abl. EG vom 11.09.2002, S. 243.
57. See Chinese newspaper: *National Business Daily*, 13 April 2006. Price Waterhouse Cooper was charged in 2001 for issuing an auditing report for a fraudulent financial scheme made by Jingzhou Port; and Deloitte was charged in 2006 for approving the fraudulent financial scheme of Kelong Electronics.
58. Issued on 25 February 2006 by the Ministry of Finance. From 1 January 2007, all the Chinese stock companies, whether listed in the domestic market or abroad, shall apply the new standards.
59. Art. 63 of the Security Law stipulates joint liability of issuer, portfolio firms in the case of a fraudulent financial statement or other documents. Art. 212 of Corporate Law and Art. 177, 202, 181 of Security Law stipulate administrative liability of institutions and relevant parties. Arts 160, 161 and 229 of Penalty Law extend the criminal sanction against people who conduct serious fraudulent activities.
60. The revised Security Act was examined and approved by the People's Congress on 23.10.2005. The new Security Law is effective together with the new Corporate Law on 01.01.2006.
61. Art. 173 and Art. 210 of Chinese Security Act (2006).
62. Chapter 11, Chinese Security Act.
63. Gomard (1985, p. 209).
64. Zhou and Luo (2000, p. 66).

65. For example, Art. 115 imposes civil liability in the case of breach of fiduciary obligations with some wording such as 'civil liability cannot be exempted'. But, as a civil right, the law shall also respect private autonomy and allow the exemption of the litigant or claimer.
66. <http://finance.people.com.cn/GB/1041/3815096.html>. According to the principles of collective action in security law, litigation cost can be borne by each party; small shareholders are allowed not to pay litigation cost, except when they win the case; an individual small shareholder can sue the corporation, and all other shareholders can benefit from winning the case.
67. See Chinese newspaper, *Nan Fang Zhou Mo*, 6 April 2006. In the report, Deloitte China was accused of wrong-doing in approving the fraudulent financial report made by the electronics firm Kelong. Lawyers went further to hold the accountant and auditor liable for misconduct.
68. A practical and detailed decision-making procedure is necessary. It should define the scope of decision making of the board. Also, the law shall also rule that the directors and managers shall bear insurance costs partly or completely so that the penalty will be plausible and effective. See Baums (2001, p. 75). Not like other countries, such as Germany, liability insurance for directors and managers is not regulated in Chinese law. Compare Die Uebersicht bei Kaestner (2000, pp. 113–14).
69. Art. 150 of Chinese Corporate Law (2006).
70. Art. 152 of Chinese Corporate Law (2006).
71. BGHZ 135, 244.
72. Art. 147 of Aktiengesellschaft (AG).
73. Easterbrook and Fischel (1983, pp. 407ff.). The existence of a large shareholder may signal to the market that the firm's stock is valuable. Studies show that the firm's share price rises when a shareholder accumulates large block of shares. Also see Shleifer and Vishny (1986, pp. 461, 465–71).
74. A valuable consideration is to relieve the burden of small shareholders in derivative lawsuits. Because of the consideration of high litigation cost, small shareholders may hesitate to bring the cases to the court. In Britain, the law requires the company to pre-pay the costs. Even if the litigant loses the case, the British court has the discretion to exempt the litigant from paying the costs, since the court holds that the claim of the litigant could be reasonable and the company has more information than the litigant. See Shou and Jiang (2003, p. 114).
75. Compare Lowy (2005, pp. 79–80).
76. Compare Wang (2004, p. 6).
77. Art. 152 of Chinese Corporate Law (2006).

REFERENCES

Alchian, A.A. and H. Demsetz (1972), 'Production, information costs, and economic organization', *American Economic Review*, **62**, 777.

Baums, T. (ed.) (2001), *Bericht der Regierungskommission Corporate Governance*, Cologne: Otto-Schmidt.

Berle, A. and G. Means (1932), *The Modern Corporation and Private Property*, New York: The Macmillan Company.

Clark, R.C. (1979), 'Vote buying and corporate law', *Case Western Reserve Law Review*, **29**, 776, 780–85, 807.

Clark, R.C. (1986), *Corporate Law*, Boston: Little, Brown and Co.

Clark, R.C. (1995), 'Agency costs versus fiduciary duties', in J. Pratt and R. Zeckhauser (eds), *Principals and Agents: The Structure of Business*, pp. 55–79, 65–8.

Dent, G.W. (1981), 'The revolution of corporate governance, the monitoring board, and the director's duty of care', *Boston University Law Review*, **61**, 623, 629.
Dent, G.W. Jr (1989), 'Toward unifying ownership and control in the public corporation', *Wisconsin Law Review*, 883, 892–903, 898–9.
Die Uebersicht bei Kaestner (2000), *Die Aktiengesellschaft (AG)*, pp. 113, 114.
Dodd, E.M. (1932), 'For whom are corporate managers trustees?', *Harvard Law Review*, **45**, 1145.
Easterbrook, F.H. and D.R. Fischel (1984), 'Mandatory disclosure and the protection of investors', *Virginia Law Review*, **70**, 695–6.
Eisenberg, M. (1976), *The Structure of the Corporation I*, Boston: Little, Brown and Co., pp. 1, 141–3, 162–70.
Fama, E.F. (1980), 'Agency problems and theory of the firm', *Journal of Political Economy*, **88**, 288.
Gao, X.J. (2003), 'Independent directors in Chinese public corporations', in X.J. Gao (ed.), *Comparative Research on Corporate Governance between Chinese and German Firms*, Shanghai: Bai Jia Publication, p. 71.
Gao, J.K. and H.J. Tang (2003), 'Some considerations on the transplantation of independent directors in China', *China Commercial Law Journal*, 232.
Gomard, B. (1985), 'Board members' liability for damages', in K.J. Hopt and G. Teubner (eds), *Corporate Governance and Directors' Liabilities (Legal, Economic and Sociological Analysis on Corporate Social Responsibility)*, Berlin: Walter de Gruyter & Co., p. 209.
Gu, X.R. (2003), 'The way of improving Chinese corporate governance', in X.J. Gao (ed.), *Comparative Research on Corporate Governance between Chinese and German Firms*, Shanghai: Bai Jia Publication, pp. 126–8.
Hu, H.G. (2003), 'Questioning the feasibility about the introduction of independent directors in China', in X.J. Gao (ed.), *Comparative Research on Corporate Governance between Chinese and German Firms*, Shanghai: Bai Jia Publication, pp. 54–61.
Jensen, M.C. and W.H. Meckling (1976), 'Theory of the firm: managerial behavior, agency costs and ownership structure', *Journal of Financial Economics*, **3**, 305.
Liang, N. (ed.) (2000), *Corporate Governance: Chinese Practice and American Experience*, China: Renmin Universtiy Publication.
Lowy, M. (2005), *Corporate Governance for Public Company Directors*, Chinese version, trans. Liu Yan, Law Press China.
Manning, B. (1958), 'Review of "The American Stockholder"', *Yale Law Journal*, **67**, 1477–96.
Peltzer, M. (2003), *Deutsche Corporate Governance, Ein Leitfaden*, C.H. Beck.
Shleifer, A. and R.W. Vishny (1986), 'Large shareholders and corporate control', *Journal of Political Economy*, **94**, 461, 465–71.
Shou, X.B. and Y.Y. Jiang (2003), 'Corporate governance: system design and international experience', in *Faxue*, Shanghai 114.
Wang, B.S. (2004), 'The revision of corporate law shall pursue applicability', in *Faxue*, Shanghai **272**, 6.
Zhou, Y.S. and H.L. Luo (2000), 'Civil liability in security law', in *China Legal Journal (Zhong Guo Fa Xue)*, **4**, 66.

9. The stable self-enforcement and distribution of property right: the right to virtual property in MMORPG

Jian Wei and Shanguo Xue

1. INTRODUCTION

As a new type of property, virtual property in MMORPG (Massive Multiplayer Online Role Playing Game) has attracted more and more attention. Disputes over malicious fraud and theft concerned with virtual property are also increasing gradually. The first lawsuit of MMORPG in China, *Hongchen Li* v. *Beijibing Company*, is as follows: in more than two years, Hongchen Li, a cyber game player, spent thousands of hours and more than ten thousand of game currency in playing Red Moon, a MMORPG, and thus purchased and accumulated dozens of types of virtual biochemical weapons in the game. On 17 February 2003, he was astonished to find that all virtual equipment that was stored under the ID 'state chairman' in the game server was lost. Afterwards he contacted the defendant, the Beijibing Company, to inquire after the equipment's whereabouts and detailed information on the thief, but the defendant refused his request in the name of 'the protection of player's information as privacy'. Therefore, Hongchen Li sued the game's manufacturer for infringing his private property.

A large number of virtual property disputes have shown that the source of dispute between players and manufacturers is the loss of virtual property for unknown reasons, for which each side blames the other and they finally engage in a lawsuit. Who should be responsible for the loss? What kind of property right arrangement can solve this problem effectively? Which basis of principle can guide the distribution of property right?

2. ALTERNATIVE AVAILABLE PRINCIPLES OF RIGHT DISTRIBUTION

In the economics literature, the concept of 'property rights' basically refers to all kinds of economic rights. Generally, property rights include those rights whose sub-rights are all economic, for instance the right to property, and those whose sub-rights are partly economic, like the right to portrayal for commercial purpose. In addition, 'property rights' not only indicate one economic right, but also one group of economic rights. This thesis will apply the latter indication of 'property rights' to most conditions.

The distribution of property rights is one of the most significant problems of mankind and society, for the reason that it is not only concerned with the distribution of wealth, but also plays a decisive role in producing wealth. In order to solve this problem, the law has established three principles. The first one is the principle of first possession; that is, a person who first finds the property owns it. Typically, the first occupier of ownerless land will be its owner. The second is the principle of tied ownership; that is, the ownership of appurtenances belongs to the one who owns a major piece of property to which the appurtenances are attached. For example, the owner of a house enjoys the ownership of the house's key. The third is the creation principle; that is, a person owns what he or she creates, like the patent that belongs to its inventor.

Nevertheless, all these three principles have their own drawbacks. The principle of first possession often arouses competition in pre-occupancy and excessive investment; the principle of tied ownership lacks feasibility, for it is difficult to clearly define the boundary between different rights, and the creation principle frequently initiates disputes over who first creates the property. So these three principles are only effective within a certain area.

Using the Coase theorem, Posner[1] put forward the efficiency-evaluating principle; that is, the property right should be entitled to the person who values the property the most. According to the Coase theorem, if transaction costs are zero, it does not matter who is entitled to the property right, because people can obtain what they want by costless bargaining; while the distribution of property rights will influence the efficiency of resource distribution if the transaction costs are more than zero, as transaction costs prevent people from obtaining the property right they expected. To allocate the entitlement of the property right to the person who values it the most will save transaction costs and also achieve the highest efficiency in terms of use of resource. The reason for this is that the one who values the property most highly will also use it most effectively. However, this is merely an inspiring and theoretical principle, for it is quite difficult to make an exact choice on who values it the most. Although the owner can be determined by auction, it remains a questionable point whether he or she will have the greatest efficient use in practice.

Demsetz[2] analysed the economic precondition of property right distribution and argued that scarcity relatively increases the price of the property object, which exceeds the original cost of obtaining the property. Therefore the right holder has an incentive to obtain and protect the property right. The elements that lead to the relative increase of a property object's price include technology, population and change in society. Demsetz's contribution is that he advanced the precondition of property right distribution; that is, that people have incentives to affirm property rights only when their interests from the property right distribution exceed the costs.

Libecap[3] made a comprehensive analysis on the political games among parties concerned with the process of property right distribution, and suggested that the results of these games are not always the realization of the rational utilization of resources, but depend on the balance of political forces between parties concerned with property right distribution. Robert Higgs'[4] research on salmon fishery in Washington not only proved Libecap's argument, but also emphasized the influences that political games brought to technology advancement. As implied by the literature of Libecap and others, the rule makers (government, Congress and other legislators) have incentives to allocate entitlements to property rights only when the interests of entitlement activities exceed their cost, while the rule makers will not commit themselves to these activities when they face oppressive political pressure (the strong protest of the people who were deprived of their right or their vote) that directly threatens their interests, or when the allocation of entitlements will do direct harm to the public interests which indirectly threaten rule makers' interests.

William H. Riker and Itai Sened[5] came to a further conclusion on the preconditions of property right distribution. The first precondition is scarcity. The scarcity of property determines that the value of the property right exceeds its cost. Without scarcity, the controlling of property rights will be meaningless. The second one is the right-holder's desire for the right. Without desire, the right-holder will not seek the right, and the property right will have no reason to exist. The third is the rule maker's desire to recognize the right. If the right is not an official formal entitlement, the rule maker is unable to put the right into operation. The fourth is the duty-bearer's respect of the right. This is a necessary yet often neglected condition. To sum up, only when the entitlement interests of each party (right-holder, rule maker and duty-bearer) concerned exceed, or at least equal, their respective costs can a property right be entitled and implemented.

Thus the precondition of property right establishment is multi-balanced, that is, the interests of each party exceed their costs, under which the right-holder, the rule maker and the duty-bearer have incentives to promote the entitlement and enforcement of the right. The essential requirement and purpose for the entitlement of a right in society is successful self-enforcement, which promotes the most efficient use of the property and achieves the maximum of social welfare. Therefore, the multi-balance is also a basic precondition for a right's stable self-enforcement.

Full self-enforcement of a right is unrealistic. However, if the enforcement of the right is continually disturbed so that the cost of enforcement becomes quite high, the entitlement of right will become meaningless. If the parties' gain from exercising their right is far lower than the cost, the right will become valueless and no one will exercise it. In the same way, if the cost to hold the right exceeds the corresponding gain, people will not be interested in the entitlement of the right. Furthermore, if a person thinks that the cost to bear a duty is greater than what he can get from it, he will make continuous efforts to evade his duty, so that it is difficult fully to enforce the right. So, in order to enforce some rights, society must pay high costs in order to solve various disputes, so that the total social cost exceeds the total social gains.

Consequently, we take the stable and successful self-enforcement of a property right as the basic principle for allocating a right; that is, concerned parties have an incentive to implement the right or to promote the benefits of the right. The incentive is that the benefits gained from enforcement are more than, or at least the same as, the costs. When entitlement to a property right needs to be given officially, there exist many alternatives. The alternative that results in maximum self-enforcement will be chosen as the distribution plan. This distribution principle is a principle aiming towards the right result.

As stated above, existing studies have realized that the multi-balance among concerned parties with property rights is a key condition of property right distribution. This chapter takes the multi-balance among concerned parties as an essential principle of property distribution. In fact, the First Possession Principle, the Tied Ownership Principle and the Creation Principle have implied the meaning of stable self-enforcement of property right. All these three principles are intended to ensure that the property right can be accepted by society and is carried out successfully. The intention of using these three principles as the core principles of distributing rights is to use social common understanding in order to establish a good base which will reduce obstacles in the process of implementing the property right. Therefore we can see that self-enforcement of property right and the above three principles do not conflict with each other. On the contrary, they are compatible with and complement each other. Posner's efficiency-evaluating principle implies that the right-holder must have the most efficient use of the property in order to make the benefits gained from implementing the right exceed costs maximally; therefore it also has something in common with the property right stable self-enforcement principle.

However, existing studies have not performed in-depth analysis in examining the elements that influence the cost–benefit judgment of concerned parties. This chapter chooses the property right to virtual property in MMORPG as a research object, it explains that the stable self-enforcement of property rights should be the basic principle of property right distribution, and analyses the elements that influence the cost–benefit judgment of concerned parties.

3. INFLUENTIAL ELEMENTS OF PROPERTY RIGHT DISTRIBUTION

How to define the boundaries and specific forms of the rights that belong to each concerned party in order to achieve the multi-balance? To put it more precisely: which elements influence the choice of boundaries of rights, specific forms and cost–benefit judgment of concerned parties?

3.1 The Physical Attributes of a Property Object

3.1.1 MMORPG and virtual property

As a newly emerging thing, network games, growing out of Multi-User Dungeons, exist in many forms. This chapter chooses the virtual property in MMORPG (Massive Multiplayer Online Role Playing Game) as the research object, but the conclusion can apply to other types of games. In MMORPG, a player plays a favourite role in a virtual world, grows from his role in the game, and communicates, cooperates and fights with others for mental happiness and satisfaction. The basic rule is that a player gradually acquires game skills, experiences and ranks in the process of the game, and the next stage of the game is based on the previous stage. The MMORPG is operated by two parts, the client part and the server part. Through the Internet, a player enters the game from the client part into the server part, and plays the game. All of the player's data will be kept in the server part.

The virtual property that players can obtain in MMORPG is divided into two categories: one is the virtual status, including the role's virtual attributes (the figure, experience, rank and other attributes), virtual social connections (for example, guild connections, hail-fellow system and so on) which are attached to the player's account; the other category is virtual articles, including all kinds of virtual articles that are independent from the player's account, such as game currency, virtual equipment, virtual pets, virtual props and so on.

Now the majority of research considers these two categories of property as their research objects, for these are essential for players to begin and act in games. For example, Juhua Liu and Weide Zhou define virtual things in MMORPG as 'some things that have certain usage values in MMORPG, include virtual persons of players' accounts, virtual currency and other things that virtual persons gained in the virtual world by all possible means. Virtual currency is a universal equivalent for virtual trade in Internet space. Virtual things include treasures, weapons, tools, experience and other things used in games'.[6]

However, virtual articles can be separated from a player's account and can be traded in games, so cases involving transactions of this type of virtual property are far more than those about virtual status. As a result, more attention is paid to virtual articles. This chapter also mainly considers virtual articles as the research object.

3.1.2 Physical attributes of virtual property in MMORPG

MMORPG satisfies a player's thirst for exploration, war and other experiences through the Internet game. In order to carry out these experiences, virtual property is the most important medium and tool. Virtual property has two important physical attributes: intangibility and the inability to be transferred physically.

Intangibility means that virtual property has no physical form and only exists in the form of an electromagnetic record for conserving equipment in a computer. There are two preconditions for the emerging of virtual articles: one is the games programme of manufacturers. The other is the players' activity in games. Under the game rules constituted by firms (including devising the time, place, probability of virtual article emergency and so on), players can trigger the emergence of virtual property. The former (manufacturer's activity) is creative production, while the latter (players' activity) is the production of games, although the players invest a lot more money and time in order to acquire virtual property.

Inability to be transferred physically means that the virtual property only exists in games and is unable to be separated from the games, and therefore cannot actually be held, used and enjoyed by parties outside of the games. Because all virtual property in MMORPG is conserved in game-operating computers, players are unable to hold this virtual property after the game is closed, and are hardly able even to prove their possession of their virtual property. Virtual property only exists at given times and in given spaces. The given space means that the value and function of the virtual property can only appear in certain games and on certain Internet servers' computers. The given time means that the virtual property will become meaningless after the MMORPG is shut down (the games will be closed when the operating merchant becomes insolvent, the game server is attacked, the player voluntarily gives up, and so on).[7] What is more important is that the existence and transaction of virtual property are unable to be separated from a certain game. As soon as the game begins, on the one hand, players cannot withdraw from the game according to the large sunk costs, such as the large amount of time, money and effort invested. Also the increasing involvement established through the process of playing will also make the player unwilling to withdraw.

Nevertheless, virtual property can be traded amongst the same game players, which has been shown by the development of MMORPG. Especially the emergence of professional players has enlarged the scope of virtual property transactions. The market for off-line transactions, namely different players from the same game trading in the virtual property, has developed on a huge scale.

3.1.3 The influences of virtual property's physical attributes on the distribution of the property right

The physical attributes of the object of the right are basic influential elements that directly determine the distribution of property rights. For game manufacturers, virtual property in MMORPG, conserved in the computer programmes, is created by collective labour. For players, virtual property is obtained under the pre-occupancy rule through the investment of a lot of time, money and energy. According to the creation principle, both manufacturers and players should be entitled to a property right for virtual property. But the two characteristics of virtual property mentioned above determine that the rights of manufacturers and players should differ. Supposing that players have the ownership of the virtual property in MMORPG, according to the ownership conception, players have the right to remove their virtual property and trade with it, after they withdraw from the game and stop consumption. Yet the two features of virtual property determine this to be impossible, so that it is unfeasible and impossible to entitle players to the ownership of virtual property.

In fact, players' consuming activities in MMORPG only establish a consumption contract between players and manufacturers. The virtual property is only a medium for the player's consumption activities and a tool that the manufacturer provides to the players for consumption, such as the dishware that the restaurant provides to consumers. Therefore what the player owns is the right to use virtual property at a given time and place. Although players need to make certain efforts (even comparatively great efforts) to gain the virtual property, it is the game manufacturer, the owner of game, and not the player who has ownership.

In MMORPG the ownership of virtual property entitled to the manufacturer accords with the creative principle. With such ownership, the manufacturer's massive investment in developing the game will not be eroded by players who are falsely entitled to ownership. In particular, the manufacturer need not pay ransom money to get the virtual property back after the game is over. Hence the manufacturer has an incentive to constantly add more virtual property in order to enrich the game and attract more players and enlarge profits. The players are granted the use of the virtual property, but their rights are limited; that is, the use of virtual property is limited in certain games and requires manufacturer's authentication in advance. The user rights guarantee the player the consumption of the experiences that the virtual property supplies, and give him protection when the proper usage is infringed. The usage rights build upon the manufacturer's duty to guarantee a players' use of virtual property under proper conditions. At the same time, the manufacturer's ownership also confers a duty on players to consume appropriately and protect their game information cautiously.

3.2 The Technical Level of Property Right Protection

3.2.1 The lack of effective techniques to judge harm caused is the source of disputes as regards virtual property in MMORPG

Property rights will not be self-enforced successfully after primary entitlement. The technical level for protecting a property right is the second important influential element. A right that lacks effective protection is an incomplete right and will cause high protection costs which may even exceed the benefits of the right, and therefore make the entitlement meaningless. The protection techniques of rights include the technique of protecting a right's boundaries, tort judgment technique, tort investigation and fixation technique and so on. The technique of protecting a right's boundaries, including the techniques of fencing, usage of a patrol system, an electro-monitor system and so on, ensures that the right is not invaded by outsiders. The tort judgment technique is to identify the tortfeasor by means of such techniques, such as the mark testing technique, checking technique and so on. The tort investigation and fixation technique is to ensure that the punishment is implemented strictly, for example through the restriction of individual freedom and the closure of accounts. Among these techniques, the tort judgment technique is the key. The disputes concerning virtual property are initiated by the lack of effective techniques to judge the actual cause of torts.

The possible causes of loss of virtual property include three instances. Firstly, players' activity, such as improper conduct or neglecting caution, will cause loss. For example, players do not take care of their accounts and passwords, which are revealed to others intentionally or unintentionally; when aware of someone's intention to steal their information, players also consistently take the risk of trading with this person; the level of protection of the players' computers is very low, and often cannot even resist basic viruses; or some voluntarily download illicit software, which may include such Trojan viruses.

Secondly, the activity of the manufacturer causes loss. For example, the latent faults in the game itself result in chaos or loss of data in a game; the operating computers of the manufacturer's server are not stable and, as a result, the player's role in the game may be ended and virtual property lost; the game manager makes use of bad management to steal players' virtual property; actions taken directly by the manufacturer in order to restore and alter attributes of virtual property cause the loss of virtual property; the manufacturer stops operating the game, which makes players' whole virtual property become ineffective.

Thirdly, activities undertaken by a third party can also cause loss. There are three cases of third parties' interference that harm virtual property. The first case is that the server computers of the operation merchant are invaded and the invaders steal the players' virtual equipment. The second case is that the player's own PC is invaded or the thief uses Hacker software installed in Internet café computers in advance, in order to steal players' user names and passwords. Owing to the difficulty of invading the server of the operation merchant, personal information becomes the centre of invasion. The last case is that players possessing virtual property are lured by others through fraud, concealment, threat and force to agree to a trade. The forced trade cheating procedure and illegal copy of virtual property are used in the course of the transaction to rob others' virtual property. This frequently happens to players.

Of course loss caused for different reasons brings different duties. The duty of damage will be self-evident if we can find out the reasons for loss at no or at lower cost. However, the problem is that we cannot find out what is the real cause of a loss. After the loss occurs, the reasons for the losses will become private information. Even if it is individual activities of the manufacturer or the player that cause loss, neither of them will admit to it. More importantly, there are no effective techniques for preventing 'Hacker invading' or a 'forcedly cheating procedure'. Existing techniques are unable to investigate and fix the reasons causing virtual property loss, and say nothing of identifying whose fault causes the loss. As a result, in the case that loss occurs, the manufacturer and the player will criticize each other and require the other side to take responsibility for the loss.

Because of the lack of effective techniques to protect rights, manufacturer's ownership and players' rights of use are threatened by torts. How is one to distribute risks caused by insufficient techniques among parties, in order to promote a successful self-enforcement of property right? One needs to analyse the source of risks. MMORPG is a growing industry, through which the manufacturer provides a virtual experience to players and charges them according to the times they played. For the manufacturer, the main pattern of gaining profits is to charge players according to how long they spend on the game. That is to say, MMORPG is a mere medium for the manufacturer to gain profits. Thus the technical risks that cannot investigate the reason for loss exist in the process of the manufacturer's seeking profits. Without MMORPG, there would be no such risks. In other words, the risks result from the manufacturer's rent-seeking. Consequently the manufacturer should bear the responsibility for this risk.

Further, from a social development perspective, although games function through the entertainment of people and promote economy, they are not necessities for the advancement of human society and need not be given special encouragement for development. The burden of the loss caused by limited techniques should be borne by the game's manufacturer and should not be imposed on the consumers. In this regard, it is the complete opposite of the medical service, because the medical service is necessary for human society. In order to promote the progress of medical techniques continuously, it takes considerable encouragement to increase its development. So it is not the doctor but the patient who should bear the risks and losses caused by limited medical techniques.

3.2.2 Distribution of duties under manufacturer taking technical risks

The requirement that the manufacturer bears the technical risks caused by a lack of sufficient techniques means that the manufacturer should be responsible for the loss of virtual property and should therefore restore it free of charge, except where the loss is caused by a player's own fault. For the manufacturer, the direct cost is very small when only restoring the missing virtual property. In general, on the condition that the procedure of the game functions normally and data interface exists, recovery of virtual property only needs to change some data's attributes (as when changing data 1010 in a binary system) so as to change aspects of property in the game such as the type, time, location and so on when the virtual property appears in the game. This can hardly cost the manufacturer. For the manufacturer, the indirect costs consist of two aspects. One is the rising investment in management, safety and customer service and so on, which helps the manufacturer not only to reduce inner management holes and prevent in-house staff from infringing players' interests, but also to enhance safety levels and reduce the possibility of loss caused by Hacker attacks. The other is compensation cost; that is, the manufacturer compensates players for the lost virtual property.

The requirement that the manufacturer should take all technical risks and pay for the loss will change the players' expectations. As long as virtual property is lost, players will ask the manufacturer to restore and compensate the loss, which will cause players themselves to invest less in safety and reduce their caution to avoid attacks. Under such conditions, the possibilities of losing virtual property and the compensation claims towards the manufacturer will increase. This situation is what worries the manufacturer most. Moreover, compensation for loss will create two markets of virtual property. One is the proper market, namely, the off-line trade market where players and manufacturer trade virtual property. The other is the compensation market after the loss. In order to obtain virtual property in the proper market, players have to pay, while in the compensation market property costs the players nothing. For that reason, arbitrage of virtual property between two markets may occur. To gain profits, malicious players probably sell their virtual property in the proper market and then falsely claim a loss and ask for compensation. If such activities are unable to be detected and stopped effectively, more players will be induced to defraud the manufacturer of virtual property. As a result, virtual property will increase without foundation, be overprovided and be devalued, which will affect the all-round balance of the game, and even run into an awkward situation that is out the control of the manufacturer.

The source of the above situation is the manufacturer's bearing excessive duties that simultaneously decrease the benefits of property right and give chances of arbitrage to players. The policies for solving the problem are as follows: firstly, the manufacturer can request all virtual property transactions, except those gained properly from the game, to be registered in the register office set up by the manufacturer. Through this register, the manufacturer can identify and verify virtual property and partially eliminate improper property produced by Hacker. Those passing the registration are proper property and will be restored in a case of loss, while those having no registration or without manufacturer's verification are considered to be improper property and will be given no protection; nor will they be restored. The registration system not only strengthens the players' level of care and reduces harm to players and the manufacturer caused by improper property, but it also limits the arbitrage activities and ensures that trading virtual property in a different market becomes impossible. Moreover, to establish a registration system does not cost the manufacturer too much and is easy to administer; secondly, the manufacturer's duties are limited to restoring virtual property completely or partly, rather than handing out compensation. Restoration of virtual property is the players' main claim, and limited manufacturer's duty will prevent this risk from expanding excessively.

In this way, the cost to the manufacturer will not increase much for taking the technical risks; on the other hand, the manufacturer will gain profits for doing this. First, players will get more satisfaction out of the game and invest more time in the game, and other players will be attracted by the game; second, with the development and standardization of the virtual property market, the manufacturer, the defender of the market and commodity seller, will gain more benefits from selling and from the appraisal of virtual property. To sum up, for the manufacturer, the benefits of taking the above-mentioned duties should exceed costs of doing so.

However, what the manufacturer compares is not the benefits and the costs before and after taking the duties, but the benefits and the costs with or without the duties. Without the above duties, the results are the decline in players' satisfaction, less game playing time, and the reduction of manufacturer's profits. Under competitive circumstances, the manufacturer will lose competitive superiority if he ignores the players' interests over a long period. Moreover, being sued frequently by players for compensation will affect the manufacturer's regular management and reputation. In addition, without taking on the duties the manufacturer can hardly make any profit, and is merely saving some time by not having to restore the virtual property.

In conclusion, the manufacturer has an incentive to take on the risk caused by a lack of sufficiently advanced techniques, under which the players' right of usage can get better protection. The distribution of property right, so that the manufacturer has the ownership of the virtual property and players own a limited right of usage, can be explained more precisely in that the manufacturer has the ownership right and takes on limited duties as regards losses, and players own the right of usage under certain conditions. This distribution ensures that the concerned parties have incentives to enforce their rights.

3.3 Valuation of Society

The above analysis has illustrated the structure of property right distribution in a situation where the gain exceeds the cost through emphasizing people's interests and duties. It is also concluded that the emergence and stable self-enforcement of property rights need to be determined from the rule maker's perspective.

According to Libecap and others, it is the potential right-holder that participates in the political game, and the legislator appears as a dependent party whose choice depends on games among different constituency groups. However, government is an independent party, although influenced by other interest groups. Especially in nations such as China, the legislation activities of government are, to a great degree, self-determining. As the rule maker of property rights, government has its own opinion as to the comparison of costs and interests. According to the general hypothesis that government represents the public interests, before being given an entitlement to a right, what the government is most concerned about is the social costs and social interests resulting from that entitlement.

For the government, the social interests resulting from allocating a property right of virtual property in MMORPG are mainly reflected by the contributions that MMORPG brings to economic growth, and the main part of the corresponding social cost is the harm done to some people who indulge themselves and become addicted to the games – especially some youngsters who are less self-disciplined and become addicted to the cyber games that distort their development.

In 2002, the overall contribution of Chinese Internet games added up to RMB128.4 hundred million, which accounted for 0.1225 per cent of GDP in the same year. The Chinese Internet game market has reached a scale of RMB9.1 hundred million, the telecom industry RMB68.3 hundred million, the IT industry RMB32.8 hundred million, and the media and publishing industry RMB18.2 hundred million. The overall contribution of the internet industry to the Chinese economy totalled RMB128.4 hundred million and represented 0.1225 per cent of GDP in the same year.

Therefore, realizing the promising potential of network games, the Chinese government has established many supportive policies for their development. In the year 2003, the project of developing network games was incorporated into the Chinese National 863 Plan. And four 'National network games and cartoon development bases' were founded in Beijing, Shanghai, Chengdu and Guangzhou in the same year.

On the other hand, because more and more youngsters have become addicted to network games, the government also has taken some restrictive actions. In August 2005, the National Press and Publishing Office announced that it would be 'developing a system that will prevent people from becoming addicted to network games', and declared that this system would be developed by 30 September of the same year. In October 2005, this system was tested in seven Internet game companies, SOHU, SINA, DONEWS, NETEASE, SHANDA, KINGSOFT and so on, and after that it was put to the test in 11 Internet games, such as the Legend, WARCRAFT and MU. From early 2006 onwards, this system will be mandatorily incorporated in all Internet games, which will restrict the time of playing to five hours.

The evidence above shows that the government holds an ambivalent attitude to the development of MMORPG. On the one hand, the government encourages it to become a new opportunity to increase economic growth. On the other hand, the government also worries that the healthy growth of youngsters is impaired through an addiction to MMORPG. To entitle the manufacturer to the ownership of the virtual property will help protect the manufacturer's intellectual property and promote the development of the game industry. To entitle the players to use the right of virtual property will safeguard players' interests and speed up the virtuous development of the game industry. In particular, a favourable off-line market can provide better and quicker access to virtual property, in order to obtain more enjoyment from the game and effectively to reduce the on-line time of unprofessional players, as well as to assist youngsters to raise their monetary threshold and entering threshold for playing the game. Meanwhile, the risk taken by the manufacturer as regards a lack of advanced techniques may help to heighten the entering threshold of the whole industry, thereby allowing the survival of manufacturers owning real techniques and positive designs. Consequently, the above-mentioned property right structure, under which the manufacturer has ownership and players have right to use, can help the government to keep a stable balance between the increase in the economy and the healthy growth of youngsters, so that social interests exceed social costs.

4. CONCLUSION

Virtual property in MMORPG is a new type of property. The problem of the way to distribute rights rationally among concerned parties is crucial to the development of the Internet game industry. On the basis of reviewing literature of property right distribution, this chapter argues that the stable self-enforcement of property rights is the basic principle underlying the distribution of property right, and that the core of the stable self-enforcement of property rights is the multi-balance of interests among the right-holder, duty-bearer, rule maker and other concerned parties. According to this basic principle, the following legislation suggestion should be taken into consideration:

1. To give the entitlement of ownership of the virtual property to the manufacturer;
2. To give a limited right of usage at a given time and place to players, and furthermore, following a specific procedure, the right of usage to be transferrable among players in the same game;
3. The manufacturer takes the risk caused by lack of sufficiently advanced techniques and takes on the duty of restoration of the lost virtual property completely or partly, when the cause of the loss was very clearly

not the player's own fault; however, the manufacturer is to take no duty of compensation.

As the rule maker, the government also has incentives to support the above-defined property right structure, for it strikes the right balance between promoting the economy and the healthy growth of youngsters.

NOTES

1. See Posner (1992, pp. 52–4).
2. See Demsetz (1964; 1967, pp. 347–59).
3. See Libecap (1989).
4. See Higgs (1982, pp. 55–86).
5. See Riker and Sened (1991, pp. 951–69).
6. See Liu and Zhou (2004).
7. See Li (2005).

REFERENCES

Cooter, R. and T. Ulen (1998), *Law and Economics*, vol. 3, Reading, Mass.: Scott, Foresman and Company.

Demsetz, H. (1964), 'The exchange and enforcement of property rights', *Journal of Law and Economics*, **11**, 26.

Demsetz, H. (1967), 'Toward a theory of property rights', *American Economics Review*, **57**, 347–59.

Higgs, R. (1982), 'Legally induced technical regress in the Washington salmon fishery', *Research in Economic History*, **7**.

Hu, Z. (2005), 'A survey of Chinese first suing player of internet game' (Chinese edition), *TOMScience and Technology*, www.tom.com.

Li, M. (2005), 'On virtual property' (Chinese edition) (<www.chinaeclaw.com>).

Libecap, G.D. (1989), *Contracting for Property Rights*, New York: Cambridge University Press.

Liu, J. and W. Zhou (2004), 'On the value attribute of virtual things in MMORPG and its legal protection' (Chinese edition), *He Bei Law Review*, **12**.

Posner, R.A. (1992), *Economic Analysis of Law*, Boston: Little, Brown.

Riker, W.H. and I. Sened (1991), 'A political theory of the origin of property rights: airport slots', *American Journal of Political Science*, **35**(4), 951–69.

Wang, H. (2005), 'The legal problems of virtual properties in the Internet' (Chinese edition) (<www.chinaeclaw.com>).

PART III

China in the world economy

10. Intellectual property law and policy and economic development with special reference to China

Anselm Kamperman Sanders

1. INTRODUCTION[1]

Few areas of law have known such a rapid growth in importance as intellectual property law has. Not so long ago this area of law was practised by a few specialists only. Even now, some of the finer aspects of the acquisition of patents and trademarks form the exclusive prerogative for specialist agents. Still, with the advent of the information age, intellectual property law has come crashing down on the oblivious business and legal community and is now pervading everyday life. With the elevation of intellectual property (IP) law to the world stage through the World Trade Organization (WTO) trade-related aspects of the intellectual property rights (TRIPS) treaty, IP law has become prominent in the political arena, where part of the discussion seems to centre on the neo-colonial tendencies of the Western world.

In today's business game in the world market, where production is moved to low-cost countries, licensing intellectual property appears to be one of the tools to exercise continued control. Where high investment know-how and information becomes the prime ingredient of today's modern products, which are cheaply reproduced in mass, intellectual property becomes the prime method to ensure a high return on investment. It comes as no surprise, then, that in the global economy intellectual property law has gone global too. Treaties, harmonization efforts and the WTO framework all contribute to the emerging IP world order, which obscures the paradox inherent in IP law, namely, that rights remain predominantly territorial.

A myriad of international agreements (for example, the Paris Convention, 1883, Berne Convention, 1886, Patent Cooperation Treaty, 1970, TRIPS Agreement, 1994, World Intellectual Property Organization (WIPO) Copyright Treaty and WIPO Performances and Phonograms Treaty 1996) enable right holders to apply for and to enforce intellectual property rights in multiple jurisdictions.

This contribution explores whether implementation and execution of the obligations of the TRIPS Agreement have indeed contributed to economic development in developing economies, most notably in China. This contribution traces the economic rationale of the intellectual property system in the context of implementation of TRIPS obligations and international trade. It also explores the flexibilities available under the TRIPS Agreement that may be used to find local legal instruments to foster creative and industrial development and asks the question why China is conspicuously inactive when it comes to formulating new intellectual property initiatives fostering economic development and technology transfer. With a WTO case of the US against China looming over TRIPS standards requiring criminal prosecutions and transparency of rules, the combat of production and trade in counterfeit goods remains a hot topic.[2]

2. TRADE-RELATED ASPECTS OF INTELLECTUAL PROPERTY RIGHTS

Since its adoption in 1994, the WTO's TRIPS Agreement has become the de facto norm that shapes multilateral, regional, bilateral and national intellectual property laws and practices. It is the basis for all current and future standard setting in the area of IPR. An authoritative UK Government Commission on Intellectual Property Rights has noted that introducing higher standards of protection and enforcement of IPR put a considerable strain on the resources and economies of developing countries.[3] Further increases could have a negative impact on agriculture, education, public health, innovation and technology transfer and commonly raise the cost of administration and enforcement for developing nations.

Still, TRIPS implementation is a prerequisite for WTO members, with pay-offs in respect of market access and foreign direct investment. In fact, TRIPS standards are now a permanent fixture in international trade, as they are integral to many bilateral trade and investment agreements.[4]

2.1 Cornerstones of the TRIPS Agreement

The two central provisions of the TRIPS Agreement can be found in articles 3 and 4. They concern the principle of national treatment and most-favoured nation treatment. Both are principles of non-discrimination: foreign nationals have to be treated like one's own nationals, and any advantage, favour, privilege or immunity offered to nationals of another member must also be offered to nationals of all other members (albeit with exceptions). The TRIPS Agreement incorporates the obligations from pre-existing main intellectual and industrial property treaties, most notably the Paris and Berne Convention. Furthermore, unlike these older treaties, all disputes on implementation and interpretation of treaty obligations are subject to a dispute settlement mechanism before the WTO.

The TRIPS agreement covers minimum obligations in respect of most of the subject matter recognized as intellectual or industrial property: copyright and related rights, industrial designs, patents, layout-designs (topographies) of integrated circuits, confidential information, trade marks and geographical indications. Other subject matter, such as plant varieties, trade secrets and expressions of folklore and utility models, is covered by the TRIPS Agreement only partially, or by reference, or not at all.

2.2 Subject Matter

Intellectual property law serves to protect intellectual and industrial human creativity and recognizes rights in relation to the following:

1. literary, artistic and scientific works;
2. performances of performing artists, phonograms and broadcasts;
3. inventions in all fields of human endeavour;
4. scientific discoveries;
5. industrial design;
6. trade marks, service marks and commercial names and designations;
7. protection against unfair competition.[5]

2.3 Term of Protection

Generally intellectual property laws provide the right holder with the right to exclude others from appropriation (depending on the subject matter, the rights may comprise copying, reproduction, diffusion, use in commerce, deceptive use, making, using, offering for sale, selling and/or importing) of the protected subject matter over a certain period of time.

TRIPS requires minimum terms of protection for the following:

1. copyright: the life of the author plus 50 years;
2. performers and producers of phonograms: 50 years from fixation of an unfixed performance;
3. broadcasting: 20 years from the first broadcast;
4. trade marks: renewable term for a minimum of seven years;
5. famous marks: always available irrespective of registration;
6. geographical indications: always protection against misleading the public; wines and spirits: extra protection against expressive use;

7. industrial designs: 10 years;
8. patents: 20 years from filing;
9. lay-out designs of integrated circuits: 10 years from filing/first commercial exploitation;
10. undisclosed information: for as long as it remains secret.

3. THE RATIONALE OF INTELLECTUAL PROPERTY RIGHTS

All intellectual and industrial property rights provide a form of private property that enables the holder of such a right to exclude others from using it. The justification for this lies in the notion that everyone is entitled to reap the benefits of their own labour in creating scientific, artistic and literary works, as well as market recognition. In addition, there is a more profound moral notion that the author or inventor is entitled to recognition as author or inventor (paternity). Overall these notions can be encapsulated by an incentive-by-reward (monetary or reputation/honour) theory. The benefit for society lies in the advancement of science and the arts that this incentive offers. This is also expressed in Article 7 of the TRIPS Agreement, which outlines the objective as 'protection and enforcement as a contribution to the promotion of technological innovation and the transfer and dissemination of technology to the mutual advantage of producers and users of technological knowledge in a manner conducive to social and economic welfare and to the balance of rights and obligations, which are qualified by public interest considerations'. It is in light of a balance of interests of creators, users, and society that the scope of intellectual property rights and limitations and exceptions thereto can be judged. Each intellectual or industrial property right has its own (sub)rationale.

1. Copyright and related rights concern protection and exploitation of the expression of ideas in a tangible form. Once an idea has been expressed in an original way (as bearing the stamp of its creator), we can speak of a copyright work. Certain uses of this work require authorization from the right holder. These acts usually comprise copying, reproduction, performance in public, making a sound recording, making a motion picture, broadcasting, translating or adapting a work. In modern copyright systems (and following the 1996 WIPO Copyright and Performances and Phonograms Treaties), communication to the public of a work also requires authorization. The Berne Convention furthermore recognizes certain 'moral rights', such as a claim to authorship and the right to object to any distortion, mutilation, modification or

other derogatory action in relation to the work that is harmful to the author's honour or reputation. Whereas others have always been free to use the idea, upon expiry of the copyright the work becomes part of the public domain and the original expression of this idea is free to be used as well.

2. Trademarks concern the protection of distinctive symbols that are capable of distinguishing the goods or services of one trader from those of another. As long as a trademark is actually fulfilling this role, its confusing use by others is not permitted. Since trademarks enable consumers to make rational choices about what they buy (type and quality) from where (source), search and transaction costs remain low. The creation of confusion not only diverts trade away from the legitimate right holder to another, but it also increases search and transaction costs. Famous marks and marks that are well known often receive a higher level of protection over and above the presumption or onus to show confusion. Protection against dilution (the gradual whittling away of the distinctive character or repute of the mark) is then offered even though the consumer is not confused as to the origin or quality of the product.
3. Geographical indications concern the protection of indications of provenance of a product. The rationale for protection is the same as that for trademarks.
4. Industrial designs: *vide* copyright and patents.
5. Patents concern the protection of novel inventions that are not part of or foreseen by the state of the art. A patent is a statutory privilege whereby an exclusive right is conferred upon the inventor or another who derives his rights from the inventor for a fixed period of time and in return for the disclosure of an idea, that offers the solution for a specific problem in the field of technology. The exclusive right in question is broad and covers the manufacture, use or sale of a patented product or process. Upon expiry of the patent right all others are free to use the invention; it becomes part of the public domain.
6. Layout designs of integrated circuits concern the protection of semiconductor chips. They are not really inventive, neither are they true original copyright (let alone literary and artistic) works. The problem here is one of market failure if they are left unprotected, since they are costly to design, but easy to copy. This explains their inclusion as a separate category of subject matter and a hybrid form of protection that veers between protection against copying, and low-level patent protection.
7. Undisclosed information attributes value to keeping business secrets and know-how secret.

3.1 The Economic Rationale of Intellectual Property

Free and unrestricted competition lies at the heart of the generally accepted Western economic theory. Free play of market forces and free competition between enterprises are thought to be the best means to satisfy supply and demand and to maximize wealth in society as a whole. Central to this proposition is the axiom that market participants can compete on a level playing field, so that all competitors face the same market barriers, thus facilitating freedom of entry in the market. From this point of view, legal interference in the market should be kept to a minimum. This does not mean, however, that the policy towards markets should be one of *laissez faire*. There is a compelling argument for *laissez faire* in that interference in the market brings with it administrative costs that are incurred from the transfer of the costs of competition from one market participant to the other. Market intervention should result therefore in a clear social benefit. In the competitive game, the process of spreading market information facilitates the shaping of the opinion of market participants with regard to profit-making activities,[6] and is seen as socially beneficial. Government intervention to enhance this aspect of competition is generally accepted, even in classical economic theory. This adage has given rise to the premise in neo-classical theory that perfect knowledge induces a situation in which the spontaneous interaction between knowledge possessors leads to a state of equilibrium, the optimum distribution of resources in society. This means that disturbances in knowledge creation, leading to imperfect knowledge, need to be countered. Legal intervention should therefore be aimed at providing a level playing field of 'market information' in which perfect knowledge induces perfect competition.

Laws on the protection of intellectual property and competition can be seen in this light. Entitlements are allocated to specific creators, to safeguard their information against expropriation, so that bargaining can facilitate an exchange and a market is created. With most intellectual and industrial creations, the establishment of a market for ideas is possible only if the value of the idea can be assessed in advance. This generally means revealing that idea to a potential buyer, who will then already have acquired the idea at no cost.[7] Government intervention through the creation of a property right facilitates the bargaining process and the creation of a market for copyright materials and the information contained therein. After the creation of the entitlement, the role of the State is finished, leaving the transfer of the entitlement to the market, where a voluntary bargain can be made between buyer and seller. This implies that the value of the entitlement is also determined by the market and not by the State. This means that the value determination and maximization require the least State intervention.[8] According to the Coase Theorem,[9] even the allocations of initial entitlements by the State are unimportant, since they will be transferred to their highest value use through private bargaining, leaving the total output of the economy unaffected. One system of property rights is no more efficient than another in this view. This means, however, that the transaction costs of the (re)allocation of property rights and the rules governing the exchange determine the efficiency of one system over the other.[10] In addition, the cost effectiveness of a protective regime depends on the social costs that are incurred when protection is afforded in error and when the likelihood of overprotection by the system is real.

The economic rationale for the patent system,[11] commonly described as a system of incentives and rewards, can, for example, more aptly be described as a monopoly that creates a barrier to entry,[12] forcing a licensing practice to evolve. This serves two ends. First, the competitor faces a market barrier equivalent to that encountered by the first market entrant, that the competitor would not encounter as a free-rider, thus levelling the playing field and inducing him to be creative himself. Second, the creator produces a wider variety of works that the public may be willing to pay for, since creativity is stimulated. This gives the consumer more choice and facilitates the creation of new markets. Without the protective regime of the patent system, which excludes free-riders, a situation of asymmetric market failure could emerge. Market failure is a situation where creators are not rewarded for their creative efforts. This makes it economically more attractive to copy than to create, resulting in creators producing fewer works than the public would be willing to pay for. The aspect of asymmetry is the situation where one party, the creator, faces a market barrier and the other, a copyist, does not.[13] If a combination of market failure and asymmetry occurs, a pattern emerges that holds true for all forms of intellectual property law.

Just like the patent system, which serves to stimulate disclosure of the invention and thus encourages further development, the copyright system[14] should allow for utilization of information, either by addition to the public domain or by rights acquisition on a licensing basis. Where new work relies on prior work and ideas, the new work should not benefit the copyright holder in monopoly rents in excess of the value the copyrighted work has added to total welfare.[15] The other situation would lead to wasteful competition[16] to gain those rights that dispel the value of the underlying work, which often consists of contributions by others that may already be in the public domain or have never been susceptible to copyright.[17] In addition, if there are many potential users of the work, which is especially true when works have become de facto industry standards,[18] it may become too costly to negotiate individual licences for every use that is made of it. Disclosure of the information and the fair use doctrine in copyright law can redress the economic imbalance that this increase in transaction costs entails.[19] The trademark system displays different characteristics,[20] in that it was not envisaged as a system of incentives and rewards, but as a regulation of marketing efforts. As an identifier of products and their sources, a trademark performs the role of a communicator, a messenger that spreads information about what is best, the level and consistency of quality, and what is cheapest. Protection of trademarks ensures that the consumer can make correct purchasing decisions,[21] thus lowering the transaction costs.[22] The confusion rationale is also expressed in the doctrine of passing off, where it also serves to prevent the consumer from incurring increased transaction costs, guaranteeing to the marketeer that his or her message is heard without interference.

Protection of trade secrets is again underpinned by the notion of incentives and rewards, but may be located in the realm of unfair competition law.[23] As an item of sensitive information, it may have commercial value and so may attract the interest of competitors. Here lies one of the major differences from the fixed costs associated with obtaining a patent, in that the value of the trade secret and the costs that have to be incurred in order to protect it are directly related to the willingness of another to try to steal it. The parties do not bargain themselves, neither are they able to, since one of the parties intends to keep the asset secret. A regime that protects trade secrets, therefore, veers towards a liability rule-based system in which the transfer of an entitlement is protected and its value is determined by the State.

In the patent system, independent invention, reverse engineering and public disclosure do not detract from the proprietary right in the patent,[24] but in the case of trade secrets they do. Someone who sets out to uncover and apply another's trade secret may bring about social gain by increasing competition, but he may equally reduce the incentive to invent by inducing asymmetric market failure.[25] Trade secrecy protection serves to reduce the social costs that comprise expenditures for protection of trade secrets on one hand, and the cost of 'not investing resources designed to effect a transfer of wealth',[26] on the other. In balancing those costs associated with the upkeep of a protective regime and the costs associated with the absence of a market structure that facilitates bargaining and sale of information, trade secrecy protection is limited to tortuous interference with an entitlement that is not absolute in nature. An inventor relying on a trade secret cannot prevent the application of independent research and, if the resulting invention is patentable, he cannot even prevent a second market entrant from patenting the invention, forcing the original inventor out of the market. In the first instance, all market entrants face the same market barriers. This places reverse engineering in a peculiar position. It is not a method of independent research and may be considered theft. Friedman et al. (1991),[27] advance two reasons against liability for reverse engineering, namely the administrative cost associated with proof that independent research did not take place, and the public disclosure argument. The line between piracy and acceptable reverse engineering then lies in the presence of substantial investment and innovation. This means that reverse engineering does not create a monopolistic barrier to entry and the investment and innovation associated with it do not induce asymmetry in the market since all market entrants face similar market barriers.

3.2 Property Rules and Liability Rules

The differing rationales of patent and trade secrets or confidential information regimes may also be used to demonstrate the justification in an economic sense for each particular protective regime. The incentive and reward rationale can be found in both the patent and confidential information regimes, but it is modified by the property rule and liability rule dichotomy, which underlines the varying economic considerations that shape either regime. The work of Calabresi and Melamed (1972),[28] demonstrates the economic considerations that are relevant to make a considered choice between the regimes.

The patent system is based on a property rule, where the State-sanctioned monopolistic entitlement enables the proprietor in advance to set a price for the use of his asset by others. From an economic point of view, this system makes sense if transaction costs are low, there are few parties and the value of the asset is difficult to assess.[29] In view of a legal entitlement, legitimate use of the asset can be made only after bargaining with the owner of the property right.

A liability rule, on the other hand, does not rely on a bargaining process prior to the transfer of an intangible asset, but the situation is assessed ex post in order to determine the correct amount of compensation for appropriation. A liability rule is economically effective in those cases where there are many parties and high transaction costs, which interfere with the bargaining process.[30] The economic efficiency of the liability rule is further heightened if the value of the asset can be easily assessed by the arbiter who has to settle a dispute. In view of the valuation problems that courts face in liability and property rule systems alike, damages and restitution rates are often assessed on an equitable basis, resulting in the 'reasonable royalty'. The reasonable royalty should be set at a level that makes the copyist face the same market barrier as the creator, by remedying the market failure the creator suffers.

In the free market, the property rule appears to be the most liberal, since it minimizes State intervention in the valuation of assets, leaving it to the market to maximize wealth by voluntary transaction. Despite the fact that a property rule is often the most cost-effective, since it stimulates party autonomy as opposed to State intervention in the transaction process, the policing of the property rule may require so much State intervention that the system is less cost-effective than in a liability rule-based system. This is increasingly true in the information society, where assets develop the characteristics of public goods, owing to the fact that information-based assets are costly to develop, but vulnerable to rapid and widespread duplication.[31] Furthermore, within the property rule system, barriers to entry are created, which may stifle competition. The absolute nature of property rights also does not take into account that some forms of 'infringement' may be economically desirable for society. Economic theory has come up with two tests to determine whether the act of appropriation of an asset in the face of a monopolistic claim is efficient. The first, the so-called Kaldor–Hicks test,[32] is a test of whether the 'infringer' can pay off the inventor and still find parties who are willing to value the infringer's product more highly. If this is the case, the exercise of a monopoly to the detriment of another is not economically justifiable. Where protection of intangible assets is concerned, this means that an injunction preventing the appropriation of an asset is not a correct option.

This test, however, does not take into account that benefits and costs are not independent of the distribution of wealth. If the asset is appropriated without compensation, wealth is redistributed, but this does not mean that the situation that then comes about is efficient. Efficiency may in fact dictate that the old monopolistic situation be restored, for example, because the original developer is better placed to benefit society in the light of incentive- and reward-based innovation considerations. To avoid this paradox one also has to test whether the monopolistic claimant can pay the potential 'infringer' to cease and desist from appropriation of the intangible that is the bone of contention. If the answer is negative, then exercising monopoly power is not economically efficient. This so-called 'Scitovszky test'[33] serves to remedy that asymmetry and can be taken in tandem with the Kaldor–Hicks test. If both tests are passed, appropriation of an intangible is efficient and monopoly power should not be exercised in order to obtain injunctive relief. In effect the tests serve to determine whether copying results in the creation of *new* products that society is willing to pay for, without destroying the market for the source product.

When making a choice between a liability and a property rule, the desirability of the application of the Kaldor–Hicks and Scitovszky tests is also a consideration. The absolute nature of intellectual property rights does not leave room for the tests. However, statutory exceptions to the monopoly are the elements that can be tested for their effectiveness. It is equally clear that the elasticity of the liability rule-based doctrine of misappropriation facilitates the assessment of fact on the basis of the Kaldor–Hicks and Scitovszky tests in a way that property rule systems cannot. This means that, if a choice is made for a liability rule, and party autonomy in the assessment of the value of an asset by means of transfer bargaining is diverted to an arbiter, the efficiency of the transfer as such can be tested.

4. CHINA'S WTO MEMBERSHIP

The World Trade Organization (WTO) at present has 150 members and soon the 151 number will be passed. China's WTO entry on 11 December 2001 was preceded by feverish activity in updating China's IP statutes and enforcement mechanisms.[34] The body of Chinese IP legislation comprises copyright, trademark, patents, utility models and industrial design protection. These laws, where amended,[35] implement a TRIPS-plus regime rather than minimum treaty obligations.[36] For example, where copyright protection is concerned, Article 47 (6) of the Chinese Copyright Act provides for anti-circumvention rules in respect of technological measures.[37] This measure was introduced in 2001, ahead of the WIPO Copyright and Performances and Phonograms Treaties of 1996, which China has ratified in 2007.

4.1 China's Attitude Towards Intellectual Property Law

China's accession to the WTO at marked the end of a 15-year battle for China's acceptance as a serious partner committed to free trade. But the country still had a long way to go in the development of an open market economy, and in the protection of intellectual property rights in particular. It is important to realize where the People's Republic of China (PRC) 'came from' in terms of free trade. China's intellectual and industrial property laws have long been seen to be lacking, both in substance and in practice. After the 1966 Cultural Revolution, they were all but abrogated. By the 1980s, efforts were being made to implement international conventions, an obligation stemming from membership of the WIPO. Yet large-scale piracy and counterfeiting activity continues to this day.

As pressure mounted on the Chinese administration to comply with the TRIPS Agreement, an overhaul of the laws on patent, trademark and copyright, related rules of procedure and the effective enforcement of intellectual and industrial property rights took place. But public perception and practice were (and still are) lagging. Moreover, matters worsened before they improved. Pirates and counterfeiters took advantage of the increase in trade volume and associated market turmoil that WTO membership entailed, and this strained the capacity of enforcement agencies as well as the court system.

China's patent and trademarks acts to some extent still discriminate against foreigners by obliging them to engage a limited number of designated agencies for application and enforcement matters. What is more, the procedure for filing a lawsuit to enforce IP rights is also more costly and burdensome for foreigners.

It is changes in public perception, however, that still present the greatest challenge to China's successful implementation of intellectual property rights. Emulation is traditionally considered a form of flattery in China and, even in the emerging free market economy, copying is not perceived as wrong.[38] Private property rights in intangible creative ideas and artistic expression remain alien concepts in a society that has long viewed intellectual creations as social, rather than individual, products.

In both Imperial and Communist China, IP systems were also used as mechanisms of State control. Trademark regulation, for example, controlled the quality and consistency of products on a nationwide basis. In an economy long characterized by scarcity and State-controlled production, such notions as the use of trademarks for private brand marketing, product positioning and the reduction of search costs for consumers are novel indeed.

The key problem for the rule of law, however, lies in the long-established practice of doing business through informal network (*guanxi*) relationships, which provide economic security in exchange for privileges, favours, commodities and services. Not only do *guanxi* networks foster what westerners perceive to be corruption, they also raise anti-trust concerns.

Thanks to *guanxi*, local dignitaries, administration and enforcement officials have often become stakeholders in newly privatized enterprises, compromising their ability to act on outside complaints about counterfeiting or lack of respect for IP rights. Furthermore, with the emphasis now on compliance with international norms, the issues of fair trade practices, licensing of IP rights, and access to essential facilities have taken a backseat. Thus far, complaints about a lack of market transparency raised by EU trade delegations to China have long fallen on deaf ears and a draft Chinese competition act is still under consideration. However, market access for goods and services is the key to economic cooperation within the WTO framework.

4.2 First Sale Doctrine

The right of a holder of an intellectual property right enables the right holder to control whether and how a product subject to such a right (most notably for trademarked goods and copyright works) is marketed. Once a right holder has voluntarily put such a product on a given market, it is a generally accepted principle of intellectual property law that he can no longer object to the further commercialization of the product on that market. His intellectual property rights in relation to the particular product are deemed to be exhausted and he cannot object to trade of goods that were marketed with his consent in the same, or in the case of international exhaustion, parallel importation from other markets. This principle is also referred to as the 'first sale doctrine'. For the purpose of defining the relevant market, the borders of national member states, of free trade zones, or the international market are used. Open market economies employ the principle of international exhaustion, whereas more protectionist economies use the principle of national exhaustion. In all it is a choice that is determined by specific market and price conditions and industry interests.

TRIPS is silent on this matter. In fact Article 6 TRIPS indicates that disputes on the application of the doctrine cannot be subject to dispute settlement under the TRIPS Agreement. This means that WTO members can decide for themselves whether to apply national, international or regional (free trade area) exhaustion. Economic research into parallel trade and restrictions thereto have so far not yielded any evidence that there is a need for harmonization in this area.[39] Aban on parallel trade always benefits the manufacturer,[40] because he can segment the market. However, policy, competition, trade and commerce issues indicate that global welfare is not likely to benefit from a multilateral rule on national exhaustion.[41]

The regime of exhaustion in China is not at all clear yet. The patent statute contains no provision on whether national or international exhaustion is the norm. There are only a few trademark cases on parallel trade. These involve the illegal importation of goods into the Chinese market, where an exclusive licensee was active. The defendants failed to prove that their goods were produced elsewhere (in Thailand) under licence,[42] and so the court did not have to rule on the issue of parallel trade in genuine goods. The Chinese Anti-Unfair Competition Law provides relief in cases where parallel trade involves goods of lower quality or with fundamental differences to goods traded under the same brand in China.[43] Although this indicates that creating consumer confusion will not be tolerated, it does not provide a fundamental decision on whether parallel trade is subject to national or international exhaustion. In the domains of patent and copyright, no cases are reported.[44] The reason is that parallel trade into a low-cost manufacturing country such as China is not likely to be profitable. The legal situation in Macau S.A.R. appears to be similar in that no express provision on exhaustion of rights has been included in Macau's IP statutes.[45] Still, a policy on the legitimacy of parallel trade should be stated at some point in time. When such a choice is finally made, arguments of intellectual property policy will have to be in alignment with economic principles of economic efficiency and welfare considerations.

4.3 More Effective Protection

Despite the enactment of an extensive framework of intellectual property rights, however, the enforcement of intellectual property in China remains problematic.[46] For years, commentators have argued that lax enforcement of intellectual property rights will harm Chinese interests.[47] Direct reference has been made to negative effects poor enforcement will have on domestic development, foreign direct investment and opportunities to enter into free trade agreements.[48]

A recent World Bank publication on Intellectual Property and Development,[49] however, shows that neither strong IPR, nor bilateral investment or free trade agreements (FTAs) automatically yield an increase in technology transfer and foreign direct investment (FDI).[50] Figures show that countries with weak protection or enforcement of IPR, like Brazil and China, have been more successful in attracting FDI than many developing countries that have made strong IPR central to their development strategy.[51] Brazil and China are high-growth, large market economies with an increasingly adequate regulatory system involving taxes, investment regulations, production incentives, trade policies and even a hint of competition rules. The strength of IPR protection is clearly not the only factor in investment decision making. Empirical economic studies show that the relationship between IPR and FDI in developing countries varies highly in respect of industry type, the stage of economic development factors (for example transparency, openness, stable financial institutions, sound economic governance, competition law, low corruption) and the natural and labour resources of the country in question. Although econometric evidence of positive effects of strong IPR on FDI and technology transfer is not conclusive,[52] strengthening IPR and providing effective enforcement is seen as a strong signal indicating that a country is willing to provide a more business-friendly environment that is capable of absorbing and safeguarding foreign investment and technology transfer interests.[53] This is particularly relevant in view of the fact that, in 2005, China breached the top ten list of countries submitting the most Patent Cooperation Treaty patent applications. On its website, the World Intellectual Property Organization (WIPO) puts the USA at the top of this list, with its PCT applications amounting to 45 111. For the first time, China is among the top ten countries, with its PCT applications totalling 2452. This is a clear indication that China is becoming a frontrunner in technological development. Applying for a patent is, however, but the first step in innovation, as innovation is only successful if patented technology is successfully applied in a marketable product. The number of patents applications as such does not say very much about the rate of innovation. It is the inventor's ability to recoup his investment, enabling him to engage in further research and development, that is much more relevant. This is where protection of intellectual property rights is of paramount importance.

The steps that China has taken in bringing its domestic intellectual property regime up to speed are significant. Although the myriads of protective regimes, civil, administrative and criminal, that are in operation in China are not yet streamlined,[54] the efficacy of enforcement is slowly improving.[55] This is partly due to the fact that awareness of intellectual property protection and litigation is heightened. Successes of domestic companies in challenging the validity of patents held by multinational corporations have paradoxically led to an increased acceptance of the court system as a means to settle disputes.[56] It is this domestic use of the intellectual property system that will be instrumental to the development of intellectual property law and doctrine in civil litigation. In short, China is still finding a place for private enforcement of intellectual property rights in its domestic system.[57]

The exception to unease with intellectual property as a means of settling disputes or as a policy for fostering local industrial creativity can be found in the treatment of traditional Chinese medicine.[58] Here China makes use of the fact that utility models and petty patents are not covered by the TRIPS Agreement, leaving scope for WTO members to establish a domestic system of quasi-patent protection for inventions that are not necessarily novel or do not display an immense inventive step. When China brought its patent act in line with TRIPS obligations it included pharmaceutical products as patentable subject matter. New applications of a known chemical substance are patentable and traditional Chinese medicine has benefited from this fact to some extent. More helpful, however, is a *sui generis* regime designed specifically for the protection of traditional Chinese medicine that overcomes the problems of novelty and inventive step inherent in established and traditional practices and supplements the patent system. This system that rewards disclosure by offering intellectual property protection fosters innovation and aids the transition from secretive traditional knowledge systems to an open product-based market.

5. CHALLENGES FOR DEVELOPING COUNTRIES

5.1 TRIPS, the Development Agenda and IPR Policy[59]

As far as TRIPS obligations are concerned, the development issues which dominated the agenda at the 2005 WTO Hong Kong Ministerial Conference concern finding flexibility in the implementation of TRIPS obligations and balancing the monopoly of the intellectual property right holder with the interests of third parties and of society as a whole. Flexibility is, however, something that sits uneasily with the current trend in intellectual property policy. This trend has been one of strengthening of IP rights to stamp out serious issues of piracy and one of harmonization to provide a one-size-fits-all 'level playing field' of rights. Flexibility to curb the full exercise of the intellectual property monopoly to accommodate the interests of users, competitors or developing countries is not popular among industrialists. Still, following a decision reached by member governments on 29 November 2005, least-developed countries have been given an extension until 1 July 2013 to provide protection for trademarks, copyright, patents and other intellectual property under the WTO's TRIPS Agreement.

The call of the Development Agenda[60] is to come up with a humane policy that takes into account the needs of developing nations. The recognition of access to medicine as a human right was seen as a first step in formulating this humane policy. However, the adoption by the UN Commission of Human Rights of a declaration on the right of access to medicine remains merely symbolic if the IPR system remains unclear on the appropriate balance of rights and interests. Rather than looking to other or higher legal principles such as human rights[61] to forge humane IPR policy, the IPR system needs to internalize the recognition of the interests of all stakeholders. The recognition of interests of both developed and developing nations is therefore part of a wider concern on the fundamentals of the IPR system. Individual right holders, consumers, citizens and society at large all share a common interest in innovation and development of and access to industrial and intellectual creativity. WIPO, as the UN's bureau on the development of IPR, should take a leading role in tailoring the IPR system to accommodate the needs of all stakeholders.

A cooperation Agreement with the WTO in 1995 has put the WIPO in charge of providing technical assistance for TRIPS implementation to developing country members of the WTO. Providing assistance is after all one of the areas in which WIPO specializes. WIPO is now able assist the WTO by offering expertise in the area of intellectual property law so as to ensure a successful implementation of the TRIPS Agreement.

5.2 WTO Ministerial Conference (Hong Kong 2005)

In the period leading up to the Hong Kong Ministerial Conference, the WIPO General Assembly agreed to adopt a decision (4 October 2004) to examine further the Development Agenda proposal originally presented by Brazil and Argentina (and subsequently sponsored by many developing countries) to integrate in a more systematic manner the development dimension in all of WIPO's work. Prior to the General Assembly meeting, hundreds of non-profit organizations, scientists, academics and other individuals had signed the 'Geneva Declaration on the Future of WIPO'[62] in support of the Development Agenda's aims to engrain in WIPO's policies the practice of using IPR as tools for the development of nations as opposed to the mere safeguard of the interests of individual right holders. Despite the apparent support in the WIPO General Assembly for the Development Agenda, no new bodies to discuss matters raised in the proposal were created, because, after all: 'WIPO had always been sensitive to the concerns of developing countries.'

An intersessional intergovernmental meeting in the Development Agenda for WIPO was held on 11 to 13 April 2005. Brazil, now heading the 'Group of Friends of Development', comprising Argentina, Bolivia, Brazil, Cuba, Dominican Republic, Ecuador, Egypt, Iran, Kenya, Peru, Sierra Leone, South Africa, Tanzania and Venezuela, raised the stakes in a more elaborate proposal on the Development Agenda for WIPO.[63]

This document reads as an indictment of all that is wrong within WIPO. The issue that stands out is WIPO's effort to standardize IPR to the highest norm at the expense of least developed and developing nations. The document reiterates that WIPO should be driven by a policy recognizing that

> Intellectual property should be regarded not as an end in itself, but as a means for promoting the public interest, innovation, and access to science, technology and the promotion of diverse national creative industries – in order to ensure material progress and welfare in the long run. Promotion of intellectual property protection alone is not sufficient if unaccompanied by policies that respond to the specific development needs of each country.[64]

A proposal submitted for discussion by the United Kingdom[65] recognizes the needs of least developed and developing countries and points to the burdens associated with TRIPS implementation on these countries. It indicates that there ought to be flexibility to the point of a clear opt-out for least developed and developing countries to implement and reform their IPR system at a pace in line with their rate of development. However, the UK submits that the WTO and not WIPO is the appropriate forum to address these complex issues of technology transfer.

This explains the resurfacing of the Development Agenda's issues at the WTO Ministerial Meeting. One of the hot topics concerns access to educational and cultural works protected by copyright. Another is the implementation of the Doha Declaration on access to essential medicines.

5.3 Access to Educational and Cultural Works

The global copyright system is being tailored to meet the worries of media industries by means of the WIPO Copyright and Performances and Phonograms treaties. These treaties have introduced the right to control communication to the public of copyright works and provide right holders with the possibility to act against the removal or alteration of digital rights management information, and technical protection mechanisms.

Although not part of the WTO TRIPS Agreement, these WIPO treaties are fast becoming the de facto world standard, not because countries voluntarily sign up to these agreements, but through inclusion in Bilateral Investment Treaties (BITs) and Free Trade Agreements (FTAs). The United States is exporting its version of the WIPO treaties, the Digital Millennium Copyright Act (DMCA), not because it fulfils the needs of citizens and industry in developing nations, but, because of economic and political pressure it can exert through BITs and FTAs.[66]

Criticism of the unilateral focus on strengthening of rights is rife.[67] The problem stems from the fact that international copyright harmonization has focused on the protection of copyright, not on establishing common standards on limitations and exceptions. National law predominantly determines the scope and number of these limitations and exceptions. Limitations and exceptions can be found in statute, as is the case in Europe, or in jurisprudence by means of an intricate case-by-case fair use analysis, as is the case in the USA.

The inclusion of IPR in BITs and FTAs means that countries that lack access to even the most elementary educational materials are confronted with the demand that their copyright statutes be tailored to meet the highest Western norm. Exceptions and limitations enabling fair use of copyright works, however, are not part of that international standard setting to the same extent as heightening protection levels are. There is little guidance on the appropriate limitations and exceptions, let alone special concessions for developing countries, other than the WTO-endorsed mantra that the economic interests of right holders should not be harmed.[68] The fact that the media industry has long been inapt and unwilling[69] to replace outdated CD and DVD disc technology with adequate Internet distribution methods only reinforces the feeling that stronger IPR merely serve to preserve the stranglehold of Western big media industry on new global distribution methods. It is not surprising, therefore, that developing countries feel they have been forced to adopt a copyright system that enables Western media conglomerates to maintain a position of global dominance.

A study by Consumers International's Asia and Pacific Office[70] shows that many Asian countries, including China, have seen a rise in public expenditure on education as a direct result of rising standards in copyright protection. Educational works protected by copyright are prohibitively priced to the extent that the scope and duration of rights and a lack of teaching exceptions to copyright act as a barrier to access to knowledge. The study provides a number of suggestions for modification of China's statutes that would, in keeping with China's international obligations, increase access to copyright materials that are important to education.

It is this type of study into the flexibilities of WTO and other intellectual property treaty obligations that can provide a positive impulse to tailoring intellectual property rights to domestic needs.

5.4 Access to Essential Medicine

Compulsory licensing of patented pharmaceuticals has been a hot topic for quite some time.[71] Most notably, the issue of providing access for the poor to drugs to combat AIDS made headlines in the global media and was the subject of intense lobbying at the WTO. Governments of South Africa and Brazil, and major drugs companies together with industrialized nations, found one another on opposite sides of the fence. If anything, the media coverage has also made the general public aware that drugs companies prefer to concentrate on the tourists rather than the developing nations they visit in increasingly greater numbers when it comes to making available much-needed medication for diseases such as malaria, tuberculosis and HIV. These three diseases alone kill five million people every year.[72] Although less than 5 per cent of the drugs on the World Health Organization (WHO) Essential Drugs List[73] are patented,[74] and patent protection in many developing countries is less stringent than TRIPS otherwise requires,[75] the drugs are still not available. It is estimated that two billion people cannot get adequate treatment.[76] Lack of distribution channels and high cost of drugs relative to the gross domestic product (GDP) and average wage make up half of the explanation why this is so. When it comes to the availability of the latest, more effective or complex drugs, patent rights and the lack of production facilities make up the other half. Increasingly, traditional producers and suppliers of cheap generic drugs, such as India, the world's leading supplier of generic medicines,[77] have been under pressure[78] to adopt TRIPS-compliant patent acts that protect pharmaceutical products, processes and products directly obtained by use of this patented process.[79] India is also a nation where as many as one in seven people may be infected with HIV.[80] A recently adopted[81] Indian patent act will provide heightened protection for medicines invented after the implementation date, but also for those that have been patented outside of India since 1 January 1995. According to TRIPS,[82] India was required to establish a 'mailbox' when it became a member of the WTO. Foreign applicants could already file patents between 1995 and 2005 for later consideration. There are some 4000 patent applications for medicines that are now waiting to be examined by the Indian Patent Office. Patents eventually granted may affect generics currently available on the market, unless they are made subject to a compulsory licence.

5.5 Compulsory Licensing and the Flexibility of the TRIPS Agreement

The TRIPS Agreement offers WTO members a broad discretion on government use of compulsory licensing. There are no limitations on the grounds upon which a government can authorize use of a patent by third parties. Grounds explicitly mentioned in Article 31 TRIPS are national emergency, anti-competitive practices, public non-commercial use and dependent patents. Further grounds can be found in Article 8(1), which allows members to adopt measures necessary to protect public health and nutrition, and to promote the public interest in sectors of vital importance to their socioeconomic and technological development. Furthermore Article 8(2) permits members to take necessary measures to prevent the abuse of IPR by right holders and practices that unreasonably restrain trade or adversely affect the international transfer of technology. There are, however, a number of procedural requirements, that can be summarized as follows:

1. cases have to be judged on their individual merits, thus excluding blanket advance approval for patents in a particular field of technology;[83]
2. prior to authorizing third party use there should be an effort to negotiate a voluntary licence on reasonable commercial terms;
3. government must provide for adequate remuneration, taking into account the economic value of the authorization;
4. use shall be authorized predominantly for the supply of the domestic market;
5. the scope and duration of the licence is limited to the purpose for which it was authorized, a requirement which is supplemented by the 'Intel clause', limiting the compulsory licensing of semiconductor

technology to public non-commercial use and judicial remedies for anti-competitive behaviour;

6. licences must be terminated if and when the circumstances which led to it cease to exist and are unlikely to recur.

Exemptions can be found in Article 31(b), which allows a waiver of the requirements for negotiation for a voluntary licence on reasonable commercial terms (a) in case of a national emergency or other circumstances of extreme urgency; or (b) in cases of public non-commercial use. In short, the TRIPS rules on compulsory licensing seemingly already offer the necessary flexibility that proponents of the WIPO Development Agenda seek. However, nations, most notably Brazil and South Africa, trying to use this flexibility for the purpose of supplying generic anti-retroviral AIDS drugs produced under (threat of) compulsory licences, found that their interpretation of this scope of the flexibility that TRIPS offers differs from Western notions of fair licensing.

The United States, in particular, were quick to point to the general nature of the compulsory licensing provisions in the patent statutes of these countries and in 2001 took action against Brazil before the WTO.[84] The USA complained:

> Brazil has asserted that the U.S. case will threaten Brazil's widely praised anti-AIDS program, and will prevent Brazil from addressing its national health crisis. Nothing could be further from the truth. For example, should Brazil choose to compulsorily licence anti-retroviral AIDS drugs, it could do so under Section 71 of its patent law, which authorizes compulsory licensing to address a national health emergency, consistent with TRIPS, and which the United States is not challenging. In contrast, Section 68 – the provision under dispute – may require the compulsory licensing of any patented product, from bicycles to automobile components to golf clubs. Section 68 is unrelated to health or access to drugs, but instead is discriminating against all imported products in favour of locally produced products. In short, Section 68 is a protectionist measure intended to create jobs for Brazilian nationals.[85]

In the ensuing public relations battle, Brazil put itself ahead of the game in that it capitalized on the AIDS drugs patent dispute in South Africa[86] and brought its successful national STD/AIDS programme to the attention of the world.[87] Brazil even managed to get a resolution adopted by the UN Commission of Human Rights on the right of access to medication.[88] The 53-member body passed the resolution by a 52–0 vote, with the United States abstaining.

At the WTO Doha Ministerial Conference of November 2001 in Quatar, consensus on the compulsory licensing issue was seen as imperative for the successful conclusion of a new round of world trade negotiations.[89]

Ironically, the anthrax crisis in the USA and the reaction of the US government in face of this national emergency to obtain the drug CIPRO at the lowest price possible was a godsend for developing countries. They felt empowered to push within the WTO for a deal on compulsory licensing.

Owing to the continuing media exposure of the lack of availability of anti-retroviral AIDS drugs for the poor, of the fact that profit margins for Big Pharma are the highest of any industry,[90] and of the Anthrax crisis in the USA,[91] a breakthrough was possible in the post 9/11 world. The result was a joint declaration on the TRIPS Agreement and Public Health.[92] The Ministerial Declaration amounts to an understanding that members will not bring action under the WTO Dispute Settlement Understanding over compulsory licensing of essential patented drugs.[93] It also reiterated that the least-developed country members[94] will not be obliged, in respect of pharmaceutical products, to implement the patent section[95] or to enforce rights provided for under these sections before 1 January 2016, thus alleviating any pressure on the compulsory licensing issue.[96] The Ministerial Declaration hinges on the interpretation of TRIPS Article 8(1) and its exception for the institution of measures necessary[97] to protect public health that are consistent with the TRIPS provisions.[98] In the face of adversity (the US and Big Pharma tried to limit the scope of the Declaration to drugs for the treatment of HIV/AIDS, tuberculosis and malaria), the WTO members took some two years to agree on measures that would lead to a satisfactory arrangement to give effect to the Declaration. The supply of essential drugs under compulsory licences to least-developed WTO members and WTO members with insufficient or no manufacturing capacity in the pharmaceutical sector was finally guaranteed in the WTO General Council Decision of 30 August 2003 on the Implementation of Paragraph 6 of the Declaration of the TRIPS Agreement and Public Health.[99] The Decision will see the WTO begin routinely to review the issuance of individual licences for pharmaceutical products and will look at the terms of individual licences. It will evaluate the basis for deciding that manufacturing capacity is insufficient, or review any of the new terms and obligations for the issue of compulsory licences of patents on medicinal products. The conditions for a compulsory licence will then also include measures to ensure tiered pricing and measures on parallel imports. This means that cheap medicine destined for developing nations is not imported back to developed nations to be sold at a premium price.

We are currently witnessing the first proposals on the implementation of the WTO Decision in the EU and Canada.[100] These proposals provide for a two-pronged approach to the issue of compulsory licensing: first, that essential medicine may be produced under compulsory licence in the EU and Canada for the purpose of export to WTO members with insufficient production capacity; second, that these drugs are so distinctive that customs can easily detect illegal parallel reimportation. The EU and Canada seem intent on protecting their own pharmaceutical industry base by allowing production of generics in the EU and Canada under strict conditions by making use of the WTO system. European and Canadian production and control over distribution of drugs will after all prevent technology transfer to developing countries.

The latest development in this saga is an amendment to the TRIPS Agreement, designed to implement paragraph 6 of the Doha Declaration. The members of the WTO quietly agreed to it on 6 December 2005, only days ahead of the WTO Hong Kong Ministerial Conference. This was a fortunate move, since this decision did not become hostage to the overall failure of the Ministerial Conference.

6. A WTO CASE AGAINST CHINA?

Speculation is rife about the fact that the US is about to bring a case against China over its failure to meet its TRIPS obligations.[101] With US companies claiming to lose out to Chinese piracy and counterfeiting to the tune of $250 billion annually, it is hardly surprising that Washington is thinking about flexing its muscles. Yet the volume of illegal goods is extremely difficult to quantify and hard data showing systematic piracy in China are not easily obtained. Similarly, and as shown above, it is also not easy to obtain information on court decisions and government crackdowns, making it difficult to gauge whether the Chinese government's promise to step up intellectual property protection has indeed been met. US companies themselves, despite all their complaints, are themselves reluctant to provide the US government with piracy details and statistics. They fully realize that hard-earned *guanxi* is quickly lost. Without *guanxi* it is impossible to do business in China at all. In view of the scale of economic development, it is therefore often preferable to accept Chinese piracy rates in the Chinese market for the time being and try to prevent exports from China to other markets. There is, however, an additional problem. Despite China's economic might, it is easily forgotten that China's wealth is in the hands of a relatively few. Outside the economic development zones, China still is a developing and in some respects an underdeveloped country. A complaint on non-enforcement grounds may therefore not yield the desired result, as WTO Member States are not required to devote more resources to intellectual property enforcement than to other areas of law enforcement.[102] In other areas of law enforcement, including those that are subject to WTO membership obligations, China's record is similar to that of many developing nations. To argue therefore that China should spend more resources on combating piracy and counterfeiting than, for example, on tax collection, is not tenable. The strategy of taking a case to the WTO is a risky one. A formal decision of the WTO in favour of China is harmful to US and Western interests in China. It therefore makes more sense for Western industry to support and stimulate its local Chinese partners by using the new Chinese IP framework. As shown earlier in this chapter, the acceptance of IP laws at a local level yields many more results than outside pressure.

7. CONCLUSION

What is remarkable is that, despite its economic might and despite its increasing share of patent applications, China has yet to find its place when it comes to formulating policy initiatives in the field of intellectual property law. Chinese IP laws and doctrine have yet to develop within Chinese business culture. Where Brazil and Argentina are forging ahead and are making their views on the role of intellectual property for developing economies known, the PRC is still focusing on domestic enforcement of intellectual property rights. It should also do so in order to foster the acceptance of IP protection with the domestic business community and its population. However, the PRC's relative absence from the international policy arena is remarkable considering the fact that China is both an economic giant and a developing country. China requires inbound investment and technology transfer if it is to succeed in maintaining its economic growth. Intellectual property law and the enforcement of IP rights are instrumental in fostering a climate that attracts innovation. Simultaneously, China needs to explore the flexibilities inherent in the TRIPS Agreement in order to make sure it is able to provide access to essential medicine and educational materials. Furthermore, China is well placed to claim a leadership role when it comes to new initiatives in the area of the protection of traditional medicine and culture.

NOTES

1. In part, the section on the economics of IP law is based on Kamperman Sanders (2006). The section on access to essential medicine is based in part on Kamperman Sanders (2005).
2. On the grounds for and wisdom of bringing a case against China under the WTO Dispute Settlement Understanding, see Bloomberg's new reporting: 'There is still a lack of a meeting of the minds over how China is dealing with the issue,' said James Jochum, a former U.S. Commerce Department official who now works on China issues at the law firm of Mayer, Brown, Rowe and Maw LLP in Washington. The US thinks it is

going poorly, and the Chinese think it is going well. There is an incredible disconnect. (<http://www.bloomberg.com/apps/news?pid=10000087&sid=av4hVAmF1bp 4&refer=top_world_news><f"MathematicalPi 1">).

3. Commission on Intellectual Property Rights (2002). Bilateral agreements entered into between the EC and their Member States and various partners require these partners to ensure adequate and effective protection of intellectual property rights 'in conformity with the highest international standards'; see Drahos (2002), study prepared for the UK Commission on Intellectual Property Rights, all available at www.iprcommission.org.
4. Vivas-Eugui, Regional and Bilateral Agreements and a TRIPS-plus World: the Free Trade Area of the Americas (FTAA), TRIPS Issues Papers No. 1 (2003, QUNO/QIAP/ICTSD, Geneva).
5. Convention Establishing the WIPO, Art. 2 (viii).
6. Hayek (1937, p. 106): 'Competition is essentially a process of the formation of opinion: by spreading information [i]t creates the views people have about what is best and cheapest.'
7. Arrow (1962, pp. 609–15).
8. Calabresi and Melamed (1972, pp. 1089, 1092, 1105).
9. Coase (1960, p. 1).
10. Merges (1994, p. 2655).
11. See Kaufer (1989) and Heald (1991, p. 959).
12. See Demsetz (1982): 'The problem of defining ownership is precisely that of creating properly scaled legal barriers to entry.'
13. For a definition of asymmetric market failure and the role of intellectual property law in providing a remedy against the resulting loss in wealth, see Gordon (1992, p. 853).
14. For a representation of classical patent and copyright protection and the varying level of creativity required, see Mackaay (1994, p. 2630).
15. See Landes and Posner (1989, p. 325) where the economic rationale for not protecting ideas is given.
16. Besen and Raskind (1991, p. 3).
17. Warren-Boulton, Baseman and Woroch (1994).
18. *US* v. *Microsoft* The findings of fact of the district court are reported at 84 F. Supp. 2d 9 (J.S. App. 46–246). The conclusions of law of the district court are reported at 87 F. Supp. 2d 30 (J.S. App. 1–43). The final judgment of the district court is reported at 97 F. Supp. 2d 59 (J.S. App. 253–279). The order of the district court certifying the case under the Expediting Act (J.S. App. 284–285) 20 June 2000. For further developments, see <http://www.usdoj.gov/atr/cases/ms_index.htm>.
19. See Gordon (1992, p. 1600) as to the extent of the fair use doctrine. See also Landes and Posner (1989, p. 325). However, see also *Sony Corp. of America* v. *Universal City Studios* (1984), 464 U.S. 417, in which the US Supreme Court found that distributors of Grokster and Morpheus P2P file-sharing software, although capable of being used for no infringing uses, are liable for users' copyright violations.
20. Cornish and Phillips (1982, p. 41); Economides (1988, p. 523); Landes and Posner (1987, p. 265).
21. According to Diamond (1980, pp. 528–9), the consumer is the 'unnamed third party in every action for trademark infringement,' since the interest of the consumer lies in the ability of the trademark to facilitate choice on the basis that a trademark guarantees uniformity of quality at a consistent level.
22. Akerlof (1970, p. 488) demonstrated that this also applies to the quality function of the trademark. In his work, he succinctly describes the market breakdown that occurs when the consumer can no longer trust the quality message a mark conveys.
23. Besen and Raskind (1991, p. 3, at pp. 23–4).
24. Provided that the entitlement is enforced by the state.
25. Friedman, Landes and Posner (1991), p. 61 at pp. 69–70.
26. Landes and Posner (1987, ch. 6).
27. Friedman, Landes and Posner (1991), pp. 61–70.

28. Calabresi and Melamed (1972), p. 1089.
29. Merges (1994), p. 2655, at pp. 2664–7.
30. High transaction costs induced by market failure lead to a situation in which a liability rule is more efficient. See Reichman (1994), p. 2432 and also Merges (1994), p. 2655, at p. 2668, who distinguishes another situation in which an exception to the property rule for intellectual property rights is efficient. Compulsory licence regimes defer the bargaining process and valuation of intellectual property away from party autonomy.
31. Reichman (1994), at p. 2443.
32. Kaldor (1939), p. 549; Hicks (1939), p. 696.
33. De Scitovszky (1941), p. 77.
34. On China's accession problems see Dressler (1995), p. 181, 224.
35. Yonehara (2002), p. 389; Ran (2002), p. 231; Hong (2004), p. 1; Greene (2004), p. 437.
36. For an overview of the obligations of the TRIPS Agreement, see the UNCTAD Course on Dispute Settlement World Trade Organization 3.14 TRIPS (available at:) <http://www.unctad.org/Templates/Page.asp?intItemID=2102&lang=1>).
37. Li (2006), p. 100.
38. Alford (1995).
39. Maskus (2000).
40. Ibid., at 214.
41. On the economic (non) sense of parallel import see Vautier (2003), pp. 185–217.
42. Liang (1995), p. 85 at p. 87.
43. Xiang (2004), pp. 105–12.
44. Ibid., at pp. 105–6.
45. Teixeira Garcia (2003), pp. 219–27.
46. See statistical information on piracy rates of the Business Software Alliance, (<http://www.bsa.org/globalstudy/pressreleases/, the Recording Industry Association of America>, <http://www.riaa.com/news/newsletter/020905.asp> and the Motion Picture Association of America, <http://www.mpaa.org/anti-piracy/content.htm>).
47. Yu (2000), p. 131; Bejesky (2004), p. 437.
48. See Maskus, Dougherty and Mertha (2005), who have been updating their findings since presenting an early version of their paper in 1998. They seem to have become milder on the need for strong intellectual property rights. Instead, they now point to the need for embedding intellectual property in a wider framework of stimulating innovation and competition.
49. Fink and Maskus (2005). See also Braga, Fink and Sepulveda (2000).
50. Correa (2004), p. 3, available at <www.grain.org>.
51. Maskus (note 39, p. 54), where examples cited comprise Sub-Saharan Africa and Eastern Europe.
52. Ibid., pp. 63–6.
53. Schiappacasse (2004), p. 164, who concludes that China's need to acquire growth-enhancing intellectual property through technology transfer should provide the incentive for strengthening IP protection.
54. Shah (2005), p. 69; Chynoweth (2003), p. 3.
55. Bachner (forthcoming).
56. Bai and Cheng (2005), p. 31.
57. Lu (2005), pp. 323–32; Kennedy and Wheare (2005), pp. 333–56; Cabral (2001).
58. Bachner (2005), pp. 1–36.
59. See Kamperman Sanders (2005).
60. Menescal (2005), p. 761.
61. Geiger (2004), p. 268; Ostergard (1999), p. 156.
62. See <www.cptech.org/ip/wipo/futureofwipo.html>.
63. Proposal to Establish a Development Agenda for WIPO: An Elaboration of Issues Raised in Document WO/GA/31/11, WIPO document IIM/1/4/ of April 6, 2005 (available at <www.wipo.int>).
64. Ibid, p. 4.
65. WIPO document IIM/1/5 of April 7, 2005 (available at www.wipo.int).

66. See Correa (2004), note 50 above; Drahos (2003) (both available at <www.grain.org>).
67. Boyle (2004), p. 1.
68. See the WTO Dispute Settlement Body Panel Report on United States – Section 110(5) of the US Copyright Act WT/DS160/R of 15 June 2000, providing interpretation on the Berne Three Step test dealing with appropriate exemptions to copyright.
69. See Alderman (2001); Lessing (2004).
70. Consumers International Asia Pacific Office (2006) (available at <www.ciroap.org/A2K>).
71. See also Kamperman Sanders (2003), pp. 163–84; (2004), pp. 337–46.
72. See AIDS Epidemic Update December 2004, UNAIDS/04.45E (2004, UNAIDS/WHO) (available at <www.unaids.org>).
73. See <www.who.int/medicines/organization/par/edl/procedures.shtml> for the selection criteria of essential medicines, which do not include the patent status of the drug in question, but do give consideration to cost, thus potentially excluding therapeutically important, but expensive, drugs; for the list see mednet3.who.int/eml/eml_intro.asp; see also Velásquez (2001), p. 41 and Dumoulin (2001), p. 49.
74. IFPMA Press Release, Geneva, 20 December 2001 (available at <www.ifpma.org>).
75. The Doha WTO Ministerial Declaration on TRIPS and Public Health of 14 November 2001 (WT/MIN(01)/DEC/2) reiterates that the least developed members are exempted from implementing, employing and enforcing pharmaceutical product and test data protection and may refrain from granting exclusive marketing protection during the period patent protection is not provided until 1 January 2016 (see <www.wto.org>).
76. See <www.europa.eu.int/comm/trade/issues/global/medecine/index_en.htm>.
77. 66.7% of India's drug exports go to developing countries.
78. See report of the WTO Dispute Settlement Body Panel on India – Patent Protection for Pharmaceutical and Agricultural Chemical Products, WT/DS79/R of 24 August 1998.
79. Patents Bill (Bill No. 32-C of 2005), of which TRIPS compliance is still an issue.
80. On the contentious issue whether India is the most HIV-dense country see <www.theglobalfund.org> and HIV is 'out of control' in India', news.bbc.co.uk/1/hi/world/south_asia/4461999.stm and 'India rejects HIV infection claim', news.bbc.co.uk/1/hi/world/south_asia/4463899.stm. See also Médecins Sans Frontières (<www.msf.org/countries India>).
81. The bill was passed by the Indian parliament in March 2005.
82. Art. 70 (8).
83. Further reinforced by Art. 27(1), which states that patents shall be available and patent rights enjoyable without discrimination as to the place of invention, the field of technology and whether products are imported or locally produced.
84. On 1 February 2001, a WTO panel was established to hear the case (WT/DS199/1). The US position was that the compulsory licensing provision for non-working is in violation of Art. 27(1) TRIPS, which prohibits members of the WTO from requiring the local production of the patented invention as a condition for enjoying exclusive patent rights. The United States asserted that the 'local working' requirement contained in the Brazilian Patent Act can only be satisfied by the local production – and not the importation – of the patented subject matter. This position is fuelled by the impression that working of the patent needs to take place in the territory of Brazil. Furthermore, the US takes issue with the fact that failure to work the patent also comprises incomplete manufacture of the product or a failure to make full use of the patented process.
85. US Special 301 report, 2001 (<www.ustr.gov/enforcement/special.pdf>) on the dispute before the WTO with Brazil.
86. See Seeman (2001) (<www.nationalreview.com/nr_comment/nr_commentprint032101a.html>); Mutetwa (2001) (<www.fingaz.co.zw/fingaz/2001/April/April 26/1429.shtml>), Reuters, 'Cuba Backs Brazil in AIDS Drugs Patent Dispute', 3 April 2001, and 'Cuba Seeks Third World Challenge to Patent Rules' (news.findlaw.com/legalnews/s/20010323/cubausapatents.html).

87. See Commission on Intellectual Property Rights (2002), p. 43 (available at <www.iprcommission.org>).
88. See the resolution adopted by the UN Sub-Commission on the Promotion and Protection of Human Rights (2000), UN Doc. E/CN.4/Sub.2/Res/2000/7. See also UN Commission on Human Rights Resolution (2001), UN Doc. E/CN.4/RES/2001/33, of 23 April 2001, which was proposed by Brazil (available at <www.unhchr.ch/>).
89. Moore, former director-general of the WTO, indicated in a statement that 'resolving the TRIPS and public health issue might be the "deal-breaker" for a new trade round', see Banta (2001), pp. 2655, 2656 (available at <jama.ama-assn.org/issues/v286n21/fpdf/jmn1205.pdf>).
90. In terms of profit ranked by percentage return on revenues, pharmaceuticals rank first at over 18%. By way of comparison, commercial banks achieve rates of 14%, mining and crude oil production 9%, household and personal products 8%, and insurance and securities 7%. See 362 New Internationalist (2003) (available at <www.newint.org>).
91. See 'Double Standards', *Nature*, 1 November 2001, vol. 4141, p. 1: 'The Bush administration . . . proceeded to extract agreement from Bayer to supply the drug at one-fifth of its previous price. The health secretary, Tommy Thompson, even boasted that the threat of compulsory licensing had helped to clinch the deal.'
92. Adopted on 14 November 2001, WT/MIN(01)/DEC/2, 20 November 2001.
93. Vandoren (2002) and Abbott (2002).
94. For a list of least developed countries, see <www.unctad.org/Templates/webflyer.asp?docid=2929&intItemID=1634&lang=1>.
95. Section 5 TRIPS Agreement.
96. On the issue of the role of the patent system as a motivator or hindrance to innovation in the pharmaceutical area, see Muennich (2001), p. 73, and Mossinghoff (1996), p. 38.
97. See Canada, where stockpiling of drugs in the last six months of patent term was permitted. Rogers, 'The Revised Canadian Patent Act, the Free Trade Agreement, and Pharmaceutical Patents: An Overview of Pharmaceutical Compulsory Licensing in Canada' [1990], 10 EIPR 351. See WTO Dispute Settlement Body Panel Report in Canada – Patent Protection of Pharmaceutical Products WT/DS114/R of 25 April 2000. Canada had to comply with the DBS's rulings and recommendations by 12 August 2001, abolishing the stockpiling practice.
98. See Art. 27(1) TRIPS, which states that any measures adopted cannot discriminate as to the place of invention, the field of technology and whether products are imported or locally produced; also Art. XX of GATT 1994, indicating that any measures under TRIPS necessary to protect health also cannot amount to 'arbitrary or unjustifiable discrimination between countries where the same conditions prevail, or a disguised restriction on international trade'.
99. WT/L/540 of 2 September 2003.
100. Proposal for a Regulation of the European Parliament and of the Council on compulsory licensing of patents relating to the manufacture of pharmaceutical products for export to countries with public health problems COM (2004) 737; Similarly see Canadian Bill C-9, An Act to amend the Patent Act and the Food and Drugs Act (The Jean Chrétien Pledge to Africa), 3d sess., 37th Parl., 2004, and the 'Regulations Amending the Food and Drugs Regulations (1402–Drugs for Developing Countries,' *Canada Gazette*, **138** (40), 2 October 2004, pp. 2748–60.
101. Yu (2005, p. 20).
102. See Art.41 (5) TRIPS.

REFERENCES

Abbott, F.M. (2002), 'The TRIPS Agreement, access to medicines, and the WTO Doha Ministerial Conference', *Journal of World Intellectual Property*, **5**, 15–52.

Akerlof, G. (1970), 'The market for "lemons", quality uncertainty and the market mechanism,' *Quarterly Journal of Economics*, 488–500.
Alderman, J. (2001), *Sonic Boom – Napster, MP3, and the New Pioneers of Music*, Cambridge, MA: Perseus.
Alford, W.P. (1995), *To Steal a Book is an Elegant Offense: Intellectual Property Law in Chinese Civilization*, Stanford: Stanford University Press.
Arrow, K.J. (1962), 'Economic welfare and the allocation of resources for invention', *The Rate and Direction of Economic Activity Economic and Social Factors*, Princeton, NJ: Princeton University Press, pp. 609–15.
Bachner, B. (2005), 'Back to the future: intellectual property rights and the modernisation of traditional Chinese medicine', in C. Heath and A. Kamperman Sanders (eds), *New Frontiers of Intellectual Property Law, IP and Cultural Heritage, Geographical Indications, Enforcement and Overprotection*, Oxford/Portland: Hart, pp. 1–36.
Bachner, B. and M. Jiang (forthcoming), 'Righting civil wrongs: enforcement of intellectual property rights in China', in A. Kamperman Sanders (ed.), *International Intellectual Property Enforcement and Competition*, Special issue, *International Journal of Intellectual Property Management*.
Bai, B. and H. Cheng (2005), 'Are your Chinese patents at risk?', *Intellectual Property Today*, 31.
Banta, D. (2001), 'Public health triumphs at WTO Conference', *Journal of the American Medical Association*, **286**, 2655–6.
Bejesky, R. (2004), 'Investing in the dragon: Managing the patent versus trade secret protection decision for the multinational corporation in China', *Tulsa Journal of Comparative and International Law*, **11**, 437.
Besen, S.M. and L.J. Raskind (1991), 'An introduction to the law and economics of intellectual property', *Journal of Economic Perspectives*, **23** (4).
Boyle, J. (2004), 'A manifesto on WIPO and the future of intellectual property', *Duke Law and Technology Review*, **9** (1).
Braga, C.A.P., C. Fink and C.P. Sepulveda (2000), *Intellectual Property Rights and Economic Development*, World Bank Discussion Paper No. 412, Washington: World Bank.
Cabral, G. (2001), 'Macau's intellectual property system in the digital age', in C. Heath and A. Kamperman Sanders (eds), *Intellectual Property in the Digital Age*, The Hague/London/Boston: Kluwer Law International.
Calabresi, G. and D. Melamed (1972), 'Property rules, liability rules, and inalienability: one view of the cathedral', *Harvard Law Review*, **85**, 1089, 1092, 1105.
Chynoweth, G. (2003), 'Reality bites: how the biting reality of piracy in China is working to strengthen its copyright laws', *Duke Law and Technology Review*, **3**.
Coase, R. (1960), 'The problem of social cost', *Journal of Law and Economics*, **3** (1).
Commission on Intellectual Property Rights (2002), *Integrating Intellectual Property Rights and Development Policy*, London: Commission on Intellectual Property Rights.
Consumers International Asia Pacific Office (2006), *Copyright and Access to Knowledge, Policy Recommendations on Flexibilities in Copyright Laws*, Kuala Lumpur: Consumers International.
Cornish, W.R. and J. Phillips (1982), 'The economic function of trademarks: an analysis with special reference to developing countries', *International Review of Industrial Property and Copyright Law*, **13**, 41.

Correa, C. (2004), 'Bilateral investment agreements: agent of new global standards for the protection of intellectual property rights?', *GRAIN*.
De Scitovszky, T. (1941), 'A note on welfare propositions in economics', *Review of Economic Studies*, **77**.
Demsetz, H. (1982), 'Barriers to entry', *American Economic Review*, **72**, 47.
Diamond, S. (1980), 'The public interest and the trademark system', *Journal of the Patent Office Society*, **62**, 528–9.
Drahos, P. (2002), *Developing Countries and International Intellectual Property Standard Setting*, **14**, 8.
Drahos, P. (2003), 'Expanding intellectual property's empire: the role of FTAs', *GRAIN*.
Dressler, J. (1995), 'China's intellectual property protection: prospects for achieving international standards', *International Law Journal*, **19**, 181, 224.
Dumoulin, J. (2001), 'Patents and the price of drugs', *Revue Internationale de Droit Economique Special Edition: Pharmaceutical Patents, Innovations and Public Health*, 49.
Economides, N. (1988), 'The economics of trademarks', *Trade Mark Reporter*, **78**, 523.
Fink, C. and K. Maskus (eds) (2005), *Intellectual Property and Development – Lessons From Recent Economic Research*, New York: World Bank/Oxford University Press.
Friedman, D.D., W.M. Landes and R.A. Posner (1991), 'Some economics of trade secret law', *Journal of Economic Perspectives*, 69–70.
Geiger, C. (2004), 'Fundamental rights, a safeguard for the coherence of intellectual property Law?', *International Review of Intellectual Property and Competition Law*, **35**, 268.
Gordon, W. (1992a), 'Asymmetric market failure and prisoner's dilemma in intellectual property', *University of Dayton Law Review*, **17**, 853.
Gordon, W. (1992b), 'Fair use as market failure: a structural and economic analysis of the Betamax case and its predecessors', *Columbia Law Review*, **82**, 1600.
Greene, N. (2004), 'Enforceability of the People's Republic of China's trade secret law: impact on technology transfer in the PRC and Preparing for Successful Licensing', *IDEA*, **44**, 437.
Hayek, F. (1937), 'Economics and knowledge', *Economica*, **IV**, 33–54.
Heald, P.J. (1991), 'Federal intellectual property law and the economics of preemption', *Iowa Law Review*, **76**, 962–5.
Hicks, J. (1939), 'Foundations of welfare economics', *Economic Journal*, **49**, 696.
Hong, X. (2004), 'Domain name dispute resolution in China: a comprehensive review', *Temple International and Comparative Law Journal*, **18**(1).
Kaldor, N. (1939), 'Welfare propositions of economics and interpersonal comparisons of utility', *Economic Journal*, **49**, 549.
Kamperman Sanders, A. (2003), 'Patents – antitrust, compulsory licensing and research exceptions', in C. Heath and A. Kamperman Sanders (eds), *Industrial Property in the Bio-Medical Age*, The Hague/London/New York: Kluwer Law International, pp. 163–84.
Kamperman Sanders, A. (2004), 'Compulsory licensing and public health', *Maastricht Journal of European and Comparative Law*, **11** (4), 337–46.
Kamperman Sanders, A. (2005), *The Development Agenda for Intellectual Property, Rational Humane Policy of 'Modern-day Communism*', inaugural lecture, Maastricht: Unigraphic.

Kamperman Sanders, A. (2006), 'Limits to database protection: fair use and scientific research exemptions', *Research Policy*, **35**, 854–74.

Kaufer, E. (1989), *The Economics of the Patent System*, Chur: Harwood Academic Publishers GmbH.

Kennedy, G. and H. Wheare (2005), 'The enforcement of intellectual property rights in Hong Kong', in C. Heath and A. Kamperman Sanders (eds), *New Frontiers of Intellectual Property Law, IP and Cultural Heritage, Geographical Indications, Enforcement and Overprotection*, Oxford/Portland: Hart, pp. 333–56.

Landes, W.M. and R.A. Posner (1987a), *The Economic Structure of Tort Law*, Cambridge, Mass.: Harvard University Press, ch. 6.

Landes, W.M. and R.A. Posner (1987b), 'Trademark law: an economic perspective', *Journal of Law and Economics*, **30**, 265.

Landes, W.M. and R.A. Posner (1989), 'An economic analysis of copyright law', *Journal, of Economic Studies*, **18**, 347–61.

Lessing, L. (2004), *Free Culture: How Big Media Uses Technology and the Law to Lock Down Culture and Control Creativity*, New York: Penguin.

Li, L. (2006), 'Legal protection of technical measures in China', *European Intellectual Property Review*, **2**, 100.

Liang, Y. (1995), 'Judicial decision on a case of infringing the exclusive right to use the "Lux" registered trademark', *China Patents and Trademarks*, **1**, 87.

Lu, G. (2005), 'Recent developments in judicial protection for intellectual property in China', in C. Heath and A. Kamperman Sanders (eds), *New Frontiers of Intellectual Property Law, IP and Cultural Heritage, Geographical Indications, Enforcement and Overprotection*, Oxford/Portland: Hart, pp. 323–32.

Mackaay, E. (1994), 'Legal hybrids: beyond property and monopoly?', *Columbia Law Review*, **94**, 2630.

Maskus, K. (2000), *Intellectual Property Rights in the Global Economy*, Washington, DC: Institute for International Economics.

Maskus, K., S.M. Dougherty and A. Mertha (2005), 'Intellectual property rights and economic development in China', in K. Maskus and C. Fink (eds), *Intellectual Property and Development – Lessons from Recent Economic Research*, New York: World Bank/Oxford University Press.

Menescal, A.K. (2005), 'Changing WIPO's ways? The 2004 development agenda in historical perspective', *Journal of World Intellectual Property*, **8**, 761.

Merges, R. (1994), 'Of property rules, Coase, and intellectual property', *Columbia Law Review*, **94**, 2664–7.

Mossinghoff, G.J. (1996), 'The importance of intellectual property protection to the American research-intensive pharmaceutical industry', *Columbia Journal of World Business*, **31**, 38.

Muennich, E. (2001), 'Pharmaceutical patents and availability of drugs', *Revue Internationale de Droit Economique Special Edition: Pharmaceutical Patents, Innovations and Public Health*, 73.

Mutetwa, S. (2001), 'HIV/AIDS: is Zimbabwe doing enough?', *Financial Gazette*, 26 April.

Ostergard, R. (1999), 'Intellectual property: a universal human right?', *Human Rights Quarterly*, **21**(1), 156.

Ran, R. (2002), 'Well-known trademark protection in China: before and after the TRIPS amendments to China's trademark law', *University of California at Los Angeles Pacific Basin Law Journal*, 231.

Reichman, J. (1994), 'Legal hybrids between the patent and copyright paradigms', *Columbia Law Review*, **94**, 2432.
Schiappacasse, M. (2004), 'Intellectual property rights in china: technology transfers and economic development', *Buffalo Intellectual Property Law Journal*, **2**, 164.
Seeman, N. (2001), 'Patently wrong', *National Review*, 21 March.
Shah, M.J. (2005), 'Problems with sharing the pirates' booty: an analysis of TRIPS, the copyright divide between the United States and China and two Potential solutions', *Richmand Journal of Global Law and Business*, **5**, 69.
Teixeira Garcia, A. (2003), 'Parallel Imports and IP rights with specific regard to Macao', in C. Heath and A. Kamperman Sanders (ed.), *Industrial Property in the Bio-Medical Age – Challenges for Asia*, The Hague/London/New York: Kluwer Law International, pp. 219–27.
UN Commission on Human Rights Resolution (2001), *Access to Medication in the Context of Pandemics such as HIV/AIDS*.
UN Sub-Commission on the Promotion and Protection of Human Rights (2000), *Intellectual Property Rights and Human Rights*.
Vandoren, P. (2002), 'Médicaments sans Frontière? Clarification of the relationship between TRIPS and public health resulting from the WTO Doha Ministerial Declaration', *Journal of World Intellectual Property*, **5**, 5–14.
Vautier, K. (2003), 'The economics of parallel imports', in C. Heath and A. Kamperman Sanders (2003), *Industrial Property in the Bio-Medical Age – Challenges for Asia*, The Hague/London/New York: Kluwer Law International, pp. 185–217.
Velásquez, G. (2001), 'Pharmaceutical patents and accessibility to drugs', *Revue Internationale de Droit Economique Special Edition: Pharmaceutical Patents, Innovations and Public Health*, 41.
Warren-Boulton, R., K. Baseman and G. Woroch (1994), 'The Economics of Intellectual Property Protection for Software: The Proper Role for Copyright', paper prepared for the American Council on Interoperable Systems, June, Washington, DC.
Xiang, Y. (2004), 'The regime of exhaustion and parallel imports in China: a study based on the newly amended Chinese laws and related cases', *European Intellectual Property Review*, **3**, 105–12.
Yonehara, B. (2002), 'Enter the dragon: China's WTO accession, film piracy and prospects for the enforcement of copyright laws', *University of California at Los Angeles Entertaiment Law review*.
Yu, P. (2000), 'From pirates to partners: protecting intellectual property in China in the twenty-first century', *American University Law Review*, **50**, 131.
Yu, P. (2005), 'Wrong time, wrong venue; the United States shouldn't take complaints about Chinese IP enforcement to the WTO', *Intellectual Property Law and Business*, **3**, 9, 20.

ANNEX 1: ARTICLE 31BIS TRIPS AGREEMENT

(As agreed to by WTO Members on 6 December 2005)

1. The obligations of an exporting Member under Article 31(f) shall not apply with respect to the grant by it of a compulsory licence to the

extent necessary for the purposes of production of a pharmaceutical product(s) and its export to an eligible importing Member(s) in accordance with the terms set out in paragraph 2 of the Annex to this Agreement.

2. Where a compulsory licence is granted by an exporting Member under the system set out in this Article and the Annex to this Agreement, adequate remuneration pursuant to Article 31(h) shall be paid in that Member taking into account the economic value to the importing Member of the use that has been authorized in the exporting Member. Where a compulsory licence is granted for the same products in the eligible importing Member, the obligation of that Member under Article 31(h) shall not apply in respect of those products for which remuneration in accordance with the first sentence of this paragraph is paid in the exporting Member.
3. With a view to harnessing economies of scale for the purposes of enhancing purchasing power for, and facilitating the local production of, pharmaceutical products: where a developing or least-developed country WTO Member is a party to a regional trade agreement within the meaning of Article XXIV of the GATT 1994 and the Decision of 28 November 1979 on Differential and More Favourable Treatment Reciprocity and Fuller Participation of Developing Countries (L/4903), at least half of the current membership of which is made up of countries presently on the United Nations list of least-developed countries, the obligation of that Member under Article 31(f) shall not apply to the extent necessary to enable a pharmaceutical product produced or imported under a compulsory licence in that Member to be exported to the markets of those other developing or least-developed country parties to the regional trade agreement that share the health problem in question. It is understood that this will not prejudice the territorial nature of the patent rights in question.
4. Members shall not challenge any measures taken in conformity with the provisions of this Article and the Annex to this Agreement under subparagraphs 1(b) and 1(c) of Article XXIII of GATT 1994.
5. This Article and the Annex to this Agreement are without prejudice to the rights, obligations and flexibilities that Members have under the provisions of this Agreement other than paragraphs (f) and (h) of Article 31, including those reaffirmed by the Declaration on the TRIPS Agreement and Public Health (WT/MIN(01)/DEC/2), and to their interpretation. They are also without prejudice to the extent to which pharmaceutical products produced under a compulsory licence can be exported under the provisions of Article 31(f).

11. Economic analysis of compensation for oil pollution damage in China

Michael Faure and Wang Hui

1. INTRODUCTION

In recent years, almost all continents have suffered severely from damage as a result of oil spills. Many of the very well-known ones occurred in Europe. Accidents with the *Torrey Canyon*, *Amoco Cadiz* and many others are still remembered even though they occurred in the 1960s and 1970s. As a result of the *Torrey Canyon* incident, The International Convention on the Civil Liability for Oil Pollution Damage of 1969 was adopted, together with a fund convention in 1971.[1] The goals of these international arrangements were to guarantee some compensation to victims of oil pollution incidents. However, ever new incidents, *inter alia* with the Amoco Cadiz showed that the amount available in the existing regime were not sufficient to guarantee an effective compensation to victims. Therefore, the legal regime has changed continually. The most recent change took place in 2003, when a supplementary fund was established to provide a third tier of compensation in addition to the liability convention and the existing fund. This supplementary fund was promulgated after the *Erica* caused enormous pollution off the coast of Brittany in 1999 and the *Prestige* did the same in 2002, off the coast of Gallicia.

The problem of oil pollution is not at all limited to Europe or to the US (which also adopted an Oil Pollution Act in 1990 after being severely affected in 1989 by the *Exxon Valdez* incident). The demand for oil is also rapidly increasing in Asia. As a result, the seaborne trade in oil has grown enormously Asia as well. China, with its vastly developing economy, has also turned from an oil exporter into an oil importer, thus increasing the demand for oil. Many Asian countries, including China, have recently been the victims of serious oil spills. However, the legal regime with respect to oil pollution damage in China is not clear at all.[2] As we will explain below, there is a variety of domestic laws (China Maritime Code, Marine

Environmental Protection Law and other regulations) that apply. In addition, even though China has adopted the 1969 CLC convention, its application in China is a matter of different interpretation by the Chinese courts. The majority opinion today seems to hold that the CLC convention is applicable to China only when a foreign element is involved, meaning in practice that it would apply only when the oil pollution was due to an incident involving at least one non-Chinese vessel. This interpretation, also in case law, makes it difficult to assess the precise scope of Chinese law in this respect. Moreover, some features of the international regime, such as compulsory insurance and an additional layer of compensation via a fund, are missing in China.

Within the perspective of this volume the goal of our chapter is to provide an economic analysis of Chinese law with respect to the compensation for oil pollution damage. We will thus expressly not address the international regime, even though this may in certain circumstances also be applicable to incidents in China.[3] We will thus merely address some features of the current Chinese compensation regime from the traditional economic literature. Of course, even though we will not discuss the international regime in detail, we will briefly address some aspects of Chinese law where this regime differs from the international conventions. This concerns, for instance, the fact that Chinese law has no compulsory insurance and lacks a compensation fund. The question of course arises how one can address these issues from an economics perspective. What is striking, both for the international as well as for the Chinese regime, is that the compensation for oil pollution damage differs from the way traditional damage is dealt with in most legal systems. This concerns, for instance, the fact that a strict liability applies, but also that there is a so-called 'financial cap' (a limitation) on liability.[4]

The goal of our chapter is to examine critically the compensation for oil pollution damage under Chinese law from a law and economics perspective. We will first describe the compensation regime in China and then use the well-known economic literature to critically analyse this regime. To some extent we will also address the question at the normative level, whether the current Chinese regime could be improved to bring it more in line with the lessons of economic analysis.

Hence, the chapter will be structured as follows: after this introduction (section 1) a brief overview of Chinese law will be provided (section 2). As mentioned, we will only briefly refer to the international regime, insofar as it is applicable in China, without discussing it in detail. Of course not every aspect of the compensation regime can be addressed, but particular aspects, such as the applicable liability rule (strict liability or negligence), the financial limit on liability, insurance or other solvency guarantees and the possibility of an additional fund will be highlighted. Next, a critical economic analysis of these interesting aspects of Chinese law will be provided (section 3) and some policy recommendations will be formulated (section 4), indicating how Chinese law might benefit from the lessons of economic analysis.

2. LEGAL REGIME IN CHINA

2.1 International Regime in General

The international regime on compensation for marine oil pollution damage was originally set up through two international conventions, the International Convention on Civil Liability for Oil Pollution Damage (referred to as the Civil Liability Convention, or the CLC), 1969 and the International Convention on the Establishment of an International Fund for Compensation for Oil Pollution Damage (referred to as the Fund Convention), 1971. The CLC 1969 has imposed a strict liability on tanker owners, capped to a certain amount and has imposed a requirement to purchase compulsory insurance. The Fund Convention 1971 has introduced an International Oil Pollution Compensation Fund (the IOPC Fund, or the Fund) to provide additional compensation on top of the compensation provided under the CLC. The Fund is contributed by oil-importing companies in the Contracting States of the Fund Convention.[5]

These two Conventions have been amended several times, the most important changes taking place in 1992, 2000 and, most recently, 2003.[6] In the 1992 Protocols, these two conventions were amended to expand the scope of compensation and to increase the amount of compensation. In 2000, the amount of compensation under the 1992 regime was increased by 50.37 per cent. In 2003, a Supplementary Fund was established and this came into force in March 2005. This disrupted the original balance under the two conventions whereby the shipping industry and the oil industry shared the costs of oil transportation by sea. As a result of the Supplementary Fund, the oil industry has to contribute to two compensation funds for marine oil pollution compensation, the 1992 Fund and the Supplementary Fund. So far, only some European states and Japan have ratified the 2003 Protocol.

2.2 International Conventions Ratified by China

2.2.1 CLC

China acceded on 30 January 1980 to the 1969 CLC Convention, which entered into force in China on 29 April 1980. Owing to the compulsory denunciation procedure, China has denounced the 1969 CLC and joined the 1992 CLC Convention, which had been effective in China since 5 January 2000. When the 2000 Amendment to the CLC came into effect on 1 November 2003, since the Chinese government had raised no objection or announced any reservations, under the tacit acceptance procedure, the 2000 Amendment to the CLC became effective in China as well.[7]

2.2.2 Fund Convention

As for the Fund Convention, different rules apply to mainland China on the one hand and Hong Kong (Special Administrative Region of China) on the other hand. Mainland China is not a party yet to the Fund Convention; while Hong Kong is a party to the Fund Convention.

For historical and political reasons, Hong Kong was under the jurisdiction of the UK until 1997. The UK is a party to both the 1992 CLC and the 1992 Fund Convention. Since the transfer of sovereignty of Hong Kong to the Chinese government in July 1997, Hong Kong has become an administrative region of China. However, the Chinese government promised to maintain the original system in Hong Kong for 50 years and also, in order to keep legal consistency in Hong Kong, the Chinese government decided that the Fund Convention should continue to apply, and only to Hong Kong. Hence Hong Kong remains a party to the 1992 Fund.

2.2.3 Domestic legislation

General principles in Chinese law related to marine oil pollution compensation
The application of national laws in China follows the principle of *lex specialis derogat lex generalis.* As far as domestic legislation on oil pollution compensation is concerned, there is no particular legislation which specializes in dealing with the marine oil pollution issue, but there are statutes which contain provisions related to the oil pollution problem. Thus, the *lex specialis* which may be considered includes the Marine Environmental Protection Law and the China Maritime Code, although there are debates on which of the two should be considered first. In addition, there is Regulations Concerning the Prevention of Pollution of Sea Areas by Vessels. In case no provision in these specific laws or regulations can be applied, one might need to consult the General Principles of the Civil Law of the People's Republic of China.

The MEPL The Marine Environmental Protection Law of the People's Republic of China (referred to as the MEPL) was originally adopted in 1982, and revised in 1999.[8]

The revised MEPL contains in Article 66 the provision which requires the state to implement a civil liability system for marine oil pollution damage and to ensure the establishment of oil pollution insurance and a compensation fund.[9] This is the first time in Chinese legislation that the principle of compensation for marine oil pollution damage shared between the ship owner and the cargo owner (which corresponds with the international regime) has been explicitly established. However, it only states such a general principle and only requires the State Council to formulate implementing measures. So far, no specific measures have been implemented by the State Council. As a result, the principle of joint liability between the ship owner and the cargo owner remains at a theoretical stage, the requirement of compulsory insurance is not effectively implemented and there has been no compensation fund set up in China so far.

Another important provision in the MEPL is Article 90,[10] which imposes strict liability on those who cause pollution damage and sets up the principle that natural resource damage suffered by the state is recoverable. However, owing to lack of accuracy, problems exist concerning the application of this article. One problem has to do with the fact that there is no provision concerning a limitation of liability of any party in the MEPL. Hence the first paragraph of Article 90, 'Those who cause pollution damage to the marine environment shall . . . compensate the losses' is interpreted as a duty to compensate the actual loss to the full amount. However, in practice, the ones who are accused of discharging oil often refer to the provisions of the China Maritime Code to limit their liability. Moreover, the MEPL only specifies in Article 90 paragraph 2 that the natural resource damage is compensable; concerning other damages, for instance, economic losses sustained by the private parties, there is only general reference to the 'losses' that should be compensated. It remains unclear how this provision has to be interpreted.

It seems Article 66 imposes liability for oil pollution damage compensation on the ship owner, while Article 90 imposes the liability on the oil discharger, which is not exactly the same as the owner of the ship. So, according to Article 90, liability can in theory be imposed on anyone responsible for the pollution, whether charterer or operator. However, in practice, the maritime courts in China often interpret Article 90 of the MEPL as implying that the ship owner is the one who is responsible for the ship and therefore also responsible for the pollution damage caused by the vessel.

A result of the provisions in the MEPL is that, when a claimant brings an action for compensation for oil pollution damage in practice, the MEPL alone does not suffice to provide a complete solution to the oil pollution compensation problem. Hence one has to call on other legislation, such as the CMC, as well.

The CMC As we have already mentioned, oil dischargers, when confronted with claims for compensation, often tend to refer to the China Maritime Code in order to benefit from the right of limiting their liability to a certain amount. Chapter XI of the China Maritime Code deals with 'the limitation of liability for maritime claims'.

The only explicit reference in the China Maritime Code to oil pollution compensation can be found in Article 208 which stipulates that 'The provisions of this Chapter shall not be applicable to the following claims: . . . (2) Claims for oil pollution damage under the International Convention on Civil Liability for Oil Pollution Damage to which the People's Republic of China is a party; . . . .'[11] It specifically provides that the limitation of liability as contained in the CMC shall not apply where the CLC applies. Hence, the goal of this provision is to give priority to the international conventions. However, the application of international conventions in China is a very complicated issue, which will be discussed in further detail below.

In order to examine the limitation of liability for oil pollution compensation, several articles shall be considered. The parties who can be granted the right to limit their liability are not restricted to the ship owner, as provided in Article 204; the charterer and operator of a ship and salvors may also limit their liability when complying with the conditions laid down in this chapter.

The parties responsible for oil pollution damage may be allowed to limit their liability if this complies with one of the conditions in Article 207.[12] As far as the compensation for oil pollution damage is concerned, it may constitute loss or damage to the property related to the operation of the ship under sub-paragraph (1), or other loss resulting from torts related to the operation of the ship under sub-paragraph (3). Thus the compensation for oil pollution damage may be limited under Chapter XI. However, there are two exceptional situations under which the limitation right is not granted as stipulated in Articles 208 and 209. Article 208[13] includes the provision, as just mentioned, that the CLC shall have priority over the CMC. Article 209[14] specifies that the intentional act of the liable party will lead to the loss of right of limitation.

As for the amount of limitation, Article 210 provides a detailed method of calculation.[15] This article makes a distinction between the 'loss of life or personal injury' and 'claims other than loss of life or personal injury'. Interestingly, the limits of liability for 'loss of life or personal injury' are almost twice as high as those of the 'claims other than loss of life or personal injury'. It seems the legislator attaches far more importance to the human life and personal injury than to other damages such as economic losses.

In the case of claims for oil pollution damage, this mostly concerns damages other than 'loss of life or personal injury'. Thus the limitation amount under the CMC is actually lower than the limitation under the CLC.[16] Take as an example a tanker of 5000 tons: under the CMC the owner of such tanker can limit his liability to 0.9185 million SDR, while, under CLC 1992, his limit would be 3 million SDR.

There are, however, different opinions holding that the CMC should not be applicable to oil pollution compensation caused by tankers.[17] The main argument given by the advocators of this approach is that, since the application of law in China follows the principle of *lex specialis derogat lex generalis*, the *lex specialis* in the case of marine oil pollution compensation should be the MEPL. Since there is no provision holding that the oil discharger can limit his liability to a certain amount, the discharger should compensate the victim to the full amount. Although there are provisions concerning a limitation of liability in the CMC, it does not specify that it shall be applicable to oil pollution compensation as well. A limitation seems to be contradictory to the principle of actual compensation to the full amount incorporated in the MEPL. In practice, owners of tankers often refer to the CMC to limit their liability and most of the time they are successful: the maritime courts grant such a right of limitation.

Regulations Another legal document of relevance to oil pollution compensation is the Regulation of the People's Republic of China Concerning the Prevention of Pollution of Sea Areas by Vessels. It was originally enacted in 1983[18] (referred to as the Regulations) in order to enforce the MEPL of 1982.[19] Since the MEPL was revised in 1999, the Regulation is obviously outdated, and it is now in the process of revision to keep it in line with the new provisions in the MEPL 1999.

There are several provisions in the Regulation that merit special attention. Article 7 provides that the ship owner shall bear the costs of clean-up and compulsory actions taken by the authority.[20] Article 39 provides that the vessels which cause pollution shall pay 'the cost of eliminating pollution and compensate for the losses suffered by the state'.[21] As far as the scope of compensation is concerned, only the clean-up costs and the losses suffered by the state are specifically mentioned. As for the private parties who suffer losses, there is still no clear provision indicating whether and in what manner their losses can be compensated.

Article 13 specifically requires that 'Vessels engaged in international trade with a bulk oil carrying capacity of 2000 tons shall, besides observing these Regulations, be bound by the provisions of the International Conventions on Civil Liability for Oil Pollution Damage, 1969.' As a result of this article, tankers involved in international trade all have to meet the requirements of the CLC, as far as compulsory insurance is concerned.

Maritime courts in China In China, the claims for marine oil pollution compensation are dealt with by the maritime court.[22] There are so far nine maritime courts in China, with their respective geographic jurisdictions.[23]

The intention of the Chinese government in establishing the maritime courts is to resolve maritime disputes in a professional and impartial manner through the establishment of a specialized maritime judiciary.[24] The existence of several maritime courts does contribute to some extent to the settlements of maritime disputes, but on the other hand, especially as far as marine oil pollution compensation is concerned, the different judicial interpretation leads to confusion in practice.

2.2.4 Existing problems

Application of relevant international conventions in China The Chinese approach in dealing with the relationship between the international conventions and domestic law, strictly speaking, is neither the monistic nor the dualistic approach.[25] One may find different approaches in various Chinese statutes dealing with specific areas of law.[26]

A frequently adopted approach, as far as maritime affairs are concerned, is to embrace the principles of the international conventions that China has acceded to in the related Chinese law, which is a monistic approach.[27] In this respect, Article 66 of the MEPL 1999 obviously embraced the general principles of the CLC and the Fund Convention, although there are criticisms concerning these provisions, as will be discussed later.

There is no specific provision on how to apply the international conventions joined by the Chinese government in the Constitution. One may find a reference in the General Principles of the Civil Law, more particularly in Article 142(2), which has established the supremacy of international conventions when provisions in national law differ from the convention. Such a principle is that, in case of conflict between the international convention to which China is a party and the domestic law, the international convention shall prevail, unless a reservation has been made by the Chinese government. The China Maritime Code[28] and the Marine Environment Protection Law[29] both follow such a rule to give priority to international conventions.

The application of this seemingly obvious and simple principle is problematic in practice. Legal scholars and courts have different opinions on the application of this principle. There are two major opinions in this respect. The first opinion holds that the Chinese law should apply in purely domestic issues and the international convention applies only when a 'foreign element' is involved.[30] The arguments to justify this opinion are as follows: Article 268 of the China Maritime Code, which recognizes the supremacy of international conventions, is provided in the Chapter titled 'Application of Law in Relation to Foreign-related Matters'.[31] This implies that the international conventions shall apply only when there is a 'foreign element' involved.[32] As for the purely domestic issues, it is only the Chinese law that shall be applied. This can be further confirmed by the sovereignty of states that should not be interfered with.[33] Some scholars also argued that the reason behind the newly added Article 66 of MEPL is to avoid the direct application of CLC in China to all cases, and to stress the importance of domestic law in the process of handling marine pollution cases.[34] Another argument which is employed as legal basis for this opinion is found in the Regulations of the People's Republic of China Concerning the Prevention of Pollution of Sea Areas by Vessels. Article 13 of the Regulations stipulates that 'Vessels engaged in international trade with a bulk oil carrying capacity of 2,000 tons shall, besides observing these Regulations, be bound by the provisions of the International Conventions on Civil Liability for Oil Pollution Damage, 1969.' As a result, for the vessels not navigating on international lanes, these being the offshore and inland water navigating ships, national law shall apply. There are many scholars in favour of this opinion and this opinion is mostly followed in practice.[35]

The second opinion holds that the CLC should apply in all cases. The argument given is that, although the rule that international conventions prevail is indeed provided in a separate chapter on foreign-related issues in the General Principles of the Civil Law and the China Maritime Code, it does not necessarily mean that the international convention should not apply to cases where no foreign elements are involved. The Regulation of 1983 does not state to the contrary either. Moreover, the Marine Environment Protection Law 1999 does not even have a separate chapter dealing with the so-called 'foreign-related' issues, which implies that the same rules shall apply in marine environmental protection. A third argument can be found in the preamble of the CLC Convention where it is stated that the convention was aiming to 'adopt uniform international rules and procedures for determining questions of liability and providing adequate compensation'. Thus the international convention was designed for uniformity, not differentiating between internationally navigating vessels and offshore vessels. Hence the international convention shall apply to all cases to avoid complications and to maintain uniformity – so it is held.[36]

It indeed happens in practice that, in cases where only Chinese offshore vessels are involved, different maritime courts apply different rules: those laid down in the international convention or those in the Chinese law. This leads to confusions as court decisions are not consistent with each other. For instance, in two cases where all parties involved are Chinese, the Qingdao maritime court ruled, in 1994, that the request to apply the CLC should be rejected because there is no foreign element involved, whereas the

Guangzhou maritime court in the *Min Ran Gong 2* case in 1999 granted the limitation under the CLC to the ship owners and refused the application of Chinese laws.[37]

Compulsory insurance Problems exist in practice concerning the compulsory insurance requirement, no matter if the CLC is uniformly applied to all cases or the CLC and Chinese laws apply respectively in different cases, depending on whether there is a foreign element involved.

Where the international conventions and domestic law apply in different cases, depending on whether a foreign element is involved, problems arise due to the fact that the MEPL contains only a general principle in Article 66 requiring the state to establish the compulsory insurance mechanism, which is not effectively implemented in practice.

Where the international convention applies to all oil spill compensation cases, the problem of liability insurance still exists. According to the CLC, tankers of less than 2000 tonnes are not under an obligation to obtain insurance. However, the practice in China is that the small tankers are often employed by private owners for coastal service or on domestic lines. The owners of such vessels very often have only one ship, or they erect a separate legal entity for every ship in order to evade liability. Moreover, these small tankers are often badly maintained and pose the biggest risk of oil spills in Chinese waters. According to statistics, among the 2300 tankers operating on domestic lines, 80 per cent of them are below 1000 gross tons.[38] Thus, even when the CLC is uniformly applied in China, there will still be a large number of small tankers of less than 2000 tons operating in Chinese waters without maintaining liability insurance. When they spill oil in the water and cause damage, their owners are often financially incapable of paying sufficient compensation because of a lack of insurance.

Limitation of liability Despite the debate on whether the limitation right shall be granted to those who cause oil spillage, there are more problems in this respect, as the limitation amounts under the CMC and the CLC are different.

When the limitation amount under CLC applies to cases where foreign elements are involved, and CMC applies to purely domestic tankers, tankers of the same size may be confronted with different limits. Moreover, as we have shown, the limitation under the CMC is much lower than that under the CLC. The lower limitation amount under the CMC is very likely to be insufficient in many cases.[39]

Even when the CLC applies in all cases of oil pollution compensation in China, as far as the limitation of liability is concerned, it may provide a higher amount of compensation to the victims only under the strict assumption that the compulsory insurance mechanism is well implemented as well. Although the limitation amount provided under the CLC is higher, compared to the CMC, if the ship owner is not insured up to this amount, he will not be able to pay such a high amount owing to his restricted financial capacity. As a result, the high limitation amount, without any form of financial guarantee, is imposed in vain.

Compensation fund in China So far, there is no oil pollution compensation fund in China. There are at least two reasons for this. First of all, mainland China has not yet acceded to the Fund Convention. This might have to do with the fact that, according to the Fund Convention, the oil industry has to pay a contribution to the Fund. In China many oil companies are state-owned. For instance, Sinopec and PetroChina, which control 85 per cent of the country's total crude import, are state-owned.[40] To join the Fund Convention would mean that they would have to contribute financially to the Fund. If calculated on the basis of the annual report of the Fund of 2004, the contribution of the oil industry in China would be the third among all countries (only after Japan and Italy), which would amount in total to 58.1 million RMB.[41] This may explain China's reluctance to join the Fund Convention.

Second, there was no requirement for a compensation fund in the Chinese domestic law until 2000, when the revised MEPL came into force. Thus, the establishment of a compensation fund now has a legal foundation through the revision of the Marine Environment Protection Law.[42] However, Article 66 of the MEPL only contains a general requirement which is not effectively implemented as yet.

At present, spills from small ships seem to be the more problematic ones, but there is of course an increasing risk, given the huge increase in volumes of imported oil and the growth of the shipping industry, that a major spill will exceed the owner's limits provided for in the CLC, giving rise to problems of inadequate compensation under the CLC Convention as well.[43]

Summary The result of no clear provisions in Chinese law on compulsory insurance or on the compensation fund, in combination with the low limits of liability under the China Maritime Code, is that victims of oil pollution in China are often left in a disadvantageous position with insufficient compensation or no compensation at all. Even when the CLC is uniformly applied, for a purely domestic issue as well, given the particular situation of China, problems still arise. Indeed, in China, small tankers are mostly employed, and the compulsory insurance requirement is not obligatory for these small tankers. Therefore, the higher limitation amount under the CLC seems better in theory, but may not be effective to influence the practice in

China, given the fact that the requirement to purchase compulsory insurance under the CLC only applies for tankers above 2000 tonnes.

Moreover, among the ships carrying oil on domestic lines, a large number are small tankers which are privately owned. Some of these ship owners have only a single vessel registered under their names, which lowers their financial capability in case of liability. Some of these tankers are badly maintained old tankers, or with single hulls, which increases the potential accident risk.[44] In this situation, the ship owner is often insolvent, so that he is unable to pay the full compensation; when the pollution damage exceeds the ship owner's liability, the surplus part cannot be paid.

China has not yet established a complete system for oil pollution compensation that can constitute a definite financial source for oil pollution damage. The pollution damages are often inadequately compensated, and thus great social losses are incurred. As a consequence, clean-up activities and preventive measures are not encouraged either.[45]

Realizing the serious problems caused by marine oil pollution, the Chinese government organized, between 2000 and 2001, research on 'the establishment and implementation of Chinese compensation system for ship source oil pollution damage'. This research was carried out by the Institute of Scientific Research of the Ministry of Communication. The research report was submitted to the State Council to be considered for legislation. Some of the proposals in this research will be analysed in comparison with the current system from an economic perspective.

3. ECONOMIC ANALYSIS

We will now address various aspects of the oil pollution compensation system from an economics angle. Of course we can only focus on the main features. We will provide some of the lessons from economic theory and then compare these with Chinese law, as described in the previous section.

3.1 Coase Theorem

The starting point for many economic analyses of the compensation for marine oil pollution damage is of course the Coase theorem.[46] The Coase theorem may apply when the party representing the ship and the party representing the cargo interests are in a contractual relationship, whereby they agree to transport the oil cargo by sea. Applying the Coase theorem to such a contractual bargaining setting, parties could in principle *ex ante* agree on the optimal amount of care to be performed by the tanker owner, which could be related to the specific preferences of both parties and, for example, to their ability to seek insurance coverage. In that case, the agreement concerning the distribution of risk might also be reflected in the contract price that has to be paid for shipping the oil (the freight).[47]

As a result, it should in theory make no difference whether liability is allocated to the tanker owner or to the cargo interests. As long as free negotiations (in a low transaction cost setting) are possible, shifting the liability, for example to the tanker owner, would simply mean that the price charged for transport would be increased. In the alternative, it would be the cargo owner (on the assumption that that would be the presiding rule) that would bear the liability. In any event, the cargo interests will pass on the costs of liability for oil pollution damage to the end user of the cargo, those who have a demand for oil-related products.

The same conclusion could also be reached with respect to another issue closely related to liability for oil pollution damage, this being a financial cap on liability. In such a contractual setting, the financial caps should not pose any problem either, because the division of risk bearing between the cargo owner and the tanker owner can be signalled in the contract, and a limited liability will be reflected in the transport price.

However, the Coase theorem applies only when the passing on of costs is possible. In reality, the victim of oil pollution is a third party and does not stand in a contractual relationship with the injurer and, owing to legal and practical restrictions, the transaction costs are prohibitive. Thus the Coase bargaining may not provide a solution and legal instruments will be necessary to remedy the externality caused by the oil pollution risk. Of course Shavell's criteria[48] indicate that regulation will be necessary to prevent the oil pollution risk. However, since the focus of our chapter is on the compensation issue rather than the prevention, we will primarily focus on liability rules, since they are also the rules governing the international and Chinese compensation systems for oil pollution damage.

3.2 Liability Rules

3.2.1 Economic theory

Given the fact that the victim of oil pollution damage most of the time does not stand in a contractual relationship with the tanker owner, Coase bargaining is not feasible; thus, no solution is provided through the Coase theorem. Hence, a legislative intervention is necessary to remedy the externality resulting from oil pollution damage. A legal rule should therefore be put in place to give the parties involved appropriate incentives to follow an optimal care level. The economic literature on accident law has largely demonstrated that liability rules may be put in place to serve this goal.[49]

The literature holds that, in a so-called 'unilateral accident case', being one where only one party (usually referred to as the injurer) can influence the accident risk, both negligence and strict liability lead to efficient care levels, but only strict liability leads to an efficient activity level of the injurer as well.[50] However, in a bilateral accident, where the victim may also influence the accident risk, it is held that no liability rule is optimal.[51] The result is that it is usually held that, in order to develop some kind of a test for strict liability, one should examine whether it is more important to control the injurer's activity than the victim's. If it can be held that the injurer's influence on the activity is far more important than the victim's, this may be an argument in favour of strict liability.[52] It is, however, important to stress that, from the economic literature, it follows that whenever the victim can have its influence on the care level as well (the bilateral accidents), a liability rule should be chosen that provides incentives to the victim for taking optimal care as well. This may be either a negligence rule or a defence which has to be added to the strict liability rule (comparative or contributory negligence).[53]

Applying these basic insights to the case of oil pollution damage, one can hold that there may be a strong economic argument in favour of a strict liability rule. Oil pollution damage is certainly not purely unilateral. Also, victims (such as coastal states) may be able to take preventive measures once an oil pollution incident has occurred. However, the influence on the accident risk of the tanker owner seems to be far more important than that of the victim. Hence, according to the economic test, it seems far more important to control the injurer's activity than the victim's, which may create a preference for strict liability.[54] A condition is, as indicated, that the victim's care level would be controlled by adding a comparative or contributory negligence defence to the strict liability rule.

Moreover, it should be added that the economic literature has also indicated that strict liability provides incentives for prevention only in the case where the injurer has assets at stake to pay for the damage. In case of insolvency, strict liability may lead to underdeterrence. Indeed, under a negligence rule, underdeterrence will only arise when the costs of taking efficient care are higher than the injurer's wealth, whereas, under strict liability, underdeterrence already arises as soon as the magnitude of the damage is higher than the injurer's wealth.[55] This means that this economic advantage of strict liability holds only in the hypothesis of full solvency of the injurer. If the injurer (the tanker owner in the case of oil pollution damage) were judgment-proof, a regulatory solution would have to take care of the danger of underdeterrence resulting from the insolvency.[56]

3.2.2 Application to the Chinese system

The Marine Environment Protection Law 1999 imposes a strict liability rule on the party who causes the damage resulting from oil pollution. In this respect, the strict liability on the polluter under Article 90 of the MEPL seems largely to correspond to the economic literature.

Moreover, Article 90 of the MEPL also contains a provision on contributory negligence, which specifies that, if the damage results entirely from the intentional act or fault of a third party, the third party shall be liable for the compensation. Hence, the required defence is added to the strict liability rule to provide the victim with incentives to take care as well. Also, this corresponds to the economic principles sketched above.

Also it is stipulated, in Article 92 of the MEPL,[57] that there is no liability for pollution damage in case of *force majeure* or war. The exclusion of liability in case of *force majeure* is reasonable since the economic analysis assumes that liability will provide incentives to increase the level of precaution. Hence, attaching liability also in the situation where the tanker owner could not influence the accident risk and could therefore not have affected his incentives does not make sense from an economic perspective.

A major weakness of the Chinese system is, however, as we shall indicate below, that there is no sufficient guarantee against the insolvency of the injurer. Hence, strict liability may lead to underdeterrence. There is, moreover, an interesting feature in Chinese law, namely that the liability for oil pollution under the MEPL is imposed on the polluter and hence on anyone who contributes to the pollution. This constitutes a great advantage compared to the international system under the CLC. In that system, only the tanker owner is liable, excluding liability of all others who may also have contributed to the risk. This is referred to as the 'channelling' of liability.[58] This 'channelling', which has been held inefficient in the economics literature,[59] is missing in Chinese law. In that particular respect, Chinese law seems more efficient than the international regime.

3.3 Compulsory Insurance

3.3.1 Economic theory

We have already mentioned that a strict liability rule can be considered efficient only if there is no insolvency risk. Indeed, insolvency may pose a problem of underdeterrence. If the expected damage largely exceeds the injurer's assets, the injurer will only have incentives to purchase liability insurance up to the amount of his own assets. He is indeed only exposed to the risk of losing his own assets in a liability suit. The judgement-proof problem may therefore lead to underinsurance and thus to underdeterrence. Jost has rightly pointed to the fact that, in these circumstances of insolvency, compulsory insurance might provide an optimal outcome.[60] By introducing a duty to purchase insurance coverage for the amount of the expected loss, better results will be obtained than with insolvency whereby the magnitude of the loss exceeds the injurer's assets.[61] In the latter case, the injurer will indeed only consider the risk as one where he could at most lose his own assets and will set his standard of care accordingly. When he is, under a duty to insure, exposed to full liability, the insurer will obviously have incentives to control the behaviour of the insured. Via the traditional instruments for the control of moral hazard, the insurer can make sure that the injurer will take the necessary care to avoid an accident with the real magnitude of the loss. Thus, Jost and Skogh argue that compulsory insurance can, provided that the moral hazard problem is resolved adequately, provide better results than under the judgement-proof problem.

This economic argument shows that insolvency may cause potentially responsible parties to externalize harm: they may be engaged in activities which may cause harm that can largely exceed their assets. Without financial provisions, these costs would be thrown on society and would therefore be externalized instead of internalized. Such an internalization can be achieved if the insurer is able to control the behaviour of the insured. The insurer could set appropriate policy conditions and require an adequate (risk-related) premium. This shows that, if the moral hazard problem can be settled adequately, insurance even leads to a higher deterrence than a situation without liability insurance and insolvency.[62]

3.3.2 Application to the Chinese system

It is not difficult to argue that the introduction of a duty on the liable tanker owner to seek liability insurance to meet his obligations, as stipulated in Article 66 of the MEPL 1999, fits into the economic framework. However, as we have mentioned before, this provision on a compulsory insurance mechanism is too general to be effectively implemented in practice and, so far, more specific implementing measures as required in this article are not in force.

The current situation in China is that all tankers of more than 2000 tons navigating on international lanes have taken out oil pollution liability insurance. As for ships engaged in coastal or inland water shipping, and tankers under 2000 tons, such insurance is not effectively implemented. For coastal tankers, approximately 10 per cent of them are insured against oil pollution liability, while, for inland water tankers, it is reported that almost none of them takes out the oil pollution liability insurance.[63] Moreover, among the ships transporting oil on domestic lines, a large number are owned by small private enterprises. Some of these private owners have only a single vessel registered under their names, or they set up one company especially for one vessel to lower their financial capability in case of liability. The insolvency problem of the Chinese tanker owners is thus intensified by this practice. It confirms the well-known result of economics that limited liability of a corporation may lead to an externalization of harm to third parties.[64]

According to a statistical overview of major oil spills (more than 50 tons of oil spilled) between 1973 and 1996 in China, all the spills involving internationally trading ships have been compensated; on the other hand, for the spills involving only ships navigating on domestic lines in China, only 37 per cent gained compensation.[65] This evidence shows that the absence of an effective financial security for cabotage vessels leads to insufficient compensation of oil pollution damage. The result will also be an underdeterrence and thus, potentially an insufficient effect towards prevention. Hence, the question on how to ensure that the small privately owned ships are also properly insured, and can meet the costs of pollution claims when they occur, is a crucial one for the compensation regime in China.[66]

The research carried out by the Ministry of Communication, as we mentioned before, proposed in the final report a particular Chinese system, taking into account the current situation in China. It proposed that the minimum tonnage requirement for compulsory insurance (for example, in the CLC, the minimum tonnage is 2000 tons) should be abolished, and tankers of all sizes operating in Chinese waters shall be required to obtain insurance.[67] The amount of insurance will thus be divided into four categories, depending on the tonnage of the tankers,[68] and there is also a difference made between tankers navigating offshore and in inland waters. Thus, for tankers carrying persistent oil, the oil pollution liability insurance amount shall be as follows.

1. For tankers of not more than 100 tons, the insurance amount for offshore tankers shall be 2 million RMB, and for inland water tankers shall be 500 000 RMB;
2. For tankers between 101 and 200 tons, the insurance amount for offshore tankers shall be 2 million RMB, and for inland water tankers shall be 1 million RMB;
3. For tankers between 201 and 500 tons, the insurance amount for offshore tankers shall be 2 million RMB, and for inland water tankers shall be 1.5 million RMB;
4. For tankers of more than 500 tons, the insurance amount for offshore tankers shall be 2 million RMB, and for inland water tankers shall be 1.5 million RMB plus 1000 RMB per ton for the amount over 500 tons.

The overall ceiling shall be 10 million RMB for offshore tankers and 5 million for inland water tankers.[69] Such a compulsory scheme seems to correspond better to economic theory, if it can be adopted and implemented in China.

3.4 Financial Caps

3.4.1 Economic theory

As we showed above, an important feature of the international liability convention ratified by China (the CLC) is that the tanker owner is not exposed to full liability, but that his liability is capped to an amount which might be substantially lower than the amount of damage an average oil pollution incident may cause.[70] This is also one of the central debates concerning the Chinese system for oil pollution compensation.

A distinction can be made between the situation where the victim stands in a contractual relationship with the injurer, and the one where the victim is a third party. As we have briefly indicated, discussing the Coase theorem, financial caps on liability may be efficient in the contractual setting. In that case, they could simply signal the division of risk bearing between, for example, the cargo owner and the tanker owner. Traditionally, in maritime law, there were always financial caps on the liability of the ship owner as maritime transporter. A limited liability will of course be reflected in the transport price. In this particular contractual setting, where informed parties agree to cap liability, this should not cause major worries from a policy perspective.

The situation is of course different when, as in the case of oil pollution damage, victims are third parties and hence the Coase solution cannot apply. Above we indicated that, in the case of oil pollution damage, strict liability may be warranted on the condition that a defence is introduced to give incentives for optimal care to victims as well. Only under strict liability would the potential injurer have an incentive to adopt an optimal activity level. This full internalization is obviously only possible if the injurer is effectively exposed to the full costs of the activity he engages in, and is therefore in principle held to provide full compensation to a victim. An obvious disadvantage of a system of financial caps is that this will seriously impair the victim's rights to full compensation. If the cap is indeed set at a much lower amount than the expected damage, this would not only violate the victim's right on compensation, but the above-mentioned full internalization of the externality would not take place either. From an economic point of view, a limitation of compensation therefore poses a serious problem since there will be no internalization of the risky activity.

Indeed, if one believes that the exposure to liability has a deterrent effect, a limitation of the amount of compensation due to victims poses another problem. There is a direct relationship between the magnitude of the accident risk and the amount to be spent on optimal care by the potential polluter. If the liability therefore is limited to a certain amount, the potential injurer will consider the accident as one with a magnitude capped at the limited amount. Hence, he will not spend the care necessary to reduce the total accident costs. Obviously, the amount of care spent by the potential injurer will be lower and a problem of underdeterrence will arise. The amount of optimal care, reflected in the optimal standard, being the care necessary to reduce the total accident costs efficiently, will be higher than the amount the potential injurer will spend to avoid an accident equal to the statutory limited amount.[71]

The conclusion, however, is different in the case of bilateral accidents, where the victim's behaviour may also affect the accident risk. The standard argument against providing full compensation to victims in the case of bilateral accidents is that victims can take precautionary measures which are not always observable by judges and which can therefore not be fully accounted for in contributory or comparative negligence defences.[72] A limit on the compensation in the case of bilateral accidents may therefore be useful in cases where victims should be given additional incentives to reduce the accident risk. Whether caps are efficient in specific bilateral accident cases will depend on the circumstances. The question arises (*inter alia*) whether exposing the victim to risk is indeed necessary to provide these additional incentives or whether the victim's incentives can be optimally controlled via the contributory negligence defence. Also, the amount of the cap remains important. If the cap were set too low this would give incentives to the victim, but it could equally lead to serious underdeterrence of the injurer.

3.4.2 Application to the Chinese system

In this respect we can also be brief: the economics literature showed that a strict liability rule is efficient only if the potential injurer is fully exposed to the potential damage which may result from his activity. A financial limit on the (strict) liability of the tanker owner will have the same effect as the insolvency of the tanker owner: underdeterrence. The tanker owner will consider the accident only as one where the limited amount of liability is the maximum damage that can be suffered and a corresponding (lower) level of preventive measures will be chosen. A financial cap on liability can therefore be considered inefficient, more particularly since it concerns here a situation where damage is suffered by third parties, so that Coasean bargaining is not possible.

A possible justification for the cap could be found in the situation where one would argue that the contributory negligence defence would not provide victims with adequate incentives. In that case, one could argue that lower than full compensation for the victims may provide additional incentives for victim care. However, given the fact that it is more important to control the injurer's incentives than the victim's, and considering the fact that the Chinese law (the MEPL 1999) does provide for a contributory negligence defence, there is no reason to assume that this defence cannot adequately provide victims of oil pollution damage with incentives for care. Moreover, the positive effects a cap may have on a victim's incentives would probably be totally countered by the negative effects this would have on the tanker owner's incentives for prevention.

The fact that, principally, a financial limit on liability as contained in the China Maritime Code (which is even lower than the limit under the CLC) should be considered inefficient does not necessarily mean, however, that the cap will in practice also lead to a higher level of oil pollution incidents. First, for many (smaller) oil pollution incidents the damage may well be lower than the limit on liability. The risk of underdeterrence may therefore only arrive in those (catastrophic) cases where the amount of the damage actually was higher than the cap. Second, the prevention of oil pollution incidents is today primarily dependent upon regulation aiming at an optimal tanker design to prevent spill risks. Liability rules therefore, have at most an additional deterrent effect to back up this regulation. The fact that the cap may create underdeterrence can thus affect this additional incentive effect of the liability regime, but should not necessarily lead to an increase in pollution incidents. That will depend upon the effectiveness of the regulatory system and the extent to which liability rules thus have to provide supplementary incentives.

Some may argue that a financial cap is necessary to keep the oil pollution risk insurable. That argument, however, is not very convincing since the duty to insure could have been limited to an (insurable) amount, whereas the liability itself could have remained unlimited. The shipping industry may be strongly against such a provision, since they are afraid they will be confronted with a too heavy financial burden without the protection of the right on a limitation of liability. This also shows the interest group's influence on the Chinese legislation.

Another problem with the current system is that the limitation amount is simply built on the basis of the tonnage. The tonnage of the ship could indeed influence the scale of potential damage caused by it, but there are other factors that will also influence the pollution risk. Thus such a provision does not make the limitation amount correspond to the potential risks.

3.5 The Compensation Fund

3.5.1 Economic theory

From the above it follows that, if one fears that those on whom liability for oil pollution damage is placed (for example, the tanker owner) might be insolvent (in the sense that the amount of the damage which they may cause could be higher than their wealth) a duty to seek financial coverage (through insurance or alternative mechanisms)[73] should be introduced. However, the amount of oil pollution damage may be so large that even traditional insurance mechanisms or pooling by operators (Protection and Indemnity (P&I) Club) may not provide sufficient coverage. The question then arises whether supplementary funding should be provided through, for example, a compensation fund, and what can be suggested as far as the efficiency of such a fund mechanism is concerned.

First, no matter how a compensation system is organized, the incentives for prevention of pollution damage should always remain untouched. Liability rules can only have a preventive effect if the duty to compensate is put on the one who actually contributed to the risk. The same applies to compensation funds. This means that a duty to contribute to the fund should in principle only rest upon the one who actually contributed to the risk.

A second, related, principle is that this duty to contribute should also be related to the amount in which the specific activity or entrepreneur contributed to the risk. This principle is usually automatically respected in liability law. The duty to compensate under tort law is indeed usually limited to the damage that the specific tortfeasor himself caused.[74] However, also if a collectivization of the compensation takes place, it remains important to guarantee that the tortfeasor only contributes financially in relation to the amount in which he contributed to the risk as well. This is reflected in insurance policies in the idea of risk differentiation. It simply means that bad risks pay a higher premium than good risks. This principle should also be applied if a compensation fund is installed, meaning that bad risks should contribute more to the compensation system than good risks. This remains important, since it will give incentives for prevention to the contributors to the fund. Bad risks will be punished and good risks should be rewarded.

These principles are not only important from an efficiency point of view (providing optimal incentives for prevention), but also include a fairness element. Indeed, if these principles were not followed, it would mean that good risks would have to pay for the bad risks as well and would therefore in fact subsidize bad risks. This negative redistribution should be avoided and therefore, the compensation mechanism, fund or insurance should be financed principally by the ones who really contributed to the damage.

To summarize, the (supplementary) compensation mechanism should aim at a differentiation of the contributions due. This differentiation is only possible if the insurance company or agency administering the fund also possesses information on the amount in which the specific activity contributed to the risk. One key element to determine the choice between insurance or funds is therefore who possesses the best information to control the risk.

3.5.2 Application to the Chinese system

We have shown above that, whenever an alternative compensation mechanism like a fund is installed, in principle a risk and premium differentiation should be applied as well in order to provide optimal incentives for prevention. One may question whether the financing structure of the current International Oil Pollution Compensation Fund corresponds to these principles. The Chinese Domestic Fund to be set up is proposed mainly to follow the international model with a lower amount. Hence, the Fund will be financed by levies on the oil received at Chinese ports and will be paid by the oil receivers. An interesting point is that, as a result of this financing of the Fund by the oil interests, the compensation regime consists on the one hand of the (limited) liability of the tanker owner and supplemented by a Fund which is financed by the oil receivers on the other, which strictly follows the model of the international regime. It is interesting to note that, at the 1969 conference, it was only because part of the compensation would be provided through the oil interests via the Fund that the liability of the tanker owners was considered acceptable.[75]

However, given the financing structure of the Fund, one may doubt whether this actually provides the oil interests with incentives for prevention. Indeed, their financial burden towards the Fund is merely determined on the basis of the amount of oil discharged, not on the basis of preventive measures taken or actual oil pollution incidents. Hence, the oil receivers are not rewarded, for example, for choosing safer ships or punished (with a higher contribution) for choosing riskier ones. Their contribution to the Fund merely varies with the amount of oil transported. In terms of the economic analysis, one can argue that the financing structure merely provides the oil industry with incentives for reducing the activity level (transporting less oil), but not for an efficient level of care. Moreover, the legal analysis made clear that the Fund (in the normal case) only intervenes for the amount which is not covered by the limited liability of the tanker owner,[76] which is of course a small part of the total costs of an oil pollution incident. It was held during the 1969 conference to prepare the Fund that only 5 per cent of large-scale oil casualties could not be dealt with under the existing rules.[77] In China, given the fact of a large amount of small tankers operating in Chinese waters, the portion of large-scale oil spills may be less than at the international level. This means that the oil interests would effectively only intervene for a relatively small part of the oil pollution incidents, albeit that the incidents where the Fund intervenes can of course usually be considered as catastrophic.

In sum, if compensation of oil pollution damage is set as a policy goal and it appears that traditional insurance markets (or pooling through P&I Clubs) cannot provide more or less full compensation, alternatives will have to be developed through (public or private) compensation funds. However, the economic literature has generally held that also in structuring such a compensation fund a cost reduction should be achieved and the duty to contribute to the compensation mechanisms should in principle be laid on those that create the risk and in the proportion in which they create the risk. It seems that these principles are only to a small extent followed in the design of the Fund Convention. The drafters apparently attached more importance to balancing the contribution of tanker owners and cargo interests, instead of designing a system that would provide optimal incentives for the prevention of oil spills by all those who created those risks.

4. CONCLUDING REMARKS AND POLICY RECOMMENDATIONS

So far, we have applied some well-known economic theory to analyse the compensation for marine oil pollution in the particular context of China. The notion stressed here is that laying a duty on those who cause the pollution will, with luck, have a deterrent effect. However, we did not examine the aspects of prevention or regulation, whereas regulation has a primary role to play in the prevention of oil pollution damage. It has been indicated in the literature, more particularly by Shavell, that, especially as far as environmental risks are concerned, regulation may be a more appropriate instrument than liability rules.[78] The criteria are well known: if information on optimal safety devices can better be acquired through the government than through private parties, if there is a serious insolvency risk and if the threat of a liability suit may be low, there is a strong argument in favour of regulation. All of these arguments may apply in the case of oil pollution damage.[79]

It is, moreover, indeed the case worldwide, and in China as well, that regulations concentrating on prevention through better tanker design and other safety measures have received more attention in recent years. Of course increased safety designs will lead to (a small) increase in oil prices, which has been calculated in various empirical studies.[80] This is not the place to discuss the efficiency and effectiveness of these tanker design regulations.[81] More interesting is the question whether, in addition to this regulation, any additional deterrent effect can be expected from liability rules. Lacking empirical evidence, it is not possible to provide hard data on the effectiveness of liability rules in supplementing safety regulation.

By applying the economic theory, we have sketched what an optimal regime could look like from an economic perspective. From the economic analysis of the Chinese system of marine oil pollution compensation, we found that, to some extent, the Chinese oil pollution compensation regime follows the predictions from the economic model, at least as far as the imposition of a strict liability rule adding a contributory negligence defence is concerned. Moreover, the Chinese system is more efficient than the international regime in the sense that there is no channelling of liability, thus all parties involved in the activity will be given an incentive to take preventive measures. However, the Chinese system also deviates from the economic theory in several respects.

First, the financial caps imposed on the liable party for marine oil pollution compensation are inefficient as this will lead to insufficient compensation of victims and underdeterrence of the potential polluter. However, it can be argued that, in a bilateral accident, the financial caps may have the advantage of giving additional incentives to the victims to take out prevention. But whether such caps are efficient will depend on whether exposing the victim to risk for additional incentive is necessary, or whether the victim's incentive is optimally controlled via the contributory or comparative negligence defence. Now that the Chinese law does provide for a contributory negligence defence, there is no reason to assume that this defence cannot adequately provide incentives for the victims to take out prevention. Moreover, the situation is worsened in the context of the Chinese system, which provides an even lower limitation amount than the CLC. If the cap were set too low, this would give incentives to the victim but it could equally lead to serious underdeterrence of the injurer. Given the fact that it is more important to control the injurer's incentives than the victim's, a cap as stipulated in the Chinese system probably has more negative effects on the injurer's care level than benefits of additional care for victims.

Second, the fact that no compulsory insurance is effectively implemented in China (especially for tankers navigating on domestic lines) largely deviates from economic theory. The economic analysis shows that the insolvency of the potential injurer (the polluter in the case of marine oil pollution) will lead to underdeterrence and underinsurance. In such a case, compulsory insurance up to the amount of expected losses can provide better results than under the judgement-proof situation, provided that the moral hazard problem is adequately controlled. The introduction of a duty to insure on the tanker owner in Article 66 of the MEPL 1999 thus fits into the economic framework despite some critiques. The critiques concerning this provision mainly focus on the difficulty in implementing such a provision in practice. Some proposals on the specific implementing measures are now under consideration by the legislative authority. One proposal which resulted from research carried out by the Ministry of Communication suggested a compulsory insurance system related to the tonnage of the vessels. This may overcome some inefficiencies of the international regime, for instance the minimum tonnage requirement that only tankers carrying more than 2000 tons of oil in bulk as cargo are obliged to take out insurance. However, there are serious doubts with respect to the proposed amount, which seems too low to reflect the expected losses that could be caused.

Third, the economic analysis indicated that the lack of a compensation fund in China is inefficient. The decision of the Chinese government not to join the Fund Convention can be explained as a result of effective lobbying by interest groups, more particularly the state-owned oil industry in China. The proposal from the research carried out by the Ministry of Communication on a Chinese domestic fund may be useful in improving the efficiency of the whole compensation system in China. The financing of the domestic fund in China as it has been proposed would only to a small extent be related to the risk which is created. Economic analysis would require that contributions to the fund would be risk related.

Hence, at the normative level, some recommendations may be deduced from economic analysis for Chinese policy with respect to compensation for oil pollution damage, although they seem rather straightforward: the limitation amount should be increased substantially or completely abolished, compulsory insurance should be effectively implemented and the compensation fund should be introduced and should be structured in a more risk-related way.

NOTES

1. For a critical analysis of this regime, see Faure and Wang (2003, pp. 242–53).
2. See, on the legal regime in China, Faure and Wang (2005, pp. 11–37).
3. For an economic analysis of the international regime, see Faure and Wang (2006a).
4. For an economic analysis of financial caps in the international convention, see Faure and Wang (2006b).
5. For further details, see Gold (1985); De la Rue and Anderson (1998); Wu (1996).
6. For an overview of these developments, see Faure and Wang (2003, pp. 242–53).
7. The tacit acceptance procedure was introduced in the 1992 Protocols to allow for an easy amendment of the conventions. It means that the Protocol would come into force unless a certain number of States raised objections to the Protocol within a certain period of time (different from the traditional ratification procedure which requires that a Protocol would come into force when a certain number of States ratified it).

8. The MEPL 1982 was adopted on 23 August 1982, and had come into effect on 1 March 1983; the MEPL 1999 was adopted on 25 December 1999, and had come into effect on 1 April 2000. For a detailed analysis of the MEPL 1982, see Broedermann (1984, pp. 419–53, 539–84, and 1985, pp. 65–99).
9. Article 66 of MEPL 1999 reads 'The state shall make perfect and put into practice responsibility system of civil liability compensation for oil pollution by vessel, and shall establish insurance system of oil pollution by vessel, compensation fund system of oil pollution by vessel in accordance with the principles of sharing of owners of the vessel and the cargo of the compensation liabilities for oil pollution by vessel.'
10. Article 90 of the MEPL 1999 reads: 'Those who cause pollution damage to the marine environment shall eliminate the damage and compensate the losses; in case of pollution damage to the marine environment resulting entirely from the intentional act or fault of a third party, third party shall eliminate the damage and be liable for the compensation. If the State suffers heavy losses from the damages to marine ecosystems, marine aquatic resources and marine nature reserves, the departments invested by this law with the power of marine environment supervision and administration shall, on behalf of the State, put forward compensation demand to those who are responsible for the damages.'
11. It is contained in Chapter XI, which is titled 'Limitation of Liability for Maritime Claims'.
12. Article 207 of the CMC reads: 'Except as provided otherwise in Articles 208 and 209 of this Code, with respect to the following maritime claims, the person liable may limit his liability in accordance with the provisions of this Chapter, whatever the basis of liability may be:
(1) Claims in respect of loss of life or personal injury or loss of or damage to property including damage to harbor works, basins and waterways and aids to navigation occurring on board or in direct connection with the operation of the ship or with salvage operations, as well as consequential damages resulting therefrom;
(2) Claims in respect of loss resulting from delay in delivery in the carriage of goods by sea or from delay in the arrival of passengers or their luggage;
(3) Claims in respect of other loss resulting from infringement of rights other than contractual rights occurring in direct connection with the operation of the ship or salvage operations;
(4) Claims of a person other than the person liable in respect of measures taken to avert or minimize loss for which the person liable may limit his liability in accordance with the provisions of this Chapter, and further loss caused by such measures.
All the claims set out in the preceding paragraph, whatever the way they are lodged, may be entitled to limitation of liability. However, with respect to the remuneration set out in sub-paragraph (4) for which the person liable pays as agreed upon in the contract, in relation to the obligation for payment, the person liable may not invoke the provisions on limitation of liability of this Article.'
13. Article 208 of the CMC reads: 'The provisions of this Chapter shall not be applicable to the following claims:
(1) Claims for salvage payment or contribution in general average;
(2) Claims for oil pollution damage under the International Convention on Civil Liability for Oil Pollution Damage to which the People's Republic of China is a party;
(3) Claims for nuclear damage under the International Convention on Limitation of Liability for Nuclear Damage to which the People's Republic of China is a party;
(4) Claims against the ship-owner of a nuclear ship for nuclear damage;
(5) Claims by the servants of the ship-owner or salvor, if under the law governing the contract of employment, the ship-owner or salvor is not entitled to limit his liability or if he is by such law only permitted to limit his liability to an amount greater than that provided for in this Chapter.'
14. Article 209 of the CMC reads: 'A person liable shall not be entitled to limit his liability in accordance with the provisions of this Chapter, if it is proved that the loss resulted from his act or omission done with the intent to cause such loss or recklessly and with knowledge that such loss would probably result.'

15. Article 210 provides that:
(1) In respect of claims for loss of life or personal injury:
(a) For a ship from 300 to 500 gross tonnes, 333 000 SDR;
(b) For a ship of more than 500 gross tonnes, 333 000 SDR plus the amount as follows:
For each ton from 501 to 3000 tons: 500 SDR;
For each ton from 3001 to 30 000 tons: 333 SDR;
For each ton from 30 001 tons to 70 000 tons: 250 SDR;
For each ton in excess of 70 000 tons: 167 SDR;
(2) In respect of claims other than loss of life or personal injury:
(a) For a ship between 300 and 500 gross tonnes, 167 000 SDR;
(b) For a ship of more than 500 gross tonnes, 167 000 SDR plus the amount as follows:
For each ton from 501 to 30 000 tons: 167 SDR;
For each ton from 30 001 tons to 70 000 tons: 125 SDR;
For each ton in excess of 70 000 tons: 83 SDR.
16. Article V.1 of the 1992 CLC provides: 'The owner of a ship shall be entitled to limit his liability under this Convention in respect of any one incident to an aggregate amount calculated as follows:
(a) 3 million units of account for a ship not exceeding 5000 units of tonnage;
(b) for a ship with a tonnage in excess thereof, for each additional unit of tonnage, 420 units of account in addition to the amount mentioned in sub-paragraph (a); provided, however, that this aggregate amount shall not in any event exceed 59.7 million units of account.'
17. Liu (2002, p. 27).
18. Promogated by the State Council of the People's Republic of China on 29 December 1983.
19. Article 1 of the Regulations reads: 'These Regulations are hereby formulated for the enforcement of the Law of Marine Environmental Protection of the People's Republic of China, the prevention of pollution of sea areas by vessels and the preservation of marine ecological environment.'
20. Article 7 reads 'Where a marine accident has occurred to a vessel which has caused or is likely to cause environmental pollution damage, the Harbour Superintendency Administration may decide to take whatever compulsory steps necessary to avoid or mitigate any pollution damage, such as compulsory cleaning-up or compulsory towage. All the expenses incurred therefrom shall be borne by the owners of the vessels concerned.'
21. Article 39 reads 'The Harbour Superintendency Administration may order vessels violating the Environmental Protection Law of the People's Republic of China and these Regulations and causing marine environment pollution damages to pay the cost of eliminating pollution and compensate for the losses suffered by the state.'
22. For the historical background of the establishment of the maritime courts in China, see Zheng (1987, p. 251).
23. These nine maritime courts are Guangzhou, Shanghai, Qingdao, Tianjin, Dalian, Wuhan, Haikou, Xiamen and Ningbo.
24. Tang (1994, pp. 254–8).
25. Yu, X., 'Case on limitation of liability for oil pollution damage compensation', Guangzhou Maritime Court Cases, 24 March 2003; the same view was upheld by Yang and Hu (2006).
26. See Zheng (1987, p. 261). There are opinions that the government should enact a code of private international law; see Huang (1985, p. 3); also Li (1986, pp. 62–6).
27. Take the China Maritime Code, for instance. Chapter 8 on the collision of ships is de facto based on the principles set up by the Collision Convention 1910 which was ratified by China, although there is no reference to this convention. See Faure and Hu (2006).
28. Art. 268 (1) of China Maritime Code reads: 'If any international treaty concluded or acceded to by the People's Republic of China contains provisions differing from those contained in this Code, the provisions of the relevant international treaty shall apply,

unless the provisions are those on which the People's Republic of China has announced reservations.'

29. Art. 97 of Marine Environment Protection Law 1999 reads: 'If the provisions provided in an international treaty regarding environment protection concluded or acceded to by the People's Republic of China are not consistent with the provisions provided in this law, the provisions of the international treaty shall apply, unless the People's Republic of China has announced reservations.'
30. See Zheng (1987, p. 233).
31. Article 142 of the General Principles of Civil Law which recognizes the same principle is also under a separate chapter, 'Chapter VIII Application of Law in Civil Relations with Foreigners'. Article 189 of the Civil Procedure Law follows the same model.
32. The Supreme Court in its 'suggestions concerning certain question relating to the application of the General Principles of the Civil Law' explains in Article 178 that foreign-related relations include those where the subject, object or content is foreign-related. See Han and Si (2004, p. 32).
33. The Vienna Convention on the Law of Treaties stipulates, in the preamble, 'Having in mind the principles of international law . . . the sovereign equality and independence of all states, of non-interference in the domestic affairs of states . . .'.
34. Yang and Hu (2006).
35. Zhao (2001).
36. See Yu, X., 'Case on limitation of liability for oil pollution damage compensation', Guangzhou Maritime Court Cases, 24 March 2003; Yu (2001, pp. 19–23).
37. Han and Guan (2006).
38. Liu (2002, p. 27).
39. See Xia (2001, p. 148).
40. *Lloyd's List Maritime Asia*, Spring 2004, 19.
41. Wang (2005, p. 10). The contributing oil of Hong Kong in 2004 is 3.9387 million tons.
42. See, on the procedure to assess the damage to the marine environment in China, Wang, Liu and Shen (1993, pp. 29–31).
43. For a discussion of the Chinese position, see also Xia (2001, pp. 148–9).
44. Wang (2005, p. 10).
45. Liu and Zhou (2001).
46. Coase (1960, pp. 1–44).
47. See, for an application of the Coase theorem to the issue of products liability, Oi (1973, pp. 3–28).
48. See Shavell (1984a, pp. 357–74; 1984b, pp. 271–80; 1987, pp. 277–90).
49. For a summary of this literature see Shavell (1987; 2004, pp. 175–287).
50. See Shavell (1980, pp. 1–25) and for a summary Schäfer and Schönenberger (2000, pp. 597–624).
51. For the simple reason that strict liability with a contributory negligence defence will give optimal incentives for care and activity level to the injurer, but not to the victim (no optimal incentives to follow an optimal activity level), whereas negligence will give optimal incentives for care and the activity level to the victim, but not to the injurer (because the optimal activity level is not incorporated into the negligent standard). See, on this issue also, Shavell (2004, pp. 182–93).
52. See, for a test for strict liability, the classic contribution by Landes and Posner (1981, pp. 877–907).
53. In both cases the contribution of the victim to the accident risk is taken into account and the victim's claim on damages will be reduced wholly (contributory) or partially (comparative negligence). For a discussion of the difference between both rules, see, e.g., Haddock and Curran (1985, pp. 49–73).
54. See Shavell (2004, pp. 188–9).
55. See, on these underdeterrence effects of strict liability, Landes and Posner (1984, pp. 417–34).
56. See also Shavell (1986, pp. 43–58).

57. Article 92 of the MEPL 1999 reads: 'Those who cause pollution damage may be exempted from the liability if the pollution damage to the marine environment by any of the following circumstances cannot be avoided, despite prompt and reasonable measures taken:
(1) War;
(2) Natural calamities of *force majeure*;
(3) Negligence or other wrongful acts in the exercise of functions of competent authorities responsible for the maintenance of light-towers or other navigational aids.'
58. See Brans (2001); Mitchell (1994); Ozcayir (1998).
59. See, for an analysis of the channelling in nuclear liability, Trebilcock and Winter (1997, pp. 232–5). For more recent critical economic analysis of the channelling of nuclear liability, see Van den Borre (1997, pp. 329–82; 2001, pp. 693–701).
60. Jost (1996, pp. 259–76). A similar argument has recently been formulated by Polborn (1998, pp. 141–6 and by Skogh (2000, pp. 521–37). Skogh has also pointed out that compulsory insurance may save on transaction cost.
61. See also Kunreuther and Freeman (2001, p. 316).
62. There are, however, also a few dangers that should be taken into account when a duty to insure is introduced. One of them is that the moral hazard problem should be cured; another is that there may not be concentration on insurance markets. For these potential dangers of compulsory insurance, see Faure (2003a, pp. 185–9).
63. Wang (2005, p. 9).
64. Faure (1995, pp. 21–43).
65. Research conducted by the Institute of Scientific Research under the Ministry of Communications in Beijing. This was also highlighted at a seminar on compensation regime for ship-source marine pollution damage, organized by the Shanghai Maritime Safety Administration in June 2001.
66. This was also the main topic at a recent seminar at the London Shipping Law Centre. It was reported at this seminar that the European Commission suggested that one of the criteria for deciding whether a compensation regime is satisfactory should be whether it discourages operators from using vessels of less than top quality, see *Lloyd's List, Law Section*, 3 July 2002.
67. Liu, H. and Z. Zhou, 'Establishing a Chinese compensation mechanism for ship oil pollution', Institute of Scientific Research under the Ministry of Communications, Beijing, 2002.
68. Speech from Xu Guoyi (from MSA), Wang (2005, p. 11).
69. See Wang (2005, p. 9).
70. For an economic analysis of financial caps, see equally Faure, Fenn and MacMinn (2000).
71. See Faure (1995, pp. 21–43).
72. This point has been made by Rea (1982, pp. 50–52), but also by Adams (1989, p. 214) and by Ott and Schäfer (1990, pp. 564–5).
73. See Faure (2004, pp. 455–89).
74. Unless there would be joint and several or channelling of liability. For an economic analysis of these phenomena, see Faure (2003b, pp. 79–98).
75. See the comments made at the 1969 Conference by various delegates in Official Records of the International Legal Conference on Marine Pollution Damage 1969, Document LEG/CONF/3, IMO, 2-11.
76. An exception is the case where the tanker owner would be insolvent. In that case the fund would de facto act as a guarantor towards the victim.
77. Official Records of the International Legal Conference on Marine Pollution Damage 1969, Document LEG/CONF/C.2/SR12, IMO, 685-6.
78. See Shavell (1984a, pp. 357–74; 1984b, pp. 271–80; 1987, pp. 277–90).
79. See Faure and Wang (2006a).
80. For an early one, see Pedrick (1978, pp. 377–95).
81. For an overview of developments in this respect at the EU level, see Wang (2004, pp. 292–303).

REFERENCES

Adams, M. (1989), 'Warum kein Ersatz von Nichtvermögensschäden', in C. Ott and H.B. Schäfer (eds), *Allokationseffizienz in der Rechtsordnung*, Berlin: Springer, p. 214.

Brans, E. (2001), *Liability for Damage to Public Natural Resources – Standing, Damage and Damage Assessment*, The Hague: Kluwer Law International.

Broedermann, E. (1984, 1985), 'China and Admiralty – an introduction to Chinese maritime law and U.S.–Chinese shipping relations', *Journal of Maritime Law and Commerce*, **14**, 419–53, 539–84, **15**, 65–99.

Coase, R.A. (1960), 'The problem of social cost', *Journal of Law and Economics*, 1–44.

De la Rue, C. and C. Anderson (1998), *Shipping and the Environment Law and Practice*,: LLP.

Faure, M. (1995), 'Economic models of compensation for damages caused by nuclear accidents: some lessons for the division of the Paris and Vienna Conventions', *European Journal of Law and Economics*, 21–43.

Faure, M. (ed.) (2003a), *Deterrence, Insurability and Compensation in Environmental Liability. Future Developments in the European Union*, New York: Springer.

Faure, M. (2003b), 'Causal uncertainty, joint and several liability and insurance', in H. Koziol and J. Spier (eds), *Liber Amicorum Pierre Widmer*, Vienna: Springer, pp. 79–98.

Faure, M. (2004), 'Alternative compensation mechanisms as remedies for an insurability of liability', *The Geneva Papers on Risk and Insurance*, **29**(3), 455–89.

Faure, M. and J. Hu (eds) (2006), *Prevention and Compensation of Marine Pollution Damage. Recent Developments in Europe, China and the US*, The Hague: Kluwer Law International.

Faure, M. and H. Wang (2003), 'The international regimes for the compensation of oil pollution damage: are they effective?', *Review of European Community & International Environmental Law (Reciel)*, **12**, 242–53.

Faure, M. and H. Wang (2005), 'Compensation for oil pollution damage: China versus the international regime', *Asia–Pacific Journal of Environmental Law*, **9**, 11–37.

Faure, M. and H. Wang (2006a), 'Economic analysis of compensation for oil pollution damage', *Journal of Maritime Law and Commerce*, **37**, 179–217.

Faure, M. and H. Wang (2006b), 'Financial caps for oil pollution damage: China and the international conventions', in M. Faure and J. Hu (eds), *Prevention and Compensation of Marine Pollution Damage. Recent Developments in Europe, China and the US*, The Hague: Kluwer Law International, pp. 317–47.

Faure, M., P. Fenn and R. MacMinn (2000), 'Economic analysis of financial caps in accident law', paper presented at the annual conference of the European Association of Law and Economics in Ghent (September).

Gold, E. (1985), *Handbook on Marine Pollution*, Assuranceforeningen Gard, Norway.

Haddock, D. and C. Curran (1985), 'An economic theory of comparative negligence', *Journal of Legal Studies*, 49–73.

Han, L. and Z. Guan (2006), 'The enforcement of international conventions for the prevention of pollution from ships and compensation for pollution damage in China', in M. Faure and J. Hu (eds), *Prevention and Compensation of Marine Pollution Damage. Recent Developments in Europe, China and the US*, The Hague: Kluwer Law International, pp. 181–91.

Han, L. and Y. Si (2004), 'The issues concerning civil liability for oil pollution damage caused by collision of ships', *China Maritime Law Association Newsletter*, 32 (June).
Huang, J. (1985), 'Concerning the scope of private international law and other theoretical issues', *Journal of China's Legal System* (*Zhong Guo Fa Zhi Bao*, 11 November, 3.
Jost, P.J. (1996), 'Limited liability and the requirement to purchase insurance', *International Review of Law and Economics*, **16**(2), 259–76.
Kunreuther, H. and P. Freeman (2001), 'Insurability, environmental risks and the law', in A. Heyes (ed.), *The Law and Economics of the Environment*, Cheltenham, UK and Northampton, MA, USA: Edward Elgar, pp. 302–18.
Landes, W. and R. Posner (1981), 'The positive economic theory of tort law', *Georgia Law Review*, 877–907.
Landes, W. and R. Posner (1984), 'Tort law as a regulatory regime for catastrophic personal injuries', *Journal of Legal Studies*, 417–34.
Li, S. (1986), 'Several issues in the theoretical research and legislation of private international law in our country', *Forum of Law and Politics*, **3**, 62–6.
Liu, H. (2002), 'Liability system on marine oil pollution in China and suggestion on the ratification of the Bunker Convention', *China Maritime Law Association Newsletter*, **65** (September), 27.
Liu, H. and Z. Zhou (2001), 'Setting up the Chinese characteristic compensation system for oil pollution damage from vessels' ('Jian Li You Zhong Guo Te Se de Chuan Bo You Wu Sun Hai Pei Chang Ji Zhi'), International Seminar on Compensation Regime for Ship-source Marine Pollution Damage, Shanghai (June).
Mitchell, R. (1994), 'International Oil Pollution at Sea – Environmental Policy and Treaty Compliance', Massachusetts Institute of Technology.
Oi, W.Y. (1973), 'The economics of product safety', *Bell Journal of Economics*, **3**, 28.
Ott, C. and H.B. Schäfer (1990), 'Schmerzensgeld bei Körperverletzungen. Eine ökonomische Analyse', *Juristenzeitung*, 564–5.
Ozcayir, Z.O. (1998), *Liability for Oil Pollution and Collisions*, LLP.
Pedrick, J.L. (1978), 'Tank ship design regulation and its economic effect on oil consumers', *Journal of Maritime Law and Commerce*, 377–95.
Polborn, M. (1998), 'Mandatory insurance and the judgement-proof problem', *International Review of Law and Economics*, **18**, 141–6.
Rea, S. (1982), 'Non-pecuniary loss and breach of contract', *Journal of Legal Studies*, **50**, 2.
Schäfer, H.B. and A. Schönenberger (2000), 'Strict liability versus negligence', in B. Bouckaert and G. De Geest (eds), *Encyclopaedia of Law and Economics, II Civil Law and Economics*, 597–624.
Shavell, S. (1980), 'Strict Liability versus Negligence,' *Journal of Legal Studies*, 1–25.
Shavell, S. (1984a), 'Liability for harm versus regulation of safety', *Journal of Legal Studies*, **3**, 357–74.
Shavell, S. (1984b), 'A model of the optimal use of liability and safety regulation', *Rand Journal of Economics*, **15**, 271–80.
Shavell, S. (1986), 'The judgment proof problem', *International Review of Law and Economics*, **6**(1), 43–58.
Shavell, S. (1987), *Economic Analysis of Accident Law*, Cambridge: Harvard University Press.

Shavell, S. (2004), *Foundations of Economic Analysis of Law*, Cambridge: Harvard University Press.

Skogh, G. (2000), 'Mandatory insurance: transaction costs analysis of insurance', in B. Bouckaert and G. De Geest (eds), *Encyclopedia of Law and Economics*, Cheltenham, UK and Northampton, MA, USA: Edward Elgar, pp. 521–37.

Tang, Z. (1994), 'Maritime jurisdiction of the People's Republic of China: legal framework, recent developments, and future prospects', *Journal of Maritime Law and Commerce*, **25** (April), 254–8.

Trebilcock, M. and R. Winter (1997), 'The economics of nuclear accident law', *International Review of Law and Economics*, **17**(2), 232–5.

Van den Borre, T. (1997), 'Transplantatie van "kanalisatie van aansprakelijkheid" van het kernenergierecht naar het milieu (aansprakelijkheids)recht: een goede of een gebrekkige zaak?', in M. Faure and K. Deketelaere (eds), *Ius Commune en Milieurecht, Actualia in het Milieurecht in België en Nederland*, Antwerp: Intersentia, pp. 329–82.

Van den Borre, T. (2001), *Efficiënte preventie en compensatie van catastrophe risico's. Het voorbeeld van schade door kernongevallen*, Antwerp: Intersentia.

Wang, H. (2004), 'The EU marine oil pollution regime – recent developments', *European Environmental Law Review*, **13**, 292–303.

Wang, H. (2005), 'Ships' oil pollution fund is coming into being – China will establish the compensation system suitable for the country's situation for damage caused by ships' oil pollution', *China Maritime Safety*, **1**(8 August).

Wang, M., S. Liu and M. Shen (1993), 'The normal procedure of assessment of damage to the marine environment in Chinese judicial practice', in C. De La Rue (ed.), *Liability for Damage to the Marine Environment*, London: Lloyds of London Press, pp. 29–31.

Wu, C. (1996), *Pollution from the Carriage of Oil by Sea: Liability and Compensation*, The Hague: Kluwer Law International Ltd.

Xia, C. (2001), *Limitation of Liability for Maritime Claims. A Study of US Law, Chinese Law and International Conventions*, The Hague: Kluwer Law International, p. 148.

Yang, B. and J. Hu (2006), 'Application of law in civil liability for oil pollution damage caused by coastal vessels in China', in M. Faure and J. Hu (eds), *Prevention and Compensation of Marine Pollution Damage. Recent Developments in Europe, China and the US*, The Hague: Kluwer Law International, pp. 193–205.

Yu, X. (2001), 'Oil pollution liability of colliding vessels in China', *Lloyd's Maritime and Commercial Law Quarterly*, 19–23.

Zhao, L. (2001), 'Legal issues in marine oil pollution' ('Hai Shang You Wu Chu Li Zhong De Ruo Gan Fa Lu Wen Ti'), International Seminar on Compensation Regime for Ship-source Pollution Damage, Shanghai (June).

Zheng, H. (1987), 'Private international law in the People's Republic of China: principles and procedures', *Texas International Law Journal*, **21**, 251.

PART IV

Concluding remarks

12. Conclusions

Thomas Eger, Michael Faure and Zhang Naigen

1. INTRODUCTION

This book focuses on the application of the law and economics approach to Chinese law and to the development of the economic analysis of law in China. What is the 'economic analysis of law'? Let us quote a well-known textbook on law and economics (Cooter and Ulen, *Law and Economics*, 4th edn, 2004, pp. 3–4): 'Economics provided a scientific theory to predict the effects of legal sanctions on behaviour. To economists, sanctions look like prices, and presumably, people respond to these sanctions much as they respond to prices. . . . Generalizing, we can say that economics provides a behavioural theory to predict how people respond to changes in laws. This theory surpasses intuition, just as science surpasses common sense.'

2. IS THE ECONOMIC ANALYSIS OF LAW A USEFUL APPROACH TO STUDY CHINESE LAW?

Law and Economics has been developing in the US (a common law country) since the late 1960s, and has also gained importance in continental European civil law countries since the late 1980s. But does it make any sense to apply the law and economics approach to a country like China that is, in many respects, totally different from Western common law and civil law countries? At first glance, the correct answer seems to be 'no'.

The Chinese economy is still characterized by a high degree of state involvement. There is no Western-style democracy and no political competition, and there is a low degree of judicial independence. Lower court judges especially are typically not well trained and are, to a considerable extent, dependent on local political authorities. The law in the books is, in many respects, poorly enforced, and the behaviour of the market participants is to a large extent channelled by informal institutions ('guanxi').

However, this is not the whole story. Although there is still a high degree of state involvement and a political predominance of the CCP, the Chinese economy is characterized by fierce competition among provinces and lower-level political entities over resources and economic power. This competition was partly initiated by the central government's decentralization of economic decision-making power and tax revenues. The competitive behaviour of local authorities compensates, at least to some extent, for the lack of private property and developed market institutions. Although China still suffers, especially at the local level, from problems of law enforcement, foreign and domestic market participants have been putting pressure on the local political authorities to comply with formal legal rules. The growing demand for legal protection against IPR infringement is a case in point. With China's accession to the WTO, the central government has started to put more weight on the enforcement of trade-related aspects of intellectual property rights (TRIPS) by the local level.

All in all, it really makes sense to apply economic analysis of law to analyse recent achievements and problems in China. Of course, when doing so, one has to take into account the specific social and cultural constraints as perceived by the addressees of the formal legal rules and the specific problems of law enforcement via the courts. But this does not constitute an impediment to applying law and economics in order to better understand the functioning of the Chinese economic and legal system. It is rather the normal way to apply law and economics to the particular problems of a specific country.

3. LAW AND ECONOMICS AS AN AREA OF RESEARCH AND TEACHING IN CHINA

Chinese university scholars themselves have become interested in law and economics since the early 1980s. The books of Oliver Williamson and many Law & Economics scholars were translated into Chinese in the later 1980s. The textbook by Richard Posner was translated into Chinese several times; the translation of other textbooks such as the one by Robert Cooter and Thomas Ulen followed. Since the mid-1990s, law and economics has become a growing area of research and teaching in China. Workshops and conferences have been organized by several Chinese universities such as Fudan University, Beijing University and Shandong University, and an increasing number of books and articles in the Chinese language have been published.

4. FINAL RESULTS

What are the results of our conference, held in March 2006 at the Fudan University in Shanghai, and of the contributions to our conference volume? First of all, we have found that the application of the economic analysis of law is a useful tool for explaining and describing the Chinese legal system in its present form. The contributions by the Chinese colleagues who used law and economic models to analyse some particular features of the Chinese legal system today were able to demonstrate this very clearly. Secondly, it has been elaborated that the European experience with law and economics can be used, *mutatis mutandis*, in order to give Chinese policy makers recommendations as to how to change their legal system towards efficiency if they should wish to do so. According to our knowledge, it was the first attempt explicitly to make use of the findings by European scholars in the field of law and economics in order to give recommendations relating to particular policy areas, such as competitive federalism, tax policy, competition law, professional regulation, regulatory capture, intellectual property law and compensation for harm from oil pollution, to Chinese policy makers. The results of this Chinese–European cooperation are promising and thereby constitute a sufficient reason for continuing our joint venture in the future.

Index